Workbook of Accounting Standards

Workbook of Accounting Standards
Third Edition

Alan Sangster

for Dad

PITMAN PUBLISHING
128 Long Acre, London WC2E 9AN
A Division of Pearson Professional Limited

First published in Great Britain 1991
Second edition 1993
Third edition 1995

© Pearson Professional Limited 1995

British Library Cataloguing in Publication Data
A CIP catalogue record for this book is available on request from the British Library.

ISBN 0-273-61420-7

10 9 8 7 6 5 4 3 2 1

Printed in England by Clays Ltd, St Ives plc

The Publishers' policy is to use paper manufactured from sustainable forests.

Contents

12 Presentation Standards

13 Taxation and Grants

Preface

This book arose out of some research into computer assisted learning at Strathclyde University in 1988. The teaching of Statements of Standard Accounting Practice (SSAPs) and, more particularly, the testing of student understanding of them, had been identified as being an ideal area for the application of *expert system* technology based computer-assisted learning. However, conventional questions were found to be inappropriate to the expert systems environment - they are too long and tend to deal with the generalities, rather than specific points in the area being examined. What was needed was a bank of short questions, each covering a particular point contained in an SSAP, but in a way that did not make the exercise trivial or the answer obvious.

At the same time as the questions were being developed, it was recognised that it would be advisable for students to approach the exercises with a clear picture of the main rules of the SSAP which they were studying. A flowchart approach to SSAP rule analysis had been used by, among others, John Blake in his book '*Accounting Standards*' (Pitman) and students had expressed their appreciation of these diagrams. It was felt that this approach would be appropriate in the exercise, and flowcharts were prepared for each of the four SSAPs involved in the original experiment.

Subsequent analysis of exam performance showed it to be significantly superior for those students who had been exposed to the short question and flowchart approach. The idea for this book came about soon after, when a colleague suggested that I might consider expanding the method to cover all the accounting standards, and then publish the material.

In writing this book, it has been assumed that students have access to the text of the accounting standards they are studying. While it would be possible to use this book's narrative and questions to learn what each standard is concerned with, it is intended primarily as a tutorial workbook, and as a self-tutoring guide. For this reason, reference to a theoretical text, such as John Blake's '*Accounting Standards*', would probably be helpful in the initial stages of the learning process. Having said that, as a supporting text for a course of lectures, this book should be well able to stand on its own as a reinforcing, developing and diagnostic tool. It would probably be fair to suggest that any student who could successfully complete all the exercises on a particular accounting standard, would be equipped to handle virtually any accounting treatment exam question relating to that topic.

In the main, compared to accounting treatment, disclosure is straightforward, and students should not need any more assistance than the accounting standards themselves provide. This book has, therefore, concentrated upon the accounting treatment aspects of the accounting standards. It has not ignored the disclosure requirements - in some cases they are covered in great detail - but it has assumed that students can usually see these quite clearly for themselves, either in the accounting standards, or in a theoretical text.

Accounting standards are central to many of the examinations set by the main UK and Irish accountancy bodies, for example, ICAS Professional level paper in Financial Accounting, and the TPC1 level paper in Financial Reporting; ICAEW Auditing and Financial Reporting papers at both PE1 and PE2 levels; ICAI Professional Two/Three/Final; ACCA papers 1, 10, and 13; CIMA papers in Financial Accounting (stage 2) and Financial Reporting (stage 3); and CIPFA papers in Accounting Theory and Practice (P1), Auditing (P1), and Tax and Treasury Management (P2).

This book is intended to be used by those studying for professional examinations and by undergraduates whose subject involves accounting standards.

All 25 current (February 1995) accounting standards are covered in the book - 18 SSAPs and 7 Financial Reporting Standards (FRSs). In addition, one interim statement and nine Urgent Issue Task Force Abstracts (UITFs) are covered where appropriate (the others were withdrawn upon the issue of FRS 3 [UITF 2], and FRS 4 [UITFs 1 and 8]). In addition, the Companies Act 1985 requirements, as amended by the Companies Act 1989, have been included wherever appropriate. For each standard, there is a summary of the accounting treatment requirements, followed by a discussion of problems of interpretation and grey areas. Flowcharts are provided for each standard; and each of the main chapters contains 45 short questions (solutions are provided for the first 25 and the publishers will supply any tutor who contacts them with answers to the others) dealing with specific points in the standard(s) it contains. In some cases, longer questions are also provided which test, in a broader sense, the application of the accounting standards. There is also one composite chapter comprising another 40 short questions covering all the standards.

Since the first edition was published in 1991, the Accounting Standards Board (ASB) has replaced four SSAPs (6, 10, 14 and 23) with Financial Reporting Standards; and has issued twelve Urgent Issue Task Force Abstracts; a major replacement of SSAP 2 is imminent (through the proposed *Statement of principles*); and many of the 18 remaining SSAPs appear likely to be significantly modified and/or replaced over the next few years. This is an extremely volatile area, and it is hoped that through the provision of this book readers will be well placed to both interpret the current clutch of standards and to identify how any subsequent ASB pronouncements affect and are affected by them.

Many users of the first two editions felt that they got most benefit from the book after they had read the brief section on pages xiii and xiv on how to use it. I would strongly urge anyone who has not used the book previously to read that section before tackling any of the main text.

Finally, I would welcome any comments on the material contained in the book, and any suggestions on ways that it may be altered or improved.

ALAN SANGSTER

Department of Accountancy
University of Aberdeen
Dunbar Street
Aberdeen AB9 2TY

email: a.sangster@abdn.ac.uk

February 1995

Acknowledgements

While continuing to express my thanks to all those who helped with the first two editions, I cannot let the publication of the third edition pass without expressing my gratitude once more to George Georgiou for the benefit of his expertise in cash flow accounting and accounting for business combinations. However, as always, notwithstanding all the help I have received over the three editions, any remaining inaccuracies are my own.

I must also thank my wife Eunice for putting-up with becoming an 'authoring widow' once again. Even more importantly, Dinho and Manueli, especially now that you are both old enough to be conscious of my absence at this time, for your patience, thank you.

How to Use this Book

Chapters 2-14, which between them cover all 25 current accounting standards, are organised into four principal sections: the summaries of accounting treatment requirements; discussion of problems of interpretation and grey areas; flowcharts; and questions. Each of these chapters contains 45 short questions and, in some cases, longer questions are also provided. The questions are comprehensive in their coverage of the standards and are of varying degrees of difficulty, the most difficult tending to come in the latter part of the chapter. The last chapter (chapter 15) contains a further 60 short questions, covering all the standards. Suggested solutions to the first 25 short questions in each main chapter and to all the long questions are given after chapter 15. (Solutions for the remaining 20 short questions per main chapter are available free to *bona fide* tutors from Pitman Publishing.)

It is intended that students should read the chapter on the standard which they are studying, then look at the flowchart(s), and finally answer the questions which follow. There is, however, no reason why this has to occur. The questions do not rely on the student having done either of the other activities first, though there are some that students may find easier if they have done so.

The values used in the questions have been kept within reasonable limits so as to aid computation. *In every case, the information given **must** be assumed to be material.* If it were not material, the standard would not be applicable and it could be argued that non-application was appropriate. At all times, it should be remembered that the primary objective of the questions is to demonstrate correct application of the relevant accounting standard. This can be done irrespective of the materiality of the sums involved, and the question of materiality should be put to one side while the problems are being attempted.

Where this book is being used by a tutor with a group of students, it would be a worthwhile exercise to use some completed questions as the basis of a discussion of the concept of materiality. Chapter 1 considers the meaning of the term 'material', and it should be read by students before any such exercise is undertaken.

At least one flowchart is provided for each SSAP and FRS and, in some cases, there are four or five. While they do not always present all the possible permutations, they are as exhaustive as practicable and cover those aspects most relevant to the particular standard under review. One useful exercise is to try to identify any possibility not covered by a given flowchart, and amend it accordingly. Such an exercise, methodically undertaken, will increase understanding of the topic considerably, and is an ideal way for students struggling to come to terms with a standard to overcome their difficulties.

The short questions in this book are statements of items and circumstances. Students should indicate how the information in the question would be dealt with according to the SSAP or FRS under review. As previously mentioned, materiality should not be considered when tackling the questions, however, it may be useful for tutors to do so from time to time when discussing them with students. These questions can be used in many ways: in tutorials for discussion purposes, as exam revision tools, and as exam questions. Because each one deals with a specific aspect of an accounting standard, tutors wishing to concentrate on a particular area of a standard can select those questions most relevant to it, returning to the others if and when required. Students working on their own with this book would be best advised to work through the relevant chapters, tackling each of the questions in the order given. It would defeat the objective of the exercise to look at the solution to a question before attempting to answer it, and students are strongly advised not to do so.

Accounting standards contain a considerable amount of imprecise guidance and provide many opportunities for subjective interpretation in their application. By being as prescriptive as possible, the suggested solutions have attempted to overcome the difficulties that this creates for students. There will be occasions when tutors and/or students may disagree with, or over, some of the suggested solutions. This should be welcomed: students can only benefit from a discussion of the thinking behind a suggested solution which is the subject of disagreement.

1   Materiality

What is 'material'?

Nowhere in any of the accounting standards is the term 'materiality' defined, not even in SSAP 2 (*Disclosure of accounting policies* - chapter 12), though it does come close to a definition when it states: 'management should identify those items .... *judged* material or *critical for the purpose of determining and fully appreciating the company's profit or loss and its financial position*' (SSAP 2, paragraph 12, italics added).

Some standards include a suggestion of what would be material in the context in which they are being applied. For example, SSAP 3 (*Earnings per share* - chapter 12) states that a 5% dilution of basic earnings per share is material; and SSAP 25 (*Segmental reporting* - chapter 12) states that a segment is significant (i.e. material) if its third party turnover is 10% of total third party turnover. However, most use phrases such as 'and the effect is material', 'need not be applied to immaterial items', and 'should be treated as an extraordinary item where material'. As a result, it is essential that anyone attempting to interpret and apply accounting standards has a clear understanding of what is meant by the term 'material'.

There have been a number of attempts to define or clarify what is meant by 'material'. These include, in chronological order, the statements of the Institute of Chartered Accountants in England and Wales (ICAEW); the US Financial Accounting Standards Board (FASB); the ICAEW; the International Accounting Standards Committee (IASC); and the Accounting Standards Board (ASB). (SSAP 2 was issued after the first ICAEW statement.)

In Statement of Fundamental Accounting Concept 2 (SFAC No. 2), the FASB state that the omission or misstatement of an item in a financial report is material if, in the light of the surrounding circumstances, the magnitude of the item is such that it is probable that the judgement of a reasonable person relying upon the report would have been changed or influenced by the inclusion or correction of the item.

In response to the use of 'material' in the Companies Act 1985, the ICAEW document '*The Interpretation of Material in relation to Accounts*', originally issued in 1968, was revised to state that 'a matter is material if knowledge of the matter would be likely to influence the user of the financial or other statements under consideration'. (The original document had stated that a matter can be considered material if its non-disclosure, misstatement or omission would be likely to distort the view given by the accounts.)

The IASC Framework (July 1989) states that information is material if its omission or misstatement could influence the economic decisions of users taken on the basis of the financial statements.

The Exposure Draft on the *Statement of principles*, issued by the ASB in (July 1991) provides a definition which is identical to that given in the IASC Framework. It goes on to state that 'materiality depends upon the size of the item or error judged in the particular circumstances of its omission or mis-statement [and that] materiality [therefore] provides a threshold or cut-off point rather than being a primary qualitative characteristic that information must have to be useful'.

The five statements referred to above and SSAP 2 have one key factor in common: they all relate materiality to the effect an item has upon the user of the financial information in which it is included or from which it is omitted. Thus, it would appear to be generally accepted that an item would be considered 'material' if its inclusion or omission would significantly affect the understanding of the financial performance and position of the reporting enterprise *of any user of the financial statement in which it may be included or omitted.*

Acceptance of this analysis leaves two questions unanswered: (a) who are the users of financial statements? and (b) what criterion should be adopted when deciding whether or not an item is material?

There are so many classes of users of financial statements (e.g. private investors, corporate investors, charities, shareholders, prospective shareholders, government departments, pension funds, unit trusts, investment trusts, lenders, potential lenders), and such a range of needs and uses within those classes (e.g. UK companies, overseas companies, public companies, private companies, small companies, large companies, customer companies, supplier companies) that it is impossible to incorporate the needs of all the possible users in the determination of what is material. However, a good attempt can, and must, be made.

Materiality could be defined in the following way: an item is material if it is considered that its inclusion in or omission from a financial statement would cause a user of that statement to make a different decision from that which might otherwise be made.

This definition is compatible with the UK Accounting Standard Committee's explanatory foreword to the Statements of Standard Accounting Practice which states that accounting standards need not be applied to items *whose effect is judged to be immaterial to an understanding of the financial statements.* (In other words, if the item does not change the understanding of the financial statements, then it is not material.) It follows that if the understanding is unaffected, so are any decisions based on that understanding.

Conclusion

Materiality is a key factor in the application of accounting standards. As a general rule, if the inclusion or omission of an item would affect the decisions of those who use financial statements, the item is material.

It is not simply a question of magnitude - £5 to a millionaire is not material, but it is to a four year old child. Rather, it is a question of significance to decision making. When attempting to determine whether an item is or is not material, it should always be considered from the perspective of the users of the financial statements. It should not be assumed that merely because an item is of small value, it will be immaterial in the context of the financial statements. For example, the sale of £10,000 of goods to Iraq would not seem important in the context of a company's total turnover of £20m. However, many users of the undertaking's financial statements would make different decisions were that information included rather than excluded from those statements.

2 FRS 3: Reporting Financial Performance

Summary of the accounting treatment requirements

The profit and loss account should show extraordinary items separately after the after-tax profit on ordinary activities attributable to the members of the company. The amount of each extraordinary items should be shown individually, either on the face of the profit and loss account or in a note, and an adequate description of each extraordinary item should be given to enable its nature to be understood. (Paragraph 22)

The following ordinary items which are of exceptional size or incidence should be shown separately on the face of the profit and loss account after operating profit and before interest, and included under the appropriate heading of continuing or discontinued operations:
   a)   profits or losses on the sale or termination of an operation;
   b)   costs of a fundamental reorganisation or restructuring having a material effect on the nature and focus of the reporting entity's operations; and
   c)   profits or losses on the disposal of fixed assets.
In calculating the profit or loss in respect of these items, consideration should only be given to revenue and costs directly related to them. (Paragraph 20)

Other ordinary items which arc of exceptional size or incidence should be included in the ascertainment of profit or loss on ordinary activities under the statutory headings to which they relate. They should be attributed to continuing or discontinued operations as appropriate and the amount of each item, either individually or as an aggregate of items of a similar type, should be disclosed separately by way of note, or on the face of the profit and loss account if that degree of prominence is necessary in order to give a true and fair view. An adequate description of each exceptional item should be given to enable its nature to be understood. (Paragraph 19)

Tax on extraordinary items should be shown separately, as should any minority share of extraordinary items, as either a part of the extraordinary item on the face of the profit and loss account, or in a note (paragraph 22).

Items relating to prior periods will normally be recognised in (i.e. included in the financial statements for) the period in which they are identified. However, when they arise from the correction of fundamental errors or changes in accounting policy they should be treated as prior period adjustments. That is, they should be accounted for by restating the comparative figures for the preceding period in the primary statements and notes, and adjusting the opening balance of reserves for the cumulative effect. The cumulative effect of the adjustments should also be noted at the foot of the statement of total recognised gains and losses of the current period. The effect of prior period adjustments on the results for the preceding period should be disclosed where practicable. (Paragraph 29)

A note (or a primary statement) should be presented reconciling the opening and closing totals of shareholders' funds of the period (paragraphs 28 and 59). If included as a primary statement, the reconciliation should be shown separately from the statement of total recognised gains and losses (paragraph 59).

The profit and loss account should be layered to highlight: the results of continuing operations (including the results of acquisitions); the results of discontinued operations; profits or losses on the sale or termination of an operation, costs of a fundamental reorganisation or restructuring and profits or losses on the disposal of fixed assets; and extraordinary items.

The analysis between continuing operations, acquisitions (as a component of continuing operations) and discontinued operations should be disclosed to the level of operating profit. The analysis of turnover and operating profit is the minimum disclosure required in this respect on the fact of the profit and loss account. Gains and losses may be excluded from the profit and loss account only if they are specifically permitted or required to be taken directly to reserves by an accounting standard or, in the absence of a relevant accounting standard, by law (paragraph 13). However, any recognised gains or losses excluded from the profit and loss account in this way, e.g. foreign currency exchange rate gains on investments, must be included in the statement of total recognised gains and losses. The results of acquisitions included in continuing operations should not include those that are also discontinued in the same period (paragraph 14). [The requirements of paragraphs 13 and 14 do not apply to the financial statements of insurance companies or insurance groups. Nor do they apply to the consolidated financial statements to the extent that they include insurance companies or insurance group. (Paragraph 31A)]

A memorandum note of historical cost profits and losses should immediately follow either the profit and loss account or the statement of total recognised gains and losses. Its primary purpose is to present the profits or losses of reporting entities that have revalued assets on a more comparable basis with those of entities that have not. And is an abbreviated restatement of the profit and loss account which adjusts the reported profit or loss, if necessary, so as to show it as if no asset revaluations had been made. The note is required whenever there is a material difference between the result as disclosed in the profit and loss account and the result on an unmodified historical cost basis. Where full historical cost information is unavailable or cannot be obtained without unreasonable expense or delay, the earliest available values should be used. The note should include a reconciliation of the reported profit on ordinary activities before taxation to the equivalent historical cost amount and should also show the retained profit for the financial year reported on the historical cost basis. In consolidated financial statements, the profit and loss account figure for minority interests should be amended for the purposes of this note to reflect the adjustments made where they affect subsidiary companies with a minority interest. (Paragraph 26, 54 and 55)

Earnings per share (- see SSAP 3, chapter 12) is defined as the profit in pence attributable to each equity share, based on the profit (or in the case of a group, the consolidated profit) of the period after tax, minority interests and extraordinary items and after deducting preference dividends and other appropriations in respect of preference shares, divided by the number of equity shares in issue and ranking for dividend in respect of the period (paragraph 25).

Problems of interpretation and grey areas

The following items are discussed: extraordinary items and earnings per share; prior period adjustments; terminated activities; revaluation and the profit or loss on disposal of an asset; and primary statements.

Extraordinary items and earnings per share

The standard defines *extraordinary items* as: 'material items possessing a high degree of abnormality which arise from events or transactions that fall outside the ordinary activities of the reporting entity and which are *not expected to recur*. They do not include exceptional items nor do they include prior period items merely because they relate to a prior period' (paragraph 6, italics added). Ordinary activities are defined as: 'activities which are undertaken by a reporting entity as part of its business and such related activities in which the reporting entity engages in furtherance of, incidental to, or arising from, these activities' (paragraph 2); and they include the effects on the reporting entity of any event in the various environments in which it operates, including the political, regulatory, economic and geographical environments, irrespective of the frequency or unusual nature of the events.

A significant problem with the standard's predecessor, SSAP 6 (*Extraordinary items and prior year adjustments*), was that the determination of whether or not an item was *extraordinary* was largely dependant on the judgement of the directors. Prior to the amended definition of *earnings per share* contained in paragraph 25 of FRS 3, treating an item as extraordinary could have had a significant impact on many of the ratios used for analysis of profitability. Despite the definitions given in SSAP 6, and even in spite of the inclusion of lists of examples of exceptional and extraordinary items in that standard, there remained too great an opportunity for creative accounting and it was generally conceded that undertakings often used the distinction between *exceptional* and *extraordinary* items to improve the financial picture. The revised definition of *earnings per share* contained in FRS 3 effectively negated much of the EPS-derived benefit which could accrue if an item were classified as *extraordinary*. At the same time, the ASB also amended the definition of *extraordinary items* to be far more restrictive than the definition contained in SSAP 6. These two revised definitions effectively mean that not only will it only be in extremely rare circumstances that an *extraordinary item* will be found to exist, but that the EPS-related benefit of classification as *extraordinary* no longer exists.

Prior period adjustments

Two situations can give rise to prior period adjustments: changes in accounting policy and fundamental errors. Despite its apparent simplicity, the treatment of the correction of errors is a far more complex concept than it appears to be. Sweeping aside all the surface issues, paragraph 61 of the standard makes clear that the key question to be answered in determining whether an error may be treated as a prior period adjustment (other than that it relates to a previous period) is whether *additional* experience, knowledge or information has been acquired since the financial statements were approved which reveals that an error *in an estimate* occurred which could not have been detected from the experience, knowledge or information held at that time. If the answer to that question is 'yes', the item *is not* a prior period adjustment, but rather it is a normal recurring correction or adjustment of an accounting estimate made in prior periods. Among those occurrences which would not, therefore, qualify as prior period adjustments are changes in the rate of bad debt provision where the previous rate had been found to have been inappropriate; and changes in long term contract loss provisions believed to have been underestimated in the light of information which has become available since the previous period's financial statements were approved.

Having passed the *possibility of detection* test, correction of the error can only be treated as a prior period adjustment if the error is of such significance that it destroyed the true and fair view of the previous financial statements - that is to say, a 'fundamental error'.

Error correction is also relevant to changes in accounting policy. Aside from accounting policy changes resulting from the issue of a new or revised accounting standard, a change in accounting policy may only be made if it will give a fairer presentation of the results and financial position of the business (paragraph 62). A correction of an accounting estimate can lead to a change in accounting policy: for example, a switch from a policy of writing off development expenditure to a policy of deferral and amortisation may occur because the previous trading life forecast (of, say, two years) in respect of products being developed was incorrect (it should have been, say, 20 years); and, in the light of this discovery, the company believes that a change of policy would result in a fairer spread of the costs and benefits of the development expenditure than would result from immediate write-off. Such changes in accounting policy would be treated as prior period adjustments. However, the circumstances of the error in the previous estimate must be considered before it too may be applied retrospectively as a prior period adjustment. If the error is a correction or adjustment to an accounting estimate which could not have been detected when the previous financial statements were approved (in this case, the forecast of product trading life), the change in accounting policy would qualify as a prior period adjustment, but the error would not. Thus, if the forecasting error in the above example arose because a software bug caused the figures used to be inaccurate, and the error could not be detected with the knowledge, experience or information available at that time, this would not qualify as an error-based prior period adjustment (i.e. any retrospective amortisation required would be based on a two year trading life, not 20). However, if the company employed a statistician who should have detected the error, but failed to do so, this would (assuming it was a fundamental error) qualify as an error-based prior period adjustment (and any retrospective amortisation would be based on a 20 year trading life).

To summarise, in order for an item to be treated as a prior period adjustment it must *either* be a correction of a fundamental error which was detectable from the information available at the date on which the previous financial statements were approved, *or* it must be a change in accounting policy. It is not surprising that the standard states (paragraph 60) that prior period adjustments are rare.

Paragraph 33f of FRS 3 uses the term 'prior year adjustment' as, for example, does the standard's example of the *Statement of Total Recognised Gains and Losses*. This is the terminology which was used in SSAP 6 and should be read as being the same as 'prior period adjustment'.

Terminated activities

One of the most contentious issues surrounding SSAP 6 related to the treatment of discontinuation and reorganisation. One reporting entity, faced with identical circumstances, would treat such items as exceptional, another would treat them as extraordinary. Entities even contradicted their own treatment from one accounting period to the next (although they were always able to justify the approach adopted). FRS 3 sought to address this issue by prescribing the treatment of any such material items as exceptional and requiring their separate disclosure on the face of the profit and loss account (after operating profit and before interest) *and* by their classification under either *continuing* or *discontinued* operations, as appropriate. (Paragraph 20)

The standard also tightened-up the situation relating to decisions to sell or terminate an operation. Under SSAP 6, once a decision had been taken to discontinue a business segment, a provision was required for the consequences of all the decisions taken up to the balance sheet date. All that was required before a provision could be made was an agreed intent (by the board) to terminate an activity. In contrast, FRS 3 requires that before any consequential provisions can be made, there should be evidence in the form of a binding sale agreement or a detailed formal plan for termination from which the reporting entity cannot realistically withdraw. In addition, the provision should only cover the direct costs of the sale or termination and any operating losses of the operation up to the date of sale or termination. In both cases, this should be calculated after taking into account the aggregate profit, if any, to be recognised in the profit and loss account from the future profits of the operation or disposal of its assets. In the case of an intended sale for which no legally binding sale agreement exists, no obligation has been entered into by the reporting entity; accordingly, provisions for the direct costs of the decision to sell and for future operating losses should not be made. (Paragraphs 18 and 45)

There is also the problem of what to do when the provision for discontinuance made in a previous period turns out to be overstated. Assuming the provision had been treated as an exceptional item, should the reversal of the provision be similarly treated, treated as a prior period adjustment, or treated as an ordinary item? Consistency would normally require that it be treated as an exceptional item, though it may qualify as a prior period adjustment if it could have been detected from the information available when the previous financial statements were approved.

Interestingly, only once sold or terminated should the effects be shown under the discontinued operations category. Until that time, any provisions made should be shown under continuing operations. However, comparative figures in the profit and loss account should include in the continuing operations category only the results of those operations included in the current period's continuing operations (paragraph 30). In addition, to be treated as 'discontinued', the sale or termination may occur up to three months after the balance sheet date (or the date when the financial statements are approved, if earlier) (paragraph 4a) - i.e. it qualifies as an 'adjusting event' as defined by SSAP 17 (*Accounting for post balance sheet events* - chapter 6) even though the decision to discontinue may only have been made after the balance sheet date.

Finally, should provision be made for the consequences of a decision to terminate an activity when no binding sale agreement or detailed formal plan exists? Paragraph 45 states that none should be made (although permanent diminutions in asset values should be recorded). This would seem to contradict the requirements of SSAP 18 (*Accounting for contingencies* - chapter 7). As there is no reference to SSAP 18 in FRS 3, no clear guidance exists as to the whether FRS 3 is excluding this type of contingency from the application of SSAP 18, or whether it is merely stating the 'normal' position. On balance, the true and fair view should be the deciding factor, which effectively means that SSAP 18 should be applied.

Revaluation and the profit or loss on disposal of an asset

Paragraph 21 states that 'the profit or loss on the disposal of an asset should be accounted for in the profit and loss account of the period in which the disposal occurs as the difference between the net sale proceeds and the net carrying amount, whether carried at historical cost (less any provisions made) or at a valuation'. This could be interpreted as meaning that the depreciation provided on revalued assets should be ignored and the valuation, whenever made, should be used in the calculation. However, the use of the term 'net carrying amount' makes it clear that this interpretation would be inappropriate and the net carrying amount (i.e. revaluation amount less cumulative depreciation provided to date) should be used.

Primary statements

FRS 3 introduces two new primary statements: the statement of total recognised gains and losses (that shows the extent to which shareholders' funds have increased or decreased from all the various gains and losses recognised in the period, and enables users to consider all recognised gains and losses of a reporting entity in assessing its overall performance; an example of what would be included in the statement would be unrealised gains on fixed asset revaluations) and the reconciliation of movements in shareholders' funds (which highlights changes in shareholders' funds which do not appear in the other primary statements whose disclosure can assist in understanding the change in the financial position of the entity). Whereas the statement of total recognised gains and losses is required (except where the reporting entity has no recognised gains or losses other than the profit or loss for the period; in which case, a statement to this effect should be made immediately below the profit and loss account - paragraph 57), the movement in shareholders' funds can be included as a note rather than as a primary statement, indeed paragraph 28 refers to the use of a note.

Comparative figures should be given for all items in the primary statements and such notes thereto as are required by the FRS (paragraph 30). However, the analysis of comparative figures between continuing and discontinued operations is not required on the face of the profit and loss account (paragraph 64).

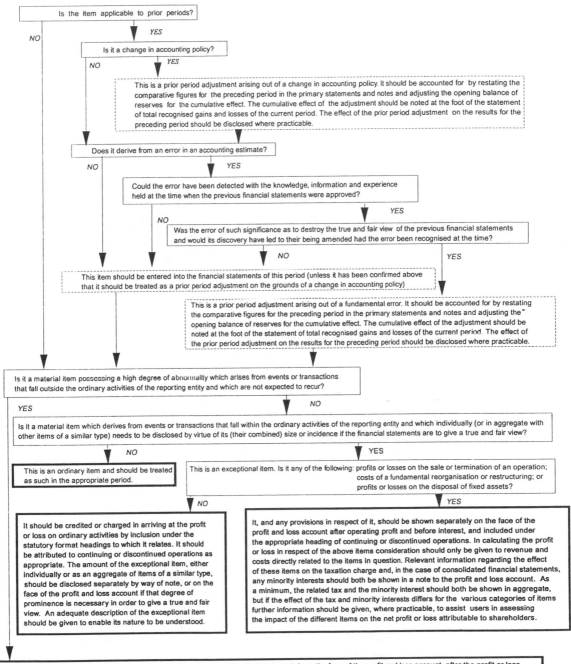

FRS 3 Prior period adjustments, exceptional items and extraordinary items

Short Questions

*ASSUME THAT MATERIALITY EXISTS IN **EVERY** CASE*

Questions 1-18 relate to a household furniture manufacturing and retailing plc with current turnover of £8m and draft pre-tax profit of £1.4m. (Last year £6.6m and £1.1m respectively.) The company's financial year ends on 31st December. (Ignore the taxation effects.)

1   Normally the company breaks even on its currency exchange dealings but this year a currency exchange surplus amounting to £180,000 arose on a remittance from an overseas depot.

2   In September, the company entered into a contract with the Brazilian government for the supply of wood from the Queimar tree (which grows only in Brazil) to be used in the construction of an exclusive range of outdoor furniture. The company started work on the project in January and had spent £110,000 developing the product until, in November, the Brazilian government was replaced and all foreign contracts were cancelled. There is no possibility of reinstatement of the contract and no other source for the wood. Work on the project ceased immediately the supply contract was cancelled.

3   Eighteen months ago the company was informed that a shop that it had constructed the year before, at a cost of £12,000, had been built without proper planning permission and that it was going to be issued with a directive to destroy it. As a result, it was held prudent at the time to write-off, as an exceptional item, the £11,400 book value of the building. (The company policy is to depreciate buildings over twenty years using the straight-line method.) The directive has never been issued and the shop has been used continuously since it was first built. During the last year a new local council was elected, and it now transpires that the destruction order will definitely not be issued.

4   Previously, *development* expenditure was written-off over 5 years. The company has changed its policy this year and now writes it off as it is incurred. In last year's balance sheet, *development* was shown as £320,000. (This year's new [net] *research and development* costs were £145,000.)

5   In May, the company made an extra £200,000 contribution to the employees' pension fund.

6   In April, the company entered into a contract to refurbish all hospitals in Strathclyde Region. It was expected to take two years to complete at a cost of £900,000. The contract price was £1.8m. Cost was expected to be spread evenly over the two years. Since the start, serious problems have been encountered due to the unforeseen complexity of the design of hospital interiors. As a result, costs are running at a rate of £100,000 per month and are not expected to fall. Completion is still on schedule.

7   An overall cost of £800,000 was incurred in terminating production at the company's Edinburgh factory during the year.

8   Over three years ago, the company bought four weaving machines, which are exclusively manufactured in the far east, for £10,000 each. The currency of their country of origin

has consistently weakened against the pound since its government was overthrown by the army in the middle of the previous year (50% in the last 12 months). As a result, the current UK price of a machine is £4,000. The company had the machines professionally revalued at the end of the current year. The revalued amount is £3,000 per machine. They have an estimated useful economic life of 20 years (from when they were first used) and are being depreciated using the straight-line method. The estimated residual value at the time of purchase was £1,000 per machine. As a result of the change in the price of the machine, this is now felt to have been an overestimate and £600 is considered more appropriate. No revaluation has taken place previously.

9   Equipment which had a net carrying value of £128,000 had been written-off (as an exceptional item) in the previous period's financial statements (when the decision had been taken to terminate production of an old product). An overall profit of £320,000 arose when the termination was completed in May, including proceeds of £135,000 from the sale of the equipment. Apart from the asset write-down, no provisions in respect of the termination had been made in the previous period's financial statements.

10   In September, an art expert who was visiting the company secretary discovered that one of the paintings in the company boardroom was a valuable masterpiece. It was sold at auction in December for £300,000. No value had ever been placed on the painting in the company's financial statements. (Assume that company policy has never been to revalue its fixed assets.)

11   If the company decided not to sell the painting in question 10, what would be the appropriate treatment?

12   What would be the treatment if the painting sold in question 10 had been received as a gift from the founding chairman 150 years ago, at which time he had entered in the board minutes that it was the work of a famous artist, but that no-one had ever believed his claim? (Assume that company policy has never been to revalue its fixed assets.)

13   Assume all the information concerning the painting referred to in questions 10, 11 and 12. However, if it was not sold, but valued by the art expert valued it at £250,000 when he saw it and also, for this question only, assume that the company policy had always been to revalue its fixed assets every five years and incorporate the revalued amount in the financial statements. What would be the appropriate treatment?

14   As a result of a reorganization of its distribution network, the company incurred redundancy costs of £50,000.

15   Due to an error in raw material ordering, the company used the wrong grade of material in its production of lounge suites for two weeks during the summer. As a result, the entire production for that period had to be recalled and re-upholstered. The cost of the error has been estimated at £70,000.

16   All the company's cloth cutting machines were wrongly set for the last three months of the year. As a result, £30,000 more raw material was used in production than would normally have been the case.

17   Last year's accounts included in turnover an amount of £700,000 relating to sub-contracted manufacturing of a product for *Sonno Plc* who went into liquidation in the first month of the current year still owing the entire amount. No payment is expected and the whole debt has been written-off as bad. (Total bad debts for this year are £745,000.)

18   During the year, as a result of public pressure, the government banned the use of kangaroo skin in household furniture. As a result, the company had to scrap £40,000 stock of kangaroo skin suites. The company recovered this amount from their insurers, along with a further £55,000 for loss of profits resulting.

Questions 19-20 relate to an industrial holding company with current group turnover of £19.3m and draft pre-tax profit of £4.65m. (Last year £18.2m and £3.1m respectively.) The company's financial year ends on 31st December. (Ignore the taxation effects.)

19   In June, the company disposed of a small portion of its shareholding in a subsidiary company resulting in a loss of £70,000.

20   In September, the company disposed of its 100% shareholding in a company which it had acquired in the previous financial period. As it was acquired solely with the intention to resell it, the company had not been consolidated as a subsidiary into the previous period's financial statements. A gain of £220,000 was made when the holding was sold.

Questions 21-25 relate to a chemicals company with current turnover of £11m and draft pre-tax profit of £4.8m. (Last year £11.6m and £4.6m respectively.) The company's financial year ends on 31st December. (Ignore the taxation effects.)

21   As a result of changes in the rules relating to the availability of capital allowances on scientific research, the company made an adjustment of £300,000 to its deferred taxation account.

22   Some highly specialised equipment that the company used in its research laboratory was found to emit a highly dangerous form of radiation. As a result, the equipment was scrapped. The makers went into liquidation just before the dangerous nature of the equipment was detected and no compensation is likely to be received. The net book value of the equipment at the start of the year was £120,000.

23   As a result of the equipment having to be scrapped (see question 22) the company spent £200,000 replacing it.

24   In October, the company sold a sterilisation purifier for £125,000. The machine had cost £60,000 exactly four years earlier and had been revalued to £140,000 at the end of the previous financial period (net carrying amount £120,000 after depreciation of £20,000). Straight-line depreciation is applied to all the company's equipment.

25   The company moved its laboratory to new premises during the year and made a gain of £210,000 when it sold the old building.

Additional Questions

*ASSUME THAT MATERIALITY EXISTS IN **EVERY** CASE*

Questions 26-37 relate to a company which is an industrial and domestic oil distributor in Scotland with current turnover of £7.8m and draft pre-tax profit of £0.65m. (Last year £7.2m and £0.9m respectively.) The company's financial year ends on 31st December. (Ignore the taxation effects.)

26   In March, the company moved its head office to Dunfermline. Under the terms of the rental agreement of the previous head office building in Bo'ness, the company was liable to compensate the owners if they could only sell it for a book loss. The company duly paid the owners compensation of £140,000.

27   Twelve employees were made redundant on the transfer from Bo'ness to Dunfermline. The cost to the company was £168,000.

28   At the start of the year, the company invested £150,000 in a North Sea oil exploration site. The site was later found to be worthless.

29   For almost 100 years, the company had been treating a building which it uses as a sales office in St Andrews as heritable property. They recently discovered that the original entries through the books had been incorrect and that the office is held on a 99 year lease which expires in the middle of next year. For the first 88 years no depreciation was charged on the property. In each of the previous ten years it has been depreciated at 2% per annum. The original cost was £500. The building was revalued at £100,000 during the year when it was first depreciated.

30   A tanker owned by the company was a complete write-off after a crash for which its driver was entirely to blame. The company only carried third party insurance on its tankers and was thus unable to obtain any compensation from its insurers for the loss of the vehicle. The tanker was new and had cost £50,000.

31   As a result of the loss incurred when the tanker crashed (see question 30), the company decided it would be better to have its remaining fleet of five tankers comprehensively insured. This was arranged at a cost of £10,000.

32   The company made an out-of-court settlement of £60,000 to a motor cyclist who was seriously injured and whose vintage motor bike was destroyed in the tanker crash described in question 30.

33   The company sacked the driver involved in the tanker crash (see question 30) as he was found to have been drunk at the time. As a gesture of sympathy for the two broken legs he sustained, they gave him three months wages in lieu of notice (£4,000).

34   Some petrol which the company had stored prior to distribution to its customers was contaminated by vandals during the year and had to be disposed of. The company had no insurance cover and the net cost of clean-up and replacement was £53,000.

35   At the end of June the company ceased marketing its own brand of motor oils. This had been a consistent money loser over the past four years. Net losses, which were evenly spread over the half year, amounted to £204,000. The decision to cease marketing the product was taken at a meeting held at the end of the March.

36   The company made ten employees redundant when it ceased marketing its own brand of motor oils (see question 35). The total cost to the company was £126,000.

37   The furniture from the Bo'ness office was transferred to the new building in Dunfermline (see questions 26 and 27), but found to be inappropriate due to its old-fashioned style (most of it was more than 10 years old). As a result, it was disposed of. (The secretaries were given a free choice on what to do with it. Not surprisingly it vanished very quickly.) It had a net book value of £17,000 at the start of the year.

Questions 38-40 relate to an advertising company with current turnover of £2m and draft pre-tax profit of £0.7m. (Last year £1.6m and £0.6m respectively.) The company's financial year ends on 31st December. (Ignore the taxation effects.)

38   The company decided to change from a 70% reducing balance for office furniture depreciation, to 20% straight-line. The net book value of office furniture at the year end was £62,000.

39   In June, a director of the company (who has since resigned) was convicted of attempting to bribe the marketing director of a national supermarket chain to appoint the company as its advertising agency. Extensive publicity was given to the case, as a result of which the company spent £124,000 on a media campaign in an effort to regain its market image. The campaign was relatively successful and only a handful of established clients transferred their business elsewhere.

40   During the year, the company's equipment store was broken into and items worth £109,000 were stolen. No insurance cover was in force at the time.

Questions 41-45 relate to a variety of companies, all of which have a balance sheet date of 31st December.

41   In September an art expert who was visiting the company secretary discovered that one of the paintings in the company boardroom was a valuable masterpiece. It was sold at auction in December for £300,000. It had been received as a gift from the founding chairman 150 years ago, at which time he had entered in the board minutes that it was the work of a famous artist, but no-one had ever believed his claim. No value had ever been placed on the painting in the company's financial statements, but the art expert valued it at £250,000 when he saw it. (For this question only, assume that company policy had always been to revalue its fixed assets every five years and incorporate the revalued amount in the financial statements.)

42   In February, the company acquired the rights to produce a range of items in the UK. Between March and October, it produced and sold the items. In November, all production and selling activity ceased as a result of its selling the rights to another company.

43   In May the company received £100,000 damages for libel from the editor of a consumer magazine

44   The company transferred an extra £250,000 to the employee share scheme.

45   The company had previously capitalised a patent on an ammonia-based refining process. It was capitalised at its cost to the company and had a carrying value of £300,000. During the year, a competitor challenged the company's right to the patent. As a result the patent rights were withdrawn from the company and transferred to its competitor. The company has decided not to appeal the judgement.

3   SSAP 9: Stocks and Long Term Contracts

Summary of the accounting treatment requirements

Stocks should be stated at the total of the lower of cost and net realisable value of the separate items of stock or of groups of similar items.

In the balance sheet (or in the notes), stocks should be sub-classified so as to indicate the amounts held in each of the main categories in the standard balance sheet formats (as adapted where appropriate) of the Companies Act 1985. (These categories are *raw materials and consumables, work in progress, finished goods and goods for resale,* and *payments on account.*)

Long term contracts should be assessed on a contract by contract basis. They should be reflected in the profit and loss account by recording turnover and related costs as contract activity progresses. Turnover should be ascertained in a manner appropriate to the stage of completion of the contract, the business and the industry in which it operates. Where the outcome of the contract can be assessed with reasonable accuracy, profit should be recognised (so far as prudence permits) as the difference between recognised turnover and related costs. Any foreseeable losses identified should be immediately recognised.

The amount of long term contracts, at costs incurred, net of amounts transferred to cost of sales, after deducting foreseeable losses and payments on account not matched with turnover should be classified as 'long term contract balances' and separately disclosed within the balance sheet heading of 'stocks'. The balance sheet note should disclose separately the balances of 'net cost less foreseeable losses' and 'applicable payments on account'.

Problems of interpretation and grey areas

The following items are discussed under the heading of stocks: cost identification; normal activity levels; functional allocation of overheads; valuation bases; net realisable value; and pre-production costs. Under the heading of long term contracts, there is discussion of: the meaning of 'long term'; profit recognition; interest costs on long term contracts; the splitting of contracts into sub-contracts for the purposes of profit and loss recognition; turnover valuation; payments on account; and foreseeable losses on the contract as a whole. The limitations of the standard are also considered.

Stocks

Cost identification

Costs of stock should comprise that expenditure which has been incurred in the normal course of business in bringing the product or service to its present location and condition. Such costs will include all related production overheads, even though these may accrue on a time basis (i.e. variable *and fixed* overheads).

There are two types of cost: purchase costs and conversion costs. *Purchase costs* include purchase price, import duties, transport, handling and other directly attributable costs, less trade discounts, rebates and subsidies (paragraph 18). *Conversion costs* include directly attributable costs (e.g. direct labour, direct expenses and subcontracted work); production overheads (those incurred in materials, labour or services for production, based on the *normal* level of activity, taking one year with another); and any other overheads incurred in bringing the item to its present location and condition. Each overhead, including depreciation, should be classified by function (production, marketing, selling, administration, etc.) so as to ensure inclusion of all overheads relating to production (paragraphs 19 and 20).

Normal activity levels

The appendices to SSAP 9 are exceptionally informative. Appendix 1 considers many of the areas likely to cause problems, one of which concerns the requirement that *abnormal* conversion costs (e.g. exceptional spoilage and idle capacity) be eliminated from stock valuations. In considering how to determine what constitutes the *normal* level of activity, it suggests that reference should be made to (a) the production volume which the production facilities are intended to produce under the working conditions prevailing during the year (e.g. eight hours a day, five days a week, for 50 weeks); (b) the budgeted level of activity in the year under review, and the following year; and (c) the level of activity achieved, both in the year under review, and in previous years. Once determined, temporary changes in these factors could be ignored but persistent variations should result in a revision of the norm. These recommendations still leave room for different bases to be used, particularly the distinction between temporary and permanent changes and the point at which the former becomes the latter. Nevertheless, they at least point the way towards the type of information that should be examined before a decision is made regarding overhead allocation.

Functional allocation of overheads

According to appendix 1, overhead allocations should be done on a functional basis, the question of whether an overhead is fixed or variable being irrelevant (appendix 1, section 4). General management and central service department costs are often not directly related to production and should only be allocated to product cost when they can reasonably be said to have been incurred in conversion (appendix 1, sections 5, 6, and 7). Marginal cost-based stock valuations must be amended to incorporate those relevant production overheads omitted from that valuation. Paragraph 4 of the standard states that the methods used in allocating costs need to be selected with a view to providing the fairest possible approximation to the expenditure actually incurred in bringing the product to its present location and condition. While the information in appendix 1 helps in determining what should be included in 'cost', no guidance is given as to how to determine an appropriate basis for cost allocation. Thus, two companies with the same costs and organisational structures, producing the same products, and with the same volume of production and stock, could have very different stock valuations. For example, one could allocate overheads on the basis of labour hours, the other on the basis of machine hours, and both could be complying with the standard.

It is not stated in the standard that service department and general management costs relating to purchasing should be included in the cost of purchase. However, paragraph 18 states that the cost of purchase includes 'any other directly attributable costs'. As indicated in the previous paragraph, general management and central service department costs may be allocated to conversion; it would also be appropriate to allocate these costs to the cost of purchase when they can reasonably be allocated to the purchasing function.

Valuation bases

Another area referred to in appendix 1 is that of costing methods: standard costs, if used, should be revised regularly; base stock and LIFO are not considered appropriate (paragraph 39 of the standard indicates that LIFO can be used if necessary in order to give a true and fair view); latest purchase price is not an acceptable basis for valuing stock if some of it was purchased at another price; selling price less estimated profit margin is only acceptable as a basis for stock valuation if it gives a *reasonable approximation* of actual cost - a purely subjective yardstick which obviously leaves a lot to be desired (if the cost is unknown, how can the value used be judged appropriate?); and where by-product costs are not separable from the costs of the principal product, the by-products may be stated at their net realisable value and the costs of the principal product calculated after deducting the value placed on the by-products.

Stocks must be stated at the lower of cost and net realisable value. As a result of deterioration, obsolescence, or a change in demand, there may be no reasonable expectation of sufficient future revenue to cover cost incurred. When this is the case, the irrecoverable cost should be charged to revenue in the year under review through the use of the net realisable value for stock valuation, rather than cost. Net realisable value is the estimated proceeds from the sale of items of stock less all further costs to completion and less all costs to be incurred in marketing, selling and distribution *directly related to* the items in question (paragraph 5). Replacement cost may be used only when it is the best measure of realisable value. (The standard gives the example of materials whose price fluctuates considerably and for which no sales contract exists - paragraph 6.)

Net realisable value

Net realisable value is central to stock valuation and appendix 1 considers it at some length. Where it is applied according to a set formula (e.g. on all stock held for more than 12 months), the formula should be reviewed if special circumstances arise which it is not designed to accommodate (e.g. the sudden obsolescence of a product). If the net realisable value of materials is less than their cost, but the goods which the materials are to be used to produce can still be sold at a profit when the material cost is charged to the product, the materials should continue to be valued at cost. Where net realisable value is applied to revalue finished goods stock, the values of stocks of parts, sub-assemblies, and stocks on order need to be reviewed as well. Post balance sheet date events should be considered in arriving at the net realisable value at balance sheet date. Thus, if the sales price of finished goods stock were cut after the balance sheet date, resulting in a loss based on the original costs incurred, net realisable value may be appropriate for the finished goods stock and/or for some of its raw materials, parts and sub-assemblies, where it is lower than their cost. (SSAP 17: *Accounting for post balance sheet events* (chapter 6) should also be consulted in these circumstances.)

Pre-production costs

One minor area covered in section 2 of appendix 1 is that of pre-production costs. The option is given of including pre-production marketing and selling costs on *firm* sales contracts for goods or services *to customer's specifications*, along with the relevant design overheads. The inclusion of design overheads in stock valuations is implied by the terms of the standard. However, the inclusion of pre-production marketing and selling costs in the stock valuation is an extension of the standard and could lead to problems in determining which costs are pre-production and which are mid-production. For example, if a company which manufactures 8,000 widgets each month, entered into a contract on 1st December (when it had no stock) for delivery of 9,000 widgets on

5th January, and the contract was renegotiated on 31st December when the original order was doubled, should the renegotiation costs be included in the stock valuation at the year end, or should they be excluded as they were incurred in mid production? There is no provision in the standard for the inclusion in 'cost' of marketing/selling costs, and their inclusion would not comply with the definition of 'cost' as given in paragraphs 18 and 19. They could only be included if they complied with the exception given in the appendix. The additional marketing costs incurred would therefore not be included in the value of the stock produced up to the year end, though, in theory, they could be carried forward to be included in the value of stock produced thereafter.

(The flowchart on page 23 considers the determination of stock value.)

Long term Contracts

The meaning of 'long term'

Long term contracts form a major part of the standard and two of the three appendices are devoted to them. Appendix 2 contains some definitions, together with five examples illustrating the various rules to be applied in determining the entries to be made in respect of long term contracts. These examples are further developed in appendix 3. (The flowchart on page 24 presents these rules.) First of all, it is necessary to determine what is meant by 'long term'. In effect, any contract which spans the financial year end is 'long term'. Thus, if the company financial year end is 31st December and a contract is due to be completed on 1st January, the contract is 'long term'. Paragraph 22 of the standard states that contracts which have a duration of less than one year should be treated as long term if they are sufficiently material to the activity of the period. It also states that the company should maintain a consistent policy, from year to year, in determining whether a contract is 'long term'. Overall, given the aims of the standard relating to long term contracts - to match turnover to costs - it would be appropriate, where the amounts involved are material, to treat any contract spanning the balance sheet date as being 'long term'. Those that are completed during the post balance sheet period will usually be valued without many problems. It is only those that are still outstanding thereafter that may give rise to major problems in valuation.

Profit recognition

Two definitions relevant to any consideration of long term contracts are given in the standard: those of 'attributable profit' and 'foreseeable losses'. *Attributable profit* is that part of total profit currently estimated to arise over the duration of the contract, after allowing for estimated remedial and maintenance costs and increases in costs (so far as not recoverable under the terms of the contract), that fairly reflects the profit attributable to that part of the work performed at the accounting date. There can be no attributable profit until the outcome of the contract can be assessed with reasonable certainty (paragraph 23).

Foreseeable losses are those losses estimated to arise over the duration of the contract, after allowing for estimated remedial and maintenance costs and increases in costs (so far as not recoverable under the terms of the contract), *whether or not* work has commenced, and irrespective of both the proportion of work completed and profits expected on other contracts (paragraph 24).

The standard does not prescribe a point at which profit on long term contracts should start to be recognised. The requirement that a contract's outcome must be capable of being assessed with reasonable certainty before any profit should be recognised, leaves it entirely to individual judgment. One company may recognise profit after the first six months, while another may wait until a year has passed. As a result, inter-firm comparability is impaired. However, the standard does assist in intra-firm comparison from one year to the next as it requires consistent application of the method of ascertaining attributable profit both within the business, and from year to year (paragraph 32).

Clearly, future costs must be estimated in arriving at a figure for attributable profit or foreseeable losses. Unfortunately, no two people are likely to independently arrive at exactly the same amount. Thus, the profits and losses recognised are likely to vary considerably from one company to another, and inter-firm comparability is further impaired.

Interest costs on long term contracts

Appendix 1 considers long term contracts in some detail. Interest costs which can be identified as arising from specific long term contracts, can be included in the costs of those contracts. If this is done, the amount of interest so included must be disclosed by way of a note to the financial statements.

The splitting of contracts into sub-contracts for the purposes of profit and loss recognition

Sometimes a contract can be broken down into a series of sub-contracts. In this case, it is suggested that profit may be calculated on each of the sub-contracts and entered into the financial statements accordingly. However, the overall contract should also be viewed and where incomplete sub-contracts are expected to generate a loss, such losses should be immediately offset against the profits arising from the other completed and part-completed sub-contracts.

Turnover valuation

Turnover should be ascertained in a manner suitable to the industry and the specific contracts concerned. It is suggested that valuation of work carried out may be used to derive a value for turnover (appendix 1, section 23); and that profit should be regarded as earned in relation to the *amount* of work performed to date (appendix 1, section 24). These two approaches could often produce different results, but clarification is found in paragraph 9 of the standard which states that 'the profit taken up needs to reflect the proportion of the work carried out ... and to take into account any known inequalities of profitability in the various stages of a contract'. Consequently, when there is a work certified value, this should be used as the turnover value and the costs incurred in achieving that turnover charged to cost of sales. Where no work certified figure exists, costs to date as a proportion of total expected costs should be applied to the contract value in order to determine the figure for turnover. Where the work certified value is not available for all work completed, a combination of the two approaches would be appropriate. One further point regarding turnover, mentioned in section 27 of appendix 1, concerns settlements of claims against the purchaser arising from circumstances not foreseen in the contract: these should only be incorporated when there is sufficient evidence that payment will be received.

Turnover on long term contracts is determined by the combination of two items: costs and profit. While the amount of profit recognised in an accounting period on a long term contract is intended to reflect that proportion of profit actually earned in the accounting period under review, this will not usually be the case. Often no profit will be recognised in the early part of a contract. Thus, the accounting period when profit is first recognised will also be credited with profits relating to earlier accounting periods. In addition, circumstances change and cost and profitability patterns alter as a result. Each accounting period must absorb such changes relating to earlier accounting periods. Sometimes this will take the form of the inclusion of profits relating to earlier periods; on other occasions, the profit for the period will be offset by a reduction in profits previously recognised but subsequently believed to have been overestimated. The method used for arriving at the profit to be recognised, and the means by which turnover is determined, must be disclosed and consistently applied from one year to the next (paragraph 32).

Payments on account

Paragraph 25 states that 'payments on account include all amounts received and receivable'. If a customer who had been invoiced for £100 has only paid £80 at the balance sheet date, normal accounting practice would be to include the £20 unpaid in debtors. The examples in appendices 2 and 3 show that payments on account which exceed cumulative turnover should be included in creditors. In the case of the above example, if cumulative turnover were £80, £20 would be entered in creditors (as payments on account are £100). Consequently, there would be a £20 entry in debtors and a £20 entry in creditors. Ordinarily this would have little or no effect upon the quality of the information contained in the financial statements. However, a company might have receivable payments on account which, when combined with payments on account received, result in a substantial amount in excess of cumulative turnover: in this case, a misleading impression might be gained if working capital and liquidity ratio calculations were to be performed. In these circumstances, a more true and fair view would result if the amount of receivable payments on account which is included in both these sections of the balance sheet were, at the very least, disclosed.

Foreseeable losses on the contract as a whole

One final point relating to long term contracts concerns the term 'foreseeable losses on the contract as a whole'. Analysis of 'Project 4' in appendix 3 reveals that, while a contract will be charged through profit and loss with the whole anticipated loss, the 'foreseeable losses on the contract as a whole' value which is used to calculate the stocks, provision/accrual for foreseeable losses, and creditor balance sheet values, is that part of the whole anticipated loss which relates to future periods. Thus, if cumulative turnover is £100 and cumulative total costs transferred to cost of sales amount to £110, the £10 loss already charged to profit and loss would be subtracted from the overall foreseeable loss on the contract as a whole (of, say, £25) to provide the figure to be used in the above calculations (which, in this case, would be £15). No adjustment of the future foreseeable losses is made for profits recognised prior to the future foreseeable loss being identified. Consequently, the term 'future foreseeable losses on the contract as a whole' refers to losses which will arise in the future, *not* to all the past, present and future losses on the contract.

Limitations of the Standard

Overall, SSAP 9 attempts to cover an area which, in the absence of regulation, is open to widespread abuse. The valuation placed on stock can materially affect the performance and liquidity position reported in the financial statements. By pursuing the matching principle and applying the prudence convention, SSAP 9 attempts to ensure that a true and fair view is given in the statements. However, it does not prevent the application of individual judgment in a number of cases: in fact, it encourages it.

The selection of appropriate bases for overhead allocation is left to the individual company, with the result that comparability between companies, even within the same industry, is impaired. In addition, should a company switch from one base of allocation to another (for example, from labour hours to machine hours), there is no requirement to disclose the change: comparability is again impaired, and in this case it also affects intra-firm comparison.

While LIFO and base stock are not recommended in the standard, their use is not prohibited. Thus, companies may still use them if they believe it necessary in order to give a true and fair view. This is stated, rather unnecessarily, in the discussion of LIFO in paragraph 39: the 'true and fair' clause always overrides what is contained in any standard and does not require to be included in the text in order to be applicable.

As has been shown in the preceding sections, similar contracts may be treated as 'long term' by one company, and 'short term' by another; one company may recognise profit after six months, another may wait a year; and one company's views regarding future costs may be very different from another's. The existence of these, and other areas in which there is scope for subjective judgement, significantly affects the comparability of reported performance among companies.

The illogicality of the definition given in the standard for payments on account, and the lack of clarity concerning the term 'foreseeable losses on contract as a whole', provide much scope for confusion. Care should be exercised whenever these items are encountered.

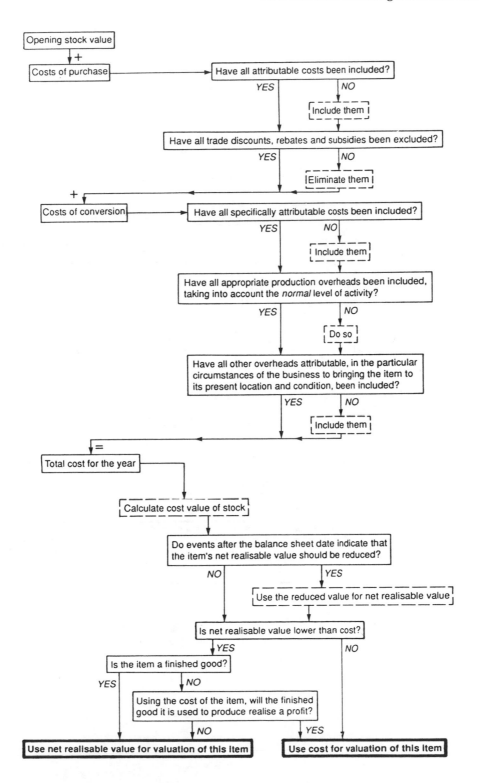

SSAP 9(1)   Determination of stock value

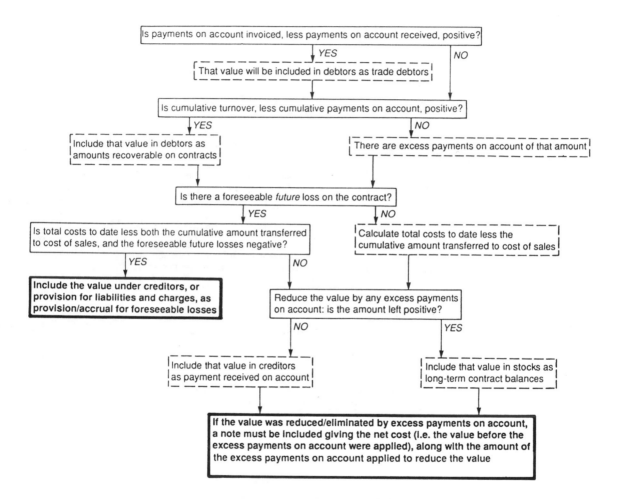

Short Questions

*ASSUME THAT MATERIALITY EXISTS IN **EVERY** CASE*

Questions 1-39 relate to a furniture manufacturing and redecoration company with current turnover of £15m and net pre-tax profit of £2.5m. (Last year £13.6m and £1.8m respectively.) The company's financial year ends on 31st December and the Board of Directors are scheduled to approve the accounts on 31st March.

1   During the year the company sub-contracted to develop a new range of garden furniture for an Australian hardware company incorporating the company's newly discovered sun-proof furniture varnish. Total costs in the year, £37,000.

2   In December the company paid £42,000 for all the remaining toilet suites from a bankrupt manufacturer. They are to be sold to the trade. In order to generate orders a circular was produced and distributed at a cost of £1,800.

3   All the company's cloth cutting machines were wrongly set for the last three months of the year. As a result, £30,000 more raw material was used in production than would normally have been the case.

4   Early in the year, the company was sub-contracted to develop a new exclusive range of bedroom furniture for Marks & Spencer. It incorporates the company's newly discovered mirrored glass effect finish. Total costs in the year were £22,000. On 31st December, the company received a cheque for £22,000 from Marks & Spencer.

5   At the balance sheet date, the company had 4,000 wooden ceiling panels in stock. Their total cost was £14,000. Due to foreign competition, the market for these panels had slumped in the last three months of the year and the balance sheet date sale price was £2.

6   In order to sell the wooden ceiling panels (see question 5), they require to be packaged and shipped. Costs per panel are £0.30 and £0.20, respectively.

7   At the balance sheet date, the company had stock of furniture fitments valued at cost of £30,000. The fitments are used in the production of kitchen units. Four fitments (total cost £5) are used in the manufacture of each completed unit. The kitchen units have a total cost of £23 and their balance sheet date sale price was £25. Net realisable value of the fitments at the balance sheet date (based on replacement cost) was £21,000.

8   Two weeks after the balance sheet date, the net realisable value (based on replacement cost) of the furniture fitments referred to in question 7 was still £21,000, but the sale price of the kitchen units was reduced to £22, as a result of increased competition. No other costs incurred in the manufacture of the kitchen units had changed since the balance sheet date. All of the balance sheet date stock of furniture fitments was still held by the company, though half of it was in kitchen units held in the company's warehouse.

9   The company has stock of 1,200 glass-topped coffee tables which was purchased direct from a foreign supplier for £14,000 over three years ago on the basis of an expected contract which never transpired. All attempts to sell the coffee tables have failed and an

offer has been received from a discount warehouse to buy them from the company for £2,000.

10   Early in the year, the company was sub-contracted to develop a new exclusive range of kitchen furniture for MFI. MFI agreed to reimburse all development costs incurred. Total costs in the year were £55,000, in respect of which £30,000 has been received to date from MFI.

11   The company produces three different beds in its Dundee factory. In each of the previous two years, the total labour hours worked in the factory was 450,000. Fixed overheads are apportioned to production on the basis of standard hours per unit. In the current year, the total labour hours worked was, as before, 450,000. The same products are being produced as in the previous two years. The standard hours per single bed is 8, per queen-sized bed 10, and per king-sized bed 12. These standards were set three years ago and have remained unchanged. Actual labour hours per bed during the current year were 9, 10 and 11, respectively. 15,000 of each type of bed were produced during the year. There was no work in progress at the balance sheet date. Stock of finished beds comprised: 3,000 single beds, 2,000 queen-sized beds, and 1,500 king-sized beds. The stocks are at a similar level to that in previous years.

12   Included in the company's stocks at the balance sheet date is a large holding of plywood boards. This stock is stored on wooden pallets and is withdrawn for use by taking the uppermost board first. Additions to stock are placed on top of existing stocks. The stock is approximately ten metres high. During the year, four consignments were received, each of 1000 boards. During the year, stocks never fell below 1,100 boards. The cost per board rose at each delivery and was £12, £13, £14, and £15 respectively. Closing stock is 1,300 boards. This is the first year the company has held stocks of these boards.

13   The company manufactures card tables. The total cost per table, as calculated by the chief management accountant, is £26. This comprises material costs of £13.50 (after deducting a 10% cash discount received from the supplier); delivery charges on the materials of £0.20; direct labour and expenses of £10; other production overheads apportioned of £1.65; £0.55 central service department costs (derived from the original apportionment to the production function of £35,000); and general administration costs apportioned at a rate of £0.10 per table. At the year end, the company had 120 finished card tables in stock.

14   There were 30 half-finished and 40 three-quarter finished card tables in stock at the balance sheet date (see question 13). All the materials are incorporated at an early stage in the production process.

15   The company sells all waste from its production of laminated worktops to a local foundry. The sale takes place every three months. The company had stock of this waste valued at a net realisable value of £1,200 at the balance sheet date. This represented the result of two months production. One months production of laminated worktops was also in stock at that date.

Questions 16 - 42 are concerned with long term contracts

16   In October the company entered into a contract to furnish and decorate every new house built in Scotland by Wimpey during the following 12 months. Costs to date are £50,000 and a further £70,000 is expected to be incurred before completion. The work done so far will be invoiced at £85,000 when the company raises an invoice at the end of the first six months.

17   During the year, the company entered into a contract to refurbish an Edinburgh concert hall. Costs to date of £120,000 have been transferred to cost of sales. A further £70,000 is expected to be spent prior to completion. The contract price is £160,000. The contract is 65% complete.

18   In March the company agreed to fully refurbish a chain of supermarkets. It is anticipated that a profit will result and the contract is expected to take eighteen more months to complete. No payment will be received until three months after the contract is completed.

Questions 19 - 21 concern a contract to redecorate all the chalets in three timeshare resorts. It was started in July and is scheduled to take two years.

19   Turnover recognised in this year's accounts is £50,000. No profit has been recognised this year. At the end of September the company raised an invoice for £10,000 and sent it to the customer, another invoice, this time for £20,000, was sent at the beginning of December. At the year end, payments on account from the customer totalled £35,000. Total costs to balance sheet date are £95,000, of which £76,000 are to be recorded as cost of sales. The remaining eighteen months of the contract are expected to break-even.

20   An error has been discovered in the amounts posted to the timeshare customer's account: the year end payments on account from the customer totalled £53,000, not the £35,000 mentioned in question 19.

21   After reconsideration of the timeshare contract, an additional £30,000 is to be provided to cover losses on the contract as a whole.

22   The company is replacing all sleeper furnishings on ScotRail trains. The contract is worth £2.6m, total costs were estimated at £1.4m and were expected to be spread evenly over twenty months. Work began at the start of April and costs so far are £0.9m due to a mistake in the price used in the contract quotation calculation. All the estimates have now been checked and it is anticipated that a further £1.1m will be incurred over the remainder of the contract. All costs to balance sheet date are to be included in cost of sales. (£200,000 payment on account has been invoiced, but has not yet been paid by British Rail.)

23   A contract to supply and fit all the restaurants in the *Dormebem* hotel chain with kitchen furniture was started during the year. The contract is expected to take a further six months to complete. Turnover recognised in this year's accounts is £80,000, including profit of £25,000. At the end of November, the company raised an invoice for £70,000

and sent it to the customer. At the year end, payments on account from the customer totalled £60,000. Total costs to date are £65,000.

24   In January the company entered into a contract to fully refurbish a chain of hotels, one at a time. It is expected to take three years. The work on each hotel is individually priced within the contract and payment of the contracted amount is due on each hotel one month after the work on it has been certified complete. The refurbishment costs estimated for each hotel varied considerably across the chain. The fourth hotel was certified complete in mid December. Of the four completed to date, three have been profitable and one was not. Work has not yet started on the next hotel scheduled for refurbishment. Payment has been received in respect of the first three hotels completed.

25   At the beginning of April the company started on a contract to refurbish all the offices of Grant Thornton in Scotland. It was expected to take three years to complete, at a cost of £590,000. The contract price was £860,000. Cost and profitability was expected to be spread evenly over the three years. Costs are running at a rate of £30,000 per month and are not expected to fall. All costs have been transferred to cost of sales. £100,000 has been received as payments on account. Completion is still on schedule.

Additional Questions

*ASSUME THAT MATERIALITY EXISTS IN **EVERY** CASE*

26   A contract which started 18 months ago is due to be completed in 20 months time. The contract amount is £28,000; costs incurred to the balance sheet date were £17,000; anticipated costs to completion are £13,000; and payments on account received at the balance sheet date were £15,500. In respect of this contract, the financial statements for the previous financial period included £9,000 turnover and cost of sales of £12,000. What figure should be entered in this period's profit and loss account for cost of sales on this contract? (All costs are charged to cost of sales.)

Questions 27 - 30 concern a 2 year painting contract which is due to be completed in May.

27   Last year's accounts included £35,000 turnover and £12,000 profit in respect of the contract. Cumulative turnover to the balance sheet date is £162,000. Cumulative costs transferred to cost of sales at the balance sheet date, are £122,000.

28   The contract is expected to incur a loss of £50,000 over its remaining five months.

29   Total costs incurred to date on the contract are £185,000.

30   Payments on account on the contract in the previous year's accounts were £35,000. The cumulative total of payments on account at the current balance sheet date is £145,000.

Questions 31 - 33 concern a factory refurbishment contract.

31   Costs to date amount to £72,000. It is anticipated that a further £48,000 will be incurred between the balance sheet date and completion of the contract. The contract value is

£180,000. It was started during the previous accounting period and the previous year's accounts included £42,000 in turnover, and £28,000 in cost of sales, in respect of the contract.

32   Cumulative payments on account at the previous year's balance sheet date were £26,000. During this year, a further £38,000 was received.

33   On the balance sheet date, an independent consultant certified the work completed at a value of £126,000. There was no part-completed work at that date.

Questions 34 - 36 concern a contract to redecorate all the cabins of an ocean going liner. The contract is scheduled to be completed in April.

34   The contract is worth £230,000, and estimated total costs were expected to be £220,000. However, in November, the contract ran into some problems. As a result, alterations had to be made to the contract, all of which were approved by the ship's owners. The alterations have directly resulted in an increase in costs of £20,000. While the alterations were approved by the ship's owners, they are disputing their liability for these £20,000 costs.

35   As a result of the variations to the original contract, completion is now expected to be ten days late. The contract has a penalty clause of £1,000 per day for each day it runs beyond the scheduled completion date.

36   The company has notified the firm thought to have been responsible for the work, which led to the need for the alterations to the contract, about the potential penalty for late completion and the additional costs incurred. The reply received refuted all responsibility for the need to alter the original contract. The ship's owners have indicated that, should the company be successful in its claim, it will not request any proportion of the amount received. Previous experience suggests that the company has approximately a 30% chance of succeeding in its claim.

37   In November the company entered into a contract worth £700,000 to fully refurbish all council houses in Dunfermline. The project is expected to take eight months. Costs to date are £100,000, all of which are to be transferred to cost of sales, and a further £600,000 is expected to be incurred before completion. The work done so far has been certified at £250,000.

38   In February, the company started on a contract to refurbish all BUPA hospitals in south west Scotland. It was expected to take two years to complete, at a cost of £960,000. The contract price is £1.8m. Costs were expected to be spread evenly over the two years. Monthly costs have been higher than expected at a consistent figure of £60,000 and are not expected to change. The work is now expected to be completed six months early.

39   Only £540,000 of the costs to date on the BUPA hospitals contract (see question 38) are to be transferred to cost of sales.

Questions 40-45 relate to a variety of companies, all of which have a balance sheet date of 31st December.

40   A contract started in March is due to be completed in October next year. The contract amount is £42,500; costs incurred to the balance sheet date were £13,500; anticipated costs to completion are £22,000; work certified at the balance sheet date was £9,500; the cost of the work certified was £7,000; and payments on account received at the balance sheet date were £11,500. As profit is earned in an uneven manner on this contract, an estimate that 40% of the profit had been earned at the balance sheet date has been agreed with the contract surveyor. What is the attributable profit on the contract at the balance sheet date?

41   A contract to repaint all the rooms in a university was started in November, when a payment on account of £75,000 was received. The contract is due to be completed in August and is expected to incur losses of £20,000 in the period between balance sheet date and its completion. Costs to balance sheet date are £95,000, of which £50,000 are included in cost of sales. Turnover for the year includes £40,000 in respect of the contract.

42   After checking the calculations, the future loss of £20,000 on the university contract (question 41) has been found to be the expected loss on the contract as a whole.

Questions 43 - 45 are concerned with valuation of stock

43   A company produces a range of six products. At the period end, it has stock of each of the products. The value of the stock of each item has been calculated on the following two bases:

Product	1	2	3	4	5	6	Total
Cost	1,000	1,400	1,250	1,050	1,750	1,450	7,900
Net Realisable Value	1,800	2,100	950	1,100	2,750	3,100	11,800

What value should be placed on this stock in the financial statements?

44   At the end of its financial year, an engineering company has stock of 2,500 lathe adjuster gauges. The manufacturing cost of each of these gauges was £12. The retail price according to the company's catalogue is £16, however, a very small proportion of its sales are to trade customers who receive a 30% discount on its published retail prices. Marketing, selling and distribution costs average £1 per gauge. What figure should be entered in the financial statements for stock of lathe adjuster gauges?

45   An electronics company allows all its trade customers a 25% discount on its published prices. At the end of its financial year it has stock of 3,000 transformer units. The manufacturing cost of each of these units was £11. The price according to the company's catalogue is £14. The company only sells to the trade and the average marketing, selling and distribution costs per transformer is £0.75. What figure should be entered in the company's financial statements for stock of transformer units?

Long Questions

(1) *Estrada Plc*

Among its long term contracts, *Estrada Plc* has three contracts to upgrade and extend motorways. At the balance sheet date each contract was developing as follows (all amounts are £m):

Motorway	M.20	M.30	M.40
Contracted Sum	8.0	10.0	5.0
Costs to date	6.8	11.0	1.0
Costs to date transferred to cost of sales	6.6	10.5	1.0
Estimated costs to complete	0.4	1.4	3.5
Certified value of work completed to date	7.1	9.0	2.5
Payments on account invoiced to date	6.0	9.0	2.0
Payments on account received to date	6.5	8.0	2.7

M20	M30	M40
This contract is proceeding according to plan and should be completed on schedule.	This contract has been a disaster from the start. Due to a lack of pre-contractual analysis, costs are running far higher than planned. Unfortunately there is no provision in the contract for recovery of additional costs. Nor is anyone but the company to blame.	Large cost savings were encountered in the first part of this contract. However, those factors which resulted in the savings, will have the opposite effect over the remainder of the contract. It has proved impossible to ascertain precisely what these additional costs will be but it is hoped that the contract will not make an overall loss.

Required:

In compliance with SSAP 9, in respect of each of these contracts:

(A) critically evaluate the profits/losses to be recognised in the financial statements

(B) show what values will be included in the profit and loss account

(C) show what values will be included in the balance sheet

(2) *Navio Ltd*

Navio Ltd is a firm of builders whose balance sheet date is 31st December. The company works exclusively on long term contracts and, at 31st December, these included three which had been started during the year, for *Anda Ltd*, *Briga Ltd*, and *Canta Ltd* respectively. The financial information relating to these contracts is as follows (all amounts are in £000s):

	Anda		*Briga*		*Canta*
Estimated total costs for the whole contract:					
Direct material	148		196		340
Direct labour	180		252		150
		328		448	490
Costs incurred to date:					
Direct material		120	182		30
Direct labour		150	228		6
		270	410		36
Value of work certified at year end (see note)		-	920		36
Progress payments invoiced		540	600		6
Progress payments received		510	540		6
Contract price		805	990		660

The total costs incurred in the year on all contracts were:

Direct material	1,000
Direct labour	800
Overheads	
Production	1,600
Marketing	200
Administration	400
	4,000

The company policy is to apportion appropriate overheads on the basis of direct labour. All costs incurred to balance sheet date are transferred to cost of sales. The value of work on Anda has not been certified to date.

Required:

In compliance with SSAP 9, in respect of each of these contracts:

(A) critically evaluate the profits/losses to be recognised in the financial statements

(B) show what values will be included in the profit and loss account

(C) show what values will be included in the balance sheet

(3) *Fazer Ltd*

Fazer Ltd is a one-product company: it produces and sells 'coisas'. During the year, it purchased 5,000 tonnes of raw material every two weeks. For the first eight deliveries, it paid £400 per tonne. For the rest of the year, the price was £420. On each delivery it had to pay VAT at 15%, and handling charges of £20,000. Three tonnes of raw material produce two tonnes of coisas. These are sold at £899 per tonne. Packaging costs are £30 per tonne. Delivery is subcontracted at an annual cost of £432,000.

Direct production costs throughout the year were £80 per tonne produced. Production capacity exists to process 4,000 tonnes per week and fixed production costs were £90,000 per week. General management costs for the year were £3.5m.

At the beginning of the year there were no stocks and at the end of the year there were 13,000 tonnes of raw material and 6,000 tons of finished goods. There was no work in process stock at that date.

The company applies FIFO for stock valuation.

Required:

In compliance with SSAP 9, calculate the value of stock at the year end. (Assume that there are 52 weeks in the year, and that the raw material stock cannot be sold other than as part of the finished product.)

4 SSAP 12: Accounting for Depreciation

Summary of the accounting treatment requirements

Depreciation should be provided in respect of all fixed assets which have a finite useful economic life. It should be provided by allocating the cost less net realisable value over the periods expected to benefit from the use of the asset being depreciated. No depreciation method is prescribed, but the method selected should be that which produces the most appropriate allocation of depreciation to each period in relation to the benefit being received in that period through use of the asset.

Useful economic lives should be reviewed on a regular basis, normally at least every five years. Where the amended asset life would materially distort future results if treated normally, it should be treated as an exceptional item as defined by FRS 3 (*Reporting financial performance*) and included under the sane statutory format heading as the ongoing depreciation charge (FRS 3 amendment to paragraph 18 of SSAP 12).

Revaluation is recommended and if a policy of revaluation is adopted, the valuations should be kept up-to-date. The subsequent depreciation charge should be based on the new valuation and the remaining useful economic life. Depreciation should be charged irrespective of when the asset was revalued. According to paragraph 21 of FRS 3 (*Reporting financial performance* -chapter 2), the profit or loss on the disposal of an asset should be accounted for in the profit and loss account of the period in which the disposal occurs as the difference between the net sale proceeds and the net carrying amount, whether carried at historical cost (less any provisions made) or at a valuation

The depreciation method may only be changed when to do so will result in an improvement in the true and fair view. A change in method does not constitute a change in accounting policy. When the method is changed, the net book value should be depreciated over the remaining useful economic life of the asset, commencing with the period when the change occurred.

UITF 5, issued in July 1992, introduced rules relating to situations where current assets are included in the balance sheet at the lower of cost and net realisable value. Specifically, it addressed the question of an appropriate transfer value when a current asset becomes a fixed asset through its being retained for use on a continuing basis. (This could arise, for example, when a motor dealer removes a second-hand car from sale and provides it as a company car to the company secretary.) To avoid entities being able to transfer from current asset to fixed asset at above net realisable value and subsequently write-down the value through a debit to a revaluation reserve, UITF 5 requires that all such transfers are done at the lower of cost and net realisable value, with any diminution in value at that point being charged in the profit and loss account.

Problems of interpretation and grey areas

The following items are discussed: the link to FRS 3; the selection of the depreciation method; non-depreciation of certain assets; revaluation: profit and loss account -v- balance sheet; review of useful economic life; permanent diminution in value of revalued assets; freehold land; disclosure of changes; and approaches to adopt.

The link to FRS 3

As can be seen from the flowchart on page 39, there are six possible treatments under SSAP 12. Of these, the final two require application of FRS 3 (*Reporting financial performance* - chapter 2) as they involve the treatment of an 'exceptional' depreciation adjustment.

Selection of the depreciation method

All fixed assets with finite useful economic lives must be depreciated in order to reflect use. The standard leaves it open to the user to decide what method to apply (though it is suggested that 'straight-line' may be the simplest), subject to the proviso that it should be the method most appropriate to the circumstances. Depreciation should be calculated so as to charge a fair proportion of cost/valuation to each period expected to benefit from use of the asset; there is nothing in the standard to indicate how to charge a fair proportion to each period expected to benefit. The calculation involves consideration of the net cost/valuation (i.e. cost/valuation less estimated residual value) and estimated useful economic life (which should be subject to review at least every five years). Emphasis is given to the desirability of avoiding fully depreciating assets which are still in use. Regular revaluation is recommended and periodic reviews of estimated useful economic life are considered essential. If both these are done, the implication is that the fairest charge possible will be applied and the chance of fully depreciated assets still operating will be virtually eliminated.

Non-depreciation of certain assets

SSAP 12 emphasises the need to depreciate fixed assets in order to charge a fair proportion of their cost or valuation to each accounting period *expected to benefit from their use*. The implication is that fixed assets which were not in use in a period should not be depreciated if non-use results in the estimated useful economic life at the end of the period being the same as it was at the start. This would apply to incomplete assets, such as buildings still being constructed. It would also apply to assets which were taken out of use before the start of the accounting period, whose useful economic life is dependent solely upon physical deterioration through use. If an asset which complies with this condition has been out of use for only a part of the period, it must be depreciated. The lack of use can be incorporated through a revision of remaining useful economic life, if it is felt appropriate to do so.

Revaluation: profit and loss account -v- balance sheet

Assets may be revalued in order to reflect their market value. The standard suggests that depreciation of such assets should be based on the new valuation and calculated by reference to their 'remaining useful economic lives' (paragraph 22). It is emphasised in the standard that depreciation should always be applied to the period when the revaluation takes place. If interpreted as meaning that the depreciation for the entire year should be based on the new valuation, and if that valuation were done at the year-end, this would result in understating the net book value at the year-end. It can be argued that this interpretation may give a fair reflection of the benefit utilised during the period but it will *not* result in the net book value of the asset in the balance sheet being a fair reflection of its value.

This can be illustrated by a simple example: if a building was revalued during the year at £200,000 with a remaining expected useful economic life of 20 years, the depreciation for the year (were straight-line adopted) would be **£10,000** [£200,000/20] and the net book value at the end of the year **£190,000** [£200,000-£10,000], on the basis that £10,000 represents the diminished value of the building as a result of its use during the year. Close consideration of this example clearly shows that the net book value is scarcely likely to be a fair reflection of the true value of the building at the year end. Indeed, it would only be 'fair' if the revaluation was done on the first day of the year. If the valuation took place on the last day of the year, the accounts would show a net book value of £190,000 compared to a true value of £200,000.

This difficulty can be eased if a slightly different view is taken of the wording in paragraph 22: if the charge for depreciation were to be based on the revalued amount in respect of the remaining useful economic life *at the date of the revaluation*, then it would only be used to calculate a proportion of the depreciation charge in the period that a revaluation takes place. If the revaluation is on the last day of the period, it will not be used at all in the calculation of the depreciation charge. The earlier part of the year's depreciation would be based on the previous carrying amount. Using this approach, the net book value at that revaluation date would be calculated and used in calculating the transfer to revaluation reserve. The depreciation for the period after revaluation could then be calculated and added to the amount calculated up to the date of revaluation, thereby producing the total depreciation transferred to the profit and loss account for the year, while only charging the new valuation with the depreciation applicable directly to it. For example, if the revaluation cited in the previous example occurred on 1st October, and the original cost were £50,000, being depreciated at 2% straight-line, the appropriate depreciation for the year ended 31st December would be **£750** [(£50,000 @ 2%) × ¾] + **£2,500** [(£200,000/20) × ¼] = **£3,250**. If the net book value at the start of the year was £20,000, the revised net book value at 30th September would be £19,250 [£20,000-£750] and the revaluation reserve transfer **£180,750** [£200,000-£19,250]. The net book value at the year end would be **£197,500** [£200,000 - £2,500].

This approach, while improving the 'fairness' of the balance sheet, causes the profit and loss depreciation charge to be less than 'fair' as it ignores the reality that the asset was undervalued for that proportion of the year when the true value was unknown. While this is an undesirable feature of the approach, the overall effect is probably as near to a true and fair view as it is possible to achieve, and it should therefore be adopted.

The task of revaluation could be considerable for those companies that revalue their fixed assets at points scattered throughout their accounting period. While computerised accounting systems do much to alleviate the problem, the simplest solution, if a more straightforward computation is required, would be to perform all revaluations at the start, or end, of the year.

It should be remembered that the standard confirms that companies should follow the balance sheet format and disclosures required under the Companies Act. These include the requirement that where assets have been revalued in earlier years, the year of valuation and the value given must be disclosed; and, in respect of current year valuations, disclosure must be made of the names or qualifications of the valuers, and the bases of valuation used.

Review of useful economic life

It is suggested that useful economic lives should be reviewed regularly. The overall impression is that assets should be depreciated to represent the reduction in their market value (due to use) over their useful economic lives, and that the net book value should fairly approximate to the market value. This would appear to rule out the use of the 'reducing balance' method when adopted on the basis that it would be fair to front-load the depreciation in order to offset the increasing maintenance cost as the age of the asset increases, thereby achieving relative uniformity in the annual cost of using the asset. However, rather than being ruled out, its use is justified on different grounds: that market value falls rapidly on certain classes of assets (e.g. vehicles and computers) and it would therefore be fair to front-load the depreciation through the use of the 'reducing balance' method. Coincidentally, those assets which fall into this category are also those for which the 'increasing maintenance' argument would be applicable.

Permanent diminution in value of revalued assets

The standard specifically refuses to give guidance in the case of a previously revalued asset whose value has now permanently diminished (paragraph 20). In such situations, common sense would suggest that the down-valuation should be offset directly to the revaluation reserve up to the value previously transferred to it in respect of the asset. Should insufficient value have been transferred previously, the remaining write-off should be charged to the profit and loss for the year. The amount transferred directly to the revaluation reserve is not 'depreciation' but an adjustment for permanent diminution in value and is not, therefore, in conflict with the requirement of SSAP 12 that no part of the depreciation charge should be set directly against reserves. It may be that such a write-off materially distorts the results for the year. In such circumstances, FRS 3 should be consulted in order to determine whether it should be disclosed as an exceptional, or extraordinary, item. Unlike depreciation, a permanent adjustment of this type can be written-back later should it prove to have been misjudged.

Freehold land

The standard explicitly states that freehold land will not be depreciated as it is not a wasting asset, *unless* subject to depletion or loss of value for reasons which may be applicable in certain circumstances, such as desirability of location. The standard specifically refers to the situation which arises where freehold land is being used as the raw material for some process, for example, earth which a builder is transferring to his house-building sites. This is depletion and the land should be depreciated accordingly.

There are occasions when freehold land may be being naturally depleted, for example, through coastal erosion. The treatment to adopt is again clearly covered by the depletion clause: it should be depreciated, although it may be difficult to select an appropriate basis. Probably the only suitable approach would be on the basis of revaluation as adopted in the hotel and catering industry when deriving the depreciation charge on linen, cutlery and crockery. This involves comparing the value of what is held at the year end with the value of what was held at the start, adjusted for additions and disposals.

The value of freehold land may be subject to material change as a result of the use to which it is being put, or may be put. Normally, land that cannot be built upon will have considerably less value than land which can. Land bought with a view to its development as a new factory site, will have been bought at a relatively high price. Should planning permission unexpectedly be refused, the market value would be likely to be significantly less than the price paid. In such circumstances the value should be reduced, not by a depreciation charge, but by a revaluation adjustment.

It is rare to encounter circumstances under which freehold land should be subject to depreciation. The problem that most often occurs is the distinction between the cost/value of freehold land and the cost/value of the buildings upon it. SSAP 12 implies that the distinction should be made as only the buildings should be depreciated. Failure to separate the two elements of the cost/value will result in non-compliance with the standard.

Disclosure of changes

While most of the disclosure requirements are clear from the disclosure section of the standard and the Companies Act requirements that follow it, two points in particular should be mentioned.

Firstly, the effect of revaluation on the depreciation charge, *if material*, should be disclosed. A similar requirement applies to the disclosure of the effect of a change in depreciation method. However, while the standard also states that the reason for the change in method should be disclosed, it is not clear if this also is subject to the materiality exemption. On balance, the correct treatment is probably to state the reason for the change irrespective of the materiality of the difference in the charge for the year.

Secondly, while the disclosure requirements include nothing relating to changes in useful economic life, any exceptional item adjustment to the accumulated depreciation resulting from an amendment of useful economic life should be disclosed.

Approaches to adopt

It is important to know what to do with the most common circumstances that are likely to be included in an examination question on this topic. In the event of a change in the estimated useful economic life, depreciation should be calculated using the net book value and the new useful economic life. If the method of depreciation changes, it may encompass a change in estimated useful economic life, and depreciation should be based on the net book value. If a fixed asset is revalued, depreciation should be calculated for the period in two parts - the pre-revaluation element (based on the previous carrying amount) and the post-revaluation element (based on the revaluation amount). The surplus/deficit on revaluation should be calculated by subtracting the net book value (after deducting the pre-revaluation depreciation for the period) from the revaluation value.

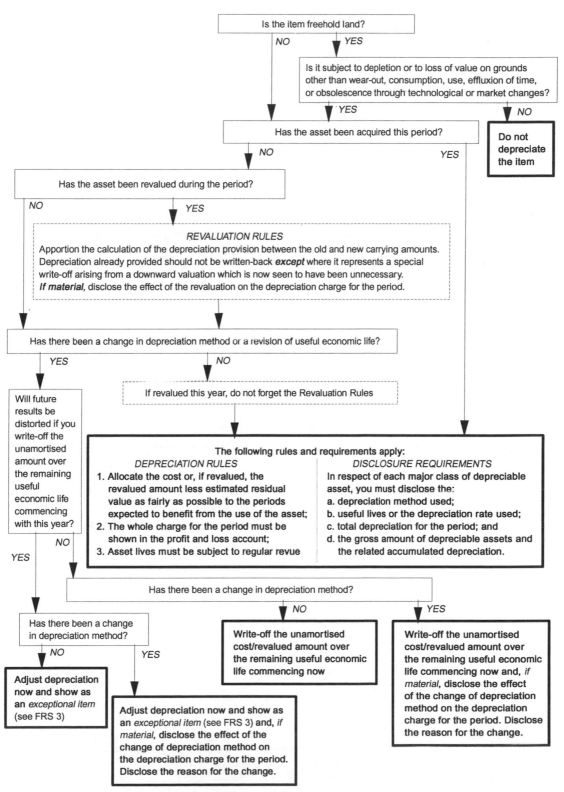

Short Questions

*ASSUME THAT MATERIALITY EXISTS IN **EVERY** CASE*

Questions 1-25 relate to a household furniture manufacturing and retailing company with current turnover of £5m and net pre-tax profit of £0.5m. (Last year £4.6m and £0.6m respectively.) The company's financial year ends on 31st December. (Unless otherwise indicated, estimated residual value is zero.)

1   During the year, the company purchased 20 acres of freehold land for £100,000.

2   The company owns a binding machine which cost £72,000 over two years ago. At the end of each of the previous two years it was depreciated using 25% straight-line. This year the company is adopting a 20% straight-line basis for all its machinery depreciation.

3   At the start of the year, the company revalued its head office at £220,000. It had cost £115,000 four years earlier and this was the first revaluation of this property the company have undertaken.

4   The depreciation method applied to the head office (see question 3) was changed during the year from 5% straight-line to 25% reducing balance.

5   During the year, the Icelandic government passed a law forbidding foreign-based companies from having sales outlets on Icelandic territory. All such outlets must be closed and vacated by the end of the year after next at which time they are to be confiscated with no compensation. As a result, the company have revised the expected useful economic life of their custom built (and now legally unsellable) shop in Iceland from 43 years to 3. The shop cost £300,000, had an original expected useful economic life of 50 years, and was being depreciated at 2% straight-line.

6   The company has previously used a 5 year life when calculating depreciation on its computers. It has now decided to change this to 10 years. The method of depreciation has not been changed.

7   One of the company's computers is now 6 years old. It originally cost £6,000 and was written-down to zero last year.

8   At the end of the year, the company, as a result of a purchasing error, had sufficient stocks of computer stationery for the next 2 years. It was valued at £19,000.

9   The depreciation method on company motor vehicles has been changed to straight-line from reducing balance.

10   The company's shop in Paisley was revalued two years ago at £22,000.

11   During the year, the company bought a furniture shop building in Greenock for £170,000. The value of the freehold was £140,000.

12   The asset values of the freehold of the Greenock shop (see question 11) were £60,000 for the land and £80,000 for the building.

13   A small shop which the company bought for £15,000 over 10 years ago was closed at the same time as the company closed its Edinburgh factory. It was being depreciated by 1% per year, straight-line. The company has no plans to re-open the shop. Instead, it plans to retain it for a few years and then sell it when its value has appreciated appreciably, probably in about five years' time. In the meantime it is allowing a local hospice to use the premises rent free.

14   The company has the leasehold of a warehouse in Greenock. The lease was originally for 30 years and still has 22 years to run. It was revalued at the start of the year from a net book value of £88,000 to a value of £132,000. No change has been made to the depreciation method (which is straight-line).

15   At the start of the year, the company renegotiated the lease on its shop in Troon. Under the renegotiation, which cost £25,000, the unexpired term was increased by 5 years. At the start of the year there was 5 years left on the old lease. After the re-negotiation, the company adopted the valuation which the lessor had undertaken at the end of the previous year and the shop is now shown at a value of £50,000 compared to the £20,000 net book value it had at the start of the year. It is to continue to be written-off using the straight-line method.

16   During the year the company purchased three new wood-steel-binding machines at a total cost of £210,000. It only has need of two and has leased the third on a 25 year lease to *Joga Fora Plc*, a company specializing in office furniture. The company has adopted a general policy of depreciating all machines over a period of 5 years, straight-line.

17   During the year the company increased its holding in *Boots Plc* to 50,000 ordinary shares. The total cost of its holding is £90,000.

18   The company's small tools are revalued every year due to the frequency with which they are lost. Prior to this year's revaluation, the small tools account was showing a value of £16,000. After the revaluation this figure was reduced to £11,500.

19   During the year, the company invested £70,000 on a new water cooling system for the administration block at head office.

20   During the year, the company spent £120,000 repairing the roof of the Motherwell factory.

21   At the end of the year, the company had almost completed the building of a new bungalow for retired single ex-employees. Total costs to date are £16,000.

22   A company car used by one of the directors, with a book value of £14,000 was stolen in December. It had only been bought the day before and, due to an error by a clerk in the office, it was not yet insured. It has not yet been recovered.

23   At the start of the year, the company revalued its Glasgow shop. Its net book value at the start of the year was £15,000 and it was revalued at £112,000. Two years earlier, the

company had reduced the useful economic life of the shop from 20 years to 5 as the local council had indicated they would condemn it as unsafe when a new inner-city motorway was built. This had caused the company to charge an exceptional depreciation write-off to that year's accounts. (The plan to built the inner-city motorway was scrapped during the year.)

24   The company has a rainwear subsidiary, *Abaixo Ltd*, which is leasing the company's old Edinburgh factory at full market rental. At the start of the year the factory had a net book value of £180,000 (cost £200,000). Previously it was being depreciated at 2% straight-line. Now it is to be depreciated at 4% straight-line.

25   The company purchased a new machine in February for £45,000. It paid for it by cheque in April but the cheque has not been cashed and has now lapsed. It transpires that the supplier (a sole trader) disappeared on a scuba-diving holiday in the Bahamas in March. The sole trader has no lawyer and no dependents and paid all his bills prior to leaving for his holiday.

Additional Questions

*ASSUME THAT MATERIALITY EXISTS IN **EVERY** CASE*

26   A car which was transferred from a car dealer's sales stock to its directors' car pool in June, was transferee back to the sales stock in November. The car had originally cost £7,600. In June, it had a net realisable value of £7,200. In November, it was £6,300. It remained unsold at the year end, when it was valued at £6,100.

27   Repeat question 26, this time the car is sold in December for £6,400.

28   *Construir Plc* is a construction company specializing in roads and bridges. Mid-way through the financial year it completed a three year contract to build a series of pedestrian subways in the centre of Glasgow. The contract has a clause stating that no payments will be made to *Construir Plc* until two calendar years after full completion of the contract.

Questions 29-36 concern Umtar Ltd, an industrial and domestic oil distributor in Scotland. Annual turnover in the last year was £4.4m and pre-tax profit £0.6m. (Previous year £4.1m and £0.4m respectively.) The company's year end is 31st December. (Unless otherwise indicated, estimated residual value is zero.)

29   The company acquired a 6% holding in a foreign distributor for £180,000. The company has been guaranteed a minimum return of £30,000 per year but expects to receive at least twice that amount as the foreign company has very good prospects. The shares were acquired under an agreement that they be sold back for a fixed price of £90,000 in 5 years time.

30   For twenty years the company has depreciated a vehicle maintenance workshop and garage at 2% straight-line on its original cost of £12,000. At the beginning of the year it was revalued at £270,000.

31   The company bought a five year license to use the trade mark *Liso* from a French distributor in order that it could market its generic product under the well known label. It cost £50,000.

32   The company has a fleet of three tankers which it has been depreciating at 20% straight-line. The entire fleet was purchased at the beginning of the previous year at a cost of £80,000. It has decided that the basis of depreciation was wrong and that it should be based on the miles travelled. The company was advised that 100,000 miles would be a reasonable estimate of useful economic life. Average mileage at the start of the year was 19,000. The average mileage during the year was 20,500.

33   The company traded-in all its computers and replaced them with low-cost micros. The original equipment had a net book value at the start of the year of £13,000. They received a trade-in allowance of £9,000. The new equipment cost £80,000, less the trade-in, i.e. £71,000.

34   The company spent £20,000 improving an office in Banchory. The office is held on a fifteen year lease. The improvements involved stripping-out the previous internal walls and fittings and re-building it to an open-plan design. It is a requirement of the lease that the office should be returned to its original state when the lease expires.

35   The company has a warehouse in central Scotland which it uses to store its surplus furniture stock. It was bought just over nine years ago for £12,000 and has been depreciated in each of the nine years at 4% straight-line. Its net book value at the start of the year was £7,680. Under the year end annual review of its fixed assets' useful economic lives it was decided that the warehouse would continue to be economically useful for a further 25 years. At the same time it was revalued to reflect its true value of £56,000.

36   £30,000 was paid in December for a garage in Dundee which is due for demolition in 2 years time. The garage is currently closed while it is prepared for its scheduled opening in February. It was bought as a publicity exercise in order to establish the company's generic petrol brand in the city. The company is currently pursuing planning permission for a new garage a mile away from this short-term purchase.

Questions 37-40 relate to an advertising company with annual turnover in the last year of £2m and pre-tax profit £0.7m. (Previous year £1.2m and £0.2m respectively.) The company's year end is 31st December. (Unless otherwise indicated, estimated residual value is zero.)

37   The company moved to a new office in Edinburgh. It was bought on a 40 year lease for £340,000. The land included in the property was valued at £80,000.

38   One of the company's advertising executives was involved in a car crash in mid-December. It was the executive's fault. His company car was seriously damaged and is likely to be declared a write-off by the insurers. The car was bought earlier in the year for £11,000. Company policy is to have all its vehicles fully comprehensively insured.

39   A new suite of accounting software was delivered to the company in November. It cost £25,000 but has not yet been used as the company accountant is still involved in installing it. It is expected to be put into use in February.

40   In October, the company purchased the right to instal advertising displays around the pitch at all cricket test matches in England over the next 5 seasons. It cost £100,000.

Questions 41-45 relate to a variety of companies, all of which have a balance sheet date of 31st December.

41   In October, a household furniture retailer re-equipped the company offices with desks and chairs from its showroom. The stock had cost £11,000 and, at the date the transfer occurred it had a net realisable value of £10,500.

42   A woolen mill revised the residual value of a stitching machine from zero to £1,500. The machine cost £37,500 over four years ago and had a net book value of £22,500 at the start of the year. Company policy is to charge 10% straight-line depreciation on this type of machine.

43   A paper manufacturer discovered an old machine in its Aberdeen factory when it was closing it down. The old machine had been written-off years earlier and should have been disposed of at that time but someone forgot. On hearing of the discovery, a Canadian millionaire offered the company £160,000 for the machine - it turned-out to be the only working example of a first generation wood-steel-binding machine which his uncle had invented. The company signed the contract to sell in February, i.e. after the end of the current year, and the machine was collected and paid for in March.

44   At the beginning of the year, a country club paid £1.7m for some adjacent land which it intended using for a golf course development. In December, planning permission was revoked and a compulsory purchase order was received valuing the land at £1.1m. The company has been advised that it has no legal grounds of appeal and that it will have to comply with the purchase order.

45   A fishing company (which has a fleet of trawlers operating around the UK) has owned a harbour on the north-east coast of Scotland since the company was founded in 1843. The harbour has never been revalued or depreciated and is shown in the company's balance sheet at cost of £150. During the year, severe gales struck the harbour causing extensive damage to it which required repairs costing £220,000 before the harbour could be put back into service. As a result of the damage and the compromising nature of the repairs, the harbour is no longer capable of servicing the company's larger vessels. It is generally agreed that it is now worth much less than was the case prior to the gales. An independent valuer has placed a value on the harbour at the year end of £425,000, and has stated that the value at the previous year end was £550,000.

Long Question

Casa Linda Plc

At the start of the current year, *Casa Linda Plc* had the following balances on its fixed asset accounts. The company's year end is at 31 December.

	Land & Buildings	Vehicles	Equipment	Under Construction
Cost	25,000	20,000	40,000	12,000
less: Acc. Depn.	800	15,000	16,000	-
Net Book Value	24,200	5,000	24,000	12,000

The company has a policy of depreciating in the year of acquisition but not in the year of disposal. It always uses straight-line and the rates applied are:

Buildings	-	2%
Vehicles	-	25%
Equipment	-	20%

During the year the following occurred:

a)   the office extension was completed at an additional cost of £8,000. It had taken 20 months.

b)   a piece of land beside the company's office was sold for £10,000 at the start of the year. (The only land and buildings owned are the company's office and the surrounding land.) All the company's land was purchased 20 years ago at a cost of £5,000. The land sold represented 10% of the land owned by the company.

c)   at the time of the land sale, the company revalued its other land at £75,000. The valuation is to be incorporated into this year's financial statements.

d)   one of the company's cars was traded-in for £3,000 when a new Volvo was bought for the chairman. The company issued a cheque for £13,000 to pay the amount due. The car traded-in had a net book value of £2,000, having originally cost £8,000.

Required: (i) prepare appropriate balance sheet notes in accordance with SSAP 12.

(ii) indicate what the profit and loss account entry will be.

5 SSAP 13: Accounting for Research and Development

Summary of the accounting treatment requirements

Expenditure on research and development (R&D) should be distinguished from non-R&D expenditure. Research expenditure should be distinguished from development expenditure and must be charged to profit and loss. Development expenditure *may* be capitalised and amortised over the period when the benefits arising from the expenditure are expected to be received; otherwise, it must be charged to profit and loss. Fixed assets used to provide facilities for R&D must be capitalised and written-off over their useful lives; the annual depreciation charge should be included in the R&D total for the period; and if it relates to development expenditure deferred, it should also be deferred. The unamortised balance of development expenditure should be examined at the end of each accounting period to ensure it still meets the criteria for deferral; if not, it must be written-off.

Problems of interpretation and grey areas

The following items are discussed: the determination of what constitutes research and development expenditure; the period in which amortisation should begin; the basis of amortisation which should be adopted; and the writing back of development expenditure previously written-off. Finally, there is a brief conclusion.

What constitutes research and development expenditure?

The standard states that 'R&D activity is distinguished from non-research based activity by the presence or absence of an appreciable element of innovation. If the activity departs from routine and breaks new ground, it should normally be included; if it follows an established pattern, it should normally be excluded' (paragraph 5). Part of the definition of research given in paragraph 21 of the standard refers to it as being experimental or theoretical work (pure research), or as being original or critical investigation (applied research). If these definitions are followed, it should not be too difficult to distinguish between research activities and non-R&D activities. (The question of whether research is pure or applied is irrelevant, as the accounting treatment is the same.) Problems only really arise when attempting to determine whether an activity is research or development; and whether an activity is development or non-R&D.

In the standard, examples are given of activities that would *normally* be included in R&D, and of those that would *normally* be excluded. The use of the word 'normally' indicates that such a classification will not always hold. While these examples can be taken as a useful guide, they must not be treated as inviolable. There will be occasions when the treatment of an item given in the examples will be the opposite of that suggested. For example, the costs of corrective action on break-downs during commercial production is in the list of examples of items normally excluded from R&D. However, if the corrective action involved returning to the design stage, or even the pre-design stage, a strong case could be made for treating that part of the corrective action as R&D. Commercial production does not necessarily mean that all related R&D activities have ceased.

Each case must be decided on its merits and, where it is unclear whether an item is research or development, a subjective judgement will be required. The same holds for situations where it is unclear whether an item is development or non-R&D.

When should amortisation begin?

The standard states that amortisation should commence in the period when production starts, and that it should be allocated on a systematic basis to each accounting period over which the product is expected to be sold (paragraph 28). What should be done when production starts in a different period from that in which sales start? Clearly, it would be inappropriate to allocate the amortisation over periods when there is no income being generated. That would not be matching expenditure to income, any more than would writing off the expenditure when it was first incurred. Alternatively, the amortisation could be started when production begins but added to the value of the stock being built up, rather than charged to the period's profit and loss. While there will often be nothing wrong with this approach, it could lead to the first period of sale being charged with more than its fair share of the development costs. Consequently, when production begins in a different period from sales, amortisation would be best delayed until the period in which income is first generated.

What basis of amortisation should be adopted?

Two bases are suggested in paragraph 28: (a) by reference to either the sale or use of the product; and (b) by reference to the total time over which the product is expected to be sold or used. If the first basis is adopted, amortisation may well be bell-shaped - low at first as the product struggles to gain a market, peaking in the middle as its market penetration is maximised, then low at the end as its sales drop off. If the second basis is used, amortisation would be by the straight-line method. Whichever is adopted, the length of time over which amortisation should occur must be selected. Given the amount of complex forecasting that may be involved, particularly in the case of the adoption of the first basis, it is very unlikely that any consistency in approach would be found between companies faced with similar amortisation decisions. (Obviously, this criticism is equally applicable to all depreciation and amortisation decisions, not just those arising under SSAP 13.)

The writing back of development expenditure previously written-off

As a general rule, once it has been written-off, development expenditure cannot be reinstated *unless* it was previously capitalised, in which case the Companies Act regulations applicable to fixed assets apply, and reinstatement may be made of provisions for diminution in value which are no longer required.

In addition, development expenditure previously written-off can also be reinstated under FRS 3 (*Reporting financial performance* - chapter 2), either as the result of a fundamental error, or as a change in accounting policy, but only if the expenditure could have been deferred under the conditions which applied at the time of the original decision to write it off.

Conclusion

The broad terminology used in SSAP 13 gives rise to problems and in many instances could lead to the adoption of widely differing treatments by different companies faced with the same conditions and expenditure. However, in a survey of 300 UK companies (the results of which are contained in the 1989-90 ICAEW survey of UK published accounts), only 1% of the 171 companies identified as having some R&D activity elected to capitalise it. If this is representative of the overall treatment of R&D expenditure, there is very little cause for concern over whether companies categorise expenditure as research or as development. Nevertheless, there remains the problem that the distinction between development and non-R&D expenditure is imprecise and open to manipulation, if there is any benefit to be gained by doing so.

Finally, the partial exemption from disclosure (given to most companies other than public limited companies under paragraph 22 of the standard) is difficult to justify. If the information is regarded as unimportant for the majority of companies, what is so special about the others that it suddenly takes on an important role? It is hard to see why the shareholders of non-public limited companies would be any less interested than the shareholders of public limited companies in knowing the total R&D expenditure charged to profit and loss, and the proportion of it which related to the amortisation of deferred development expenditure.

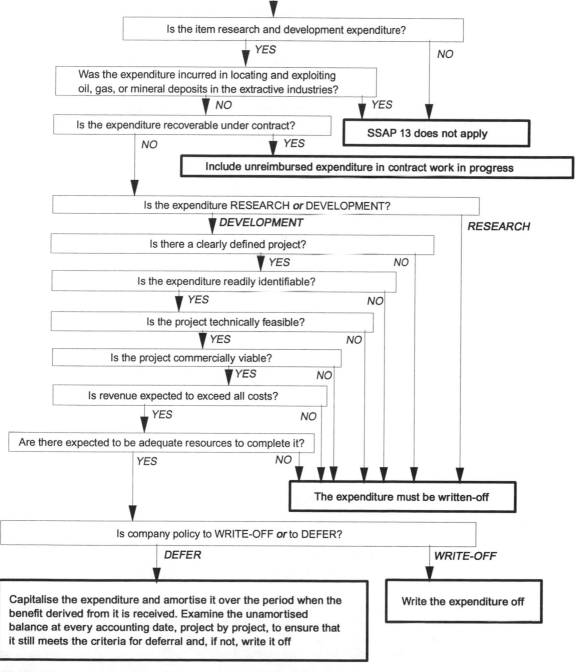

If the company has any research and development expenditure, it must state and explain its research and development accounting policy. Movements on deferred development expenditure and the amount carried forward at the beginning and the end of the period should be disclosed. Deferred development expenditure should be disclosed under intangible fixed assets in the balance sheet. If not exempt under paragraph 22 of SSAP 13, the total amount of research and development expenditure charged in the profit and loss account should be disclosed, analysed between the current year's expenditure and amounts amortised from deferred expenditure.

Is the item research and development expenditure?

YES   NO

Was the expenditure incurred in locating and exploiting oil, gas, or mineral deposits in the extractive industries?

NO   YES

Is the expenditure recoverable under contract?

NO   YES

SSAP 13 does not apply

Include unreimbursed expenditure in contract work in progress

Is the expenditure RESEARCH or DEVELOPMENT?

DEVELOPMENT   RESEARCH

Is there a clearly defined project?

YES   NO

Is the expenditure readily identifiable?

YES   NO

Is the project technically feasible?

YES   NO

Is the project commercially viable?

YES   NO

Is revenue expected to exceed all costs?

YES   NO

Are there expected to be adequate resources to complete it?

YES   NO

The expenditure must be written-off

Is company policy to WRITE-OFF or to DEFER?

DEFER   WRITE-OFF

Capitalise the expenditure and amortise it over the period when the benefit derived from it is received. Examine the unamortised balance at every accounting date, project by project, to ensure that it still meets the criteria for deferral and, if not, write it off

Write the expenditure off

SSAP 13   Accounting for research and development

Short Questions

*ASSUME THAT MATERIALITY EXISTS IN **EVERY** CASE*

Questions 1-3 concern Diga Ltd, a private independent engineering company with 100 employees, current turnover of £8m and net pre-tax profit of £700,000. (Last year £7.6m and £780,000 respectively.) The company's financial year ends on 31st December.

1   The company's accounting policy on research and development expenditure is that, where permissable, development expenditure should be deferred and amortised over the period during which the item it relates to is expected to be sold or used, starting in the first such period.

2   Until the current accounting period, research and development expenditure was written-off as it occurred.

3   The company charged £80,000 to profit and loss for the current year's expenditure on research and development, this was in addition to an amortization charge in the accounts for £10,000 relating to deferred development expenditure.

Questions 4-17 relate to Casabonita Plc, a household furniture manufacturing and retailing company with current turnover of £28m and net pre-tax losses of £3.4m. (Last year £26.6m and £3.1m [profit] respectively.) The company's financial year ends on 31st December.

4   During the year, the company bought a mobile laboratory for £42,000 which it is using to develop a new range of kitchen worktops incorporating the company's newly discovered cigarette burn resistant furniture laminate.

5   During the year, work commenced on an attempt to identify a new scratch-proof wood coating using a newly discovered process. By the end of the year, £62,000 had been spent on this work.

6   After some prototypes had been made to verify feasibility, the company entered into a contract with the Sri Lankan government for the company to be supplied with a natural furniture dye whose only source is a large forest on the Sri Lankan eastern seaboard. It was to have been used in the finishing of an exclusive range of dining furniture. The company spent £110,000 on the feasibility study and use of the dye is believed to be potentially highly profitable. In November the Sri Lankan government cancelled all foreign contracts pending a review of the methods whereby such contracts were negotiated. In view of the generous compensation payments made by the company to the Sri Lankan negotiators, it is thought unlikely that the contract will be reinstated. However, it is thought possible that another dye could be substituted: tests will be required before a decision can be taken on the use of the substitute dye.

7   During the year, £37,000 was spent developing a bright yellow pigmentation which could be added to the colours available for customers when selecting a bathroom suite from the company's range. A large demand had been identified for the colour. Unfortunately, although the pigmentation was easily developed, all attempts to

manufacture bright yellow bathroom suites have failed and the company's experts have stated that the colour cannot be incorporated using any known methods.

8   During the year, the company spent £50,000 identifying consumer preference relating to a new type of collapsible table it is developing. A large and profitable market has been found to exist.

9   During the year, the company sub-contracted to develop and then produce a new range of bedroom furniture for an American hotel chain, incorporating the company's newly-discovered cigarette burn resistant furniture laminate. Total development costs in the year were £120,000. Under the terms of the contract, the company will receive 80% of the costs incurred prior to completion and the remaining 20% after the furniture has been satisfactorily installed. The company had been reimbursed £78,000 by the balance sheet date. Production is expected to start in April or May.

10   During the year, the company took out a two-year lease on a small workshop, in order that it could develop the new range of bedroom furniture for the American hotel chain, incorporating the company's newly-discovered cigarette-burn-resistant furniture laminate.

11   The American hotel chain referred to in questions 9 and 10 went into liquidation at the end of the year. There is no prospect of any further payments being received. Under the terms of the contract, the company has full rights of disposal over any furniture produced.

12   During the year, the company spent £100,000 exploring the possibility that it had a rich seam of coal on some land it owned within the grounds of its Motherwell factory.

13   In July, the company started developing a new furniture fabric using a newly-discovered chemical, *Ficar*. The company is confident that this will enable them to lead the luxury furniture market for a number of years and are convinced they will make enormous profits on the production of furniture incorporating the fabric. The development work has been undertaken in his quiet moments by the site chemist at the Motherwell factory. No records of his time on this have been kept and unfortunately he died just after the year end before telling anyone how much time he had spent. The company believe he may have spent something between 1,000 and 2,000 hours on the project during the year.

14   The company is considering using the new flush-pan wood-waterproofing technique on a new range of garden furniture. During the year it spent £44,000 undertaking research on prototypes into the functionality of the product.

15   During the year, the company spent £45,000 on research into attitudes to waterbeds and peoples' comfort needs. This is directly related to a new type of waterbed, consisting of an air mattress within a bed of water, which the company is developing and intends to sell exclusively through its London showroom. As a result of the research, the design was changed substantially and it is believed that the research has given the company the knowledge to dominate the market for up-market beds over the next two to three years. Consequently, the bed is expected to realise a considerable profit.

16   During the year, the company started trying to identify a new water-resistant coating solution. Unfortunately, the records relating to this project were stolen and the company are unable to precisely state the amount incurred. It is thought to have been between £30,000 and £45,000.

17   During the year, the company started to develop the production process necessary in order to add its newly-discovered *Neve* fabric strengthener to its curtain and furnishing-cover range. The process is certain to be successfully implemented, but there is some doubt as to whether the costs will ever be recovered. Nevertheless, the company is carrying on with the development as it sees it as a means of field-testing the fabric strengthener as a possible future do-it-yourself product, if the recent law relating to the sale of poisonous substances were ever to be repealed.

Questions 18-34 relate to, Inventar plc, a chemicals and pharmaceuticals company with current turnover of £120m and net pre-tax profit of £19m. (Last year £81m and £13.6m respectively.) The company's financial year ends on 31st December.

18   The company spent £37,000 during the year attempting to discover whether a newly-discovered virus could be used in the treatment of toothache.

19   £60,000 was spent during the year developing a new brand of toothpaste. Most of the expense has been incurred in trying to eliminate the repulsive flavour of the newly-discovered fluoride substitute which was the reason for the new product's development. Despite all the company's efforts, the flavour is as obnoxious as ever, and the chief research chemist is of the opinion that it cannot be eradicated.

20   The company brought forward deferred development expenditure of £103,000 at the start of the year relating to the development of a new coating for emery boards. A further £54,000 was spent on development of the project during the year. The potential profits are large, and the market is certainly there for the taking. It had been felt that development work would be completed by the middle of next year, and that production could follow soon after. However, in December the Romanian government announced an export ban on *Duro*, the mineral employed in the emery board construction, as it was needed as a cheap source of raw material in the construction of the country's new motorway network. No other known source exists.

21   The company introduced a new range of breath freshener in September. It has been a huge commercial success due to the fact that it is effective for three times as long as any other product on the market. Development took place in the Spring and cost £71,000.

22   In the previous period, the company wrote off £130,000 deferred development expenditure incurred on a project which led to the marketing of a new product, *Gosto*. Sales of the product had slumped to zero in the middle of that year after a competitor brought out a similar product at one third of the selling price of *Gosto*. The company was unable to match the competitor's price and production of *Gosto* ceased. In May of the current year, the competitor's product was found to contain some very dangerous banned chemicals. As a result the product was withdrawn and, one month later, the competitor went into liquidation. The company recommenced production of *Gosto* in August and

has subsequently regained its original share of the market at the same selling price as before.

23   £39,000 was spent during the year on developing techniques for putting more toothpaste into the tube.

24   The company spent £89,500 during the year researching the durability characteristics of the five leading types of toothbrush. This was with a view to entering into a joint promotional campaign for the company's new fluoride toothpaste (see question 19) and the brush which came out best in the test.

25   The company's chief research chemist has spent £36,000 on the development of a new toothpaste preservative, or it might be a dental floss preservative, or it might be a toothpick steriliser - he's not too sure which, but he is sure that one of them will result.

Additional Questions

*ASSUME THAT MATERIALITY EXISTS IN **EVERY** CASE*

26   The company has spent £50,000 on research into the properties of a new compound, *Vista*, which its chief research chemist discovered while working late one night.

27   Development has been undertaken (over the last 10 months) of a new brand of denture polish. Production is due to start in February and a healthy profit is expected over the market-life of the product, which is going to enable users to keep their dentures clean with only one clean-up per week. Total development costs to date are £73,000.

28   During the year, £57,000 was spent on research into the heat resistance of tooth enamel, on the instruction of the managing director, whose wife had been experiencing toothache every time she had a hot drink.

29   In April, a new computer was purchased for £300,000 in order to speed-up the research work of the product development team.

30   In order to utilise the spare capacity on the new computer (see question 29), a systems engineer and a programmer were appointed to develop a computer-assisted manufacturing system for the company's proposed new product *Magre*. Their salaries and other related costs amounted to £45,000 during the year.

31   A new laboratory was built to house the new computer (see question 29) and those working with it. It was completed in April at a cost of £60,000, and is expected to have a useful life of 50 years.

32   £23,000 was spent during the year developing an improved form of tamper-proof packaging for the company's headache pills, *Batem*. So far, no progress has been made, and it has been decided to shelve the project for a few years in order to give the technology a chance to progress.

33   In September, the company discovered that liquid chemicals valued at £250,000 stored in a vat in a sealed warehouse had become contaminated. £31,000 was spent on research into why it happened, but no conclusive findings resulted.

34   £75,000 was brought forward at the start of the year as deferred development expenditure on a new range of dental floss. The scientist employed to develop the product left soon after the start of the year to join a rival company which, six months later, launched a new range of dental floss incorporating the new ingredients that the company's proposed product would have included. The market for the new product is now felt to have been permanently lost and no further development work on it is planned.

Questions 35 and 36 relate to an advertising company, Fala Plc. The company's year end is 31st December. Annual turnover in the current year was £5m and pre-tax profit £0.7m. (Last year £7.6m and £780,000 respectively.)

35   The company spent £66,000 on market research for a client in November. It still has further work to do on the client's product, which will probably be completed by the Spring.

36   The company intends to introduce a new form of advertising which it has been developing since the middle of the year. Development costs to date are £190,000. It is expected to be a great success and market research (costing £7,000) has indicated a probable doubling of profits in the first two years after its introduction.

37   *Bebendo Plc*, a brewing company, has been developing a new high-alcohol drink over the last four years which is expected to be very profitable. Development has now ceased, and the total spent to date, including the amounts deferred in the first three years, is £270,000. Production started in September and the product must be stored for twenty four months before being sold.

38   *Faliando Ltd* is a small private electronics company with an accounting policy that development expenditure be deferred and amortised over the periods during which the item it relates to is expected to be sold or used, starting in the first such period. During the current year, the company incurred development expenditure of £34,000 relating to a new product which it hopes to start producing in the middle of the year after next. A further £40,000 development costs are expected to be incurred before the product will be ready for production. The company has been experiencing some cash flow problems and its auditors are concerned about its status as a going concern.

39   *Procura Plc*, a scientific equipment manufacturing company, has spent £130,000 developing a new scanner to be used by companies engaged in the location of oceanic oil and gas deposits. Development is expected to continue over the next three years, and the total cost is expected to exceed £1m by the time the product is ready for production. The company is confident that the product is technically feasible and commercially viable, and that all the costs will be more than covered by the revenue resulting from the sale of the scanner.

40   *Cadeira Ltd* has, for many years, been in receipt of funding from a charitable trust to help it to develop medical aids for the physically handicapped. The chairman has recently fallen-out with the trust administrators, and they have informed the company that it will no longer be assisted in this way. Thanks to the previous subsidy the company has been able to afford to develop marginally profitable products which it would otherwise never have contemplated. During the current year it has spent £90,000 of its own money developing a new wheelchair. It is felt that a further £110,000 will be required to complete the project and the company has many more-profitable projects on which it would rather spend that amount of money. It is unlikely that funds will be released by the company to continue the wheelchair project in the foreseeable future.

Questions 41-45 relate to companies, all of which are 'small companies', as defined by the Companies Act, and have a balance sheet date of 31st December.

41   During the year, the operational research team of *Barco Ltd* has been working on the development of a new design for the company's ship assembly line. In December, the team announced that they had been successful and the new design was immediately put into effect. The total cost of development has been calculated at £150,000 and it is expected that the new design will substantially increase annual profits. It is anticipated that it will be five years before the design will need to be reconsidered.

42   In February, *Estrela Plc* was contracted, on a full reimbursement basis, to undertake some research and development work for *Major Plc*. In respect of this contract, *Estrela Plc* spent £90,000 on research and £170,000 on development during the year. At the balance sheet date, *Estrela Plc* had received £55,000 of the research expenditure, and £110,000 of the development expenditure from *Major Plc*.

43   A mining company spent £120,000 on the purchase of a small laboratory to conduct research into the properties and quality of the minerals it was extracting.

44   *Muitopequeno Ltd*, an independent chemicals company, has a policy of writing-off all research and development expenditure as it is incurred. It has no provision in its accounting systems to differentiate between research and non-research expenditure and can only separate the two classes of expenditure by manually examining all items charged in the accounting period. In previous years, it has employed two temporary accounts clerks to undertake the analysis but the managing director no longer wishes to do so.

45   In July, a company which specialises in building North Sea oil platforms set-up a small research team to develop a safer helicopter landing platform design. Costs incurred to the end of the period were £35,000. It is anticipated that they will be successful in developing a new landing environment, probably in another six to eight months. It is predicted that a successful project will result in savings of approximately £60,000 per annum on oil extraction companies' insurance costs on each platform built using the new design.

6   SSAP 17: Accounting for Post Balance Sheet Events

Summary of the accounting treatment requirements

This standard covers the treatment of events which occur between the balance sheet date and the date on which the board of directors approve the financial statements (the 'post balance sheet period'). It distinguishes between two classes of events ('adjusting' and 'non-adjusting') and makes it reasonably clear which category an item will initially come under. If the event provides evidence of conditions existing at the balance sheet date, or is of a type that by statute or convention is always incorporated in the financial statements (for example, dividends proposed and amounts appropriated to reserves), then it is an adjusting event. An event which does not meet one of these requirements is provisionally treated as non-adjusting, and must then be reassessed and subsequently may be reclassified as adjusting, or treated as either non-adjusting-but-disclosed, or non-adjusting-and-not-disclosed.

Adjusting events result in the figures in the financial statements being amended. Non-adjusting events do not, but they must be disclosed when non-disclosure would affect the ability of the users of financial statements to reach a proper understanding of the financial position. The disclosure is in two parts: the nature of the event must be stated along with an estimate of its financial effect; and if it is not practicable to estimate the financial effect, then this must be stated.

Problems of interpretation and grey areas

The following items are discussed: window dressing; the definition of an adjusting event; the distinction between adjusting and non-adjusting events; and post-post balance sheet events.

Window dressing

Unfortunately, for a number of reasons, SSAP 17 is not as uncomplicated and straightforward as it appears to be. A prime example concerns transactions processed before the year end, and reversed once it has passed. This will often be done in order to alter the appearance of the balance sheet. The standard attempts to preserve the true and fair view by stating that disclosure of such alterations would be required. It then comments that they include those adjustments commonly known as' window dressing' (paragraph 10). The phrase 'window dressing' is defined by the ASC, in Technical Release 398, as 'the *lawful* arrangement of affairs over the year end to make things look different from the way they usually are'. Two points arise here: firstly, what are those other alterations implicitly referred to in paragraph 10? and secondly, what is wrong with a company organising its financial affairs differently at the end of the year, as compared to the rest of the time?

Could these other alterations include the *unlawful* arrangement of affairs (i.e. fraudulent window dressing)? According to the ASC (TR 398), fraudulent falsification of the accounts, in order to make things look better than they really are, is outside the scope of SSAP 17. Consequently, it is only non-fraudulent window dressing that comes within its scope and fraudulent window dressing is not among the other implied alterations. It does appear therefore that there may be no other types of *lawful* alterations (i.e. all such alterations are what could be described as 'window dressing'). The wording in paragraph 10 appears to be a 'catch-all' implying the existence of others, just in case any should arise.

As to what is wrong with a company using lawful window dressing, it is necessary to consider what a balance sheet is: it is a snapshot of the financial affairs of a company at a point in time. It does not purport to reflect the permanent situation, though many users of accounts apply the figures contained therein as if they were permanent, making adjustments only for trends indicated by the statement of source and application of funds, and comparison with previous years' accounts. On the basis that many users of the balance sheet do make these assumptions, it would be misleading not to disclose window dressing activities.

Given that the standard is correct in tackling this issue, why require only the disclosure of window dressing? Why is it not treated as requiring restatement of the figures in the accounts? The answer is clear: the required disclosure of the nature and financial effects of window dressing will in itself provide sufficient information for the users of the accounts to make the appropriate adjustments to the balance sheet so as to produce a 'normalised' picture of the company's financial position. By its very nature, it is inconceivable that an example of window dressing will not be financially quantifiable.

What is an adjusting event?

Another problem with the standard concerns the definition of an adjusting event. Sometimes it is clear that evidence is provided of conditions existing at the balance sheet date. Examples of this include a property revaluation which indicates that the year end accounts value was incorrect; stock sold on the first day of the next year at below its balance sheet value; and a claim for damages being settled for an amount other than that incorporated in the financial statements.

However, it is often not clear if evidence has in fact been found of conditions *existing at the balance sheet date*. Consider what might cause a company to reduce its stock values in the first few weeks after the balance sheet date. It may, for instance, be the result of a fall in net realisable value caused by its competitors beginning to undercut its selling prices, or it could be because the stock was overvalued at the balance sheet date. Before any figures are revised, it is necessary to discover whether the change identified was the result of something which occurred after the company's balance sheet date, or whether it existed at the balance sheet date.

For the purposes of clarification, the appendix to the standard contains a list of adjusting events which is sufficiently wide-ranging to cover most instances where doubt could arise. A careful study of this indicates that, while it may not be immediately obvious whether something is an adjusting event, further investigation can usually determine whether or not it is.

What is the difference between adjusting and non-adjusting events?

The lists of examples of adjusting and non-adjusting events in the appendix are preceded by the comment that 'in exceptional circumstances, to accord with the prudence concept, an adverse event which would normally be classified as non-adjusting may need to be reclassified as adjusting'. (The relevant part of the definition of 'prudence' in SSAP 2 (*Disclosure of accounting policies* - chapter 12) refers to making provision for *all* known liabilities.) It could be argued that the identification of any material liability may be considered an exceptional circumstance requiring adjustment. This could be interpreted as suggesting that if something adverse arises in the post balance sheet period (and therefore the liability is now known to exist), it may need to be provided for in the financial statements, even though it may not have existed at the balance sheet date.

This has the effect of blurring the distinction between adverse adjusting and non-adjusting events and could result in non-reversing window dressing (i.e. items being recognised in an adjustment to the accounts of a period prior to that in which they arise and belong, which will not be reversed in a later period). This is surely contrary to the intention of the standard, but it is hard to see how its use can be prevented. The only limiting factor is that it arises in the appendix, not in the main body of the standard, and so has only limited status. However, whether this will prevent its being used is open to debate. Indeed, it is highly unlikely that a company will forgo the option of reclassification, where preferable, on the grounds that it is only the appendix of SSAP 17 which mentions it.

While this would not be everyone's interpretation of the introduction to the appendix, it is a possible one; and it is unfortunate that the phrase 'exceptional circumstances' was not clearly defined in the standard, thereby avoiding any possibility of inappropriate recognition of non-adjusting events.

There is little doubt that this concession was made because of the relatively narrow definition of an adjusting event. Yet, that definition seems valid and is workable, and it is hard to imagine any situation requiring adjustment of the financial statements that would not be covered by the definition of adjusting events. Indeed, only one - an event which brings into question the going concern status of the company (or, by implication, any section of it) - appears possible, and that is dealt with in paragraph 8 which states that such events may be treated as adjusting events.

Non-adjusting events require to be disclosed, unless non-disclosure would not be misleading. This applies even when they are reclassified as adjusting events under the prudence option referred to in the appendix. Consequently, the user of the accounts should always be aware of the facts and be able to draw appropriate conclusions, even if the figures in the financial statements have not been adjusted. Where any doubt exists as to whether something should be treated as adjusting or non-adjusting, the obvious solution is to treat it as non-adjusting and disclose as much detail as possible.

Post-post balance sheet events

Post-post balance sheet events are those occurring after the financial statements have been approved by the board of directors. In paragraph 4, it is stated that such events do not come within the scope of the standard. Yet, this is followed by: 'if such events are material the directors should consider publishing the relevant information so that users of financial statements are not misled'. This must surely be an example of bringing events within the scope of the standard. Clearly it is saying that anything which occurs up until the *publication* of the financial statements should be disclosed where non-disclosure would be misleading (i.e. would fail to present a true and fair view). The optional tone ('should consider publishing') is deceptive: if a company considered publishing such an event where non-disclosure would be misleading, and then decided not to disclose it, the accounts would be liable to qualification for failing to give a true and fair view. Such events should therefore be disclosed, despite the apparent option of non-disclosure given in the standard.

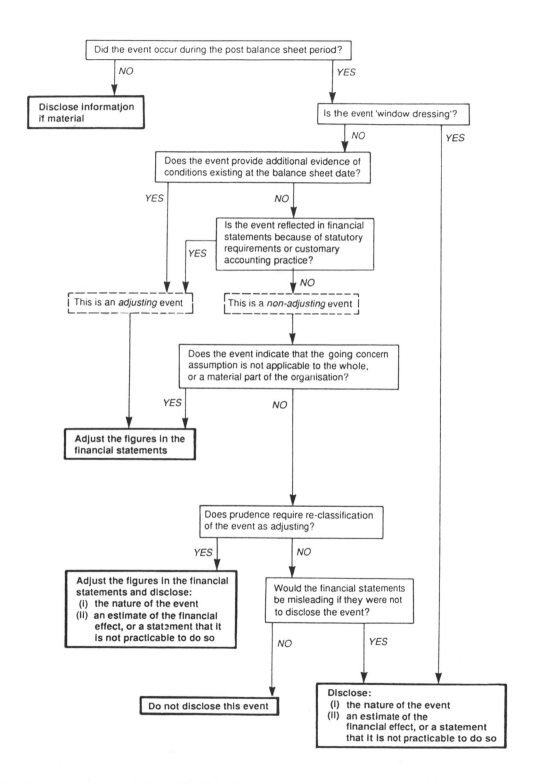

Short Questions

*ASSUME THAT MATERIALITY EXISTS IN **EVERY** CASE*

Questions 1-40 relate to a household furniture manufacturing and retailing company with 100 employees, current turnover of £8m and net pre-tax profit of £700,000. (Last year £7.6m and £780,000 respectively.) The company's financial year ended on 31st December. It is now 31st March and the Board of Directors are meeting to approve the accounts. (All references to January, February, March and April relate to the year following the accounting period under review.)

1   In February, the company bought a new warehouse for £500,000. The purchase was funded by a 10 year loan and the loan is secured by a fixed charge over the company's offices and central warehouse assets.

2   In late January, the company's entire stock of recliner chairs (which had been water damaged in a small fire in the warehouse in the first week in January) were sold for £20,000 to an overseas customer. The value in the accounts was £45,000.

3   In February, a defect was found in the material used in some batches of furniture awaiting shipment to an overseas customer. It was discovered that these were the only batches affected and that they were all manufactured in the last week of December. As a result, the customer was offered a 40% discount on the agreed price. This was accepted and the sale proceeded at a value of £60,000. (The value placed on the stock in question in the year-end accounts was £80,000.)

4   After negotiating for six months, the company finally sold its Dundee factory 2 days after the year end. It was sold for £160,000. This was £28,000 less than the value it was shown at in the accounts which was based on an independent valuation carried out in mid-December.

5   The warehouse fire in January gave rise to a claim for loss of profits with the company's insurers. In March the company received a cheque for £12,000.

6   Some land that the company owned was sold in November at a price to be set by independent valuers. It was included in the year end accounts at a figure of £23,000, pending a decision on the sale value. In January it was agreed that the land should be sold for £41,000.

7   For some years the company has been running a wallpaper division. This has never been very profitable - approximately 2% on turnover of £1.2m in the last year. In order to improve profitability of what the company then believed to be a potentially profitable venture an industrial consultant was appointed in January to undertake a feasibility study of the operation. Unfortunately he concluded that, due to the company's failure to keep up-to-date in both design and manufacture, huge losses would be incurred if it were not closed immediately. As a result, at an emergency board meeting in 18th February, the wallpaper division was disbanded and steps were taken to sell off all the equipment and plant as quickly as possible. By mid-March this had been achieved and the sale raised £129,000 as against a book value in the year end accounts of £335,000.

8   Due to the company being under-insured since it changed insurers last year, a claim for equipment worth £20,000 which was destroyed in the January fire realised only £5,000 from the insurance company.

9   In February, the company's subsidiary *Menor Ltd* declared a dividend for the year to 31st December.

10   In late December, the company sold stock worth £300,000 to a furnishing company for £350,000. In February, the company bought back all this stock for £355,000 and resold it to a foreign customer for £390,000. It has subsequently been discovered that the stock never left the company's warehouse until it was shipped overseas in mid-March - i.e. the temporary owner never had possession of the stock.

11   In January, a ship carrying a consignment of custom-built furniture which had been sold in December sank. All the furniture was lost. The company had forgotten to arrange insurance cover. The buyer demanded an immediate refund of the deposit paid and refused to accept a replacement consignment.

12   The board decided at a special board meeting on 23rd December that its investment in an associate company should be sold as soon as possible. The investment was valued in the balance sheet at £80,000. On 9th January the entire holding was sold and raised £110,000.

13   The board decided at the January 12th board meeting that, following the profitable sale of its investment in one associated undertaking it should sell its holding in another as soon as possible. The investment was valued in the balance sheet at £90,000. On 23rd February the entire holding was sold and raised £140,000.

14   The board decided at the 14th March board meeting that, following the profitable sale of its investments in two associated undertakings, it should sell another similar holding as soon as possible. The investment was valued in the balance sheet at £70,000. No sale has yet been negotiated.

15   The board also decided at the March board meeting that it should consider selling a wholly-owned subsidiary which is valued in the financial statements at £240,000. The finance director was instructed to investigate the financial implications and determine whether there may be any interested buyers. The proposal is to be discussed again at the June board meeting.

16   On 19th December, the union safety officer drew the management's attention to a potentially dangerous area in the Aberdeen factory. This was noted and it was agreed that it would be looked at. On December 29th a painter slipped and fell 30 feet, breaking an arm and a leg. He is unlikely to work for the next year and, in a letter dated February 7th, is suing the company for £60,000. The company's lawyers advise that the company was negligent and that, even allowing for contributory negligence on the part of the employee (who did know the floor was unsafe) they would be unlikely to avoid a damages payment of £30,000. The company's insurance will not meet the claim as the company had taken no steps to improve a dangerous situation. No allowance has been entered in

the financial statements as it was assumed that the company's insurance would meet any claim arising.

17   After a painter was badly injured at the end of December, some repair work was undertaken to improve the safety level in part of the Aberdeen factory. However, before it could be completed, on January 4th a security guard slipped and fell 30 feet, breaking his back. He is unlikely to ever work again and is suing the company for £350,000. The company's lawyers advise that the company was negligent and that, even allowing for contributory negligence on the part of the security guard (who did know the floor was unsafe) they would be unlikely to avoid a damages payment of £150,000. The company's insurance will meet the claim as they had approved the company's plan and timetable for the safety improvement work being undertaken.

18   On 29th December, the company repaid a £300,000 loan from an Iraq-based finance company which had been taken out in June in order to fund the establishment of an overseas distribution network. On 2nd January the loan was taken out again from the same source.

19   In order to finance the temporary repayment of the Iraq loan, trade creditors were unpaid for three months, instead of the normal one month. When the loan was reactivated in January the creditors were immediately paid.

20   A contract to supply hospital fixtures (built-in wardrobes and private rooms facilities) throughout Highland region was due to have been completed by the end of February. The company had sub-contracted the work to a highly successful, private company, *Malsorte Ltd*, and work had been proceeding on schedule up to the end of the year when profit of £20,000 was recognised in the accounts. In January the entire board, management and workforce of *Malsorte Ltd* were killed when the charter flight taking them for a week's holiday in Egypt to celebrate the company's 50th anniversary crashed. As a result of having to identify and appoint another firm to take over the sub-contract work, the expected completion date is now mid-July and an overall loss is expected of £40,000 on the contract thanks to a combination of penalty costs for late completion and the higher cost of employing the new sub-contractors compared to *Malsorte Ltd*. (There is no possibility of any contribution towards the costs being recoverable from either *Malsorte Ltd* or their insurers.)

21   A contract to supply restaurant furnishings to a fast-food chain was due to have been completed by the end of next July. The contract had been proceeding on schedule up to the end of the year when a profit of £30,000 was included in the accounts. It has just been discovered that the table tops, which were manufactured in December, are not of the correct grade of burn-resistant plastic. Consequently all the table tops will have to be scrapped and replaced with new production. It is anticipated that the contract completion date will still be met but the cost of the extra work will cause the contract to make an overall loss of £22,000.

22   At the end of December the company tendered for a contract to refurnish Holyrood Palace in Edinburgh. The price quoted would result in a loss of around £30,000 but it was felt that the publicity benefits would more than compensate for this. On 6th February the tender was accepted at the price proposed.

23   The company instructed a firm of surveyors to conduct a full structural survey of the Dundee offices following the appearance of cracks in the ceiling in mid-February. The surveyors have reported that there is considerable evidence of long-standing subsidence and have recommended extensive structural repairs be carried out. The value they place on the building is £30,000 less than the £90,000 at which it was included in the year end balance sheet.

24   Stocks of invalid furniture, which had been valued at £26,000 in the year end balance sheet, had to be sold-off at vastly reduced prices (£12,000 was received) when the market for the company's product collapsed in mid-January as a result of a competitor introducing a new range of invalid furniture using a far superior type of material. The new material is readily available but the company had had an informal agreement with the competitor that neither would use it until existing stocks of the old material-based furniture had been exhausted. (On 5th January the company sold a batch of the furniture to Grampian Health Board at the company's usual selling price.)

25   The company has, for many years, sold deck chairs to the main high street chain stores. At the year end, the stock of deck chairs was valued at £40,000. In the first week of January, the company's salesmen started to report that they were hearing rumours of cheap Taiwanese deck chairs becoming available. No sales of deck chairs were made in January - usually the peak month for deck chair sales. After making some enquiries, it was discovered that these were being offered to the stores for half the price the company charged. Not surprisingly, the stores' buyers were not keen to place any orders for the company's deck chairs. The production of deck chairs always occurs in November and December. The company never manufactures them outside these months unless a customer places an order of sufficient size to warrant production being undertaken. In response to the Taiwanese competition, the company decided to offer all the deck chairs in stock at a 40% discount to existing customers and to wait until the autumn before deciding whether or not to produce deck chairs in future. The stock has consequently now been revalued at £28,000 and sufficient orders are being received to suggest that it will all be sold by the end of April.

Additional Questions

*ASSUME THAT MATERIALITY EXISTS IN **EVERY** CASE*

26   The company had been negotiating with Fife Regional Council throughout December regarding a contract to re-furnish all the regions schools. The contract was signed on 4th January at the apparently very profitable price of £350,000. It was discovered on 18th March that, due to a miscalculation, the contract was going to produce a loss of at least £85,000. The company is legally bound to fulfil the contract and it would incur a penalty of £350,000 were it to withdraw.

27   On 5th February, after an earth tremor, subsidence was detected in the company's head office building. The market value of the building fell as a result from the £190,000 entered in the year end accounts to £120,000.

28   In November, the company sold an old factory it no longer required. The sale proceeds were entered through the books at £115,000. On 1st March a structural defect was

detected and, under a clause in the sale agreement, the company was responsible for rectifying the problem. The work was done quickly and, on 25th March, a bill was received for £20,000.

29   The profit ascribed to a long-term contract at the year end has subsequently been found to have been overstated by £34,000.

30   In December, the company started pay negotiations with its manual workers. These negotiations spread over into January and in mid-January the employees went out on indefinite strike. So far 6 weeks production has been lost. A settlement is expected within the next few days.

31   At the year end, *Ruim Ltd* a long standing customer owed the company £23,000. It has just been announced that *Ruim Ltd* has gone into liquidation and that there is expected to be no cash available to pay its trade creditors.

32   The board proposes to declare a dividend of seven pence for every ordinary share held.

33   The board has decided that £600,000 be transferred from the profit and loss account balance to a general repairs reserve.

34   Included in this year's March Budget is a change in the full rate of Corporation Tax to 30%.

35   In January, the company was contacted and asked if it would consider investing £100,000 in a small French furniture making company. After some consideration, the investment was made. In March the company was taken over and the company received £200,000 for its holding.

36   In January, the company raised some additional capital through a rights issue which had been planned and approved in November.

37   A posting error has been found in the accounts whereby £52,000 income from the sale of six delivery trucks has been credited to furniture sales.

38   As a result of the sudden and surprising collapse of the Norwegian government, the exchange rate with Norway fell from £1 = 11.5kr to £1 = 9.75kr in January. The fall has not been reversed since then and it looks as if it is likely to be long term. The company had over £500,000 sales to Norway in the last year. Since the exchange rate fell, sales to Norway have increased by 30% on those of the corresponding period last year.

39   After many years of stability, the exchange rate with Switzerland has risen from £1 = SFr2.5 to £1 = SFr3 in the period since the year end. Prior to this, annual sales to Switzerland were £150,000. Sales to Switzerland are down 50% on the same period last year. It is thought that the exchange rate will come back towards its old level within the next eighteen months but that, for the immediate future, while no further rise was expected, there was little prospect of an improvement. Items sold to Switzerland have always been from the company's main catalogue and stock unsold to Switzerland due to the fall in demand there can be channelled into other markets.

40   The government has just announced that it intends to drastically re-organise the Health Service. One of the changes that will result is that all hospitals will in future be supplied with all their furnishings from a central store facility based in Milton Keynes. The company has six months in which to tender to supply the central store. The successful manufacturers will be notified one month later, and orders will be placed at the start of the following year. No further Health Service furnishing orders are to be issued until then. The company currently has £600,000 annual sales to the Health Service and £100,000 worth of stock of hospital furnishings, of which £40,000 was held at the balance sheet date. Production of further hospital furnishing has ceased and has been replaced by increased production of items ordered from Norway.

Questions 41-45 relate to companies, all of which have a balance sheet date of 31st December. It is now 31st March and the Board of Directors are meeting to approve the accounts. (All references to January, February, March and April relate to the year following the accounting period under review.)

41   Two months after the financial year end, *Dinho Plc* acquired the entire share capital of *Minha Ltd* in exchange for 400,000 ordinary £1 shares in *Dinho Plc*.

42   Since preparing the financial statements of *Emma Ltd* for the financial period ended on 31st December, fixed assets have been increased in value by 30% following the determination of the purchase price of a new factory acquired in November.

43   Nine weeks after the 31st December financial year end (on 4th March), a major debtor balance (*Ladrao Ltd*) was renegotiated to 75% of its 31st December value.

44   After eight months negotiations, a supermarket company finally sold a vacant store which it had built in the hope of a sale materialising. It was valued in the financial statements at cost and no allowance had been made for any profit. The sale was completed five days after the financial year end, at a price that was £15,000 less than the cost value.

45   Two weeks after the end of the financial period, the managing director of a car dealership decided to reclassify six of the new cars which had been in stock for the previous eight months as salesmen's vehicles. Accordingly, the cars were withdrawn from sale and transferred to the asset register at their net realisable value (which had not changed since the period end).

7   SSAP 18: Accounting for Contingencies

Summary of the accounting treatment requirements

A contingency is a condition which exists at the balance sheet date, where the outcome will be confirmed only on the occurrence or non-occurrence of one or more uncertain future events.

A material contingent *loss* should be accrued in the financial statements where it is *probable* that a future event will confirm a loss which can be estimated with reasonable accuracy at the date on which the financial statements are approved by the board of directors. A *possible*, rather than *probable* contingent loss should be disclosed. It should not be accrued. *Remote* contingent losses should neither be disclosed nor accrued.

Contingent *gains* should not be accrued. They should be disclosed only if *probable*.

When disclosure is made, it should include the nature of the contingency, the expected uncertainties, and a prudent estimate of the *potential* financial effect *made at the date on which the financial statements are approved by the board of directors* (or a statement that it is not practicable to make such an estimate). Any estimate of the financial effect of a contingent *loss* should be reduced by any amounts accrued and by any element of the estimated amount which relates to circumstances where the possibility of loss is remote. Only the net amount need be disclosed, and it should be disclosed *before* taking account of taxation. However, the taxation implications should be explained where necessary for the true and fair view.

Where both the nature of, and uncertainties affecting a contingency are common to a number of similar transactions, the financial effect may be based on the group of similar transactions and the separate contingencies need not be individually disclosed.

Problems of interpretation and grey areas

The following items are discussed: the treatment of remote contingencies; post balance sheet period events; objective definition of contingent probabilities; the question of whether to disclose 'potential' or 'expected' financial effects; litigation contingencies; the inconsistency between the treatments of contingent losses and gains; accounting estimate uncertainties; and the question of whether compensation claims are indicative of the existence of contingent losses or contingent gains.

The treatment of remote contingencies

Paragraph 8 of the standard states that there are some contingencies (liabilities only, not gains) which are so remote that their disclosure would be misleading. It then states that the standard 'does not require disclosure of remote contingencies'. It appears to be giving the reason why it does not require the disclosure of remote contingencies and, at the same time, implying that it is easier to apply a blanket exemption than to restrict it specifically to those situations where disclosure would be misleading. This leaves a gap, for if there are some contingencies so remote that their disclosure would be misleading, there are also some less remote whose disclosure would not be misleading. This unsatisfactory situation is covered by the statutory requirement that each contingent liability must be disclosed. It would be appropriate to cite the standard for non-compliance with the statute in respect of those contingencies whose disclosure would be misleading, but not otherwise. Thus, material, non-misleading, remote contingent liabilities should be disclosed, though under statute rather than the standard.

Post balance sheet period events

Post balance sheet period events may give rise to contingencies, but the standard states (paragraph 1) that it applies to conditions existing at the balance sheet date. Thus, contingencies which arise relating to conditions which did not exist at the balance sheet date are outside the scope of the standard. What should be done when a contingency arises in the period between the balance sheet date and the date on which the financial statements are approved by the board of directors (i.e. during the post balance sheet period)? Consider, for example, a situation where a company had agreed to guarantee a loan to an ex-employee in order that he might start up his own business and it became apparent during the post balance sheet period that there was a possibility that the loan might not be repaid when due. Had this become apparent during the accounting period, it would certainly be treated as a contingency and merit disclosure. Why is the situation different just because a few weeks have elapsed? The readers and users of the financial statements will not have any idea that the company might suffer this loss and the value of the company will be overestimated if such valuation is based on the information contained in the financial statements (assuming materiality in the amount of the loan).

To overcome this apparent inconsistency, any contingency which arises in the post-balance sheet event period is covered by SSAP 17 (*Accounting for post balance sheet events* - chapter 6) and reference should be made to the disclosure requirements of that standard after identifying the appropriate treatment under SSAP 18. (SSAP 18 determines *what* is to be disclosed and SSAP 17 determines *how* it is to be disclosed.) If such a contingency were a probable or reasonably certain liability, or a reasonably certain gain, SSAP 18 prescribes provision being made for it. However, as it has arisen in the post-balance sheet period, and is unconnected with conditions which existed at the balance sheet date, it would be classified as a non-adjusting event under SSAP 17. Therefore, excepting when the contingency indicates that the 'going concern' assumption may be inappropriate, it would be disclosed, not provided for. This would also be the case for any probable contingent gain which arose during the post balance sheet period. The SSAP 17 treatment must have precedence: in these cases, SSAP 18 is only relevant as a guide as to how to arrive at the items to be disclosed.

In the case of a possible contingent gain which arises during the post balance sheet period, it would seem appropriate to follow prudence and the guidance offered by SSAP 18, and not disclose it.

Objective definition of contingent probabilities

The standard relies heavily upon a distinction being drawn between contingencies that are 'reasonably certain', 'probable' and 'possible'. To add to the complication, 'possible' contingencies must be further classified as 'remote' and 'non-remote'. There is difficulty in deciding objectively which category a contingency comes under. Without some clear yardstick, the decision on treatment is very subjective and open to abuse. One way to tackle this is to adopt the levels of probability for each likelihood of outcome as suggested in *'UK GAAP'* (MacMillan, 1994, p. 1270). That is:

0%- 5%	=	remote
5%- 50%	=	possible
50%- 95%	=	probable
95%-100%	=	reasonably certain

By adopting this approach some consistency in application will be achieved. However, the problem still remains that the derivation of the percentages themselves is a highly subjective exercise. Care must therefore be taken to ensure that all the available information is considered before an assessment of probability is made.

Should 'potential' or 'expected' financial effects be disclosed?

The standard states that the amount disclosed should be the *potential* financial effect of the contingency (paragraph 19). It does appear therefore that it would not be correct to disclose only the *expected* financial effect. In the same paragraph, it is stated that the amount disclosed should be reduced by 'the amounts of any component where the possibility of loss is remote'. This could be seen as making the 'potential' financial effect disclosure equivalent to the 'expected' financial effect, but that is not the case. Consider, for example, a situation where a company is being sued for £150,000, the maximum non-remote damages it is believed that it may sustain are £100,000 and the expected damages are £30,000. According to the standard, the financial effect to be disclosed is £100,000. The £30,000 expected financial effect could be disclosed as well as, but not instead of, the £100,000.

Litigation contingencies

Problems arise when companies are engaged in litigation, or may be in the future. The contingent losses and gains will often be very substantial. Disclosure of the company's position may jeopardise its case and, when litigation is a possibility but not yet a reality, disclosure may actually lead to the contingency materialising: if no disclosure had been made, the litigation would not have occurred. Are there any situations when not revealing details about litigation contingencies would be in compliance with SSAP 18? The answer is 'no': regardless of the potential effect of disclosure, the company must disclose if to do otherwise would constitute failure to present a 'true and fair view' in the financial statements.

The inconsistency between the treatments of contingent losses and gains

There is apparent inconsistency between the treatment of contingent losses and contingent gains (see paragraph 19). Losses are reduced by amounts already accrued; gains are not. Probable losses are provided for in the financial statements; probable gains are not: therefore it is more likely that a contingent loss will have been provided for to some extent, as only reasonably certain contingent gains can be accrued. This does not mean that there will never be an occasion when a contingent gain will be treated as partly reasonably certain (and accrued) and partly probable (and disclosed). In such a case, the standard appears to imply that all the financial effects of the whole contingent gain should be disclosed, including that part which has been accrued. However, this apparent inconsistency between the treatment of gains and losses is removed by closer examination of the standard. Paragraph 4 states that 'when the realisation of the gain becomes reasonably certain, then such a gain is not a contingency and accrual is appropriate'. In other words, those elements of a contingent gain that have been accrued no longer merit classification as contingencies and so there will never be a situation where there will be any accrual available to offset a probable contingent gain.

Accounting estimate uncertainties

Possibly the most confusing aspect of this standard is the statement, in paragraph 1, that 'it is not intended that uncertainties connected with accounting estimates should fall within the scope of this statement'. A number of examples are then cited: lives of fixed assets; amount of bad debts; net realisable value of inventories; expected outcome of long term contracts; valuation of properties; and foreign currency balances. The standard is not concerned with the ongoing possibility that any accounting estimate will prove inaccurate. The contingencies to which the standard relates are those one-off occurrences which are outside the normal range of accounting estimates. For example, bad debts are accounting estimates made on a regular basis. Companies will have a system, either formal or informal, for determining when provision for loss should be made. While the spirit of SSAP 18 could be applied to such estimates, they are outside the scope of the standard as they are routine accounting estimates prepared on a regular basis.

On the other hand, net realisable value of inventories is governed by the rules of SSAP 9 (*Stocks and long term contracts* - chapter 3). SSAP 18 would only be relevant if a contingency arose which would not normally be covered by the rules of SSAP 9. For example, if there was a possibility that the government would ban the use of a material which is held in stock, such a ban would have a material effect upon the net realisable value of that stock. A situation such as this is not covered in SSAP 9 and does not come within the normal range of accounting estimates. SSAP 18 would therefore apply.

Consequently, it should not be assumed that a contingency relating to accounting estimates will be outside the scope of SSAP 18. The exclusion from SSAP 18 depends upon the relationship between the contingency and the accounting estimate. If the contingency concerns an item which is beyond the scope of the accounting estimate, SSAP 18 will apply.

Are compensation claims indicative of the existence of contingent losses or contingent gains?

There is some difficulty in determining whether certain items are contingent gains or losses. This situation arises when a loss has been incurred and there is a possibility of compensation being received in respect of the loss. It can be viewed in two ways. On the one hand, it may be held that the loss has already been incurred and that there is no contingency of additional loss, only of a potential gain: in this case, it is a contingent gain that is being considered. Conversely, it may be held that the loss incurred is only an estimate of the loss and that its final value is contingent upon the level of compensation ultimately received: in other words, it is a contingent loss. This confusion needs to be addressed because contingent gains are disclosed only when probable and not when possible; contingent losses, on the other hand, are provided for when probable and disclosed when possible.

Paragraph 14 of the standard states that a contingency is 'a condition which exists ... where the outcome will be confirmed only on the occurrence or non-occurrence of one or more uncertain future events'. This does not help to clarify the situation: either of the two options would fit this definition.

Paragraph 6 states that 'a contingency may be reduced or avoided because it is matched by a related ... claim ... against a third party'. The initial loss in the above example is not a contingency and therefore paragraph 6 does not apply.

Paragraph 18 states that 'in respect of each contingency which is required to be disclosed ... the following ... should be stated ... [:] ... a prudent estimate of the financial effect'. This is followed, in paragraph 19, by: 'where there is disclosure of an estimate of the financial effect of a contingency, the amount should be the potential financial effect'. It could be argued that the compensation referred to in the example is the financial effect of the contingency. It will be a gain, should it be realised. If this view is accepted, it is the effect of the contingency which determines its nature and, where a situation of this type arises, the contingency is a contingent gain, not a contingent loss.

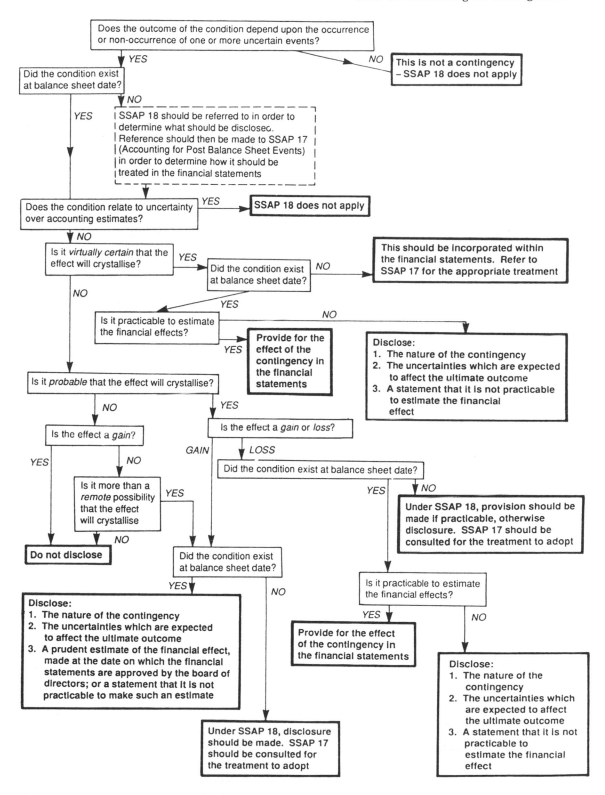

Short Questions

*ASSUME THAT MATERIALITY EXISTS IN **EVERY** CASE*

Questions 1-40 relate to a household furniture manufacturing and retailing company with 100 employees, current turnover of £8m and net pre-tax profit of £700,000. (Last year £7.6m and £780,000 respectively.) The company's financial year ended on 31st December. It is now 31st March and the Board of Directors are meeting to approve the accounts. (All references to January, February, March and April relate to the year following the accounting period under review.) **[You should ignore the taxation implications referred to in paragraphs 7 and 20 of the standard.]**

1   In February a very successful and profitable subsidiary purchased a new warehouse for £400,000. The purchase was funded by a 10 year loan and the company, under group policy, guaranteed the subsidiary's loan.

2   In December, a ship carrying a consignment of custom-built furniture, which had been sold in November, sank. All the furniture was lost. The company had not arranged insurance cover, believing it to be the responsibility of the buyer. The buyer insists that it was not his responsibility and is suing the company for a refund of the payment he made in respect of the goods. (Full payment for the goods - amounting to just over £38,000 - was required prior to shipment being sent.) The company's lawyers are of the opinion that it has a reasonable chance of success unless the buyer can produce evidence that the company agreed to insure the cargo. (The buyer has indicated that he has evidence that the company made a commitment to insure the cargo and the lawyers do find it strange that the case should be going to court unless the buyer has such evidence. The company maintains that no evidence can exist, as it is against company policy to make such a commitment.) No provision has been made in the accounts for the potential loss.

3   In December, one of the company's delivery lorries was left double parked while the driver went into a shop to buy a newspaper. The street was on a steep hill and, within seconds, sixteen cars had been damaged and the delivery lorry was a write-off. Expert examination revealed that the hand-brake had failed and that neither the driver, nor anyone else, was to blame. The company carries its own motor insurance. Repair and replacement claims received to date amount to £32,000 and there are also two court cases pending, one for consequential loss (£4,000) and another in respect of personal injury (£45,000). The company's lawyers have recommended that the company settle all the repair and replacement claims, that the consequential loss claim should be settled out of court, and would be if £1,500 were offered, and that the personal injury case should be taken to court where an award of about £30,000 was probable, though it was possible that as much as £65,000 could be awarded.

4   Some land that the company owned was sold in December at a price to be set by independent valuers. It was included in the year end accounts at a figure of £23,000 despite the expected sale value being £50,000 to £60,000.

5   In December, the company invested £100,000 in shares in a well established chain of hardware stores which had just 'gone public'. The shares are partly paid and the hardware

company is expected to make a call for the rest of the investment in the mid-April. At that time, the company will be required to pay a further £120,000.

6   Due to the company being under-insured since it changed insurers last year, a claim for building repairs costing £50,000 (which arose because of storm damage in November) remains unsettled. £20,000 has been offered by the insurers and at best this may be raised to £30,000, though the company's lawyers are doubtful that it will be increased.

7   The company is awaiting results for the year ending 31st December of a subsidiary company (*Tarde Ltd*) before deciding on the amount of dividend to declare for the year. The results, which are expected to show unusually high losses due to the excessively bad autumn weather's effect on demand for *Tarde's* products, should have arrived last week but have been delayed due to problems with a new management information system *Tarde* has recently had installed.

8   In February, a defect was found in the material used in some batches of furniture which had been made in December. Some of these batches had already been shipped to customers. There has been an insignificant return of these items so far. The company is of the opinion that the defect (a slight fault in the colour match) is unlikely to result in significant returns.

9   On 19th December the union safety officer drew the management's attention to a potentially dangerous area in the Aberdeen factory. This was noted, and it was agreed that it would be looked at. On December 29th a painter slipped and fell 30 feet, breaking an arm and a leg. He is unlikely to work for the next year and, in a letter dated February 7th, is suing the company for £60,000. The company's lawyers advise that the company was negligent and that, even allowing for contributory negligence on the part of the employee (who did know the floor was unsafe) they would be unlikely to avoid a damages payment of £30,000. The company's insurance will not meet the claim as the company had taken no steps to improve a dangerous situation. No allowance has been entered in the financial statements as it was assumed that the company's insurance would meet any claim arising.

10   In August, the Spanish government expropriated some land that the company had bought two years earlier with a view to building a factory and distribution warehouse. The land is valued in the financial statements at its cost of £50,000. Compensation amounting to between 50% and 80% of the original cost is to be paid once all the formalities have been completed. It is expected that payment will be received in June or July.

11   The company guarantees all furniture sold to the public through its own department store, and by mail order, for a period of ten years. This normally results in annual refund, repair and replacement costs of approximately 4% of these sales. Last year these sales totalled £750,000. Events in the period since the year end indicate that a similar level of claims can be expected this year.

12   In September, a special order of a new design of bedroom furniture was completed and despatched to a customer in the United States. The total value of the order was £120,000. In October, the company were contacted by the customer and informed that one of the beds on display had collapsed when lain on by an overweight prospective purchaser, and

that they were being sued for the equivalent of £80,000 for injuries sustained. The company has been advised by its lawyers to do nothing unless the American firm raises an action for compensation.

13   The company, along with three subsidiaries has a group registration for VAT purposes. (This means that the company is jointly and severally liable, along with the other three companies, for the whole of the VAT group's VAT liability.) At the balance sheet date the total VAT the company was due to remit to Customs and Excise was £70,000. The total for the whole VAT group was £160,000. All the amount due was paid. It is estimated that the equivalent figures for the quarter just ending will be £85,000 and £190,000.

14   In September, a special order of a new design of lounge furniture was completed and despatched to a firm in London. The total value of the order was £110,000. In October the company were contacted by the customer and informed that an electric bed settee on display had closed and trapped a customer inside. The customer had suffered severe trauma and a broken arm and was suing the London firm for undisclosed damages. The company examined the bed settee in question and found that the electric control on the bed settee was faulty. Further examination of the rest of the London firm's stock has revealed that all the bed settee controls were faulty, as were all those held in the company's own warehouse. No sales of the bed settee have been made to the public. The electric switch company that supplied the electric controls denies all responsibility insisting that the controls were designed for fold-down beds of the type that is concealed behind a built in panel in the wall. The company has contacted an electrical specialist who is of the opinion that the controls should have been modified by the manufacturer, if the manufacturer had been told of the use to which they were to be put. The company has a copy of the letter sent with the order to the electric switch company in which it was stated what they were to be used for. The company's lawyers feel that there is a good case for the company to sue the electric switch company for failing to supply goods as specified. They are also of the opinion that the London firm's customer will receive a substantial award and that a claim for damages will be raised by the London firm in respect of the effect the case has had upon its image and trade, in addition to the damages the court awards to the injured customer.

15   A warehouse fire in January gave rise to a claim for loss of profits with the company's insurers. There is some dispute as to how much will be received. The insurers are claiming that the company was negligent and are offering £30,000. The company is claiming £90,000. The company's lawyers have recommended that it stick to its original claim and, if necessary, take the matter to arbitration where it will be guaranteed at least the £30,000 currently on offer.

16   The company engaged a building firm to build a new multi-storey car park for employees to use at the Aberdeen factory. In November, just as the car park was due to be completed, the structure collapsed, destroying a raw material store and a works canteen. The company is suing for compensation and the case comes to court in June. The builders' insurers have offered to settle out of court for £130,000. The company is claiming £290,000. The company's lawyers belief that their claim is uncontestable and the company is proceeding with the case.

17   The company ran an advertising campaign in respect of its children's bedroom furniture during December. The campaign involved the distribution of 200,000 £20 discount vouchers for purchases made up to the end of June. Since these were issued, 4,000 vouchers have been redeemed and it is estimated that a further 2,000 will be redeemed during the remaining three months of the offer.

18   Rumours have been circulating since November that a Japanese company is close to world-wide marketing of a new synthetic wood substitute which would make the use of wood in furniture building obsolete. The company has wood valued at £150,000 (3 months supply) in stock on a permanent basis. Were the rumours to prove true, the stock value would fall to about £25,000.

19   At the year end, the company had discounted £200,000 bills of exchange without recourse. By the end of March, £50,000 were still outstanding and are due to mature in two months time.

20   On December 28th the company discounted, with recourse, a bill of exchange for £70,000 from a small private company. It is not normal practice for the company to discount bills with recourse. The bill was met when due earlier this week.

21   The company uses recourse factoring for credit sales to private individuals made through its department store, and by mail order. At the year end there was £70,000 outstanding in factored credit. Of this, £2,100 was not met when due (which was around the normal percentage level of recourse the company experiences) and the company had to purchase it back. The other £67,900 has been cleared. There is currently £110,000 of outstanding factored debt.

22   A retail customer who heard about the problem the company was having over electric controls on its bed settees, asked that the company provide a performance bond guaranteeing that the goods it bought will meet the standards stipulated. The performance bond includes a legally enforceable penalty clause which would result in the company meeting all costs of supplying replacement goods from a competitor at retail prices if more than the normal fault rate of 2% is found. If the whole consignment were to be faulty it is estimated that this would cost the company about £150,000. The contract was for toilet suites and had a value of £90,000. The sale occurred in December since when no claims have been received.

23   A contract to supply hotel fixtures (built-in wardrobes and en-suite facilities) throughout the north of England was started in May and completed at the end of November. It was discovered in December that someone in the company forgot to apply for planning permission to put in the en-suite facilities and that, as a result, the company was liable to be sued for loss of profits and all the costs related to the removal of the en-suite facilities. At that time, the contingent liability was estimated at £140,000. It has transpired that the company is being sued, but only in respect of two Newcastle hotels (where the local council has refused to retrospectively grant planning permission - all the other councils involved gave retrospective permission). The total claim is for £30,000 and the company's lawyers advise that they have no defence to it. The company has no insurance cover for this type of employee negligence.

24   A contract to refurbish a private school in Edinburgh was started in December. In the process of doing the work, one of the company's painters accidentally started a fire and the work had to be abandoned in mid-January. The school has indicated that it will be suing the company for the full costs of repair and other losses incurred. The total has been estimated at being somewhere between £50,000 and £200,000. The company's lawyers have indicated that the company is wholly liable and that there is no point in suing the painter.

25   The company bought £200,000 in German marks in December. This was done on the advice of the company's bankers who viewed the move as a good hedge against a rise in the mark versus the pound, especially as the company was due to pay that amount to a German sub-contractor in about six months time. Unfortunately the opposite has occurred and the investment is now worth about £180,000 and is expected to fall further before starting to rise again in the autumn. It is thought 20% likely that it will have risen back to its original value by the time the company is due to pay for the work done, 50% likely that it will be at about the current level and 30% likely that it will have fallen to about £160,000. The work has to be paid in marks but is priced in £sterling.

Additional Questions

*ASSUME THAT MATERIALITY EXISTS IN **EVERY** CASE*

26   The company is being sued, as a test case, by the chairman of 'Fat People of Britain' for its allegedly libelous advertising campaign which said that 'even fat people will find a bed to fit them if they buy from us'. It went on to show fat people falling through beds, bursting water beds and being unable to fit onto beds made by other manufacturers. The claimant contends that they never have any problem buying a bed and that to suggest otherwise is a gross misrepresentation of their lifestyle and habits. Were the case to succeed, it is estimated that approximately 20,000 people would be eligible to claim against the company. The amount being claimed is only £50. The campaign ran for one week at the start of December before being cancelled in view of the notification of intent to sue. The company's lawyers are unsure of how the case will go but are of the opinion that there is about a 70/30 chance of the company succeeding in its defence. Total costs of the court case are expected to be about £50,000 and may rise to as much as £200,000 if it goes to appeal, which is almost certain. The company is fighting the claim and has ruled out any out-of-court settlement.

27   In November, a special order of a new design of beach and camping furniture was completed and despatched to a customer in France. The total value of the order was £70,000. In December, the company were contacted by the customer and informed that a camp bed on display had collapsed when lain on by a prospective purchaser and that they (the French customer) were being sued for the equivalent of £40,000 for injuries sustained. The company has been advised by its lawyers to do nothing unless the French firm raises an action for compensation. The company has examined some reserve stock it was holding for the customer which was made at the same time as the batch despatched in November. It can find no evidence of faulty manufacture.

28   The company tendered in December for a contract to do all the interior decoration, and

supply the furniture for a liner being built in the north of England. It has been short-listed and a final decision is due in about one month's time. The company has priced the tender so as to break even as it wants to get a foothold in the market. Total costs are expected to be about £130,000.

29   The company has given a tender bond in respect of the tender for the work on the liner. Under the bond it guarantees not to withdraw from the contract if the tender submitted is accepted. A legally enforceable damages clause is included which would result in the company paying approximately £90,000 were it to break its bond.

30   The company has incorporated an advance payment bond (a guarantee that all advance payments made by the company will be reimbursed should the customer fail to fulfil the contract) into a contract with a Yorkshire-based partnership who are developing a new range of laminates for the company's kitchen furniture range. The company advanced £50,000 to the partnership in November when the contract was enacted. There now appear to be doubts that the Yorkshire-based partnership will be able to fulfil the contract by the due date in two months time. The chances of them fulfilling the contract are estimated at about 60%.

31   At the end of September the company tendered for a contract to refurnish part of Balmoral Palace. The price quoted would result in a loss of around £30,000 but it was felt that the publicity benefits would more than compensate for this. The company is on a short-list with one other company, and the contract is due to be awarded in about six weeks time.

32   Last May, the company guaranteed a £1m 5 year loan taken out by a subsidiary company which has been experiencing some financial and trading difficulties recently.

33   The company sacked the previous chief accountant in August. In September a claim for £70,000 damages for unfair dismissal was received. The company's lawyers belief there to be no possibility that the claim will succeed but have recommended that the company offer to settle for £10,000. No offer has yet been made. Provision for £10,000 has been entered in the accounts for the year.

34   The company has been in dispute for some six months with the Inland Revenue regarding previous years' tax computations. The Inland Revenue are arguing that the company has underpaid a total of £150,000 in tax over the previous five years. The company's tax advisor is convinced that the company has a strong case, and has urged that it appeal the latest assessment. The directors are reluctant to disclose details of this in the accounts in case it is seen as a concession that the Inland Revenue are correct.

35   The company revalued one of its warehouses in December. As a result, the balance sheet value was raised from £28,000 to £140,000. The original cost of the building was £44,000.

36   For some years the company has been running a paints division. This has never been very profitable - approximately 1% on turnover of £0.8m in the current year. In order to improve profitability of what the company then believed to be a potentially profitable venture, an industrial consultant was appointed (in February) to undertake a feasibility

study of the operation. Unfortunately he concluded that, due to the company's failure to keep up-to-date in both design and manufacture, annual profits would continue to be very low and that there was no prospect of the division ever making sufficient profit to justify the capital invested in it. The consultant recommended immediate closure and redeployment of resources at a net cost of approximately £150,000 - £200,000. At an emergency board meeting last week the directors decided to close the paints division immediately.

37   For over a year, the company has been engaged in a contract to manufacture aircraft seats for an American manufacturer. The contract is due to be completed in May. It has become apparent in the last month that the completion date will not be met, and it is expected to be one month late. There is a penalty clause in the contract which will result in the company paying out £30,000 in compensation if completion is one month late.

38   Some senior managers believe that the expected useful life of the company's plant and machinery has been overestimated and that provision will be required for major replacement within the next year. Others hold the view that the life expectancies adopted are appropriate.

39   In October a security guard slipped and fell while on night duty in the company's Dundee warehouse. He sustained a broken back and is unlikely to ever work again. He is suing the company for £350,000. The company's lawyers advise that the company was negligent and that, even allowing for contributory negligence on the part of the security guard (he should have been wearing rubber soled shoes) they would be unlikely to avoid a damages payment of £150,000. The company's insurance will meet the final settlement in full but wish the company to take the claim to court.

40   A few months ago, the company discovered that it has been in breach of another company's patent rights. No action has been taken by the other company as yet, and the product was withdrawn in November. It had only been marketed outside the UK and it is thought that the other company may not have been aware of it, even though it had been selling well for over two years. The company's lawyers believe that the company stand to pay substantial damages, probably of around £250,000 should the other company ever take them to court and have advised the company to avoid publicising the breach.

Questions 41-45 relate to companies, all of which have a balance sheet date of 31st December. It is now 31st March and the Board of Directors are meeting to approve the accounts. (All references to January, February, March and April relate to the year following the accounting period under review.) ***[You should ignore the taxation implications referred to in paragraphs 7 and 20 of the standard.]***

41   *Vidro Plc* received grants of £60,000 in September on condition that it employ 10 redundant executives over the following three years and give at least 5 of them permanent jobs. It must repay all the grant if either of these conditions is not met. To date it has employed 5, 3 of whom were useless and have been released. There has been a shortage of redundant executives for most of the last two years, but there has been a recent increase in company failures which is expected to continue for the next 12 months.

42   A company's insurers have agreed to meet all claims arising from an accident which occurred in June which resulted in serious injuries to one of the company's employees. But the company must take any claim against it (the company - legally it was responsible for the conditions which gave rise to the accident) to court. It is being sued for £375,000 and while its solicitors believe the employee was partially responsible, they also believe that the award will be in the employee's favour and that it will be for a minimum of £225,000.

43   *Devendo Ltd* is being pursued by the Customs and Excise for an underpayment of VAT amounting to £95,000 over a two year period. The company's advisers are confident that it will be found not to be liable when the case comes to court in 3 months time. However, if found liable, there is a 75% chance that penalty damages of £190,000 may also be incurred.

44   *Moveis Ltd*, a furniture retailer, suffered a loss of £110,000 when stock was destroyed in a warehouse fire on 23rd November. Unfortunately, it was under-insured at the time and the insurance company have only offered compensation of £60,000. The company's advisers believe that there is a possibility that the offer may be raised to £68,000.

45   *Terra Plc*, a supermarket chain, sold land on 28th December at a price which had still not been set by the independent valuers at the end of March. Despite the expected sale value being in the range of £140,000 to £170,000, it has been included in the draft financial statements at a figure of £87,000.

8   SSAP 19: Accounting for Investment Properties

Summary of the accounting treatment requirements

Investment properties should be included in the financial statements at their open market value and, with the exception of leasehold property, should not be depreciated. Leasehold property with 20 years or less until expiry of the lease *must* be depreciated in accordance with SSAP 12 (*Accounting for depreciation* - chapter 4); leasehold property with more than 20 years until expiry of the lease *may* be depreciated in accordance with SSAP 12.

The annual valuations need not be carried out by qualified or independent valuers. Disclosure must be made of the names or qualifications of the valuers, the bases used, and whether the valuer is an employee or officer of the company or group *which owns the property*. When the investment properties represent a substantial proportion of the total assets of a major enterprise, the valuation should be carried out by a professionally qualified and experienced valuer, and an external valuer should be used every five years.

Changes in valuation should generally be taken to the statement of total recognised gains and losses (being a movement on investment revaluation reserve), not to profit and loss, except where the change is both expected to be permanent and is a deficit (or its reversal) on an individual investment property; in which case it should be charged to (or credited in) the profit and loss account for the period. However, excess revaluation deficits of property unit trusts and of Companies Act investment companies should be shown only in the statement of total recognised gains and losses. Revaluation changes relating to the long term business of insurance companies are included in the profit and loss account. Revaluation changes of pension funds are dealt with in the relevant fund account. The carrying value of investment properties, and the investment revaluation reserve, should be displayed prominently in the financial statements.

This accounting standard does not apply to charities.

Problems of interpretation and grey areas

The following items are discussed: the conflict with the Companies Act; the partial application of SSAP 12; optional depreciation; the confusion between properties held on leases and investment properties; and the redesignation of property. Finally, there is a brief conclusion.

The conflict with the Companies Act

This standard is unique in that it is at odds with the legal requirements. It requires that freehold investment property should not be depreciated, whereas the Companies Act requires that all fixed assets with finite lives be depreciated (CA 85 Schedule 4, paragraph 18). Thus, in order to apply SSAP 19, it is necessary to disclose the way(s) in which the Companies Act requirements have not been observed, the reason for non-observance (usually a statement that it was done to comply with SSAP 19, and in order to provide a true and fair view), and the effect of the non-observance.

The partial application of SSAP 12

> It is a common mistake to assume that an investment property which is subject to SSAP 12 because it is held on a lease, should also be subject to the revaluation rules of that standard: it is assumed that SSAP 19 does not apply, and that the property should be treated in the same way as non-investment properties. However, the application of SSAP 12 to such properties is restricted to providing for depreciation. For all other purposes, the item continues to be classified and treated as an investment property.

Optional depreciation

> In addition to the mandatory application of SSAP 12 to all investment properties held on a lease with 20 years or less to run, there is also the option to depreciate any that are held on leases with more than 20 years to run. Where this option is adopted, it should be applied consistently to all leasehold investment properties (i.e., either all those with leases of more than 20 years to run are depreciated, or none of them).

The confusion between properties held on leases and investment properties

> Properties held on leases are only investment properties *if the company sub-leases them to another unrelated entity*. Otherwise, they are either treated as leasehold property assets, and depreciated and revalued according to SSAP 12 or, if held on an operating lease as defined by SSAP 21 (*Accounting for leases and hire purchase contracts* - chapter 10), the rental is treated as a revenue charge and no asset is recognised in the financial statements.

The redesignation of property

> When a company changes the use of an investment property with the result that it loses its investment property status, the balance relating to it on the investment revaluation reserve should be transferred to the revaluation reserve for non-investment properties. This may arise, for example, if the new lessee is another company in the same group, or where the new rental is not an 'arm's length rental'. The opposite treatment should be adopted when a property becomes an investment property, where previously it was not. If this approach is not adopted, the investment revaluation reserve will not be a reflection of the revaluation balance relating to current investment properties; nor will the non-investment property revaluation reserve reflect that relating to current non-investment properties.

Conclusion

> This standard was issued in response to pressure from the property industry both before and after the issue of the original version of SSAP 12 in 1977. It deals with a very specific topic and, unlike most of the other accounting standards, it will not be applicable to the vast majority of companies. Even when it is applicable, it will not usually apply to all the property assets of the company concerned.
>
> While there is an obvious justification for its depreciation exemption being applicable only to a specific class of property, it is unfortunate that the requirement to revalue investment properties annually is not applicable to non-investment properties under SSAP 12. There is no doubt that the use of current market property values provides a more true and fair view than the use of historical cost property values. The fact that the balance sheets of companies with investment properties will

contain a mixture of property at market value, at historic revaluation, and at historical cost, does nothing for the clarity of that true and fair view.

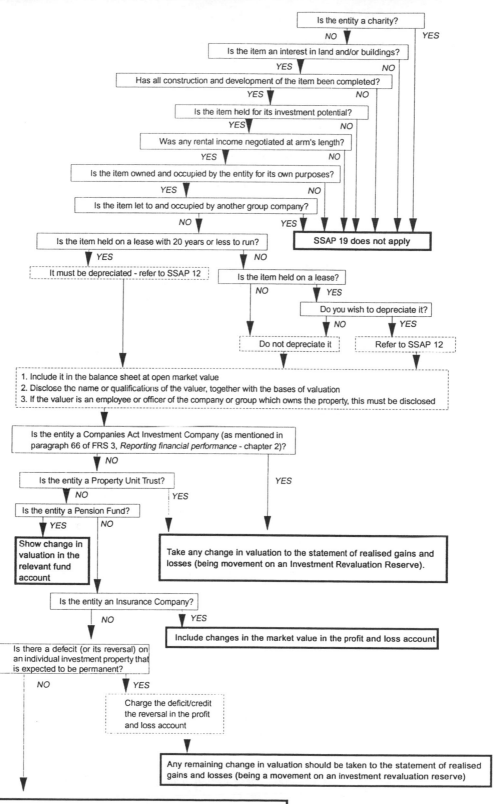

SSAP 19   Accounting for investment properties

Short Questions

*ASSUME THAT MATERIALITY EXISTS IN **EVERY** CASE*

Except where otherwise indicated, all the questions relate to a household manufacturing and retailing company with 100 employees, current turnover of £18m and net pre-tax profit of £2.7m. (Last year £16.2m and £1.9m respectively.) The company's financial year ends on 31st December and the board of directors are scheduled to approve the financial statements on 31st March.

1   The company has the leasehold of a warehouse in Greenock. The lease still has 22 years to run.

2   As a result of the closure earlier in the year of the company's Edinburgh factory, the company was left with a large empty and unused warehouse on the east side of the city. The warehouse, which was originally acquired on a 50 year lease 39 years ago, has a net book value of £120,000. The situation is causing the company some concern because no other company has expressed an interest in sub-leasing it. The main problem lies in its wording which prevents it from selling-on the lease - i.e. it has no option but to continue leasing the property itself and sub-leasing it to a third party, should it no longer have any use for it. The company's lease, which cost £5,000, also prohibits any change in use of the warehouse and requires that the company maintain it. The company is of the opinion that it will never be sub-leased.

3   The company used an independent firm of professional surveyors to determine the open market value of most of its property.

4   *A property unit trust* has revalued its investment properties this year. It had a balance of £460,000 on its investment revaluation reserve at the start of the year. Due to depressed market conditions, the revaluation showed a fall in value and a revaluation deficit for the year of £190,000 has resulted.

5   *A pension fund* found a deficit when revaluing its investment properties this year.

6   In October the company signed an agreement to lease one of its shops to the local housing association for £1 per month. It had closed the shop earlier in the year when it opened up a new one further down the same street.

7   The company has a shop in Dunblane which has a garage attached that had been converted into a small store. It was decided to rent it separately from the shop but, despite being advertised for lease, at a very competitive rental, as yet there have been no positive enquiries. The company is of the opinion that it will eventually be leased and wishes to retain the property for this purpose.

8   The company erected a number of advertising hoardings in the south of Scotland. The total cost was £59,000. These are all leased for 3 months at a time. They have an expected useful life of 50 years.

9   The company holds a 30 year lease on a shop in Dumfries which it purchased 8 years ago. The shop was a disaster and was closed and leased to a chemist on a 12 year lease which still has 6 years to run.

10   The company intends to use the year end open market value of the Dumfries shop (see question 9) which it has been supplied with by the shop's owners. The valuer was a fully qualified surveyor employed in their estates department.

11   *An insurance company* found a deficit when it revalued its long-term business investment properties this year.

12   At the start of the year, a *Companies Act investment company* had a balance of £230,000 on its investment revaluation reserve. The annual revaluation showed a fall in value and a revaluation deficit for the year of £310,000 resulted.

13   After a decision earlier in the year to buy-in more items, the company closed its Edinburgh factory. It had been acquired on a 99 year lease 81 years ago and the terms of the lease permit sub-leasing but not re-sale. The company has successfully negotiated a lease to a local co-operative at a fair rental.

14   The company acquired a 10 year leasehold on a shop in Carluke during the year.

15   On purchasing a new shop in Greenock, the company closed its existing Rothesay shop and transferred all stock and staff to the new premises. The old shop building, which has a nct book value of £15,000, was then leased to the managing director's brother at a nominal rental of £52 per year, plus all rates and upkeep costs. (The company is going to re-assess the situation in five year's with a view to re-opening the shop at that time.)

16   *A D-I-Y chain* has a number of investment properties. When they were revalued this year a revaluation deficit resulted which exceeded the balance on the investment revaluation reserve brought forward.

17   The company owns a building in Brodick which it has let on a 10-year lease to a local garage proprietor.

18   The company owns ten completed bungalows which it lets out to retired single ex-employees with more than 20 years service. The rental on these bungalows has been set by the local government rents tribunal. The bungalows, which are being depreciated at 1% straight line per annum, were built over ten years ago at a cost of £100,000 and were revalued at the start of the year at £126,000. The net book value at the end of the previous year was £90,000. No revaluation has been undertaken at the current year end as the directors do not believe it is necessary.

19   *A pension fund's* annual property revaluation resulted in an increase in value on investment properties held of £76,000.

20   The company opened a new office in Cumbernauld. A 25 year lease, which cost £80,000, is held on the property. The lease restricts the use of the building to offices and the property cannot be sub-let. The company is responsible for all maintenance and

upkeep of the property during the term of the lease. At the end of the lease, the company has no right to require renewal of the lease and full rights revert to the lessor. The property must be returned to the lessor in its present state.

21   The company has 14 years to run on a 30 year lease of a warehouse which it took out for its investment potential. It sub-let it from the start to an associated undertaking at an 'arm's length' rental.

22   In February, the company obtained, at no cost, a cottage in Wishaw on a 25 year cost-free lease from a grateful ex-employee who won £1.5m on the football pools. It rents the cottage to a local policeman at full market rental.

23   When it moved to its new Cumbernauld office at the start of this year, the company leased its old Cumbernauld branch office to an estate agent. Its net book value at that time was £17,000. It has been revalued at £35,000. The lease is for 10 years.

24   The revaluation of the old Cumbernauld branch office (see question 23) was done by the company's marketing director. She has no formal qualifications but has often been involved in property valuations.

25   A *Companies Act investment company* has purchased investment properties costing £2.1m this year. At the start of the year it had a surplus of £211,000 on its investment revaluation reserve. The annual property revaluation resulted in an increase in value on investment properties held at the start of the year of £87,000; none of the properties experienced a fall in valuation.

Additional Questions

*ASSUME THAT MATERIALITY EXISTS IN **EVERY** CASE*

26   *An insurance company* has revalued its long-term business investment properties this year. Due to a large slump in the property market, the revaluation showed a fall in value and a revaluation deficit for the year of £1.21m was found. This was the first time that a revaluation deficit had been found, and was £290,000 more than the sum of all previous revaluation surpluses.

27   As a result of the closure earlier in the year of the company's Edinburgh factory, the company was left with a two-storey office block in a prime site which it has decided to lease. Negotiations are currently in hand with a London-based insurance company who are interested in taking the property on a 15 year lease. At the moment, the company is using the offices to store some of the equipment which had been in the factory until it can be transferred to the company's Cumbernauld site.

28   During the year the company took complete possession of a new shop which it had built in Dunfermline. As the company was not yet ready to occupy and staff it, the shop was leased temporarily to the local *Oxfam* branch. No rental is being collected (the company

feel it will appreciate in value more than enough to compensate for its use by the charity), but the charity is responsible for its upkeep.

29   The company was left with a warehouseman's cottage after the closure of the Edinburgh factory. (The warehouseman accepted the offer of a transfer to the company's Cumbernauld site.) It is held on a 50 year lease which was taken out at the same time as the lease on the warehouse, 39 years ago. Under the terms of this lease the company is free to do what it likes with the property and the lease and can, if it wishes, surrender the lease to the lessor without charge and with no further liability to rental thereafter. The current rental is very low and the company decided to retain the property and place it on the market for sub-lease over the remaining period of the leasehold. A lessee was found very quickly and has been in occupation since September, at a rental which will produce a good profit for the company.

30   When the company's pension fund revalued its investment property at the end of the year, the revaluation showed a fall in value which resulted in a revaluation deficit for the year of £56,000. This was £20,000 more than the net surplus arising from all previous revaluation surpluses and deficits.´

31   The company has a 50 year leasehold on a garage in Perth. The lease has now just under 20 years to run. It has never used the garage itself and it is currently sub-let on a 10 year lease to a local businessman. The company has never depreciated the garage.

32   The company is having a factory built on an industrial site near Edinburgh. There is a considerable shortage of suitable sites in the Edinburgh area and the company are sure that it will generate a large income from leasing. The cost of the factory is £120,000 and it is anticipated that it will cost another £70,000 to complete. The first lessor has already signed the lease and is due to take possession in April of the coming year.

33   In November, the company took out a twenty year lease on a vehicle depot in Cumbernauld. The depot became available earlier than the company had wished, but the terms of the lease were too good to miss. As the company had originally intended to switch its Glasgow depot to Cumbernauld in three years time, it decided not to accelerate the changeover. Instead it has sub-let the depot on a two year lease to a local vegetable growers association at the same cost as it is paying to the depot's owners.

34   The company has a 50 year lease on a small shop in Dunkeld which has 19 years to run. It is has been let to a butcher for the previous six years.

35   The company has been leasing a shop in Wishaw to a local printing company at an 'arm's length rental' for the last 15 years. In that time it has transferred an overall revaluation surplus relating to the shop of £15,000 to the investment revaluation reserve. In

September, the lease term ended and the company took over the shop for the sale of its own products.

36   During the year the company closed an unprofitable shop in Dunblane and then leased it at full market rental to a grocer.

37   At the start of the year, *a property unit trust* had a balance of £120,000 on its investment revaluation reserve. The annual revaluation showed a revaluation deficit for the year of £190,000.

38   The Dunkeld shop (see question 34) was not valued by the external firm of surveyors as the company's marketing director had already done it (see question 24). She valued it at £20,000.

39   *An insurance company* found a surplus when it revalued its long-term business investment properties this year.

40   Earlier in the year, the company's subsidiary, *Pingando Ltd*, leased a small warehouse from the company on a 25 year lease at full market rental.

41   The company's chief accountant set a value of £120,000 on the company's Port Glasgow warehouse facility which has been leased for ten years to a motor vehicle distributor.

42   Every year, the managing director's brother-in-law revalues an office complex which he has leased on an arm's length 30 year lease from the company. He has no formal qualifications as a valuer, but is a qualified optician.

43   Two years ago, the company let an unoccupied shop to a 100% subsidiary at an arm's length rental on a 30 year lease. The subsidiary has never occupied the shop and has been trying to sub-let it ever since acquiring it.

44   Three years ago, the company let an unoccupied shop to a 100% subsidiary at an arm's length rental on a 30 year lease. For the first two years, the subsidiary used the shop as a temporary store. However, earlier this year, the subsidiary leased the shop to a newsagent on a 25 year lease.

45   For the last eight years, *Maluca plc*, whose main business is property leasing, has had all its properties revalued annually by a qualified surveyor who is employed by one of *Maluca plc*'s tenant companies.

Long Question

Devagar Plc

It is now the end of *Devagar Plc's* accounting period. The company took out a 40 year lease on a city centre office block 20¼ years ago at a cost of £1,500. For the first 11½ years it was used by the company, thereafter it has been sub-let to an insurance company.

It has been revalued from time to time, always at the end of an accounting period. It was first revalued (to £3,450) at the end of the accounting period following the end of the 4th year of the lease, thereafter it was revalued as follows at the end of the accounting periods following the:

6th year of the lease	£ 6,400
11th " " " " "	£ 16,000
12th " " " " "	£ 28,000
13th " " " " "	£ 38,000
14th " " " " "	£ 64,000
15th " " " " "	£ 88,000
16th " " " " "	£ 78,000
17th " " " " "	£ 92,000
18th " " " " "	£104,000
19th " " " " "	£108,000
20th " " " " "	£124,000

Company policy has always been to provide depreciation on its property over its useful life using the straight-line method, unless the SSAP 19 exemption can be applied. The depreciation charged on leases is related to the actual time during the accounting period when the lease was subject to depreciation. Thus, if a lease were taken out on 1st September ⅓ of a year's depreciation would be charged to that year's profit and loss.

Required:

In respect of each of the accounting periods since ownership, show the balances carried forward in the appropriate year-end balance sheet accounts and show the depreciation charge for the year. (Assume that all current accounting standards have been in force throughout the period of ownership.)

9   SSAP 20: Foreign Currency Translation

Summary of the accounting treatment requirements

Individual companies should normally translate foreign currency transactions at the rate ruling on the date of the transaction (the 'temporal method'). At the balance sheet date, all non-monetary items should normally be left at the value found when originally translated and all monetary items should be retranslated at the closing rate. Exchange gains and losses arising should normally be included in the profit and loss for the period. Any that are taken direct to reserves should be disclosed in the statement of total recognised gains and losses (- see FRS 3: *Reporting financial performance*, chapter 2).

For consolidation purposes, the closing rate should normally be used to translate the financial statements and any exchange rate gains or losses arising should normally be recorded as movements on reserves.

At both individual company and consolidated financial statement level, the cover method may be available to offset gains and losses on foreign currency borrowings against losses and gains on foreign equity investments.

Problems of interpretation and grey areas

This section begins with an introduction to the purpose of the standard and an explanation of the approach adopted in this chapter. The following items are then discussed under the heading of the individual company aspects of SSAP 20: prudence and the marketability of monetary gains; the cover method; gains or losses on borrowings which exceed, or are in the same direction as, the exchange difference on foreign equity investments; repayment of cover borrowings; forward contracts and prior contracts; and the non-definition of average rate. Under the heading of the consolidated financial statements aspects of SSAP 20 there is discussion of: foreign enterprises; consolidation translation methods; branches; hyperinflation; the consolidation cover method; net investment; and goodwill.

The purpose of the standard

SSAP 20 attempts to clarify a situation where an assortment of techniques were being used in foreign currency translation for accounting purposes. It was almost eight years after the first exposure draft on the subject (ED 16) was issued that the standard appeared. Despite the time spent in discussion and preparation, there remain a number of loose definitions and unresolved problem areas with which the practitioner has to deal.

The standard states that 'the translation of foreign currency transactions and financial statements should produce results which are generally compatible with the effects of rate changes on a company's cash flows and its equity and should ensure that the financial statements present a true and fair view of the results of management actions' (paragraph 2). In other words, the translation of foreign currency is done in order to present a true and fair view in the financial statements of the results of management action. The standard attempts to produce a true and fair view of a situation that is frequently fluid and open to abuse by setting forth a sequence of procedures to be adopted when undertaking foreign currency translation. Without such procedures, companies would be free to adopt the basis for translation which best fitted their needs.

Paragraph 1 states that there are two ways in which companies may engage in foreign currency operations:

1   directly into business transactions denominated in the foreign currency.
     (The results of these transactions will need to be translated into the currency in which the company reports.)

2   through a foreign enterprise which maintains its records in a currency other than that of the investing company.
     (For consolidation purposes, *the financial statements will need to be translated into the currency in which the investing company reports.)*

While these two broad categories of enterprise (individual companies and consolidations) are dealt with in the standard, there are obviously many occasions when both will be applicable to one company.

The approach adopted in this chapter

SSAP 20 contains many special terms, some of which are well defined, but others are vague and indefinite. There is much to digest before all the complexities can be understood and it is unlikely that the standard could be applied efficiently by someone who has not spent a great deal of time 'getting to know it' first. It has been estimated that there are over 3,000 accounting alternatives within the standard and one book on accounting practice devotes 113 pages (10% of the total content) to this one standard. In the face of this complexity, it has been necessary to adopt a simplified approach and, as a result, the flowcharts in this chapter, while complex, *are* less detailed than most of the others in the book. Only study, analysis and experience can lead to understanding of the finer details. The same holds for the examples: they cover much of the standard but there are esoteric and complex situations which are not dealt with as they are beyond the scope of the examination syllabuses. However, they are not beyond the scope of 'real life' situations and it is important to be aware that perfect knowledge of the contents of this chapter, while appropriate for examination purposes, will not necessarily be sufficient to deal with currency translation items which might be encountered elsewhere.

The Individual Company Aspects of SSAP 20

Prudence and the marketability of monetary gains

Prudence is to be applied when an exchange rate gain arises in respect of a long term monetary item and there is doubt as to the marketability of the currency involved. While it is to be applied to the total gain, or to the amount by which the gain exceeds any past losses on the same item (paragraph 50), there is no suggestion that prudence be applied in respect of the element of the gain which is being applied against those past losses. Why not? Why should a gain that is doubtful be allowed to write-back losses from prior periods? It is no less doubtful than the rest of the gain that is restricted. Nor is there any suggestion that short term monetary item gains should be similarly treated. 'Short term' can be anything up to a year from balance sheet date. Are such potentially distant settlement rates really that foreseeable? These are questions that remain unresolved within the standard itself. However, this apparent inconsistency is dealt with by the prudence requirement of SSAP 2 (*Disclosure of accounting policies* - chapter 12), which would prevent the offset against past losses if viewed as necessary in order to give a true and fair view.

The cover method

Normally, a currency translation approach known as the 'temporal method' is applied. Under this approach, the treatment for exchange gains or losses on foreign borrowings would be to include them in the profit and loss account. Similarly, the treatment for foreign equity investments is to retain them at the value in the company's local currency at which they were translated upon acquisition; they are not normally retranslated at balance sheet date. One of the more complicated aspects of SSAP 20 revolves around the use of another approach: the 'cover method'. This is first introduced in paragraph 28 where the standard states: 'when an individual company uses borrowings in currencies other than its own to finance foreign equity investments, or ... to provide a hedge against the exchange risk associated with existing equity investments, the company may be covered ... against any movement in exchange rates. It would be inappropriate in such cases to record an accounting profit or loss when exchange rates change.' Paragraphs 29 and 51 provide conditions under which the cover method may be applied.

Paragraph 28, therefore, indicates that in situations where borrowing exists because of an investment, the treatment of exchange rate differences may (dependent upon the conditions given in paragraphs 29 and 51) differ from that normally applied. However, it is not clear if paragraph 28 means that (a) in *no* case where foreign currency borrowing has been undertaken or maintained, for one of the two specified purposes, should an accounting profit or loss be recorded in the profit and loss account in respect of exchange rate differences, or (b) exchange rate differences should *not* be recorded in the profit and loss account *only* when the company is covered against *all* exchange rate changes (i.e it has made 100% offsetting gains and losses on these transactions). The 100% offset situation envisaged in interpretation (b) is less likely to arise and interpretation (a) would seem to be the one to apply (in so far as is permitted under the conditions which are given in paragraphs 29 and 51 of the standard).

It is also unclear as to whether use of the cover method is mandatory. Some analysts have stated that its use is not mandatory, but optional (or permissive); some have implied that it is mandatory through examples quoted; some have highlighted the use of the word 'may' in paragraphs 29 and 51 (i.e. they have implied it is optional) but then given an example in which the wording used implies that it is mandatory; some have steered away from giving any guidance and have merely quoted the standard and then proceeded to cover another topic. The last sentence of paragraph 28 ('It would be inappropriate [when hedging has occurred] to record an accounting profit or loss when exchange rates change.') does seem to suggest that it may not be correct to assume that the use of the cover method is optional. On the other hand, the requirement for consistent treatment given in paragraphs 29c and 51c would not be necessary if the cover method were mandatory. On balance, therefore, use of the cover method is probably not intended to be mandatory. However, paragraph 28 clearly indicates that its application is desirable and accordingly the examples relating to the cover method in this chapter have assumed that it will be applied. In each case, the answer is followed by a brief indication of what would occur were the cover method not to be applied.

Paragraph 29 (and later, paragraph 51) states that where exchange risk cover has been undertaken, foreign equity investments may be denominated in the foreign currency and translated at the exchange rate ruling at the balance sheet date, any resulting gain or loss being taken direct to reserves. The exchange gains or losses on the borrowing should then be offset, as a reserve movement, against the equity investment exchange differences. This is done subject to the conditions that (a) gains or losses on borrowing may only be offset to the extent that there are exchange gains or losses on the equity investments; (b) the foreign currency borrowings used in this way should not exceed the total amount of cash that the investments are expected to be able to generate; and (c) the accounting treatment adopted should be consistently applied from period to period.

It should be noted that the cash value of the borrowings must not exceed the cash value of the equity investment and any income deriving from it. How is that value determined? What is meant by 'the total amount of cash that the investments are expected to be able to generate, whether from profits or otherwise' (paragraph 51b)? Does it mean the expected profit for the accounting period should be included, or that for the expected life of the investment? If the investment is for an indefinite period, what value is to be included?

Foreign currency borrowings for this purpose can be up to the value that the investments are expected to achieve during the time they are retained. Or, to put it more clearly, as the market price of the investment will account for growth and future profitability, the market value of the foreign equity investment at the balance sheet date is the maximum value that the borrowings may have at the balance sheet date in order to be utilised in this way.

The exposure draft from which this standard derived (ED 27) restricted offset to situations where the same currency applied to both borrowing and investment. Following criticism by a number of commentators, this restriction was dropped and, in its place, the paragraph 51b condition was included in the standard in order to provide for those situations where different currencies are involved. It was hoped that this would result in offset only being available when there was a genuine case of exchange rate risk cover. Thus, if a company happened to have a foreign currency loan which it had no intention of using as cover for the foreign equity investment, it was hoped that this condition would prevent the cover method from being applied. This could only be possible if the intention was to exclude from the cover method any borrowing which was greater in value than the investment which it sought to cover. In other words, apportionment of the exchange differences on the borrowing, in relation to the relative values of the loan and the investment, would not be permitted. Unfortunately, application of the condition in this way can result in genuine cover arrangements being excluded from the cover method approach, as the following example shows:

> A company has an equity investment in a German company and a loan in Italian Lire. The investment cost DM 3m and the loan is for Lire 2,100m. At the balance sheet date, the rates of exchange are (rates at the previous balance sheet date in brackets): £1 = DM 2.5 (3) = Lire 1,981 (2,100). The following exchange differences have arisen:

Investment: DM 3m	@ 3	= £1,000,000	
	@ 2.5	= £1,200,000	
Exchange Gain			£200,000
Loan: Lire 2,100m	@ 2,100	= £1,000,000	
	@ 1,981	= £1,060,007	
Exchange Loss			£(60,007)

Under paragraph 51(b), if the market value of the investment is DM 3m, all of the loss can be offset against the gain. But, if the German company has been experiencing difficulties and the market value of the company is now only DM 1m (£400,000), what proportion of the exchange loss could be used to offset the exchange gain on the investment if paragraph 51b is applied? None: the loan cover (£1,060,007) now exceeds the cash value of the investment (£400,000) and there should be no offset (i.e. the cover method could not be applied). (The question of whether the carrying amount of the investment should be reduced to DM 1m would also need to be considered, but should be ignored for the purpose of this example.)

What would be the proportion of the exchange rate loss available for offset if the paragraph 51b restriction were not applied? The cash value of the investment (£400,000) is equivalent to Lire 792.4m (at £1=Lire 1,981 and so the total available for offset, using an initial loan of Lire 792.4m at £1=Lire 2,100 (£377,333), is £22,667 [£400,000-£377,333].

On balance, paragraph 51b is too vague to be truly restrictive in the way intended when SSAP 20 was drafted. In fact, as shown, it cannot be applied without affecting other situations in a way that was never intended. In keeping with the overall spirit of the standard, the appropriate treatment would be to apportion any offset along the lines given in the above example (i.e. offset an exchange loss of £22,667). This can be justified on the grounds that there are foreign exchange borrowings whose purpose is to act as hedges against exchange risk on foreign equity investment, and that the value of those borrowings whose exchange gains or losses have been used in the offset process do not exceed the total amount of cash that the investments are expected to be able to generate.

Gains or losses on borrowings which exceed, or are in the same direction as, the exchange difference on foreign equity investments

What is done with gains or losses on borrowings which exceed, or are in the same direction as, the loss or gain on foreign equity investments? Do they get taken direct to the reserves or are they declared as accounting gains or losses? Paragraph 27 of the standard indicates that they should be treated as accounting gains or losses and taken to the profit and loss account.

Repayment of cover borrowings

What happens when cover borrowings are repaid? Paragraph 28 states that where a company *has used* foreign currency borrowings to finance foreign equity investments, or to provide a hedge against the exchange risk associated with existing equity investments, then cover may exist and offset should be performed. The use of the past tense 'has used' implies that it was something done in the past. There is no indication that any subsequent reversal is relevant. Indeed, the standard requires consistent application of the cover method (paragraphs 29c & 51c) once applied. Should it be continued after the borrowing is repaid?

In the case of the year when the borrowing was repaid, the cover method, if in use previously, should continue to be applied. To do otherwise is to ignore the standard: there were borrowings at some stage of the year and the consistency requirement of paragraph 51c should be applied. However, in applying the cover method, the translation rate used for the balance sheet value of the investment should be that ruling on the date at which the borrowing was repaid.

For subsequent years, it is possible to argue that the standard is so unclear that one of a number of approaches can be adopted, of which the three most commonly suggested are: restating the investment using the original historic rate which applied when it was acquired; translating the investment at the end of the year the borrowing was repaid and continuing to do so each year thereafter; and, retaining the investment at the exchange rate ruling when the borrowing was repaid. All these approaches can be justified, but the strongest case must be for the last one. The first is rewriting the history books and would do nothing to improve the true and fair view, and some would argue that it would only serve to confuse the less informed users of the financial statements. The second is questionable because the cover method should no longer apply: it is designed to avoid a situation where the exchange gain or loss on the borrowing would appear in the profit and loss but, as the standard prescribes non-retranslation of non-monetary items, nothing would appear anywhere in respect of exchange gains or losses on the foreign equity investment. This then leaves the third approach: in a year when there is no borrowing for this purpose, the standard should be applied accordingly and the foreign equity investment should not be retranslated at the year end, but retained at the historic value set using the exchange rate ruling on the date at which the borrowing was repaid.

Forward contracts and prior contracts

A further problem area arises from the option to apply forward contract rates when translating transactions. (The alternative is to use either the transaction date rate or the average rate.) On the basis that the forward contract rate is the actual cost that will be incurred, and that it would not have been entered into were it not for the principal transaction, all the relevant questions at the end of this chapter have assumed that the forward contract rate will be used. The transaction date rate or the average rate could be used, if it were felt that doing so would give a true and fair view. It is important to be aware that these alternatives do exist.

A 'forward contract' is defined as 'an agreement to exchange different currencies at a specified *future* date and at a specified rate' (paragraph 42, italics added). The option to apply the forward contract rate does not, therefore, relate to transactions where the currency was exchanged in advance of the main transaction. In those cases, the currency is translated when obtained and then retranslated when the transaction occurs and any exchange rate difference taken to profit and loss. The transaction would then be valued at the transaction date rate. This is somewhat inconsistent when the currency has been obtained specifically to pay for the transaction (i.e. it is the equivalent of a forward contract that relates to the past). If forward contracts can be utilised in this way, why cannot prior contracts?

The non-definition of average rate

The previous section referred to an 'average rate'. This is a term that the standard uses a number of times, but nowhere does it indicate how it should be calculated. In fact, paragraph 18 of the standard states that 'no definitive method of calculating the average rate has been prescribed'. It is a matter of judgement what rate is appropriate and care should be taken to avoid a simple average of opening and closing rates: exchange rates do not often move smoothly and it is quite possible that a simple average calculated in this way will have little bearing on the 'true' average rate.

The Consolidated Financial Statements Aspects of SSAP 20

Foreign enterprises

When companies have foreign enterprises (defined in paragraph 36 as 'a subsidiary, associated company or branch'), they must translate the financial statements of the enterprises into the parent company's currency when consolidation takes place. This can be done in two ways: the 'closing rate/net investment method' (paragraphs 15-20) and the 'temporal method' (paragraphs 21-24 and 55-56), which is the same as that used by individual companies when preparing their accounts.

Consolidation translation methods

Normally the closing rate method will apply, but where 'the affairs of a foreign enterprise are so closely interlinked with those of the investing company that its results can be regarded as being more dependent on the economic environment of the investing company's currency ... the financial statements of the foreign enterprise should be included in the consolidated financial statements as if all its transactions had been entered into by the investing company itself in its own currency'. (paragraph 22) The standard provides examples of situations where this may apply (paragraph 24) and it is made clear that it should be done 'where the currency of the investing company is the dominant currency in the economic environment in which the foreign enterprise operates' (paragraph 23).

A statement by the ASC, issued as Technical Release 504 and published by the ICAEW upon the issue of SSAP 20, states that 'where the trade of the subsidiary is a direct extension of the trade of the holding company, it will be appropriate to use only the temporal method' (TR 504, paragraph 22). Clearly, companies are to apply the temporal method where circumstances fit those described in the standard. But, what happens when circumstances have changed and there is a requirement to change the method? Is a prior period adjustment required, as defined by FRS 3 (*Reporting financial performance* - chapter 2)? No: it is not a change of accounting policy but a change of circumstances that has caused the change of method. The accounting policy, to use the method prescribed by the standard, is unchanged. A prior period adjustment would not therefore be appropriate.

There is obviously considerable scope for subjective judgement as to whether an enterprise should be translated using the temporal method. For examination purposes, it would probably be best to assume that the closing rate/net investment method should be applied, and the temporal method applied only when the enterprise definitely matches the requirements given in paragraphs 22-24 and 55.

The closing rate/net investment method requires that the net worth of the foreign enterprise be used as the basis for its valuation. The balance sheet amounts should be translated using the exchange rate ruling at the balance sheet date. Any exchange differences arising because this exchange rate differs from the previous rate used should be transferred to reserves.

Profit and loss amounts should also be translated at the closing rate, though the average rate can be used instead as it can be argued that it more fairly reflects the profits and losses and cash flows as they arise to the group. Paragraph 17 of the standard indicates that either method could be used depending on what criteria were felt to be more relevant - closing rate being more likely to achieve the objective of translation as stated in paragraph 2; average rate having the qualities previously mentioned. The chosen method is adopted because it more fairly reflects the profits and losses and cash flows as they arise to the group. Whichever method is adopted should be applied consistently from period to period. What happens if the method adopted is changed, but not the circumstances: is that a change in accounting policy? Yes, and a prior period adjustment would therefore be required.

There is no guidance given on what date to use for translation when enterprises have balance sheet dates different from those of the investing company. Nor is there any guidance on how to treat cumulated exchange differences relating to an enterprise which has been disposed of.

Branches

Foreign branches are accounted for along the same lines as subsidiaries (paragraph 25), the closing rate/net investment method being used when they operate as separate businesses with local finance and the temporal method when they meet the requirements already mentioned. (The definition of a 'branch' in paragraph 37 is very broad - it may consist merely of a group of assets and liabilities accounted for in a foreign currency, for example, a ship whose income is in dollars and which was financed by a loan in dollars.)

Hyperinflation

The historical cost basis may be replaced by a current price basis in the case of foreign enterprises operating in countries with a very high rate of inflation (paragraph 26) and where it is held that the financial position of the foreign enterprise may not be capable of being presented fairly on a historical cost basis. In such situations, it may be necessary to apply inflation adjustments to the financial statements prior to translation in order to present a true and fair view. However, no guidance is provided in the standard as to how to define a 'high rate' of inflation or how to perform the adjustment to current price. UITF 9, *Accounting for operations in hyper-inflationary economies,* was issued in June 1993 in order to clarify this area.

UITF 9 confirmed that adjustments are required when the hyper-inflationary impact will affect the true and fair view. It also states that adjustments are required where the cumulative inflation rate over three years is approaching, or exceeds, 100% - effectively a 'rule-of-thumb' definition of the term *hyper-inflation.* (Paragraph 5)

It suggested two methods that could be adopted in order to eliminate the distortions caused by hyper-inflation. (If neither was deemed suitable, the reason(s) should be stated and another method should be adopted - paragraph 7.) Either the local currency financial statements should be adjusted to reflect current price levels before being translated, or a relatively stable currency (e.g. the US dollar or sterling) should be used as the currency of measurement (the *functional* currency) for the relevant foreign operations. In the latter case, the functional currency would effectively be the *local* currency as defined in paragraph 39 of SSAP 20; and, if the transactions are not initially recorded in the functional currency, they must be measured in that currency by applying the temporal method based on the functional currency. (Paragraph 6)

The consolidation cover method

The temporal method results in all exchange differences being taken to profit and loss. Under the closing rate/net investment method, all exchange differences are taken to the reserves automatically upon the retranslation of all the items in the balance sheet and profit and loss, *including* those arising from foreign currency borrowings. The cover method which applies to consolidated financial statements is different from that which applies to individual company financial statements. The individual company cover method adjustments must be reversed and recalculated using the rules applicable to consolidations. The effect of this is that the exchange differences arising from borrowings, which would normally all be taken to profit and loss in the individual company financial statements, are reduced by offset against the exchange differences arising on the net investments in foreign enterprises.

Thus, while the overall financial position of the group is the same as it would have been had the cover method not been applied, the result shown in profit and loss is not. In addition, because a greater degree of offset is permitted for consolidation purposes, the profit or loss shown in the group profit and loss account will often not be the same as the sum of all the individual company profits and losses. For example, if a company paid $100,000 some years ago for a 100% holding in an American company which at the current year end has net assets of $1m, in the company accounts the exchange difference on the investment would be based on the original $100,000 cost of the holding but, in the consolidated accounts, it would be based on $1m.

There are two aspects to the 'greater degree of offset' referred to in the previous paragraph. Within each company, for consolidation purposes, the offset of the borrowing exchange differences is against the exchange differences arising on the retranslation of the net investment (i.e. the net assets of the company). This is clearly not the same as the 'foreign equity investment' (i.e. the carrying value of the investment made) applicable to individual companies. The other factor is that in the consolidation, offset is not limited to one company in isolation: the group as a whole is considered. Thus, if one company is unable to offset all its borrowing exchange differences, they may be offset against the net investment exchange differences of other companies within the group.

Consequently, in the extreme case, one company in a group may have a foreign currency borrowing but no foreign equity investment against which to offset exchange rate differences, all such differences being taken to profit and loss; and another may have a foreign equity investment, but no borrowings: the investment would be carried at the historic translated value. In the group accounts, the equity investment would be retranslated and the exchange difference taken direct to reserves where the exchange difference relating to the borrowing would be offset against it leaving no borrowing exchange difference to appear in the group profit and loss.

Any company which has applied the cover method to foreign equity investments which were neither in subsidiaries, nor in associated undertakings (for example, in trade investments), may carry that treatment into the consolidated accounts (paragraph 58).

Exchange gains and losses arising from transactions between companies within a group are reported in the individual company's financial statements in the same way as those arising from transactions with third parties (paragraph 12). Thus, by using fixed exchange rates, companies may be able to transfer profit within a group.

Net investment

Companies may lend subsidiaries funds rather than invest in their equity. They may also defer trading balances. The standard states that these items may be part of the 'net investment' which a company has in a foreign enterprise (paragraph 43). Where such funding is long term it should be treated as if it were equity, with any exchange rate differences taken direct to reserves (paragraph 20). How long is 'long term'? A situation where there is no intention to end the funding in the foreseeable future probably complies with the phrase 'where financing by such means is intended to be, for all practical purposes, as permanent as equity' (paragraph 20). However, there is no guidance in the standard other than this phrase and so interpretation must be left to the user. As a rough guide, three to five years is generally considered as being the limit on the 'foreseeable future'.

Goodwill

The standard implies that goodwill arising on the acquisition of a foreign enterprise should be translated at the acquisition date and then not retranslated thereafter. Paragraph 53 refers to exchange differences arising from retranslation of the opening 'net investment' and paragraph 43 defines this as being the investing company's proportion of the foreign enterprise's 'net assets'. Goodwill only arises on consolidation and is not part of the foreign enterprise's net assets.

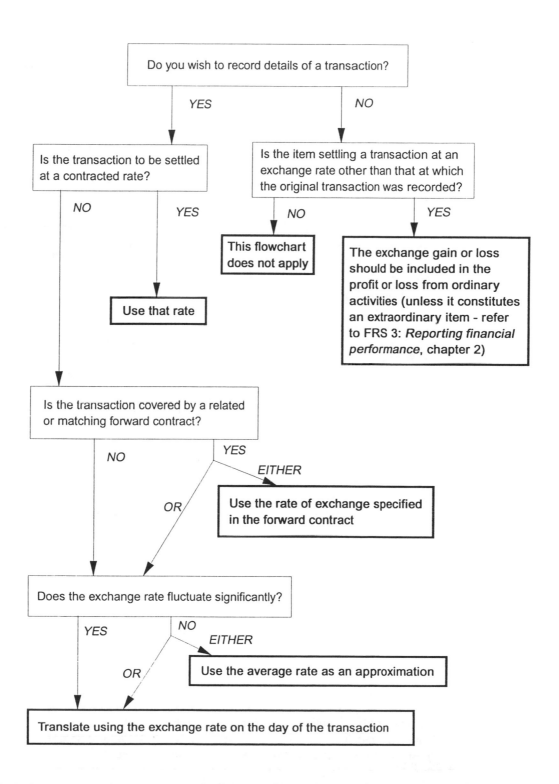

SSAP 20(1)   Foreign currency transaction recording and transaction settlement translation

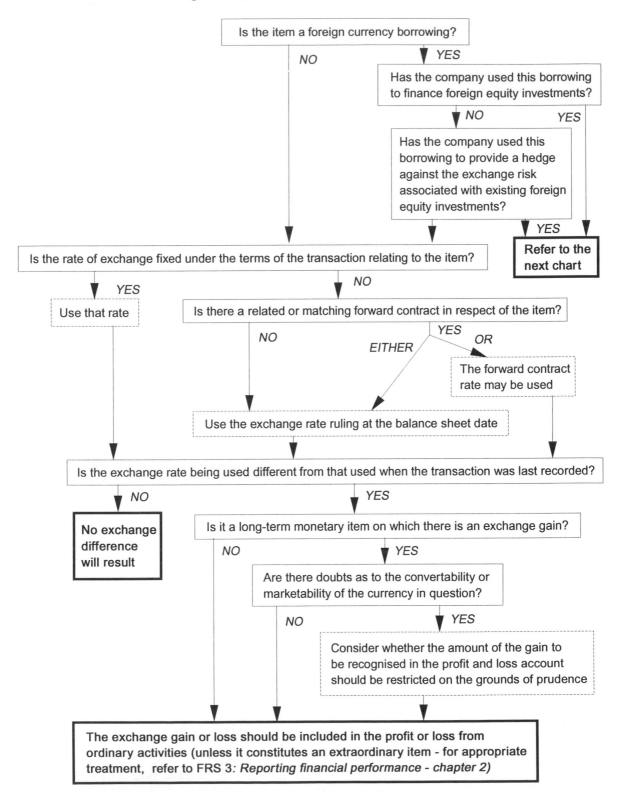

SSAP 20(2)   Balance sheet translation of monetary assets and liabilities

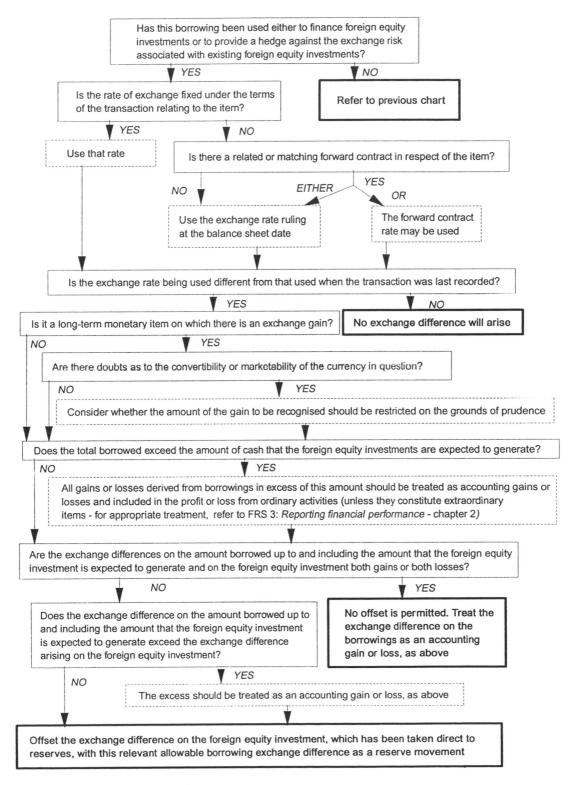

SSAP 20(3)   Balance sheet translation of foreign currency borrowing

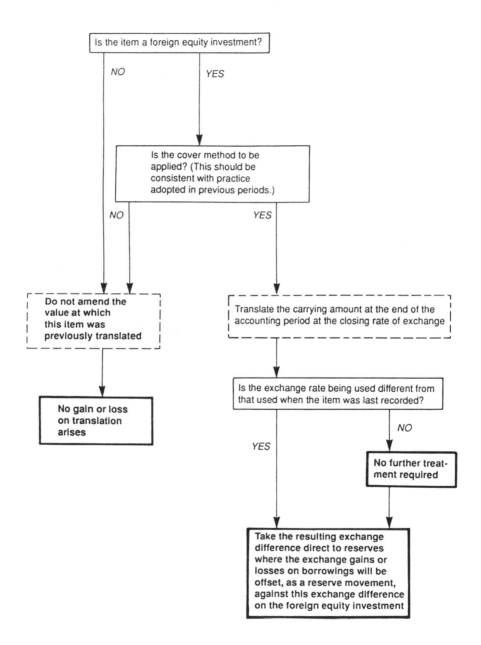

SSAP 20(4)   Balance sheet translation of non-monetary assets and liabilities

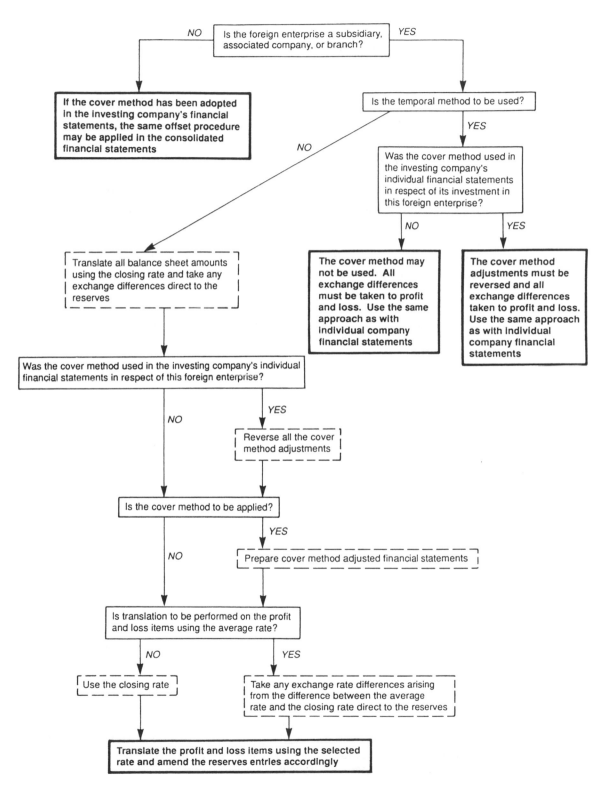

SSAP 20(5)   Consolidated financial statements

Short Questions

*ASSUME THAT MATERIALITY EXISTS IN **EVERY** CASE*

The Individual Company Stage:

Questions 1-20 relate to a large (as defined in the Companies Act) manufacturing company which has many overseas customers and suppliers. It has invested in some overseas companies and is highly geared, having both sterling and foreign currency borrowings of a long and short-term nature. The company's balance sheet date is 31st December.

1   The company purchased raw materials from a German supplier for DM 21,000. At the request of the supplier, the purchase was paid in cash the day the raw materials were delivered.

2   The company has two lorries which were bought in Denmark in June for kr420,400 when the exchange rate was £1=kr10.51. At the balance sheet date the exchange rate was £1=kr10.38.

3   The company purchased raw materials from an Italian supplier for IL400m. The goods were delivered on May 5th, when the exchange rate was £1=IL2,000. Payment was made in lire on August 15th, when the exchange rate was £1=IL2,200.

4   The company purchased raw materials from a French supplier for Ffr150,000. The goods were delivered, on September 19th when the exchange rate was £1=Ffr9.13. Payment was not made by the year end but will be paid by the due date of 19th March. The exchange rate at the balance sheet date was £1=Ffr9.16.

5   The company purchased raw materials from an American supplier for $34,000. The goods were delivered on December 14th when the exchange rate was £1=$1.70. Payment was not made by the year end but will be made on the 14th January in £sterling. £20,000 will be paid. The exchange rate at the year end was £1=$1.66.

6   The company purchased raw materials from a Portuguese supplier for esc2.4m. The goods were delivered, on December 21st when the exchange rate was £1=esc240. Payment was not made by the year end but will be made on the 11th March. The company estimate that it will cost them £10,526. The exchange rate at the year end was £1=esc220.

7   The company purchased raw materials from a Spanish supplier for pes3.1m. The goods were delivered on November 28th when the exchange rate was £1=pes240. Payment was not made by the year end and is to be made on 28th February. The company has arranged to buy pesetas on that date at an agreed rate of £1=pes245. The exchange rate at the balance sheet date was £1=pes242.

8   On 6th December, the company purchased raw materials for £110,000 from a Swedish supplier. The exchange rate on 6th December was £1=kr11.14. Payment in £sterling is to be made on 6th February. The balance sheet date exchange rate is £1=kr11.12.

9   On 3rd August, the company supplied goods with a sterling sales price of £70,000 to the Brazilian government. The exchange rate ruling when the payment was made on 8th September was £1=Cz70 (on 3rd August it had been £1=Cz60). The contract was in Brazilian cruzados and under it the company agreed to accept payment of Cz4.2m on the settlement date.

10   Having learnt from experience, when the company sold a second shipment of goods to the Brazilian government for Cz1.5m on 19th November they contracted to sell forward Cz1.5m on the settlement date (17th December). The exchange rate on 19th November was £1=Cz90. The forward contract rate was £1=Cz120. The exchange rate on 17th December was £1=Cz130.

11   The company purchased equipment from an American supplier for $34,000. The goods were delivered, on December 12th when the exchange rate was £1=$1.70. Payment was not made by the year end but will be made on the 12th March. In order to avoid exchange rate losses, the company contracted to buy $34,000 on 12th March at £1=$1.67. The exchange rate at the year end was £1=$1.66.

12   The company bought raw materials from a Belgian supplier on 21st June. The cost was BFr4m and the exchange rate on that date was £1=BFr50. Payment was made on 19th August when the exchange rate was £1=BFr46. The balance sheet date rate is £1=BFr49.

13   The company bought raw materials from a Belgian supplier on 15th February. The cost was BFr4m and the exchange rate on that date was £1=BFr50. In keeping with company policy, all foreign currency based transactions undertaken in January and February and due for payment after UK Budget Day (mid-March) are always covered by forward currency contracts. In this case, payment was due on 15th April. On 15th February the company contracted to buy BFr4m on 15th April at a rate of £1=BFr51. On 15th April the exchange rate was £1=BFr46.

14   The company bought goods valued at HK$720,000 from a Hong Kong supplier on 16th October. The exchange rate on that date was £1=HK$12. The goods were to be paid for in three monthly instalments of HK$240,000. The first payment was made on 16th November (exchange rate=£1=HK$12.2), the second was made on 16th December (exchange rate=£1=HK$12.1), the third is due to be made on 16th January. The balance sheet date exchange rate is £1=HK$11.9.

15   At the start of the year the company owed a Japanese supplier Yen7.5m. This had been translated and recorded in the financial statements at the previous balance sheet date rate of £1=Yen250 (£30,000). The supplier was paid on February 19th when the exchange rate was £1=Yen258. The balance sheet date exchange rate is £1=Yen251.

16   On September 16th, the company sold goods to a German customer for £5,000. The German customer has the option to pay for the goods in German marks. The exchange rate on the transaction date was £1=DM2.7. On the balance sheet date the customer still had not paid. The exchange rate was then £1=DM2.55. A fax was sent to the customer requesting immediate payment on December 28th and the customer's cheque is now 'in the post'.

17 All American and Canadian customers have the option to pay for goods in their local currency, but they must indicate which currency they are going to use at the date of purchase. On December 9th, the company sold a large consignment of goods to a Canadian customer for £42,000. The exchange rate on that date was £1=Cn$1.88. The customer has indicated that payment will be in Canadian dollars. Payment is due on 9th February. The company has taken out a forward contract to sell Cn$75,600 on 9th February at £1=Cn$1.87. The exchange rate on balance sheet date is £1=Cn$1.90.

18 On May 3rd, the company borrowed $200,000 from an American bank. The rate of exchange at that time was £1=$1.75. The loan was outstanding at the balance sheet date when the rate of exchange was £1=$1.66.

19 The company took a 5% equity investment in a Swiss company costing Sfr200,000 on May 7th when the exchange rate was £1=Sfr2.3. The balance sheet date exchange rate is £1=Sfr2.1.

20 The company took a 5% equity investment in an Australian company costing A$200,000 on June 7th when the exchange rate was £1=A$2.1. At the same time, as a hedge against the exchange risk in the investment, the company borrowed A$200,000. The balance sheet date exchange rate is £1=A$2.2.

The Consolidated Financial Statements Stage:

Questions 21-25 relate to groups, each of which comprises a UK holding company and many foreign enterprises. The balance sheet date is 31st December. [You should ignore goodwill on consolidation.]

21 *Menino plc* is a UK holding company. It has a wholly owned American subsidiary, *Terivel*, which it acquired four years ago for $1.2m when the exchange rate was £1=$1.9. The exchange rate at the balance sheet date is £1=$1.7. It was £1=$1.65 at the previous balance sheet date and the average rate was £1=$1.67. The profit and loss account for *Terivel* for the current year is:

	$
Turnover	1,560,000
Cost of Sales	(900,000)
Depreciation	(100,000)
Interest	(60,000)
Profit before tax	500,000
Tax	(200,000)
Profit after tax	300,000

If *Menino* adopts the policy of using the closing rate to translate the profit and loss account of subsidiaries when producing consolidated accounts, what would be the effect on the consolidated balance sheet of the above profit and loss account under the net investment method?

22   Repeat question 21, but this time assume that *Menino* adopts the policy of translating the profit and loss account at the average rate.

23   The balance sheet of *Terivel* (see question 21) at the balance sheet date is as follows (the previous balance sheet date figures are in the left-hand column):

	$(then)	$(now)
Fixed Assets	1,700,000	1,600,000
Current Assets		
Stock	300,000	520,000
Debtors & Cash	580,000	810,000
	880,000	1,330,000
Current Liabilities		
Creditors	220,000	250,000
Tax	180,000	200,000
	400,000	450,000
Net Current Assets	480,000	880,000
	2,180,000	2,480,000
Long Term Loans	680,000	680,000
	1,500,000	1,800,000
Share Capital	800,000	800,000
Reserves	700,000	1,000,000
	1,500,000	1,800,000

(The fixed assets were bought when the exchange rate was £1=$1.8)

If *Menino* applies the closing rate method when incorporating *Terivel* into the consolidated accounts, what would be the exchange rate differences arising from the incorporation of *Terivel's* balance sheet, and what treatment would apply to them?

24   Repeat question 23, but this time assume that *Menino* applies the temporal method. (You will find relevant information for this in question 21.)

25   *Poco plc* is a UK holding company. It bought a 5% equity investment in a French company which cost Ffr1.2m at the start of the accounting period, when the exchange rate was £1=Ffr10. At the same time, as a hedge against the exchange risk in the investment, the company borrowed Ffr1m. The balance sheet date exchange rate is £1=Ffr9.5 and the market value of the investment is Ffr1.3m. How should any exchange rate differences arising on this investment be treated in the consolidated financial statements if the cover method was applied when *Poco* prepared its accounts?

Additional Questions

*ASSUME THAT MATERIALITY EXISTS IN **EVERY** CASE*

The Individual Company Stage:

Unless otherwise indicated, questions 26-36 relate to a large (as defined in the Companies Act) manufacturing company with many overseas customers and suppliers. It has invested in some overseas companies and is highly geared, having both sterling and foreign currency borrowings of a long and short-term nature. The balance sheet date of all the companies is 31st December.

26   The company purchased equipment from a Greek supplier for 5.3m drachmae. The goods were delivered on September 7th, when the exchange rate was £1=dr295. Payment was not made by the year end but will be made on the 7th February. The exchange rate at the balance sheet date was £1=dr270.

27   The company sold furniture to a German company on 20th November. The exchange rate on that date was £1=DM2.45 and the goods were invoiced at £65,000. The exchange rate at the balance sheet date was £1=DM2.55. The customer was given special terms of four months credit and payment is due on 20th March.

28   On 6th May, in anticipation of a Canadian equity investment, the company took out a 20 year loan with a Canadian bank for Cn$2.2m. The exchange rate on that date was £1=Cn$1.80. The exchange rate on the balance sheet date was £1=Cn$1.90. The equity investment has encountered some problems and is not now expected to be finalised until mid-way through the next accounting period.

29   The company took a 5% equity investment in an New Zealand company costing NZ$200,000 on January 7th when the exchange rate was £1=NZ$2.8. At the same time, as a hedge against the exchange risk in the investment, the company borrowed NZ$200,000. The balance sheet date exchange rate is £1=NZ$2.7. The New Zealand company has been experiencing temporary trading difficulties and the balance sheet date market value of the investment is NZ$150,000.

30   The company took a 5% equity investment in an Irish company costing Ip200,000 on February 22nd when the exchange rate was £1=Ip1. At the same time, as a hedge against the exchange risk in the investment, the company borrowed NFL500,000 (£1=NFL3). The balance sheet date exchange rates are £1=NFL2.9=Ip1.1.

31   The company took a 5% equity investment in an Greek company costing dr20m on November 11th when the exchange rate was £1=dr260. At the same time, to finance the investment, the company borrowed dr20m and entered into a forward contract to buy dr20m three months later at an exchange rate of £1=dr265, at which time it would have sufficient other funds to meet that commitment and then use the currency purchased to repay the loan. The balance sheet date exchange rate was £1=dr270.

32   [*This question is particularly complex and requires that you consider rather more than*

the treatment as indicated under SSAP 20. Do not try to do any calculations just explain what treatment would be appropriate.]

In October, the company deposited £50,000 in Brazilian cruzados in a bank in Brazil with a view to having cash available for purchase of raw materials. The exchange rate at that time was £1=Cz75. The company spent Cz4m in the period up to the balance sheet date and the balance sheet date balance on the account was Cz3m. Due to the high rate of inflation in Brazil, the Brazilian bank pays a compensatory interest rate which is approximately equal to the inflation rate but never exceeds it, and that accounts for the increase in the cruzado balance over the period from the initial deposit level of Cz3.75m. The exchange rate at the balance sheet date was £1=Cz160.

33   On March 1st, in anticipation of an Austrian equity investment, the company borrowed sch1.9m (exchange rate: £1=sch19). On April 10th the company used sch700,000 to buy 4% of the equity of an Austrian company. The exchange rate ruling on that date was £1=sch18.5. At the balance sheet date the exchange rate was £1=sch19.7.

34   On September 1st, the company lent a small Yugoslavian company din2m. The exchange rate was £1=din20. Repayment is to be din2m in 5 years time. In mid-December, the Yugoslavian government was replaced and there was an immediate freeze on all bank accounts. The balance sheet date exchange rate was £1=din17.

35   In May, the company sold some goods valued at £175,000 to a middle eastern government. Payment was to have been made by the customer in its own currency on July 17th. In June, the customer invaded a neighbouring country and as a result, all trade contact with the middle eastern customer has been banned by the UK government.

36   On 15th August, *Merece Ltd*, a UK member of the *Maisgrande* group, sold goods valued at £75,000 to another member of the group - a Venezuelan publishing company. Group policy is that such transactions are denominated in US dollars. As a result, the transaction was invoiced at US$135,000. When payment for this amount was received eight weeks later, the bank converted it into £82,300. How would this be dealt with in company financial statements of *Merece Ltd*?

The Consolidated Financial Statements Stage:

Questions 37-45 relate to groups, each of which comprises a UK holding company and many foreign enterprises. The balance sheet date is 31st December. [You should ignore goodwill on consolidation.]

37   Refer to question 36. How would this be dealt with in the group consolidated financial statements?

38   *Silva plc* is a UK holding company. It owns 100% of the share capital of a German company, *Alpha*, which it acquired some years earlier for DM10m. The exchange rate at that time was £1=DM5. At the current balance sheet date the exchange rate is £1=DM2.8 (last year £1=DM3.1). The net assets of the subsidiary at the balance sheet date are DM12.7m (last year DM12m). The market value of the subsidiary is DM14.3m

(DM14.1 last year). What related exchange rate differences should be included in *Silva's company* financial statements?

39   Repeat question 38, but this time what related exchange rate differences should be included in the *consolidated* financial statements? (Assume the closing rate method is being applied.)

40   *Silva* has a second wholly owned German subsidiary, *Beta*, which it acquired some years earlier for DM4.5m. The exchange rate at that time was £1=DM4.5. The exchange rate at the previous balance sheet date was £1=DM3.1. At the current balance sheet date it is £1=DM2.8. Four years ago, *Silva* borrowed DM6m as a hedge against the investment which was then thought to be worth DM6.5m. The exchange rate at that time was £1=DM3.9. The net assets of the subsidiary at the previous balance sheet date were DM8.6m and they are now DM8.7m. The market value of the subsidiary is DM8.8m (DM9.9 at the previous balance sheet date). What related exchange rate differences should be included in *Silva's company* financial statements?

41   Repeat question 40, but this time what related exchange rate differences should be included in the *consolidated* financial statements? (Assume the closing rate method is being applied.)

42   Repeat question 41, but this time what related exchange rate differences should be included in the consolidated financial statements assuming the *temporal* method is being applied.

43   *Silva* has a third wholly owned German subsidiary, *Gama*, which it acquired some years earlier for DM8m. The exchange rate at that time was £1=DM4. At the current balance sheet date the exchange rate is £1=DM2.8 (last year £1=DM3.1). At the same time as the investment was made, *Silva* borrowed DM8m as a hedge against the exchange risk on the investment. The subsidiary is now in the process of recovering from a period of very poor results which started prior to its being acquired. The net assets of the subsidiary at the current balance sheet date are DM7.5m (last year DM7.2m). The market value of the subsidiary is DM7.8m (DM7.4m at the previous balance sheet date). What related exchange rate differences should be included in *Silva's company* financial statements?

44   Repeat question 43, but this time what related exchange rate differences should be included in the *consolidated* financial statements? (Assume the closing rate method is being applied.)

45   Repeat question 39, but this time include the information about the other companies in the group given in questions 40 and 43. (Assume the closing rate method is being applied for all the subsidiaries.)

Long Questions

(1) *Terivel*

Refer back to the information about the subsidiary *Terivel* given in short questions 28 and 30. Prepare a translated profit and loss account for consolidation based on the temporal method, incorporating the monetary item exchange rate difference identified in question 31. (The average exchange rates for stock are: opening £1=$1.66; closing £1=$1.69)

(2) *Cansada*

The balance sheet of *Cansada*, a wholly owned Australian subsidiary of *Dormia Plc*, at the balance sheet date is as follows (the previous balance sheet date figures are in the left-hand column):

	A$(then)	A$(now)
Fixed Assets	1,000,000	900,000
Current Assets		
Stock	600,000	550,000
Debtors & Cash	700,000	800,000
	1,300,000	1,350,000
Current Liabilities		
Creditors	600,000	320,000
Tax	210,000	280,000
	810,000	600,000
Net Current Assets	490,000	750,000
	1,490,000	1,650,000
Long Term Loans	200,000	200,000
	1,290,000	1,450,000
Share Capital	1,000,000	1,000,000
Reserves	290,000	450,000
	1,290,000	1,450,000

(The closing rate is £1=A$2.1; the previous closing rate was £1=A$1.95; the average rate for stock at the balance sheet date is £1=A$2.07; the previous balance sheet date the average rate for stock was £1=A$1.98; the subsidiary was formed six years ago when the exchange rate was £1=A$2.6; the fixed assets were bought when the exchange rate was £1=A$2.3)

Dormia Plc applies the temporal rate method when incorporating *Cansada* into the consolidated accounts. Prepare the translated balance sheets for both balance sheet dates.

10 SSAP 21: Accounting for Leases and Hire Purchase Contracts

Summary of the accounting treatment requirements

Leases should be categorised as either 'finance' or 'operating'. Hire purchase contracts will usually be of a financing nature and, if so, should be accounted for on a similar basis to that applied to finance leases. Where a hire purchase contract is of an operating nature, it should be accounted for on a similar basis to that applied to operating leases.

Both lessor and lessee should take operating lease rentals to the profit and loss account, normally on a straight line basis even if the payments are not made on that basis.

Under an operating lease, the lessor should record the fixed asset and depreciate it over its useful life.

Finance leases should be capitalised by the lessee, with a corresponding entry in creditors. The initial value used should be the present value of the minimum lease payments. Depreciation should then be provided over the shorter of the lease term and the asset's useful life, except in the case of a hire purchase contract, under which circumstances the asset should be depreciated over its useful life. As each payment is made, the proportion which relates to the creditor balance should be applied to reduce that balance. The rest of the payment should be treated as a lease charge in the profit and loss account for the period.

Lessors should initially record the amount due under a finance lease as a debtor using the amount of the net investment in the lease. As each payment is received, the proportion which relates to payment of the debtor balance should be applied to reduce that balance. The rest of the receipt should be treated as lease income in the profit and loss account for the period.

Problems of interpretation and grey areas

After considering how to identify the type of lease and reviewing the relationship between SSAP 21 and FRS 5, this section discusses the following items under the heading of accounting for the lease by the lessee: a systematic and rational basis of accounting for operating lease rentals; capitalisation of finance leases; sale and leaseback; and rental allocation. Under the heading of accounting for the lease by the lessor, there is discussion of a systematic and rational basis of accounting for operating lease rentals; sale and leaseback; manufacturer and dealer lessors and fair value; grants; gross earnings allocation; and the treatment of the lessor's cost of finance.

Identification of the type of lease

All leases are either finance leases or operating leases. The standard goes into considerable detail concerning how to distinguish between them. The principal characteristic of a finance lease is that substantially all the risks and rewards of ownership are transferred to the lessee. The various steps described in SSAP 21 should be followed in order to determine whether a finance lease exists.

These involve determining whether the present value of the minimum lease payments amount to substantially all (normally 90%) of the fair value of the asset. However, notwithstanding the results of the calculation, if the substance of the lease is to have the opposite effect, then the lease should be categorised accordingly. At the end of the day, it is the substance (i.e. what is actually happening to the risks and rewards of ownership) rather than the form of the transaction that decides whether there exists a finance or an operating lease.

The Relationship between SSAP 21 and FRS 5

FRS 5 (*Reporting the substance of transactions*, chapter 12) is particularly relevant in the context of SSAP 21. While SSAP 21 generally contains the more specific provisions for stand-alone leases that fall within its parameters (governed, of course by the general principle of FRS 5 that substance should have precedence over form when classifying a lease), for some lease arrangements, particularly those that are merely one element of a larger arrangement, FRS 5 will take precedence in the appropriate treatment to adopt.

Accounting for the Lease by the Lessee

A systematic and rational basis of accounting for operating lease rentals

The lessee should record a finance lease as an asset and as an obligation to pay future rentals (paragraph 32). An operating lease should be accounted for by the lessee by charging the rental arising from it on a straight-line basis over its term even if the payments are not made on such a basis, *unless another systematic and rational basis is more appropriate* (paragraph 37). No guidance is given in the standard as to what would be considered to be a 'systematic and rational basis'. However, as a rule of thumb, a basis which presented an improved true and fair view would probably be considered to be 'more appropriate'.

To address the special case of incentives for the lessee to sign an operating lease, UITF 12, *Lessee accounting for reverse premiums and similar incentives*, was issued in December 1994. It required that benefits received and receivable by the lessee as an incentive to sign the lease should be spread by the lessee on a straight-line basis over the lease term or, if shorter than the full lease term, over the period to the review date on which the rent is first expected to be adjusted to the prevailing market rate (paragraph 8). However, if in exceptional circumstances, another method of spreading is considered to adjust the rents paid to the prevailing market rate more accurately, that method should be used (UITF 12, paragraph 9).

Capitalisation of finance leases

One area concerning finance leases which may cause confusion is the requirement (paragraph 34) that where the minimum lease payments are less than the fair value of the asset, the amount to be capitalised should be restricted to the minimum lease payments. (This could arise, for example, from the impact of capital allowances upon the overall cost to the lessor leading to lease payments being based on a value lower than fair value.) Otherwise (paragraphs 32 and 33), it should be based upon the *present value of the discounted* minimum lease payments, for which the fair value may act as a surrogate. This latter option does not mean that the fair value *should* be used (though paragraphs 64-66 of the ASC's guidance notes on SSAP 21 could be interpreted as suggesting that that is the case), only that it *may* be used.

Sale and leaseback

Profits and losses on finance leases resulting from sale and leaseback transactions should not be recognised immediately, but should be deferred and amortised. The rules for profits and losses from operating lease sale and leaseback transactions are very different: they should be recognised immediately if the sale price approximates to the fair value of the asset; where the sale price is less than the fair value and there is a compensating element in the rental charges, an appropriate proportion may be required to be deferred and amortised; and, when the sale price is greater than the fair value, the excess over the fair value should be deferred and amortised. (The flowchart on page 119 summarises the various steps involved.) [However, it should be noted that where there is also an option for the seller/lessee to repurchase the asset, Paragraph 45 of FRS 5 (*Reporting the substance of transactions*, chapter 12) states that FRS 5 would have precedence over the treatment stipulated under SSAP 21. Application Note B of FRS 5 provides examples.]

Rental allocation

Rentals payable under finance leases should be apportioned between the finance charge and the reduction of the outstanding obligation for future amounts payable. In principle, there is no great problem in following this requirement. However, it is subject to the provision that the total finance charge under a finance lease should be allocated to accounting periods during the lease term so as to produce at least an approximately *constant* periodic rate of charge on the remaining balance of the obligation for each accounting period (paragraph 35). What is meant by a 'constant periodic rate of charge'? Is it a constant amount, or a constant proportion? The ASC guidance notes suggest three possible approaches (actuarial, sum of the digits, and straight-line), and it is clear from the examples given in those notes, that it is a constant proportional write-down of the remaining balance, rather than a constant amount written-off, that is required. While the actuarial basis is preferred, sum of the digits is considered suitable when the lease term is up to about seven years, and straight line is acceptable when the lease is relatively small - which in this context means when the lease is relatively immaterial'. These two alternatives to the actuarial method were compromise methods to be used in those situations where manual computation by the actuarial basis was impracticable, but much has changed since the standard was issued in 1984. In particular, there is now a widespread availability of cheap computers well equipped to perform the complex actuarial method calculations, with the result that there is no longer any reason to use either of the other two methods. Returning to the allocation of the finance charge, the overall effect of paragraph 35 is that the finance charge must be allocated to accounting periods *on the basis of the method adopted to write-off the initial liability*, rather than on the basis of whatever schedule may be found in the lease agreement.

Accounting for the Lease by the Lessor

A systematic and rational basis of accounting for operating lease rentals

Just as the term 'systematic and rational basis' was used in relation to the lessee's recording of operating lease rentals, so it is also used in relation to their recording by the lessor. Interestingly, the reference is altered from 'unless another systematic and rational basis is more appropriate' to 'unless another systematic and rational basis is more *representative of the time pattern in which the benefit from the leased asset is receivable*' (paragraph 43, italics added). It appears that the option to use a different basis is far more restricted for the lessor than it is for the lessee. However, as it is virtually inconceivable that appropriateness for the lessee will ultimately be determined by anything other than the time pattern of the benefits arising from the use of the leased asset, the overall effect of the two wordings is the same.

Sale and leaseback

In contrast to the lessee, who must apply special rules to leases resulting from sale and leaseback transactions, lessors should treat them in the same way as all other leases (paragraph 48).

Manufacturer and dealer lessors and fair value

When manufacturer and dealer lessors enter into a finance lease, two types of income result: the gross earnings (i.e. gross investment less cost of the asset net of any grants receivable), and the selling profit or loss (i.e. the initial profit or loss which is equivalent to that which would arise were the asset sold, rather than leased). The selling profit on operating leases should not be recognised. For finance leases, paragraph 45 states that the selling profit should be restricted to the excess of the *fair value* over the lessor's cost net of any grants receivable towards the purchase, construction, or use of the asset. The definition in the standard of fair value ('the price at which an asset could be exchanged in an arm's length transaction ....') suggests that it is the market price of the asset. However, in this case, reference to the ASC guidelines reveals that the standard is referring to the price that was used as the basis for the calculation of the leasing payments.

Applying the interpretation adopted in the guidelines, where the normal cash sale price has been used in conjunction with the normal implicit rate to calculate the rental payments, the selling profit should be restricted to the excess of that cash sale price over the lessor's costs net of related grants. However, the cash sale price is frequently not used (for example, car dealers will often give a discount for cash but base any hire purchase contract upon the full selling price). In these circumstances, the ASC guidance notes suggest that the normal implicit rate should be used in order to calculate what capital cost is being written-off in the rental being charged, and the actual capital cost (net of grants receivable) should be subtracted from that amount: the difference is the selling profit or loss and should be recognised at this point. The balance of profit will arise as gross earnings over the period of the lease. The capital cost discovered as being written-off in the rental being charged is therefore the *fair value* in this case. It represents the price at which the asset could be exchanged in an arm's length transaction of this type. Thus, there may be two 'fair values' - the cash sale fair value and the finance lease fair value.

Grants

Although the standard states that tax free grants available to the lessor against the purchase price of assets acquired for leasing should be spread over the period of the lease by treating the amount of the grant as income (paragraph 41), grants receivable by manufacturer and dealer lessors towards the purchase, construction or use of an asset should be deducted from the lessor's costs relating to the provision of that asset before calculating any selling profit arising under a finance lease (paragraph 45).

There are two important points concerning grants. Firstly, should *taxable* grants be set against costs and not treated as income, or should all grants be treated as income but, for profit recognition purposes, any related grant be subtracted from the cost (i.e. the deduction from cost is a purely computational adjustment, not a bookkeeping entry)? Consideration of the source of all the various figures relating to finance leases, and specifically, the net investment and gross earnings, reveals that grants are deducted from cost in the determination of both the profit to be recognised in a period, and the rental debtor at the end of that period. This has the effect of apportioning the grant over the period of the lease. Thus, in all cases involving finance leases, the grant is deducted from cost for the purposes of profit recognition and, as a result, spread over the term of the lease. This even applies to manufacturer/dealer leases, though the weighting of the grant's spreading pattern is towards the first year of the lease because of the grant's deduction from costs directly resulting in an increase in the initial selling profit.

The second point concerning grants relates to permissable practice under company law. In SSAP 4 (*Accounting for government grants* - chapter 13), doubt is expressed regarding the legality of deducting government grants from the costs of fixed assets for balance sheet purposes. If grants are deducted from the costs of assets in a lease, higher profits will result, some of which will be recognised in each year of the lease. However, none of the assets on which there are finance leases is included in the balance sheet of the lessor. The doubt expressed in SSAP 4 relates to paragraphs 17 and 26 of the Companies Act 1985, which has the effect of prohibiting enterprises to which the legislation applies from deducting the amount of any grant received from the cost of the fixed asset to which it relates. As finance lease lessors do not carry the assets involved as fixed assets, it would seem reasonable to suggest that the Companies Act veto does not apply. Fixed assets held for use in operating leases are included in the balance sheet of the lessor but no reference is made in SSAP 21 to the deduction of grants when determining the cost of these fixed assets for balance sheet purposes: indeed, paragraph 41 would seem to suggest that they should not be set against cost. Thus, it seems that the Companies Act veto may be irrelevant to the application of SSAP 21. Nevertheless, there remains considerable uncertainty about how far-reaching the veto may in fact be and it would be useful if this were authoritatively clarified by the ASB at the earliest possible opportunity. Until such time as clarification is given, it would be appropriate to bear in mind that such a veto may apply to SSAP 21, but in the meantime to continue to apply the standard as written.

Gross earnings allocation

The gross earnings arising from finance leases should be allocated to accounting periods so as to give a constant periodic rate of return on the lessor's net cash investment in the lease in each period. In other words, the profit should be spread across the term of the lease so as to recognise the same rate of return in each period on the balance not yet written-off. That balance will reduce as each period passes so that, while the rate of return should remain constant, the actual return should be decreasing from period to period. While the standard does not suggest the methods to adopt in order to achieve the constant periodic rate, the ASC guidelines do. The calculation should be based on the investment period principle (i.e. the calculation should take account of the tax effect on cash flows). This requirement stems from the fact that the rate of return is that on the net cash investment, a figure which is arrived at after adjusting for taxation payments and receipts. Two common methods cited are the actuarial method *after tax*, and the investment period method (IPM). The actuarial method after tax is the more accurate of the two and, when cash surpluses arise, the IPM approach is more conservative, but they generally produce broadly similar results. Other methods may also be suitable, though, as with the entries by the lessee, the sum of the digits method is not likely to be appropriate given the ease with which complex financial calculations can now be performed.

The treatment of the lessor's cost of finance

One debatable point concerning the calculation of gross earnings arises in the treatment of the lessor's cost of finance (i.e. interest) which, under paragraph 40, may be deducted from gross earnings before the remainder of the gross earnings is allocated to the periods covered by the lease. The inclusion of interest payments in this way provides a more realistic picture of both the cash flows, and of the lease. It could be argued that inclusion should be preferred on this basis. However, the standard appears to suggest that exclusion would be the more usual practice. (It cites inclusion as being an alternative to exclusion.) The approach which gives the more true and fair view should be adopted and the standard is suggesting that either might do so. It is up to the individual company to make the appropriate selection. Whether this option really should be available is debatable, and it is bound to lead to an undesirable lack of comparability.

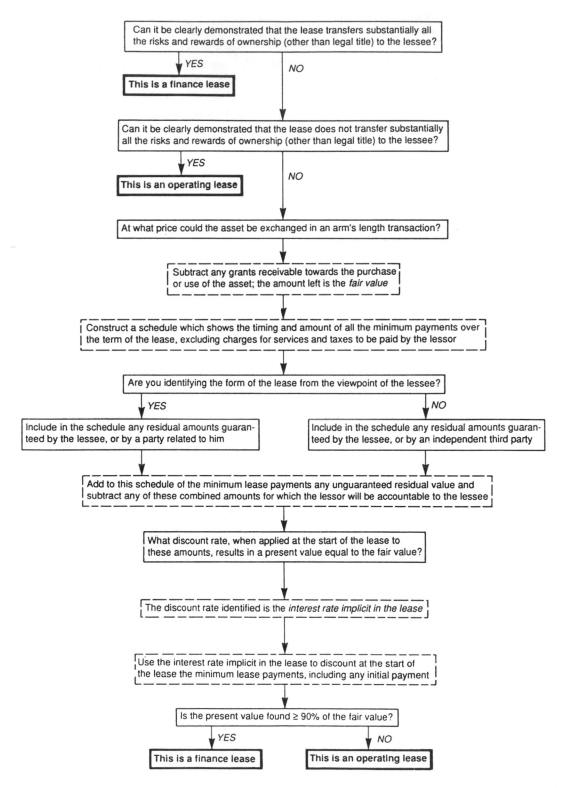

SSAP 21(1)   Form of the lease

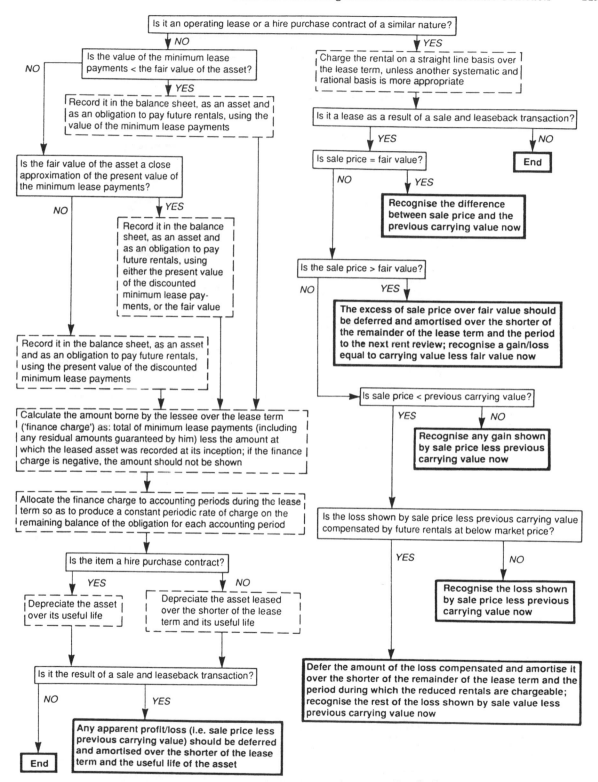

SSAP 21(2)   Initial recording and accounting by lessees

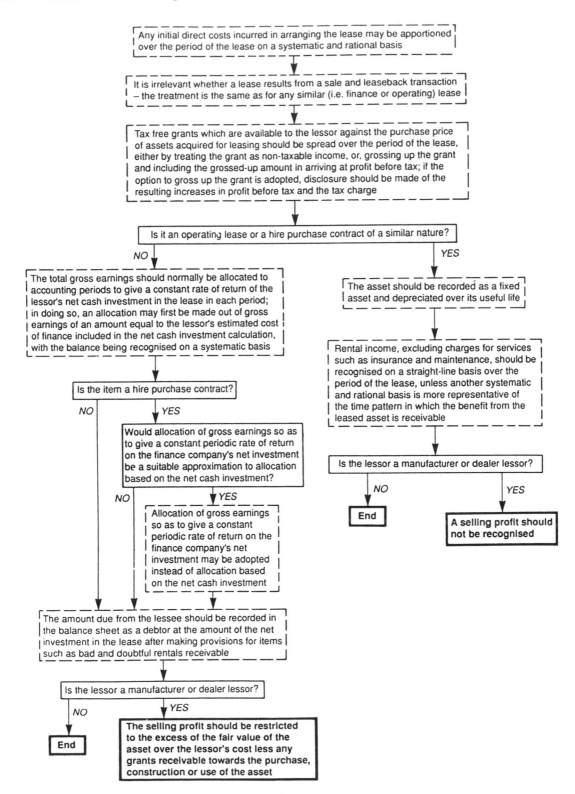

SSAP 21(3)   Initial recording and accounting by lessors

Short Questions

*ASSUME THAT MATERIALITY EXISTS IN **EVERY** CASE*

Questions 1-40 relate to an electronic engineering company with current turnover of £18m and net pre-tax profit of £3.4m. (Last year £14.3m and £1.9m respectively.) The company's financial year ends on 31st December and the Board of Directors are scheduled to approve the accounts on 31st March. [Apart from observing the principle of substance over form, unless otherwise indicated, you should concentrate upon the treatment as prescribed by SSAP 21.]

1   During the year, the company entered into a 10 year lease on a workshop near to the main company site. The lease can be cancelled at any time by the company, providing that six months notice is given. However, the company would be required to meet any deficit arising between the residual value anticipated and that which actually arose upon cancellation.

2   The fair value of an item of equipment which the company leased in February for a 3 year period, is £15,000. The company has guaranteed a residual value of £1,000 to the lessor. After discounting at an estimated implicit interest rate of 12%, the present value of the minimum lease payments, including an initial payment of £500, is £13,000.

3   The fair value of an electronic digitiser the company leased in May for a 4 year period, is £250,000. The company has the option at the end of the period to purchase the digitiser for £50,000, which it intends to exercise.

4   The company has a five year lease on a laboratory at the local university. Under the terms of the lease, the company must pay £5,000 per year and is responsible for maintaining the decor of the laboratory during the period of the lease. The laboratory is covered for insurance purposes by the university's policy. At the end of the five year term, the company has the option to extend the lease annually for the following five years. Thereafter, use of the laboratory will revert to the university. The university has the right to terminate the lease upon giving 1 month's notice, at any time within the term of the lease. In the event of such cancellation, no compensation will be payable to the company. The company has no option to cancel the lease until the end of the first five year period.

5   The fair value of a machine leased by the company in July is £12,000. The present value of the minimum lease payments is £11,000.

6   The company entered into a five year hire purchase contract on some sensory monitoring equipment. The equipment could have been purchased for £120,000. The total of the minimum lease payments is £135,000, and the present value of the minimum lease payments is £115,000. Under the contract, maintenance of the equipment is the responsibility of the seller. The contract has an option for the company to acquire title to the equipment at the end of the lease term for £80,000. It is believed that the equipment will have a useful life of 8 years. The company intends claiming 100% capital allowances on the grounds that the equipment is being used solely for scientific research.

7   A lease on an industrial lathe has a primary term of four years. It may then be extended for a further two years, if the company wishes. The lathe has an expected useful life (based on the use that the company intend to make of it) of three years.

8   A three year lease on image processing equipment, which had a fair value of £20,000 when the lease was implemented in November, has a complex clause related to the residual value of the equipment. The expected residual value is £8,000, and the lessor will sell the equipment when the lease term ends; if the lessor receives more than £8,000 the company will receive 90% of the excess; if the lessor receives less than £8,000, the company must pay the lessor the deficit subject to a limit of 1p for every time the image processing equipment was used to generate a page of output above the annual level of 50,000 pages which the company expected to produce. The equipment is expected to output 250,000 pages during its useful life.

9   Three years ago, the company leased a surplus acetator to a small manufacturing company. The lease was classified as a finance lease and at the end of the previous year the net investment debtor balance was £7,000. The manufacturing company terminated the lease during the year and paid the amount required (£3,000) under the early termination clause in the lease. The acetator is now technically obsolete and is believed to be both unreleasable and unsaleable.

10   The company leased a power modulator to another electronic engineering company six years ago. The modulator was new, and had an estimated useful life of ten years. The original lease was classified as a finance lease and, at the end of the primary term of six years, the lessee company terminated the lease. The company immediately leased the modulator to a scientific laboratory on a five year lease.

11   The fair value of a machine which the company leased from the manufacturer's agents in April, is £14,000. The present value of the minimum lease payments is £12,000.

12   Under a clause in a finance lease which the company has on some duplicating equipment it is using, should tax rates change so as to disadvantage the lessor, the company will be required to compensate the lessor by paying correspondingly higher rental charges.

13   During the year, the company sold its head office building to a property company, and then immediately leased it back. The lease is for 99 years and is a finance lease. The sale price was £240,000; the net book value at the end of the previous accounting period was £220,000.

14   The present value of the minimum lease payments on a four year lease on a sizing machine is £28,000. The company could have purchased the machine at the time the lease was signed in March, for £32,000. The quarterly payments on the lease are £2,500.

15   Five years ago, the company entered into a finance lease on some robotics kit. The lease included a clause whereby the company guaranteed to meet the first £20,000 of any deficit arising from the actual residual value being below the anticipated residual value of £80,000. The guarantee of £20,000 was included in the computation of the asset and liability amount at the start of the lease and by the end of the lease the lease asset account

had a zero balance. When the lease expired the lessor sold the robotics kit and a shortfall of £20,000 resulted, which the company duly paid.

16   During the year, the company sold an equipment store to a property company, and then immediately leased it back. The lease is an operating lease. The sale price was £70,000; the net book value at the end of the previous accounting period was £62,000; and the fair value was £65,000.

17   During the year, the company sold a filter machine to an equipment leasing company, and then immediately leased it back. The lease is an operating lease. The sale price was £20,000; the net book value at the end of the previous accounting period was £26,000; and the fair value was £24,000.

18   During the year, the company sold a computer to a leasing company, and then immediately leased it back. The lease is an operating lease. The sale price was £15,000; the net book value at the end of the previous accounting period was £16,000; and the fair value was £13,000.

19   During the year, the company sold a thermo masking machine to a leasing company, and then immediately leased it back. The lease is an operating lease. The sale price was £13,000; the net book value at the end of the previous accounting period was £11,000; and the fair value was £14,000.

20   During the year, the company sold a generator to a leasing company, and then immediately leased it back. The lease is an operating lease. The sale price was £75,000; the net book value at the end of the previous accounting period was £72,000; and the fair value was £70,000.

21   During the year, the company sold an electronic expansion chamber to a leasing company, and then immediately leased it back. The lease is an operating lease. The sale price was £55,000; the net book value at the end of the previous accounting period was £57,000; and the fair value was £61,000.

22   The fair value of a machine leased in November for five years, for use at the company's Inverness site, is £44,000. The present value of the minimum lease payments is £37,500. The quarterly payments on the lease are £1,500 in the first year, £2,000 in the second, £2,500 in the third, £3,000 in the fourth, and £3,500 in the fifth.

23   A few years ago, the company leased an unused acrylic binding machine to a chemical research company. The lease was classified as a finance lease and at the end of the previous year the net investment debtor balance was £11,000. The engineering company terminated the lease during the year and paid the amount required (£5,000) under the early termination clause in the lease. The equipment was then sold for £4,500.

24   Under a clause in a finance lease which the company has on some spacial measuring equipment, should tax rates change so as to disadvantage the lessor, the company will be required to compensate the lessor by paying a lump sum surcharge in any period where the lessor pays more tax than was anticipated at the time the lease was enacted.

25   Ten years earlier, the company entered took out a lease on a small warehouse. The lease included a clause whereby the company guaranteed to meet any deficit arising from the actual residual value being below the anticipated residual value of £30,000. The guarantee of £30,000 was included in the computation of the asset and liability amount at the start of the lease. It was estimated that a realistic value to place on the guarantee was £10,000. The warehouse lease, which was classified as a finance lease, was written-down to the £20,000 of the guarantee which was not expected to be payable. When the lease expired the lessee sold the warehouse and a shortfall of £15,000 resulted, which the company duly paid.

Additional Questions

*ASSUME THAT MATERIALITY EXISTS IN **EVERY** CASE*

26   Two years ago, the company leased an electron decoder to a chemical engineering company. The primary lease term was for five years, and it was classified as a finance lease. At the end of the previous year, the net investment debtor balance was £26,000. The lessee company terminated the lease during the year and paid the amount required (£10,000) under the early termination clause in the lease. The company leased the decoder to another company one month after the end of the current accounting period. Negotiations had started in December and at the balance sheet date it was anticipated that the lease would be enacted. The new lease is also a finance lease.

27   Under a clause in an operating lease which the company has on some reprographic equipment in use at its Forres site, should tax rates change so as to disadvantage the lessor, the company will be required to compensate the lessor by paying correspondingly higher rental charges.

28   In January, the company took out a five year lease on a machine for use at its Elgin site. The fair value of the machine was £57,000. The present value of the minimum payments is £50,300. The quarterly payments on the lease are £4,000 in the first year, £3,200 in the second, £2,800 in the third, £2,500 in the fourth, and £2,000 in the fifth. The company is responsible for all maintenance, repair, and insurance costs relating to the machine throughout the period of the lease. These costs are expected to rise as the machine ages and the rental payments have been scheduled to compensate for the extra costs that the company will incur in the later years of the lease. The machine has an expected useful life of ten years and the company has no intention of exercising the option to extend the lease for a further five years at the end of the primary term. The company has guaranteed the residual value at the end of the primary term of £20,000.

29   During the year, the company sold some heavy equipment to an equipment lessor, and then immediately leased it back. The lease is a finance lease. The sale price was £60,000; the net book value at the end of the previous accounting period was £100,000.

30   The fair value of a machine acquired on a four year lease in December, is £36,000. The present value of the minimum lease payments is £36,500. The quarterly payments on the lease are £2,000 in the first and second years, £3,000 in the third, and £4,000 in the fourth.

31   A lease on an micro circuitry modulator has a primary term of three years. It may then be extended for a further three years, if the company wishes. The modulator has an expected useful life of five years.

32   During the year, the company purchased a delivery truck on hire purchase. Under the contract, the company has the right to purchase the title at the end of the four year lease term for £100. The fair value of the truck was £11,000. The cash price of the truck was £10,500. The present value of the minimum lease payments is £12,000.

33   During the year the company sold a warehouse at its Nairn site for £100,000 (book value £90,000), and then immediately bought it back under a 10 year hire purchase contract. The warehouse has an expected remaining useful life of 30 years. The hire purchase contract is to be treated as if it were a finance lease.

34   One year ago, the company leased a laser scanner to an aeronautical engineering company. The primary lease term was for five years, and it was classified as a finance lease. At the end of the previous year, the net investment debtor balance was £6,000. The lessee company terminated the lease during the year, paid the amount required (£7,000) under the early termination clause in the lease, and assumed title of the scanner.

35   Under a clause in an operating lease which the company has on some fluid weighing equipment, should tax rates change so as to disadvantage the lessor, the company will be required to compensate the lessor by paying a lump sum surcharge in any period where the lessor pays more tax than was anticipated at the time the lease was enacted.

36   Some years previously, the company took out a lease on an office block. During the current year, the company cancelled the lease while it still had four years to run. At that time, the balance on the lease asset account (the lease had been classed as a finance lease) was £65,000. The balance on the lease obligation account was £70,000. As a penalty for early termination, the company was required to pay £30,000 to the lessor.

37   In October, the company entered into a three year hire purchase contract on some computer equipment. At the end of the term, the company has the option to acquire the title to the equipment for £1. The fair value of the equipment was £66,200. The lessor benefited from some government subsidies in relation to the equipment. As a result, the total of the minimum lease payments is £62,000, and the present value £56,000.

38   The fair value of a machine taken out on a six year lease in April, was £82,000. The present value of the minimum lease payments was £72,000. The quarterly payments on the lease are £4,000 in the first year, £4,600 in the second, £5,250 in the third, £5,750 in the fourth, and £6,500 in the fifth. The rental costs increase with time to compensate the lessor for the increased maintenance costs that will be incurred. The machine has an estimated useful life of 15 years and there is no option in the lease for any extension after the six year term.

39   In November, the company entered into a four year lease on some used radiographic equipment. The equipment has a limited useful life as some of the components ultimately fuse together and become irreplaceable. The estimated total useful life of such equipment is five years. The lease has no option to extend the term at the end of the four years. The

present value of the minimum lease payments is £61,000, and the fair value of second hand, one year old radiographic equipment like this is £70,000.

40   Under a clause in a finance lease which the company took out on some cutting equipment, should tax rates change so as to advantage the lessor, the company will be compensated by correspondingly lower rental charges.

Questions 41-45 relate to companies which have a balance sheet date of 31st December. In each case, the Board of Directors are scheduled to approve the accounts on 31st March.

41   A kitchen furniture company rents its equipment at £1,500 per month under a four-year lease. The equipment has an expected useful life of six years, and the catering company has the option to extent the lease for a further three years (at £500 per month) upon expiry of the primary four year term. At the end of the four year period, if the company does not exercise its option to extend the lease term, the equipment reverts to the lessor. If the company exercises its option to extend the lease, it has the option to buy the equipment for a single payment of £5,000 at the end of the lease.

42   Refer to question 41. If the kitchen furniture company did not exercise its right to extend the term of the lease at the end of its primary term, what would be the treatment under SSAP 21?

43   An industrial catering company rents its equipment under a five-year lease from the manufacturers. It pays £2,500 per month and has the option at the end of the five year period to buy the equipment for a single payment of £12,500.

44   In March, a pharmaceutical company agreed to lease all its computer equipment at a cost of £2,500 per month on a five year lease. Through a maintenance contract purchased at the time the lease was signed, the manufacturer is responsible for all repairs and maintenance of the equipment. The maintenance contract costs 12½% of the lease payments. The equipment has an expected useful life of eight years and the pharmaceutical company has the option to extend the lease at the end of the primary lease term for a further year on the same terms as the primary lease term. The equipment reverts to the manufacturer on the termination of the lease.

45   A shipping company leased a cruise ship on a 25 year lease from a ship building company. The fair value of the ship is £1.35m and the present value of the minimum lease payments is £1.2m. The cash price of the ship was £1.1m. The shipping company is responsible for all maintenance and upkeep of the ship throughout the 25 years of the lease. In addition, it has the right to purchase the ship for £0.1m at the end of the 25 year period. The estimated useful life of the ship is 25 years. Should the shipping company

terminate the lease before the expiry of its term, it will be required to pay £0.5m under an early termination clause in the lease. A similar condition applies to the lessor.

Long Question

Fazendo Plc

On the 1st of January, year 1, *Fazendo Plc* entered into an agreement to lease some newly acquired, two year old, computer equipment for three years, to *Usando Ltd*. The fair value, and price paid, of the equipment is £20,000. Rental of £2,500 is to be paid quarterly in advance. Tax is payable in the fourth quarter of each year. Capital allowances of 25% are receivable by *Fazendo Plc* in respect of this equipment. At the end of the lease, the equipment is to be scrapped and no residual value is expected. To purchase the computer equipment from the previous owner, *Fazendo Plc* borrowed £20,000 at 4% per quarter.

Required:

(a)   construct a table showing the actuarial method after tax computations of the net profit taken out of the lease (at 3.2132% on the average net cash invested in each quarter), tax paid, interest payments, and, the net cash investment at the end of each quarter.

(b)   calculate the gross earnings allocations using the actuarial method after tax basis.

(c)   calculate the gross earnings allocations under the investment period method.

11   SSAP 24: Accounting for Pension Costs

Summary of the accounting treatment requirements

The accounting objective of the standard is given in paragraph 16: the employer is required to recognise the cost of providing pensions on a systematic and rational basis over the period during which he benefits from the employee's services. (A slightly different objective is stated in paragraph 77: the employer should recognise the *expected* cost of providing pensions on a systematic and rational basis over the period during which he benefits from the *employees'* services.)

The charge against profits for defined contribution schemes should be the amount of contributions payable to the pension scheme in respect of the period.

The pension cost for defined benefit schemes should be calculated using actuarial valuation methods and the regular pension cost should be a substantially level percentage of the current and expected future pensionable payroll. (The two types of scheme are defined on page 129.)

Variations from regular cost should normally be allocated over the expected remaining service lives of current employees in the scheme, though prudence may require that a material deficit be recognised over a shorter period.

Problems of interpretation and grey areas

The following items are discussed: the scope of SSAP 24; the classification of pension schemes; actuarial choice and judgement; the treatment of variations; exceptions to the general spreading rule; multiple schemes; the impossibility of inter-firm comparability; and differences between amounts funded and charged, and deferred tax. Finally, there is a brief conclusion.

The scope of SSAP 24

The standard applies to all pension arrangements, no matter what the size of the scheme. Such arrangements may be formal commitments explicitly built into employment contracts, or they may be the result of custom and practice. Also covered are any *ex gratia*/discretionary payments made in the absence of any commitment, contractual or otherwise, to do so. UITF 6, issued in December 1992, extended the scope of SSAP 24 to cover other post-retirement benefits, for example, health care.

SSAP 24 does not directly relate to the contributions made by employees and whether a scheme is *contributory* (i.e. employees contribute to it) or *non-contributory* is irrelevant to the application of the standard.

The classification of pension schemes

Pension schemes can be broadly categorised as either *funded* (those whose future liabilities for benefits are provided by the accumulation of assets held externally to the employing company's business) or *unfunded* (those whose benefits are paid directly by the employer company). The difference in categorisation does not affect the application of SSAP 24, only the way in which the scheme is managed.

There are two types of scheme: *defined contribution* and *defined benefit*. (They are also known respectively as *money purchase* and *final salary* schemes.) In the case of the former, the employer's obligation is to make agreed contributions to a pension scheme. The benefits paid will depend upon the funds available at the time of payment. The funds available will be derived from contributions made, and the investment earnings arising from those contributions. The cost to the employer is measurable with reasonable certainty, as it is the amount of contributions payable in respect of the accounting period. The application of SSAP 24 is therefore relatively straightforward.

Defined benefit schemes could be said to be the reverse of defined contribution schemes. The benefits paid are set by the final salary or, less commonly, the average salary of the employee. The employer must adjust the contributions made to the scheme in order to meet this commitment. As a result, the final cost to the employer is very uncertain, and the application of SSAP 24 is correspondingly less than straightforward.

Actuarial choice and judgement

In order to determine the pension cost charge and the level of contributions required, actuarial techniques must be applied. An appropriate actuarial method must be selected, used consistently, and disclosed. Any changes in the method used must be disclosed and the effect quantified. Suitable assumptions will need to be made in arriving at the actuary's *best estimate* of the cost (the pension cost) of providing the pension benefits promised. These assumptions will, for example, be required in order to produce estimates of employee's final salary, life expectancy and number of years service, together with rates of interest and inflation. The method and the assumptions must be compatible, and must satisfy the accounting objective. Future expected increases in both earnings and pensions should be recognised and the calculation of benefit levels should be based on the situation *most likely* to be experienced. The method of providing for expected pension costs over the service lives of the employees in the scheme should result in the regular pension cost (the consistent ongoing cost recognised under the actuarial method used) being a substantially level percentage of the current and expected future pensionable payroll, based on current actuarial assumptions. It is obvious from the general wording in which these requirements are given in the standard that considerable differences may arise in methods selected and assumptions made.

The treatment of variations

There are four main ways in which variations from regular cost may arise: variations arising because events have not coincided with the actuarial assumptions made for the previous valuation ('experience variations'); changes in the actuarial method or assumptions; retroactive changes in benefits or in conditions of membership; and increases to pensions in payment or deferred pensions for which provision has not previously been made (paragraph 21). Subject to a few specific exceptions, any variations from the regular cost should be allocated over the expected remaining service lives of *current* employees in the scheme. No allowance should be made for future new entrants (though expected withdrawals should be accounted for), nor should ex-employees be included by back-dating the allocation as a prior period adjustment. An average remaining service period may be used, rather than performing the calculation on an individual employee basis. This will often be of between ten and 15 years, but the actual period to use will depend on the circumstances of each case.

Exceptions to the general spreading rule

One of the exceptions to the general spreading rule concerns surpluses/deficits arising from a significant reduction in the number of employees covered by a scheme. Such differences should be recognised as they arise, unless the reduction is *'related to the sale or termination of an operation,* [in which case] *the associated pension cost or credit should be recognised immediately to the extent necessary to comply with paragraph 18 of FRS 3'* (FRS 3 amendment to paragraph 81 of SSAP 24). The treatment of non-sale or termination employee reduction-derived surpluses and deficits should follow the funding policy: contribution reductions should not be anticipated when identified, rather they should be recognised over the period when they are being received. For example, the full effect of any contribution holidays and partial holidays arising from such circumstances should not be recognised at the start of the holiday, but spread over its duration. Thus, if a four-year contribution holiday was declared because of a £100m surplus arising from a non-sale or termination reduction in the number of employees covered by a scheme, the £100m could be recognised at the rate of £25m per year. It should not be recognised as £100m in the first year and nil thereafter.

Prudence may require that a material deficit be recognised over a period shorter than the expected remaining service lives of current employees in the scheme. To do so, three conditions must be met: a major event must have occurred which was not allowed for in the actuarial assumptions; it must be outside the scope of the assumptions (i.e. it must be more than just an oversight); and, it must have necessitated the payment of significant additional contributions to the pension scheme. An appropriate shorter period would probably be that over which the deficit was being eliminated by increased contributions.

Another exception to the spreading rule concerns refunds made to an employer which are subject to deduction of tax. In such circumstances, the refund *may* be recognised in the period it is received and the surplus or deficiency arising in that period *may* be accounted for in that period (paragraphs 29 and 83). Obviously, the choice of whether or not to take up these options means that greatly differing results can be produced from the same set of circumstances.

Finally, the treatment of the capital cost of *ex gratia* pensions, to the extent that it is not covered by a surplus, is another exception to the spreading rule. It should be recognised in the profit and loss of the accounting period when the *ex gratia* pensions are granted. This also applies where an allowance for the capital cost of discretionary or *ex gratia* increases in pensions has not been made in the actuarial assumptions.

Multiple schemes

Where a company/group has more than one pension scheme, the overall situation should be disclosed, rather than that for each scheme. However, a deficiency in one scheme should not be offset against a surplus in another.

The impossibility of inter-firm comparability

The standard, while bringing pension funding into the balance sheet and profit and loss account in a less volatile manner than was previously the case, does not facilitate inter-company comparability. It requires consistency within a company but, such is the choice available in its application, that it is less than likely that any two companies will adopt a similar approach. In addition, actuarial calculations are based on assumptions which will vary from company to company, and from actuary to actuary. Thus, two companies providing the same pension benefits to the same number and mix of employees, will tend to recognise very different pension charges and very different funding requirements.

While the greatest differences between the effects of the application of different approaches to pension funding recognition will tend to have arisen when SSAP 24 was first applied (due to the often large surpluses and deficits which were identified at that time), treatment differences of a lower magnitude will be a constant feature when inter-company comparisons are attempted, and it is unlikely that there will ever be any possibility of such comparisons being meaningful while the current version of the standard applies.

As an example of how great such a difference may be, consider a company which had an equity value at the start of 1988 of £200m; net profit for 1988, before pension adjustments, of £90m; a £100m surplus on its pension fund (identified at the end of 1987 and on which a five year contribution holiday had been declared, starting from the beginning of 1988); and a regular cost of £25m. When the standard was first introduced, companies were able to apply it immediately, or wait until the accounting period starting on or after 1st July 1988. If this company has a financial year end of 31st December, it could decide in December 1988 to do any one of at least three things: (1) defer application of SSAP 24 until the following accounting period; (2) apply SSAP 24 and spread the transitional difference over the (say) ten-year service lives of the employees; or (3) apply SSAP 24, and treat all of the difference as a prior period adjustment. (Obviously, if the first option were taken, there would still remain the option to adopt either of the other two in the following period.) The three options produce year end equity values for 1988 of £290m, £275m and £365m respectively:

	Option:	1	2	3
Net profit		90	90	90
less: Pension cost		-	25	25
		90	65	65
add: Pension surplus spread over 10 years		-	10	-
		90	75	65
Equity at start of year		200	200	200
add: Prior period adjustment		-	-	100
Equity at end of year		290	275	365

All three options produce different profit figures, equity valuations, and gearing ratios. These differences would eventually work their way out of the system by the end of the ten-year period of service life but, where pension fund surpluses can be relatively large in comparison to company equities, it is unfortunate that more prescriptive rules were not invoked by the standard so as to avoid the manipulation of the balance sheet that these alternatives made possible.

Another example of the standard's inability to standardise treatment concerns differences unamortised at the date of an actuarial valuation. Actuarial valuation usually follows a triennial pattern. Thus, whenever a surplus or deficit is being spread over expected service lives, it will be interrupted by two, three, or more actuarial valuations. When this occurs, there will usually be another surplus or deficit identified. This difference absorbs all earlier differences which have not yet been fully recognised. Consequently, the latest difference must be adjusted by the unrecognised proportion of the last difference spread, in order to determine the actual difference requiring additional adjustment. If, for example, three years earlier a surplus of £10m was found on a scheme with a standard contribution of £3m per annum; the surplus was being spread over ten years at £1m per year, resulting in annual charges of £2m instead of £3m; and in the current actuarial valuation a surplus of £4m was identified: there remains £7m outstanding from the original surplus, yet now there is only a £4m surplus. What should happen to the £3m surplus that has disappeared?

Two approaches can be adopted. In the first approach, the new surplus of £4m can first be subtracted from the amount outstanding from the previous valuation surplus (which comprises the old surplus + contributions made - the regular cost requirement in the period); the remainder is then subtracted from the old surplus less the amount of the regular cost requirement *not* charged to profit and loss; (where funding has matched the amounts charged to profit and loss, this will result in an answer equal to the new valuation surplus, otherwise it will be equal to the new surplus plus the balance sheet provision, or minus the balance sheet prepayment, brought forward); the result can then be spread over the average service life of ten years at £0.4m per year, leading to a charge of £2.6m per annum (= £26m total). In the second approach, the original spread of £1m of the surplus per annum could continue for the remaining seven years, with the intra valuation deficit of £3m spread over ten years (years 1-7 £2.3m per annum, years 8-10 £3.3m per annum = £26m total).

	Valuation ↓													
Approach 1:														
year	1	2	3	|4	5	6	7	8	9	10	11	12	13	4-13
cost	3.0	3.0	3.0	|3.0	3.0	3.0	3.0	3.0	3.0	3.0	3.0	3.0	3.0	30
less: surplus	1.0	1.0	1.0	|0.4	0.4	0.4	0.4	0.4	0.4	0.4	0.4	0.4	0.4	(4)
	2.0	2.0	2.0	|2.6	2.6	2.6	2.6	2.6	2.6	2.6	2.6	2.6	2.6	26

Approach 2:														
year	1	2	3	|4	5	6	7	8	9	10	11	12	13	4-13
cost	3.0	3.0	3.0	|3.0	3.0	3.0	3.0	3.0	3.0	3.0	3.0	3.0	3.0	30
less: surplus	1.0	1.0	1.0	|1.0	1.0	1.0	1.0	1.0	1.0	1.0	-	-	-	(7)
plus: deficit	-	-	-	|0.3	0.3	0.3	0.3	0.3	0.3	0.3	0.3	0.3	0.3	3
	2.0	2.0	2.0	|2.3	2.3	2.3	2.3	2.3	2.3	2.3	3.3	3.3	3.3	26

Of the two approaches, the first is easier to compute: it comprises the new surplus/deficit + any balance sheet balance (which will have arisen if there are differences in the timing of fund contributions and profit and loss charges), but it does mean that differences are unlikely to ever be fully amortised. The second approach is probably more directly in line with what the standard requires (i.e. that variations should be spread over the service lives of those employees in service when the variation is identified), but it does mean that amounts are being recognised which have subsequently proved to be non-existent. In addition, it could be argued that the first approach also complies with the standard's requirement that the amount recognised now should be applied to the service lives of current employees in the scheme.

There is considerable room for manoeuvre in how any variation from regular cost should be treated and such is the range of possible approaches that it is far from being simply a routine process of spreading the variance over the service lives of the current workforce. For example, the amount identified may or may not be adjusted to account for inflation/interest; the spreading could be done using any one of a number of methods including straight-line, sum of the digits (derived from the number of the current workforce expected to be in service at the end of each of the years), and a level percentage of pensionable payroll; and the service life used could be derived from the average service life of the workforce, or the specific service life of each employee, or the combination of the average service lives of groups of employees. The number of permutations is endless.

Differences between amounts funded and charged, and deferred tax

Before deciding how to spread the variation through the profit and loss account, a decision must be taken on how to arrange the funding of the scheme while the variation is being spread. Is there to be a contribution holiday, partial holiday, a mixture of the two, or a contribution excess? This will usually be decided according to the recommendations of the actuary. Unfortunately, while there may be no bookkeeping reason for the amount contributed and the amount charged to profit and loss not matching, the actuarial and accounting requirements will often dictate that they are different. Care must be taken to ensure that an inappropriate assumption is not made to the effect that the funding pattern is a suitable basis for the accounting charge. As paragraph 16 states: 'in order to comply with this statement, it will be necessary to consider whether the funding plan provides a satisfactory basis for allocating the pension cost to particular accounting periods'. When actual payments made exceed the cumulative pension cost recognised in the profit and loss account, the excess should be shown as a prepayment. Where the opposite occurs, it should be shown as a net pension provision. As the balance shown represents a cumulative timing difference, the choice that is made regarding funding and the profit and loss charge can have a significant effect upon the deferred tax position.

Deferred tax is referred to in paragraph 44 of the standard. The impact of SSAP 24 upon the calculation of deferred tax is far greater than that one paragraph would suggest. Tax relief is given for payments to pension funds and, especially where there is spreading of a surplus or a deficit involving contribution holidays/excess payments, the difference between the profit and loss charge and the actual funding contribution may be great. Consequently, a large deferred tax liability may arise when a deficit is being erased, and a large deferred tax asset when a surplus is being reduced. These differences will ultimately reverse and consequently should be accounted for under SSAP 15 (*Accounting for deferred tax* - chapter 13) when evaluating the deferred tax position.

Conclusion

SSAP 24 has been described as a disclosure standard. It certainly emphasises the need for detailed disclosure (the nature of which needs to be known for exam purposes). However, it could be argued that it does not go far enough: for example, there is no requirement to disclose on what basis any variation is being eliminated. It could also be argued that some of the disclosure requirements are more likely to confuse than to clarify: for example, the requirement in paragraph 88(h) to disclose the actuarial method used.

The standard provides a framework within which pension costs are to be determined, but it is not a measurement standard. It would be most unlikely that two independent accountants using it as their sole guide to the accounting recognition of pension fund contributions, surpluses and deficits, would adopt identical accounting entries in respect of the same company's pension fund. For example, average service periods may or may not be used; discretionary increases may or may not be recognised in the actuarial assumptions; interest may or may not be provided on balance sheet balances; and there are many possible bases which can be adopted for spreading variations, etc. Even greater is the degree of flexibility given to the actuarial calculations: for example, actuarial valuation of assets may be done using whatever approach the actuary believes to be appropriate, so long as it complies with the general requirements of the standard; the actuarial method used may be one of several; and the assumptions made involve a high degree of personal judgement. It is interesting that SSAP 24 actually admits that there will be major differences in the contribution rates calculated resulting from the flexibility it allows in the choice of actuarial method and assumptions (paragraph 8). It is a pity that more was not done to limit those differences when the standard was drafted.

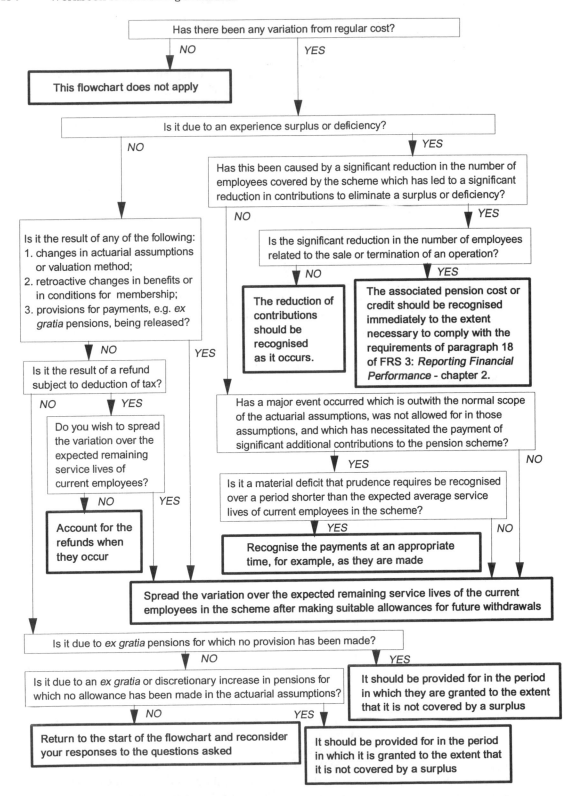

Short Questions

*ASSUME THAT MATERIALITY EXISTS IN **EVERY** CASE*

In contrast to the questions in the rest of this workbook, those on SSAP 24 are a mixture of short questions concerning disclosure requirements, treatment options, definitions, and others involving computation. Unless otherwise indicated, assume that the company involved maintains a funded defined benefit pension scheme. Also, there is no continuation from one question to another unless indicated and, unless instructed to do otherwise, each question should be considered in isolation from the rest.

In questions 1-10 you should indicate what disclosure, if any, is required.

1   The company operates a defined benefit pension scheme.

2   The latest actuarial valuation revealed a large funding deficiency.

3   At the end of the year a formal actuarial valuation was undertaken.

4   A company has a wholly owned foreign subsidiary. The subsidiary contributes to a defined benefit pension scheme which is governed by the regulations of the country in which it is based. These regulations are very different from those which are used in the United Kingdom. It is felt to be financially and realistically impractical to convert the subsidiary's obligation so as to incorporate it into the consolidated financial statements.

5   During the year, the company received a refund of surplus pension contributions subject to deduction of tax.

6   This is the first period for which SSAP 24 has been implemented.

7   The company operates a defined contribution pension scheme.

8   The company maintains two pension schemes, one for salaried staff and the other for manual staff. At the last actuarial revaluation a deficiency was found on the manual staff scheme, and a surplus was identified on the salaried staff scheme.

9   The company made contributions to the pension scheme during the year which were less than the profit and loss pension charge.

10   The profit and loss pension charge was 50% higher than the charge made in the previous period.

In questions 11-15 you should indicate what treatment(s) should be adopted.

11   For the first time since the company started its own pension scheme, an *ex gratia* pension was awarded during the year to a long serving employee who had never joined the company pension scheme. The company had not planned to make the award, and there are no current employees who are not members of the scheme.

12   The company made contributions of £500,000 to the pension scheme during the year. The profit and loss charge was £450,000.

13   During the year the company changed to an inflation proofed pension scheme. As a result, the level of the regular cost has doubled and special contributions amounting to 50% of the new regular cost will be required over the next ten years in order to take account of the deficiency that has arisen from the increased benefits being provided. There was no commitment by the company to provide inflation proofed pensions and the actuarial assumptions previously applied did not allow for their introduction. There was no surplus on the fund at the start of the year.

14   During the year, the company made 30% of the employees redundant. As a result, there has been a significant fall in the level of contributions to be made while the funding surplus which resulted is eliminated.

15   During the year, the company received a refund of £2m surplus pension contributions subject to deduction of tax.

In questions 16-21 you should define the terms listed.

16   What is the *employer's obligation* in relation to a defined contribution pension scheme?

17   What is the *level of funding*?

18   What is the difference in the assumptions used by *accrued benefit* methods and *prospective benefit* methods in order to project a stable contribution rate?

19   What is meant by the *regular cost* of defined benefit pension schemes?

20   What is the difference between an *ex gratia* pension and an *ex gratia* increase?

21   What is the *average remaining service life*?

Questions 22-25 are computational. They relate to an electronic engineering company with current turnover in excess of £100m and net pre-tax profits of approximately 30% of turnover. It has performed consistently over the last five years, experiencing profit growth of between 5 and 7% per annum.

22   In the actuarial valuation at 31st December Year 0, the company pension scheme showed a surplus of £22m. It was recommended by the actuary that this be eliminated by taking a contribution holiday in Years 1 and 2 and then paying contributions of £1m per annum for eight years. From that point onwards the standard contribution would be £3m per annum. The average remaining service life of employees in the scheme at 31st December Year 0 was ten years. What should the annual charge to profit and loss be for years 1 to 10; and what is the balance sheet amount in respect of the pension contributions and charges for years 1 to 10?

23   In the actuarial valuation at 31st December Year 0, the company pension scheme showed a surplus of £22m. Of that surplus, £8m arose because of the decision to sell a business segment and is treated as an exceptional item in Year 1. It was recommended by the actuary that the surplus be eliminated by taking a contribution holiday in Years 1 and 2 and then paying contributions of £1m per annum for eight years. From that point onwards the standard contribution would be £3m per annum. The average remaining service life of employees in the scheme at 31st December Year 0 was ten years. What should the annual charge to profit and loss be for years 1 to 10; and what is the balance sheet amount in respect of the pension contributions and charges for years 1 to 10?

24   Assume the situation and the treatment adopted in question 22. In year 3, an actuarial revaluation took place which identified a surplus of £13m. It was recommended by the actuary that the surplus be eliminated by taking a contribution holiday in Year 4, and then paying contributions of £1.5m per annum for two years, followed by seven years at £2m. From that point onwards the standard contribution would be £3m per annum. Assuming that the original accounting treatment of the elimination of the Year 0 surplus is to continue, and that the intra valuation deficit is to be treated separately, what should the annual charge to profit and loss be for years 4 to 13; and what is the balance sheet amount in respect of the pension contributions and charges for years 4 to 13?

25   Using the information from question 24, if the decision was taken to combine the old surplus with the intra valuation deficit and spread the combined figure evenly over years 4 to 13, what should the annual charge to profit and loss be for years 4 to 13; and what is the balance sheet amount in respect of the pension contributions and charges for years 4 to 13?

Additional Questions

*ASSUME THAT MATERIALITY EXISTS IN **EVERY** CASE*

In questions 26-32 you should indicate what disclosure, if any, is required.

26   The company operates a funded pension scheme.

27   The company's pension cost is assessed in accordance with the advice of the finance director, who is a qualified actuary.

28   Other than disclosing its nature, what other disclosures should be made in respect of a defined contribution scheme?

29   The actuary has determined that the actuarial method adopted in the previous valuation should be changed and has undertaken the current valuation using a different method.

30   A surplus arising from a reduction in the number of employees, which was identified at the last actuarial valuation, has been applied to reduce employees' contributions.

31   During the year, the company wound-up its pension scheme and distributed all benefits due to the schemes members and pension recipients.

32   During the year, the company contributed £200,000 to a private health scheme on behalf of retired ex-employees.

In questions 33-37 you should indicate what treatment(s) should be adopted.

33   The company maintains two pension schemes, one for salaried staff and the other for manual staff. At the actuarial review a surplus of £2.5m was identified on the salaried staff scheme, and a deficit of £1m was found on the manual staff scheme.

34   A company operates an unfunded pension scheme. On what basis should the balance sheet provision be calculated and adjusted?

35   During the year, the company wound-up its pension scheme and distributed all benefits due to the schemes members and pension recipients. What measure of cost would be appropriate under SSAP 24?

36   Over the last few years, the company had built up a provision for an increase in the general level of pensions. At the latest actuarial valuation, a large surplus was identified and it is to be used to provide the increase for which the provision had been created.

37   The company pension fund manager ignored the advice of the actuary and invested £500,000 in a company that the actuary considered to be too great an investment risk for the pension fund. Three months later the company went into liquidation and all the investment was lost. Upon discovering the existence of the investment, the actuary had informed the company that the investment was in breach of normal investment rules. As a result, the pension fund manager was sacked; but it proved too late to recover any of the sum invested. The deficiency is being eliminated by increased contributions over four years.

In questions 38-42 you should define the terms listed.

38   What is the difference between a *funded* scheme and an *unfunded* scheme?

39   What is a *hybrid scheme*?

40   What is the purpose of a *current funding level valuation*?

41   What is the 'pension cost' of defined contribution pension schemes?

42   What is the difference between a *defined benefit* scheme and a *defined contribution* scheme?

43   What four items can give rise to variations from the regular cost of defined benefit pension schemes?

44   What two factors can have a major impact upon the contribution rate calculated at each valuation for a defined benefit pension scheme?

Question 45 relates to a high technology engineering company with current turnover in excess of £110m and net pre-tax profits of approximately 30% of turnover. It has performed consistently over the last five years, experiencing profit growth of between 5 and 7% per annum.

45   In the actuarial valuation at 31st December Year 0, the company pension scheme showed a surplus of £22m. Of that surplus, £8m was due to savings arising from a redundancy programme included in a major reorganisation of the company in the period since the previous revaluation. It was recommended by the actuary that the surplus be eliminated by taking a contribution holiday in Years 1 and 2 and then paying contributions of £1m per annum for eight years. From that point onwards the standard contribution would be £3m per annum. The average remaining service life of employees in the scheme at 31st December Year 0 was ten years. The £8m redundancy surplus is included in the funding adjustments of the first three years. What should the annual charge to profit and loss be for years 1 to 10; and what is the balance sheet amount in respect of the pension contributions and charges for years 1 to 10?

12   Presentation Standards

Overview

This chapter deals with six accounting standards - SSAP 2 (Disclosure of accounting policies); SSAP 3 (Earnings per share); FRS 1 (Cash flow statements); FRS 4 (Capital Instruments); FRS 5 (Reporting the substance of transactions); and SSAP 25 (Segmental reporting), and two UITFs - UITF 7 (True and fair view override disclosures) and UITF 10 (Disclosure of directors' share options).

SSAP 2:   Disclosure of Accounting Policies

Summary of the accounting treatment requirements

The purpose of this standard is to assist in the understanding and interpretation of financial statements by promoting improvement in the quality of the information disclosed. In order to achieve this, it requires disclosure of all accounting policies adopted which are significant for the purpose of giving a true and fair view.

It is assumed that all financial statements are prepared according to the four *fundamental accounting concepts* of 'going concern', 'accruals', 'consistency', and 'prudence'. If not, an explanation should be given.

Accounting bases are the methods which have been developed for expressing or applying fundamental accounting concepts. More than one recognised accounting basis may exist for dealing with a particular item. (For example, stock may be valued using one of many accounting bases: FIFO; LIFO; base stock; replacement cost; net realisable value; the lower of cost and net realisable value; the lower of cost, net realisable value and replacement cost; etc.) *Accounting policies* are those accounting bases selected as being most appropriate for the purpose of preparing financial statements.

Problems of interpretation and grey areas

The following items are discussed: the reasons for the introduction of SSAP 2; accounting concepts, policies, and bases; the separate determination concept; the conflict with SSAP 12 regarding a change in depreciation method; the substance over form concept; and accruals -v- prudence. Finally, there is a brief conclusion.

The reasons for the introduction of SSAP 2

Of all the standards, this has the greatest influence, since it lays the foundations upon which all financial statements should be based. It could be said that there is little about it which is either contentious or problematic, that controversy only arises when its content is compared to that of other standards and the Companies Act 1985, and that, even then, there is very little reason for concern over its application. However, this is more the result of what it omits than what it contains. It is very much a foundation statement upon which other standards were intended to be built, consisting of definitions of the broad concepts upon which financial statements should be based, along with guidance on what to do if these concepts are not followed.

The standard was introduced to give users of financial statements an awareness of the main assumptions on which they were based, thereby assisting them in their assessment of the financial performance and position shown. It does so by requiring that all material accounting policies adopted be disclosed.

There are often occasions when the decision on how to include an item in the financial statements is straightforward. However, there is no class of item in the financial statements which will not at some time or another require judgement: this is the concern of SSAP 2. To quote from paragraph 12: 'the intention and spirit of this statement are that management should identify those items ... which are judged material or critical for the purpose of determining and fully appreciating the company's profit and loss and its financial position, and should make clear the accounting policies followed for dealing with them.'

Accounting concepts, policies, and bases

The standard distinguishes between 'fundamental accounting concepts' (broad basic assumptions which underlie the financial statements); 'accounting bases' (methods developed to express or apply fundamental accounting concepts to financial transactions and items); and 'accounting policies' (those accounting bases selected as being best suited to present a true and fair view). Clearly, it is a three stage process: the concepts provide the conditions which prevail when the bases are developed, the available bases are then considered, and a judgement is made of those most appropriate.

A number of areas for which different accounting bases are recognised are listed in paragraph 13 of the standard. Since SSAP 2 was issued in 1971, most of these areas have been dealt with in standards of their own (for example, depreciation, stocks, deferred tax, and foreign currency conversion). This does not mean that there is no longer a need to consider SSAP 2 when determining how to incorporate these items in the financial statements. Indeed, all these subsequent standards assume that SSAP 2 will be applied, and it must be considered concurrently with the standard developed for the specific area under review.

The separate determination concept

Schedule 4, paragraphs 10-14 of the Companies Act 1985, reveals that in addition to the four fundamental accounting concepts (going concern, accruals, consistency, and prudence), a fifth concept should be applied when financial statements are being constructed - that of 'separate determination'. The Act introduces this concept as follows: 'in determining the aggregate amount of any item the amount of each individual asset or liability that falls to be taken into account shall be determined separately.' In other words, each item must be evaluated separately before being included in the total for its class. Failure to comply with this concept would not constitute failure to apply SSAP 2 (though it could be argued that it would be contrary to its spirit), but would constitute failure to comply with the Companies Act; and details of the departure would require to be disclosed and explained, along with its effect.

The conflict with SSAP 12 regarding a change in depreciation method

Some subsequently issued standards have added to and/or qualified the requirements of SSAP 2. SSAP 12 (*Accounting for depreciation* - chapter 4), states that 'a change from one method of providing depreciation to another ... does not constitute a change of accounting policy' (paragraph

21). This completely contradicts SSAP 2 which identifies methods of depreciation as accounting bases, and the choice of accounting basis as an accounting policy. Thus, a change in the depreciation method would constitute a change in accounting policy, which should be treated as a prior period adjustment under FRS 3 (*Reporting financial performance* - chapter 2). It may be that the ASC felt that application of the definition as given in SSAP 2 would lead to too many prior period adjustments, but it is unfortunate that the exclusion of changes in depreciation methods from the remit of FRS 3 resulted in an undermining of the definition of accounting policies contained in SSAP 2. It might be better to treat this as a unique exception to the definition given in SSAP 2, while continuing to use the SSAP 2 definition of an accounting policy in all other circumstances.

Consideration of SSAP 12 also highlights another issue: SSAP 2 is very undemanding when any of the accounting concepts are not observed. It only requires that inconsistent treatment be disclosed - a change in depreciation method, or any other accounting base, would presumably fall into that category - but it does not require an explanation beyond a statement of the facts; nor does it require that the effect be quantified. SSAP 12 rectified this, but only for changes in depreciation method, by requiring disclosure of the effects of the change in method and the reasons for it. However, all changes in accounting policy could be said to be examples of failure to observe the consistency concept, and any such non-observance is now addressed in two places: paragraph 8 of the explanatory forward to the Statements of Standard Accounting Practice, which was issued in 1986; and schedule 4, paragraphs 15 and 36A of the Companies Act 1985, both of which require disclosure details, reasons, and the resulting effects of non-compliance with the requirements of any standard.

The substance over form concept

Others have commented elsewhere, for example, in the second edition of *'UK GAAP'* (Longman, 1990, p. 74), that SSAP 21 (*Accounting for leases and hire purchase contracts* - chapter 10) introduced a sixth fundamental accounting concept - that of 'substance over form': items should be incorporated in the financial statements in accordance with their economic and financial substance, not simply according to their legal form. FRS 5 (*Reporting the substance of transactions*, later in this chapter) was issued in 1994 in order to clarify this issue and the concept must now be applied generally, not just in the context of leases. Whether the issue of FRS 5 has resulted in a 'new' accounting concept in addition to those contained in SSAP 2 is irrelevant. A concept does not need to be mentioned specifically in SSAP 2 for it to exist. In fact, SSAP 2 states that 'an exhaustive theoretical approach would ... include ... many more ... than the four fundamental concepts referred to' (footnote to paragraph 2). SSAP 2 was not intended to be exhaustive. Thus, there are more than four fundamental accounting concepts, of which one (separate determination) is required by the Companies Act, and another (substance over form) is required by FRS 5 in order to provide a true and fair view. The point is that whatever fundamental accounting concepts are applied, they require the identification of appropriate accounting bases to be implemented as accounting policies. All such accounting policies must be disclosed, so that it is possible to tell if a concept has been applied. (This would arise even where the application of a concept was specifically required by a standard, compliance with which would automatically indicate observance of the concept it prescribes: such an example is FRS 5.)

Accruals -v- prudence

Two of the fundamental accounting concepts, accruals and prudence, can be contradictory. In such a case, prudence has precedence (paragraph 14).

Conclusion

Overall, this standard presents few problems. It could be improved by being brought up-to-date with the inclusion of the two additional concepts discussed above (separate determination and substance over form), and by including those legal and terminological changes (for example, the term 'financial statements') which have taken place since its issue in 1971. For consistency, the disclosure requirements for non-observance of the fundamental accounting concepts should be brought into line with those of the explanatory forward to the Statements of Standard Accounting Practice (which are slightly more demanding than those of the Companies Act). Finally, a revised version would be an ideal vehicle for an explanation of 'materiality', something which is sadly missing in the standards issued so far. It augurs well that chapter 2 of the ASB's *Statement of Principles* exposure draft (which, in its final form, shall replace SSAP 2) deals with many of these issues.

SSAP 3:   Earnings per Share

Summary of the accounting treatment requirements

Although it is SSAP 3 which is primarily concerned with earnings per share (EPS), FRS 3 (*Reporting financial performance* - chapter 2) amended the definition contained in SSAP 3 to 'the profit in pence attributable to each equity share, based on the profit (or in the case of a group the consolidated profit) of the period after tax, minority interests and extraordinary items and after deducting preference dividends and other appropriations in respect of preference shares, divided by the number of equity shares in issue and ranking for dividend in respect of the period.' At the same time, FRS 3 stated that EPS could be reported using another level of profit provided that it received no greater prominence than the required calculation, that a reconciliation between the two bases of calculation was provided and that the reasons for providing the alternative figure were explained. The reconciliation and explanation must be located beside the EPS disclosure or they must be referenced at that point. (Paragraph 25, FRS 3)

EPS must be calculated and disclosed on the face of the profit and loss account on the *net* basis, for both the current and previous periods. Where materially different, the *nil* basis EPS should also be shown.

The difference between the two bases is that under the *net* basis, the charge for taxation used in determining earnings includes any irrecoverable advanced corporation tax (ACT); under the *nil* basis it is excluded, except in so far as it arises in respect of preference dividends - the *nil* basis seeks to represent what the earnings would be if no distribution were made to the equity shareholders.

Where a company has at the balance sheet date granted options or issued warrants to subscribe for equity shares of the company; or has issued debentures, loan stock, or preference shares convertible into equity shares of the company; or has already issued equity shares which will not rank for dividends until a later date, future earnings per share may be diluted. In any of these circumstances, the fully diluted earnings per share (i.e. EPS based on the future equity ranking for dividend) must also be disclosed on the face of the profit and loss account, unless the dilution amounts to less than 5% of the basic EPS or the basic EPS is negative.

The basis of calculation of the basic EPS figure(s) must be disclosed, either in the profit and loss account or in a note. In particular, the amount of the earnings and the number of equity shares used in the calculation should be shown. In respect of the fully diluted EPS, the basis of calculation must be shown.

Problems of interpretation and grey areas

The following items are discussed: the reasons for the introduction of SSAP 3; the *net* and *nil* bases and the treatment of differences between them; inconsistencies in the disclosure requirements of *nil* basis and fully diluted earnings per share; the 5% materiality rule; and susceptibility to manipulation and distortion, and the resulting need for revision of the basis of calculation which resulted in the change in the definition of EPS contained in FRS 3.

The reasons for the introduction of SSAP 3

This standard is intended to provide a degree of comparability by regulating the way that earnings per share are calculated. EPS is a key component in the computation of the price/earnings (p/e) ratio, and it was felt that some regulation was required if consideration of this ratio was to be meaningful.

Its application is initially simple:

$$\frac{\text{earnings after tax, minority interests and extraordinary items available for equity shareholders}}{\text{the number of equity shares in issue and ranking for dividend in the period}}$$

However, complications arise when any changes in the capital structure occur during the year, or are liable to occur in the foreseeable future. The flowchart on pages 163 and 164, and the short questions on pages 171, and 174 to 176 (which deal with situations that may arise affecting the calculation of EPS), should be referred to and used as a guide to the appropriate treatment to adopt.

The *net* and *nil* bases and the treatment of differences between them

One of the issues arising from this standard concerns the option that exists to calculate EPS on either the *net* or *nil* basis. To be precise, it is not so much an option to use either, as a requirement to calculate them both, disclose the *net* basis result, but only add the disclosure of the *nil* basis result if there is a material difference between them. Under the current tax system, there will be a difference between these two figures only when a company has irrecoverable ACT. (Paragraph 6 of the standard also refers to 'overseas tax unrelieved because dividend payments restrict the double tax credit available'. However, as a result of changes in tax law since the standard was introduced, this is no longer the case.) Consequently, such a difference will not be very common. Nevertheless, it may arise, and if it does and it is a material difference, then both the *net* and *nil* results must be disclosed on the face of the profit and loss account. Whether both results, or only the *net* result, are disclosed, equivalent figures for the previous period must also be shown.

There is no guidance as to what should be done if there was a material difference in the previous year, but not in the current one. As the *nil* basis EPS is required to be disclosed only when it is materially different from the *net* basis EPS, it would be appropriate to disclose both the previous year's EPS figures, but only the *net* basis figure for the current year. On the same premise, if there is a material difference between the current year figures, but not between those of the previous year, only the *net* basis EPS should be included in respect of the previous year.

Inconsistencies in the disclosure requirements of *nil* basis and fully diluted earnings per share

There are inconsistencies between the disclosure treatment of the *nil* basis EPS and the fully diluted EPS. Firstly, the former must be disclosed *with* the *net* basis EPS, and the latter must be disclosed *as prominently as* the basic EPS (paragraph 16). Secondly, while there is no requirement to exclude the previous year's *nil* basis EPS, the previous year's fully diluted EPS should not be shown unless the assumptions on which it was based still apply (paragraph 16). The first of these inconsistencies would seem to be relatively insignificant; the second has been described as being in conflict with the purpose of the inclusion of comparatives in financial statements. This is a point of view which can be disputed: the fully diluted EPS represents the potential EPS if obligations entered into result in more shares being issued. It is of interest at the period end when it is calculated. If circumstances change it is no longer of importance. Time has moved on and a new set of circumstances exist. Unlike trends in items such as debtors, creditors, net assets, and basic EPS, it is not indicative of efficiency, profitability, or performance, and comparison with a figure in previous years, which is based on different assumptions, can do little to enhance the true and fair view. It could be argued that this non-disclosure requirement is founded on a realistic assessment of the value of providing such information: if there is no value in it, it is better not to include it rather than cause the users of the accounts to spend time considering why it has been included. If it is felt that a true and fair view would be enhanced by revealing the differences in obligations that could dilute the EPS compared to those that existed at the previous year end, the details could be included in the notes to the accounts.

As the *nil* basis EPS is disclosed only if it is materially different from the *net* basis figure, the fully diluted EPS should be calculated using the *net* basis unless the *nil* basis is also disclosed. Should this occur, the fully diluted EPS calculated on the *nil* basis should also be disclosed. Accordingly, four different EPS figures could appear on the face of the same profit and loss account.

The 5% materiality rule

Interestingly, paragraph 16 refers to a 5% level of dilution of EPS as being indicative of materiality, and thereby requiring the disclosure of the diluted EPS. The wording ('for this purpose') is such as to make it difficult to impose upon other situations where materiality is in doubt. Had it been less restrictive, the application of many standards could have been substantially different from what is currently the case.

Susceptibility to manipulation and distortion, and the resulting need for revision of the basis of calculation which resulted in the change in the definition of EPS contained in FRS 3

Apart from the general need to know the disclosure requirements of the standard, it is necessary to know how to calculate EPS, under both the *net* and *nil* bases, for each of the possible scenarios mentioned in the standard. It is also necessary to know how to calculate fully diluted EPS, under the same circumstances, and to know when not to disclose the fully diluted EPS (including the fact that it should not be disclosed when the basic EPS is negative - appendix 1, section 24).

Once the mechanics have been mastered, there is little that is difficult in the application of this standard. Prior to the issue of FRS 3 in October 1992, the major problems concerned how the EPS figure produced was subject to manipulation and distortion well in excess of that which would normally be considered acceptable if it was to be used for the purpose originally intended when the standard was draughted. Two factors gave rise to this situation - SSAP 6 and SSAP 15. Under the SSAP 3 rules, extraordinary items were excluded from the calculation of EPS. Consequently, treating an item as extraordinary, rather than exceptional, resulted in a higher EPS, and the opposite treatment produced a lower EPS. While SSAP 6 (*Extraordinary items and prior year adjustments*) sought to prevent such manipulation, it was not very successful at doing so. The determination of deferred tax, as regulated by SSAP 15 (*Accounting for deferred tax* - chapter 13), is highly subjective. One company can make a deferred tax provision many times greater (or lower) than another similarly placed company, resulting in two very different EPS figures on the basis of broadly similar operating results.

Thus the situation was less than ideal. If the original premise upon which SSAP 3 was issued still held, there was a pressing need to amend the basis upon which EPS was calculated - a basis that was devised prior to the introduction of both SSAP 6 and SSAP 15, and which had certainly fallen victim to their imprecision. With the issue of FRS 3, one of the problems was removed: EPS is now calculated *after* extraordinary items. However, the SSAP 15 problem remains. And, in addition, EPS comparability will be compromised whenever an extraordinary item *is* recognised. Extraordinary items are, by definition, 'material items possessing a high degree of abnormality which arise from events or transactions that fall *outside the ordinary activities* of the reporting entity and which are *not expected to recur*.' (Paragraph 6, FRS 3, italics added.) FRS 3 changed the definition of extraordinary items so significantly from that contained in SSAP 6 that it would now be virtually impossible to manipulate EPS in the way that was possible under SSAP 6. As a result, it may have been more appropriate to have continued to exclude extraordinary items (as amended by FRS 3) from the EPS calculation, thereby avoiding loss of EPS comparability whenever one was recognised.

FRS 1: Cash Flow Statements

Summary of the accounting treatment requirements

A cash flow statement should be included as a primary statement within the financial statements.

The objective of FRS 1 is to require entities to report their cash generation and absorption for a period on a standard basis and, by so doing, facilitate comparison of the cash flow performance of different entities (paragraph 1). For this reason, the statement should show the flows of cash and cash equivalents for the period under the headings: operating activities; returns on investments and servicing of finance; taxation; investing activities; and financing. The headings should be in that order and the statement should include a total for each heading and a total of the net cash inflow or outflow before financing (paragraph 12).

The individual categories of cash flows under the standard headings (which are specified in paragraphs 15 to 30 of the standard) should be disclosed (except where it would not be a fair representation of the activities of the reporting entity to do so - in such cases, an appropriate alternative treatment should be used). The cash flow classifications may be subdivided to give a fuller description of the activities of the reporting entity or to provide segmental information.

Where a cash flow is not specified in the categories set out in paragraphs 15 to 30 of FRS 1, the most appropriate heading should be used (paragraph 14).

Operating cash flows may be shown on either a *net* (i.e. based on the *indirect* method) or a *gross* (i.e. based on the *direct* method) basis. The notes to the statement must include a reconciliation between the operating profit reported in the profit and loss account and the net cash flow from operating activities. The reconciliation (which will be the same irrespective of the basis adopted) should disclose separately the movements in stocks, debtors and creditors related to operating activities and other differences between cash flows and profits (paragraph 17).

The notes should also contain reconciliations to appropriate figures in the opening and closing balance sheets - one for the movements in cash and cash equivalents; the other for the items shown within the financing section of the cash flow statement. They should disclose separately in each case the movements resulting from cash flows, differences arising from changes in foreign currency exchange rates (those relating to the retranslation of any opening balances of cash and cash equivalents and financing items and those resulting from the translation of the cash flows of foreign entities at exchange rates other than the year end rate) and other movements. Where several balance sheet amounts or parts thereof have to be combined to permit a reconciliation, sufficient detail should be shown to enable the movements to be understood. (Paragraph 44)

Comparative figures should be given for all items in the cash flow statement and all notes required by FRS 1 (paragraph 45). The only exception is that no comparatives are required for any note dealing with the material effects on amounts reported under each of the standard headings reflecting the cash flows of a subsidiary undertaking acquired or disposed of in the period (paragraph 42).

Problems of interpretation and grey areas

The following items are discussed: the *three month* rule; the overdraft anomaly; the wholly owned subsidiary exemption; the treatment of tax items; the treatment of capitalised interest; material non-cash transactions; the treatment of extraordinary and exceptional item-related cash flows; foreign currency cash flows; hedging transactions; deferred development expenditure; and small company exemption.

The *three month* rule

The cash flow statement reports cash flow. *Cash flow* is defined in paragraph 4 as 'an increase or decrease in an amount of *cash* or *cash equivalent* resulting from a transaction'. Anything that falls outside this definition is not a cash flow and should not appear in the statement (though it could appear in the notes). Paragraphs 2 and 3 define the two items which comprise cash flow. *Cash* comprises cash in hand and deposits repayable on demand with any bank or other financial institution, including cash in hand and deposits denominated in foreign currency. *Cash equivalents* are short-term, highly liquid investments which are *readily convertible* into *known amounts* of cash *without notice* and which were *within three months of maturity when acquired* (the *three month* rule); less advances from banks repayable within three months from the date of the advance. Cash equivalents include investments and advances denominated in foreign currencies provided that they fulfill the above criteria. Paragraph 53 extends this definition of *cash equivalents* to include a requirement that there is no significant risk of changes in value owing to changes in interest rates - i.e. if a change in interest rates could have a significant effect on the realisable value of an amount invested, it will not be possible to state that it represents a *known amount* of cash, and it should not, therefore, be included in *cash equivalents*.

The *three month* rule was established because the ASB believed it would minimise interest rate risk (paragraph 54). However, foreign exchange risk could, similarly, significantly affect the value of an item and it could be argued that even a three month period is too long in this respect. For example, between 8th September and 2nd November 1992, the £:US$ exchange rate fell by about 25% from £1:US$2 to £1:US$1.53. Nevertheless, it is the longer-term pattern of exchange rate movements which should be considered and it is unlikely that there would be any need to exclude an item denoted in US$ dollars on the basis of exchange rate risk. In contrast, an item denoted in a relatively unstable currency, like the Brazilian cruzado, would be unlikely to fulfill the criteria for inclusion in *cash equivalents*.

The *three month* rule has met with resounding opposition from industry. It has been said that it not only distorts results and confuses users, but that it is also at odds with the view that corporate treasury managers take on what should go into a cash flow statement. Quite apart from the general lack of consensus on the length of period to take, three months can comprise 89, 90, 91 or 92 days; why should whether or not a 90 day money market investment is treated as *cash equivalent* depend upon the number of days in each of the calendar months involved? (For example, a 90 day investment made on 26th January 1998 would mature on 26 April 1998, i.e. within three months. Yet, a similar investment made on 26th February 1998 would mature on 27th May 1998, which is outwith the three month period.) However, if consistency between the cash flow statements of entities is to be achieved, the basis of recognition of the items included needs to be consistently applied by all entities. Consequently, until such time as the *three month* rule is amended, it should be adopted and, if entities wish to clarify their position, they may include an explanatory note to the cash flow statement presenting the 'true' picture, as they see it.

The overdraft anomaly

Although the definition of *cash equivalents* in paragraph 3 of the standard would exclude overdrafts, paragraph 53 makes it clear that they are to be included within that category.

The wholly owned subsidiary exemption

The ASB believes that a cash flow statement is not meaningful in relation to wholly owned subsidiary undertakings (paragraph 60). As a result, wholly owned subsidiary undertakings whose parent is established under the law of a European Community member state are not required to include a cash flow statement providing that the parent publishes consolidated financial statements in English which include the subsidiary undertaking and a consolidated cash flow statement dealing with the cash flows of the group which provides sufficient information to derive the totals required to be shown under each of the standard FRS 1 headings (paragraph 8 (c)). However, while this appears relatively straightforward, when the parent is not the ultimate holding company an inconsistency in treatment may arise, leading to a wholly owned subsidiary being required to produce a cash flow statement *despite the ASB's stated view that it is not meaningful to do so*. For example, consider a group comprising a holding company (*Pae Ltd*), its 80% subsidiary (*Mae Ltd*), and *Mae Ltd's* 100% subsidiary *Filho Ltd*. *Mae Ltd* may apply for CA 85 s228 exemption from preparing its own group accounts. It would then only produce company financial statements, including a company cash flow statement. Consequently, as its parent had not produced a consolidated cash flow statement, *Filho Ltd*, the 100% subsidiary, would not be exempt from producing a cash flow statement. While it could be argued that this is merely ensuring the provision of the information concerning *Filho Ltd* which would have been found in a consolidated cash flow statement relating to *Mae Ltd*, this is in conflict with the ASB's stated view on the meaningfulness of such statements.

The treatment of tax items

Intuitively, it might be expected that all tax cash flows would be entered into the *taxation* section of the cash flow statement. However, only payments to and from tax authorities in respect of the entity's revenue and capital profits are included under this heading. Generally, the standard endeavours to relate all cash flows to the underlying transaction. Consequently, interest paid and received including any related tax is included under *returns on investment and servicing of finance*; while, in the same section, dividends paid and received are shown, but any related ACT is excluded and shown within the *taxation* section. Tax on interest is seen as relating to the original investment; whereas ACT is a tax on profits.

VAT is seen as relating to *operating activities*. Consequently, the net amount paid to or received from the tax authorities is included under that section. Generally, cash flows should be shown net of any attributable VAT or other sales tax. However, when the VAT or sales tax is irrecoverable by the reporting entity, it should be added to the originating transaction value and not distinguished from it within the cash flow statement (paragraph 34).

Tax cash flows excluding those on revenue and capital profits and VAT, or other sales tax, should be included under the same heading as the cash flow which gave rise to them; however, unlike irrecoverable VAT, there is no suggestion in FRS 1 that they be added to produce a composite value for the originating transaction (paragraph 35).

The treatment of capitalised interest

Interest paid should be included under *returns on investments and servicing of finance*, even when it has been capitalised. An approach which could cause reconciliation problems and require an adjustment in the reconciliation of operating profit to the net cash flow from *operating activities*.

Material non-cash transactions

Cash flow statements reflect transactions which result in an increase or decrease in *cash* or *cash equivalent*. Consequently, the initial purchase of a fixed asset under a finance lease will not be reflected in the statement; nor will the exchange of major assets. However, paragraph 43 states that 'material transactions not resulting in movements of cash or cash equivalents of the reporting entity should be disclosed in the notes to the cash flow statement if disclosure is necessary for an understanding of the underlying transactions'. Paragraph 83 states that this is required in order that a full picture of the alterations in financial position caused by the transactions for the period be given. While this explanation is difficult to reconcile with the objective given at the start of paragraph 1 of the statement (requiring entities to report on a standard basis their cash generation and cash absorption for a period), paragraph 1 goes on to state that 'the objective of the standard headings is to [...] facilitate comparison of the cash flow performance of different businesses'. Clearly, if one business has obtained fixed assets through finance leases and another by purchasing them for cash, the cash flows would not be directly comparable. Knowledge of such relevant non-cash transactions can, therefore, be seen to be consistent with the objectives of the standard.

The treatment of extraordinary and exceptional item-related cash flows

Cash flows relating to items classed as exceptional in the profit and loss account should be shown under the appropriate standard headings, according to their nature. They should be sufficiently disclosed in a note to the statement to allow a user to gain an understanding of the effect of the underlying item(s) on the entity's cash flows (paragraph 31). Extraordinary items should be similarly treated, *except that they should be shown separately within the headings and,* where the headings are inappropriate, the cash flow should be shown within a separate section of the statement (paragraphs 32 and 33). While this does not appear particularly complex, it is the nature of the underlying cash flows which determines where these exceptional and extraordinary items appear in the statement, not the nature of the items which gave rise to them. For example, the cash flows arising when an exceptional loss arose on the disposal of a building would be shown under *investing activities* even when the sale occurred because the company had to repay a long-term loan when the lender went into liquidation - a *financing* item.

Extraordinary items are, by definition, not part of the operating activities of an entity. It could be argued, therefore, that extraordinary items cash flows should not be shown in the *operating activities* section of the statement. However, FRS 1 requires that the nature of the item, rather than the nature of the event which gave rise to it should guide where the resultant cash flows appear in the statement. Consequently, it would be appropriate to include such cash flows under *operating activities* if that was the nature of the items involved.

In keeping with the approach of FRS 1 to taxes on revenue and capital profits, the tax flows related to extraordinary items should appear in the *taxation* section, rather than in the section where the extraordinary cash flow appears.

Foreign currency cash flows

The same basis is used to translate the cash flows of foreign entities in group cash flow statements as is used to translate their results for consolidation purposes (paragraph 36). If the closing rate method is being used (see SSAP 20 *Foreign currency translation* - chapter 9), and the profit and loss has been translated using the closing rate, only the exchange rate differences arising from retranslation of the opening balances of *cash* and *cash equivalents* and *financing items* to closing rate will have to be disclosed. However, if average rate has been used, not only will these disclosures have to be made, but the exchange rate difference on the retranslation of the net cash movement in the period from average to closing rate will also have to be disclosed. This may be difficult to derive if the cash flows are obtained from consolidated balance sheets rather than compiling them from the cash flow statements of the companies within the group.

In addition, while foreign exchange differences on intra-group transactions will be eliminated during profit and loss account and balance sheet consolidation, they will not necessarily be eliminated upon preparation of the group cash flow statement. For example, if a UK holding company borrowed £2.8m and then lent it to its US subsidiary when the exchange rate was £1:US$1.90 and the average exchange rate for the year was £1:US$1.40, the US subsidiary's cash flow statement would show a net cash inflow under *financing* of £3.8m [£2.8m translated at £1:US$1.90 = US$5.32m; US$5.32m @ £1:US$1.40 = £3.8m] and the same amount as an increase under *cash* and *cash equivalents*. In contrast, the UK parent would include a net cash inflow under *financing* of £2.8m and an outflow for the same amount under *investing activities*. Clearly, there is a residual exchange rate difference of £1m that requires to be dealt with in the statement. If the outflows which arose from the $5.32m that the subsidiary received are known, the residual would be allocated amongst the statement headings accordingly. However, if this is not known, there is no guidance in the standard as to how the residual should be treated. There is also no clearly logical place in the statement where it should be included. Given the number of entities which have intra-group cash flows with foreign subsidiaries, this is an issue which the ASB need to examine and, possibly, consider issuing a UITF announcement to clarify the position.

Hedging transactions

The statement requires that cash flows resulting from transactions undertaken to hedge another transaction be reported under the same standard heading as the transaction that is the subject of the hedge (paragraph 37). What should be done when one transaction is entered into in order to hedge a number of other transactions concurrently, and when they are not all included under the same section in the cash flow statement? In these circumstances, it would be appropriate to apportion the hedging transaction between the categories involved. However, what basis of apportionment should be used when one of the items hedged is a foreign equity investment? (See SSAP 20 *Foreign currency translation* - chapter 9.) Should the amount invested be used, or should the value that the investment is expected to achieve be used? Clearly a very different apportionment could arise depending not only on which approach were adopted, but also, where it was the preferred approach, upon the way in which the expected value was determined.

Deferred development expenditure

It could be argued that development expenditure is deferred in order to match it against the revenue arising from it (see SSAP 13 *Accounting for research and development* - chapter 5), and that it should therefore be included under *operating activities*. However, deferred development expenditure is classified as a fixed asset within the balance sheet and FRS 1 clearly requires that cash flows arising on the acquisition of a fixed asset should be included within *investing activities*.

Small company exemption

Companies entitled to the small companies exemption from filing accounts with the Registrar of Companies are not required to comply with FRS 1. Two reasons are given for this: the costs of producing the information are likely to be disproportionate to the benefits (paragraph 58) and small companies may elect to file abbreviated accounts which need not include a cash flow statement or an equivalent, and thus the information would not necessarily be within the public domain (paragraph 59). As from 16th November 1992, the Companies Act defines small companies as those which satisfy at least two of the following three conditions: their turnover does not exceed £2.8m, their balance sheet total does not exceed £1.4m, and they have no more than 50 employees. Given that the ASB believes that users of financial statements need information on liquidity, viability and financial adaptability, and that this is why they have produced FRS 1 (- see the summary at the start of the standard), it seems ironic that the majority of companies are exempt from producing such information. The cost benefit question is clearly going to be applicable in some cases. However, there can be few companies for whom information of this type would not be useful, particularly when the economy is in depression, company failures are rising and cash flow problems are frequently cited as the cause.

FRS   4:   Capital Instruments

Summary of the accounting treatment requirements

FRS 4 is concerned with accounting for capital instruments by the entities that issue them. A capital instrument is anything issued to raise finance. This includes shares, debentures, loans and debt instruments, and options and warrants that give the holder the right to subscribe for or obtain capital instruments. The term includes those issued by subsidiaries, except when held by another member of the group. Leases, warrants issued under employee share schemes, and equity shares issued as part of a business combination that is accounted for as a merger are not covered by FRS 4. Nor are investments in capital instruments issued by other entities.

The objective of FRS 4 is to ensure that financial statements provide a clear, coherent and consistent treatment of capital instruments, in particular in relation to:
- the classification of capital instruments;
- treating the costs associated with capital instruments in a manner consistent with their classification (and allocated to accounting periods on a fair basis over the period the instrument is in issue, in the case of redeemable instruments);

- ensuring that financial statements provide relevant information concerning the nature and amount of the entity's sources of finance and the associated costs, commitments and potential commitments. (Paragraph 1)

All capital instruments should be accounted for in the balance sheet within one of the following categories:

- shareholders' funds,
- liabilities, or, for consolidated financial statements,
- minority interests.

Shares and warrants should be reported as part of shareholders' funds. When issued, the net proceeds should be reported in the reconciliation of movements in shareholders' funds. When repurchased or redeemed, shareholders' funds should be reduced by the value of the consideration given. The balance sheet should show the total amount of shareholders' funds, analysed between the amount attributable to non-equity interests (i.e. the aggregate of amounts relating to all classes of non-equity shares and warrants for non-equity shares) and the amount attributable to equity interests (i.e. the difference between total shareholders' funds and the total amount attributable to non-equity interests). When the entitlement to dividends in respect of non-equity shares is calculated by reference to time, the dividends should be reported as appropriations of profit and accounted for on an accruals basis except when ultimate payment is remote (for example, when profits are insufficient to justify a dividend and the dividend rights are non-cumulative). Where the finance costs of non-equity shares are not equal to the dividends, the difference should be accounted for in the profit and loss account as an appropriation of profit. The finance costs for non-equity shares should be calculated on the same basis as the finance costs for debt. (Paragraphs 37-45)

All capital instruments other than shares should be classified as liabilities if they contain an obligation to transfer economic benefits. Otherwise, they should be reported within shareholders' funds. Convertible debt should be reported separately within liabilities from non-convertible debt. Debt should be analysed on the basis of its maturity distinguishing between debt with up to one year, one to five years, and five or more years to maturity, maturity being determined on the basis of the earliest date on which the lender can require payment. The finance cost of convertible debt should be calculated on the basis that the debt will never be converted. When converted, the amount recognised in shareholders' funds in respect of the shares issued should be the amount at which the liability for the debt is stated at the date of conversion, and therefore no gain or loss should be recognised. When issued, debt should be stated at the amount of the net proceeds and its finance cost should be allocated over the term of the debt at a constant rate on the carrying amount, charged in the profit and loss account (unless the entity is an investment company, in which case it may be included in the statement of total gains and losses to the extent that it relates to capital). The carrying amount of debt should be increased by the finance cost in respect of the reporting period and reduced by payments made in respect of the debt that period. Accrued finance costs may be included in accruals (rather than in the carrying amount of debt) to the extent that the period costs have accrued in one period and will be paid in cash in the next. However, in the event that the debt is repurchased or settled early, any such accrual should be included in the carrying amount of the debt for the purposes of calculating finance costs and gains and losses on the transaction; and any such gains or losses should be recognised in the profit and loss account in the period during which the transaction occurs. (Paragraphs 25-34)

Where subsidiaries have issued shares outside the group, those shares should be reported as minority interests, unless the group as a whole has an obligation to transfer economic benefit in connection with the shares. In such cases, they should be accounted for as liabilities within the consolidated financial statements. The amount of minority interests in the balance sheet should be split between the amounts attributable to equity and non-equity interests; the calculation of the amounts attributed to non-equity minority interests (and their associated finance costs) being calculated in the same way as those for non-equity shares. The finance costs associated with such interests should be included in minority interests in the profit and loss account. (Paragraphs 49-51)

Problems of interpretation and grey areas

The following items are discussed: the definition of non-equity shares; issuer call options; and warrants. There is also a brief conclusion.

The definition of non-equity shares

Paragraph 12 defines non-equity shares as shares possessing any of three characteristics. One of these concerns whether the rights of the shares to receive payment are for an amount that is limited and is not calculated by reference to assets, profits, or dividends on other classes of equity share. If this is the case, the share is classified as a non-equity share. Yet, despite appearing to qualify as an equity share because its holder receives a dividend that is not limited, participating preference shares are held to be non-equity shares in the Application Note to FRS 4.

The justification for this treatment, as given in the Application Note, is that as participating preference shares contain an entitlement to an amount that is fixed and has priority over the other classes of shares, they are non-equity shares. The relevant wording of the clause in the standard to which this relates is that a share is a non-equity share if *any of the rights of the shares to receive payments ... are for a limited amount* (paragraph 12a). Clearly, given the categorisation of participating preference shares as non-equity, considerable emphasis is intended for the word 'any'. It is unfortunate that the definition was not more carefully worded so as to avoid the ambiguity in the application of its literal meaning.

Issuer call options

Paragraph 16 of FRS 4 states that *if either party has the option to require the instrument to be redeemed or cancelled and, under the terms of the instrument, it is uncertain whether such an option will be exercised, the term should be taken to end on the earliest date at which the instrument would be redeemed or cancelled on exercise of such an option.* Paragraph 73 then states that this will be the case unless there is no genuine commercial possibility that the option will be exercised, implying that the call option will be exercised and that a premium will be paid. Payment of such a premium may be interpreted as being a payment that the issuer may be required to make in respect of the instrument, and hence part of the finance costs. Yet, where the option lies solely with the issuer, these are costs that issuers are not obliged to make, and will only make if they wish to at some appropriate future time. It does not seem reasonable to require them to treat the option at the outset as though it will be exercised.

In order to clarify this point, UITF 11, *Capital instruments: issuer call options*, was issued in September 1994. It relates to call options that are only exercisable by the issuer; and it states that the payment required on exercise of that option does not form part of the finance costs of the instrument (paragraph 6). Further, it states that, in the case of debt, *the gain or loss arising on any repurchase or early settlement will reflect the amount payable on exercise*; and in the case of shares, *the amount payable on exercise will be used to reduce the amount of shareholders' funds* (paragraph 6). However, UITF 11 excluded from this interpretation those cases where the effective rate of interest increases after the date at which the option is exercisable. In those cases the exercise price may be deemed to compensate the investor for forgoing such increased interest. In those cases, the total amount of the payments that the issuer may be required to make in respect of the instrument must include the amount payable on exercise of the option. (Paragraphs 5 and 9)

Warrants

The net proceeds from the issue of warrants should be credited direct to shareholders' funds (paragraph 45). However, if a warrant lapses, the amount previously recognised in respect of the warrant should be reported in the statement of total gains and losses (paragraph 47) - i.e. as a gain on a capital transaction. Yet it could be argued that this gain is a profit on a transaction with a shareholder and that, as such, it should be passed through the profit and loss account, a view that appears to be supported by the ASB's own draft *Statement of Principles*. Hopefully this issue will be clarified when the ASB finally issues the completed *Statement of Principles*.

Conclusion

FRS 4 appears at first to be fairly straightforward. If you read the summary, it contains seven short paragraphs, four of which summarise the accounting treatment required, and one diagram. Even the diagram looks straightforward:

Item	Analysed between	
Shareholders' funds	Equity interests	Non-equity interests
Minority interests in subsidiaries	Equity interests in subsidiaries	Non-equity interests in subsidiaries
Liabilities	Convertible liabilities	Non-convertible liabilities

However, while the standard is not particularly complex, the topic with which it is concerned is - hence the Application Notes which cover the treatment of 15 different capital instruments, and which are almost as long as the standard. In order to apply the standard at any more than a superficial level requires a knowledge of capital instruments beyond that generally expected of an accountant. Consequently, it is unlikely that the full complexity of the application of FRS 4 would ever be included in the examinations of any of the CCAB. What is likely to be examined are the underlying reasons concerning why FRS 4 was issued and the accounting treatments detailed in the body of the standard.

FRS   5:   Reporting the Substance of Transactions

Summary of the accounting treatment requirements

The purpose of FRS 5 is to ensure that the substance of an entity's transactions is reported in its financial statements. The commercial effect of the entity's transactions, and any resulting assets, liabilities, gains or losses, should be faithfully represented in its financial statements. (Paragraph 1)

The standard does not apply to (paragraph 12):

- forward contracts and futures;
- foreign exchange and interest rate swaps
- contracts where a net amount will be paid or received based on a movement in a price or an index
- expenditure commitments and orders placed, until the earlier of delivery or payment;
- employment contracts.

In determining the substance of a transaction, all its aspects and implications should be identified and greater weight given to those more likely to have a commercial effect in practice. Where a group or series of transactions achieve, or are intended to achieve an overall commercial effect, they should be viewed as a whole, not as individual transactions. (Paragraph 14)

The substance of a transaction depends upon whether it has given rise to new assets or liabilities for the reporting entity, and whether it has changed the entity's existing assets and liabilities (paragraph 16). An entity has rights or other access to benefits (and therefore has an asset) if the entity is exposed to the risks inherent in the benefits, taking into account the likelihood of those risks having a commercial effect (paragraph 17). Evidence that an obligation to transfer benefits (i.e. a liability) exists is shown if there is some circumstance in which the entity cannot avoid, legally or commercially, an outflow of benefits (paragraph 18).

Where an asset or a liability results from a transaction, it should be recognised in the balance sheet if there is sufficient evidence of its existence (including, where relevant, any future inflow or outflow of benefit), and if it can be measured at a monetary amount with sufficient reliability (paragraph 20).

Where transactions have no significant effect upon either the entity's rights or other access to benefits arising from a previously recognised asset, or to the entity's exposure to the risks inherent in those benefits, the entire asset should continue to be recognised (paragraph 21). When the transactions transfer *all* the significant rights or other access to benefits *and all* the significant exposure to risk, the entire asset should cease to be recognised (paragraph 22). Where a stage between nil and full effect is found, and it is a significant change, the description or monetary amounts relating to an asset should be changed and a liability recognised for any obligations to transfer benefits that are assumed (paragraph 23). However, the standard also states that this partial case arises in only three cases (paragraph 23):

(1)   a transfer of only part of the item;

(2)   a transfer of all of the item for only part of its life;

(3)   a transfer of all of the item for all of its life but where the entity retains some significant right to benefits or exposure to risk.

Where a transaction is in substance a financing of a recognised asset (whether previously recognised or not) the finance should be shown deducted from the gross amount of the item it finances on the face of the balance sheet within a single asset caption of 'linked presentation'. The gross amounts of both the item and the finance should be shown on the face of the balance sheet. (Paragraph 26) Profit on a linked presentation should be recognised on entering into the arrangement only to the extent that the non-returnable proceeds received exceed the previous carrying value of the item. Thereafter, any profit or loss arising should be recognised in the period in which it arises, both in the profit and loss account and in the notes. (Paragraph 28)

Assets and liabilities should not be offset, except where they do not constitute separate assets and liabilities (paragraph 29).

Where an entity has a quasi-subsidiary (i.e. a company, trust, partnership or other vehicle that is directly or indirectly controlled by the reporting entity, but that is not a subsidiary, and which gives rise to benefits for the reporting entity that are in substance no different from those that would arise were the vehicle a subsidiary - paragraph 7) the substance of the transactions entered into by the quasi-subsidiary should be reported in the consolidated statements (paragraph 15). The fact that a quasi-subsidiary has been included in the consolidated financial statements should be disclosed and a summary of the financial statements of the quasi-subsidiary should be provided in the notes (paragraph 38).

Disclosure of a transaction in the financial statements should be sufficient to enable the user of those statements to understand its commercial effect (paragraph 30). Where a transaction has resulted in the recognition of assets or liabilities whose nature differs from that of items usually included under the relevant balance sheet heading, the differences should be explained (paragraph 31).

Problems of interpretation and grey areas

The following items are discussed: conflicts between standards; identification of an asset or liability; and quasi-subsidiaries. There is also a brief conclusion.

Conflicts between standards

There has always been some doubt as to what to do when two standards suggest different treatments of a transaction - see, for example, the inter-relationship between SSAP 17 (*Accounting for post balance sheet events*, chapter 6) and SSAP 18 (*Accounting for contingencies*, chapter 7). In paragraph 13, FRS 5 states that where the substance of a transaction or the treatment of any resulting asset or liability falls within the scope of both FRS 5 and another standard or specific statutory requirement, the standard or statute that contains the *more specific condition* should be applied.

Identification of an asset or liability

The standard states that an asset or liability should be recognised in the balance sheet if *there is sufficient evidence of the existence of the item* and if it can be measured at a monetary amount (paragraph 20). But when does possession of evidence constitute *sufficient* evidence? Paragraph 20 also states that existence includes *evidence that a future inflow or outflow of benefit will occur*. Thus, it could be argued that ordering a new delivery truck constitutes sufficient evidence of the *existence* of the truck (the asset) to warrant its recognition in the balance sheet. This is contrary to current accepted practice (which would only recognise the truck upon receiving it) and is not likely to be an acceptable interpretation of the standard.

Quasi-subsidiaries

The inclusion of quasi-subsidiaries in FRS 5 is an interesting extension of the Companies Act definition of a subsidiary. Under the Companies Act 1985, whether or not an entity is to be treated as a subsidiary is dependent upon whether control can be exercised over it by the reporting entity. Five conditions under which an entity would be considered a subsidiary are given in the Act, none of which would be likely to be directly relevant to quasi-subsidiaries as defined in FRS 5. As a result, many more entities should be brought into consolidated financial statements than was previously the case. However, the terminology used in FRS 5 could leave it open to abuse concerning whether the existence of 'control' - the key to identification of a quasi-subsidiary - is actually acknowledged and a quasi-subsidiary recognised. To prevent manipulation, the standard suggests that control should be recognised where the benefits arising are in favour of the reporting entity. However, this could also be open to abuse and so the standard further states that whether benefits are gained by the reporting entity depends upon whether it is exposed to the risks inherent in the benefits. If it is, the vehicle should be treated as a quasi-subsidiary. (Paragraph 32) Control may appear obvious, as in the case where the reporting entity is actually directing the vehicle's financial and operating policies. However, unless it is also receiving the benefits and suffering the risks of those benefits, it would not treat the vehicle as a quasi-subsidiary. Having recognised a vehicle as a quasi-subsidiary, the only grounds for exclusion from consolidation is that it was held exclusively with a view to subsequent resale *and* has not been previously included in the reporting entity's consolidated financial statements (paragraph 101). As with the definition of quasi-subsidiary compared to that for a subsidiary, this allows far less scope for exclusion from the consolidated financial statements than is available should a reporting entity wish to exclude a subsidiary.

Conclusion

FRS 5 is an extremely complex accounting standard. Consequently, it is unlikely that the full complexity of the application of FRS 5 would ever be included in the examinations of any of the CCAB. What is likely to be examined are the underlying reasons concerning why FRS 5 was issued and the definitions and accounting treatments detailed in the body of the standard.

SSAP 25:   Segmental Reporting

Summary of the accounting treatment requirements

A segment is a distinguishable component of an entity that provides a separate product or service, or a separate group of related products or services (a 'class of business' segment); or it is a geographical area comprising an individual country or group of countries in which an entity operates, or to which it supplies products or services (a 'geographical' segment).

For each segment, turnover (analysed between sales to external customers and sales between segments), results, and net assets should be disclosed. Geographical segmental analysis should, in the first instance, be on the basis of source (i.e. the geographical location of the supplying segment). In addition, turnover to third parties should be segmentally reported on the basis of destination (i.e. the geographical location of the receiving segment).

Where associated undertakings account for at least 20% of the total results or net assets of the reporting entity, additional disclosure should be made in aggregate for all associated undertakings. This comprises segmental disclosure of the reporting entity's share of the aggregate profits or losses before tax, minority interests and extraordinary items of the associated undertakings, and the reporting entity's share of the net assets of the associated undertakings (including goodwill to the extent that it has not been written-off) after attributing, where possible, fair values to the net assets at the date of acquisition of the interest in each associated undertaking.

Problems of interpretation and grey areas

The following items are discussed: the impracticality of inter-company segmental comparison; incorporation of the Companies Act requirements; small company exemption; the hidden benefit of the preparation of segmental information; the incompatibility of the factors which determine where one segment stops and another starts; segment significance; comparatives; the use of the word 'segment'; the incomplete definition of geographical segments; transfer pricing; cost apportionment; the treatment of interest; associated undertakings; and major customer dependence. Finally, there is a brief conclusion.

The impracticality of inter-company segmental comparison

While SSAP 25 should ensure as far as possible that the segmental information reported by an entity is disclosed on a consistent basis year by year, paragraph 2 urges caution when making a comparison with similar segments in other entities. In other words, it would probably be misleading and should not, consequently, be attempted unless it is known that the figures have been prepared using similar bases and policies. On a more general note, this is a widely appreciated but often ignored facet of all financial statements and it would do no harm if a similar warning were included in every standard.

Incorporation of the Companies Act requirements

Unlike the earlier standards, SSAP 25 specifically incorporates the Companies Act requirements, separates them from the requirements specific to the standard, and states that all companies are required to comply with them (paragraph 3). It is, in effect, giving its support to the Companies Act requirements and confirming that they are consistent with standard accounting practice.

Small company exemption

While most small companies and other entities are exempted from the requirements of the standard, they are encouraged to ignore the exemptions and apply the standard to all financial statements which are intended to give a true and fair view. This is not to say that a true and fair view will not exist without the segmental disclosures of SSAP 25. Rather, it is to say that the true and fair view will be improved. Surely it would have been better if all entities had been required to comply with the disclosure requirements of SSAP 25. In this information technology age, it is probable that the preparation of information required for segmental disclosure would be neither harder, nor more expensive in relative terms, for the average small company than for the largest multinational. Given the stated purpose of segmental information (to provide information to assist the users of financial statements - paragraph 1), it is wholly inconsistent that a large proportion of reporting entities should be exempted from preparing and providing it.

The hidden benefit of the preparation of segmental information

Although segmental data are accepted as being useful to the decision-makers within a business, it is by no means certain that all companies to which segmentation would apply actually prepare such data for their internal use. Under SSAP 25, directors always have the option to declare segmental information seriously prejudicial, and thus avoid disclosure (paragraph 6). However, the standard has a hidden benefit which arises from the fact that, in order to take this decision, the directors should first calculate the segmental information. (They may not, in fact, do so but it is hard to form a truly objective opinion without all the facts.) If the information was prepared and it was decided that it should not be disclosed, internal documentation would remain containing the segmental information considered helpful to users of financial statements. The result would be an enhancement of the decision-making capabilities of those within the company who may not previously have had access to any meaningful segmental information.

The incompatibility of the factors which determine where one segment stops and another starts

There are four factors that should be used to identify where one segment stops and another starts: differences in return on investment, risk, rates of growth, and potential future development (paragraph 8). Obviously, they may not be compatible and a decision will often be required on which is to have precedence.

Segment significance

Each *significant* segment should be reported. A segment is significant if its third party turnover is $\geq$ 10% of the total third party turnover of the entity; or its profit/loss is $\geq$ 10% of the combined result of all profitable segments (or loss making segments if their total is greater); or its net assets are $\geq$ 10% of the total net assets of the entity.

This is a definition of materiality and any segment which is designated as 'significant' is reportable (i.e. should be disclosed). It should be noted that *all* segments must first be identified and then considered to determine which are 'significant'. Those not so defined should be combined with 'significant segments', or with other 'non-significant' segments until the combination becomes a 'significant' segment, or remains as a balancing adjustment on the segmental report.

It follows from the definition of 'significant' that an entity can have no more than 30 reportable business class segments, 30 reportable geographical (by source) segments, and ten reportable geographical (by destination) segments: it is likely to have many less.

Comparatives

When the segments or the accounting policies adopted for reporting segmental information are changed, the nature, reason and effect of the change should be disclosed along with comparative figures provided by restating the previous year's figures (paragraph 29). This is likely to happen relatively frequently and, while it is obviously worthwhile as it will show the change between the two periods, it does mean that information previously considered immaterial may now be considered material. In addition, in some cases, it will involve the recognition of a segment which existed in the previous period but was not considered to differ from others and so was not treated as a segment at any stage of the analysis. It would therefore be wise for companies to ensure they retain raw data, not just the previous year segmental analysis. It would also be advisable to computerise the storage and processing of the data used for segmental reporting in such a way that they may be easily accessed and reset to a new analysis basis for comparative purposes.

The use of the word 'segment'

The standard is very clumsy in the use of the word 'segment'. It uses it at both a collective level ('reportable segment') and at an individual level ('geographical segment') yet it does not use it when referring to 'classes of business'. Paragraphs 11 to 13, which deal with the determination of a class of business, highlight this confusion, particularly when compared to paragraphs 14 to 16 which consider the topic of geographical segments. It could be argued that confusion will not arise among practitioners applying the standard. This may well be the case, but there are many who use standards who are not experienced practitioners, yet who need to understand the content of standards, often to a level beyond that which many practitioners ever seek to reach. Given how easily it could have been done, it is a pity that the wording was not more thoughtfully constructed.

The incomplete definition of geographical segments

There is considerable flexibility in how classes of business may be identified. It is little wonder that the second paragraph of the standard contains a 'health warning'. Geographical segments are countries, or groups of countries, in which an entity operates, or to which it supplies products or services (paragraph 31). There may be occasions when this definition is too narrow. For example, some of the states of the USA may have taxation regulations sufficiently different from each other that there is a recognisable difference between operations conducted in one state rather than another. In addition, some of an entity's operations may take place within a subsidised region, thereby making them more profitable than other operations conducted elsewhere in the same country. In this respect, the Companies Act equivalent - 'a market delimited by geographical bounds' (CA 85, Schedule 4, paragraph 55(2)) - might have been a better choice. While it may not be in keeping with the definition in the standard, when there is a significant geographical difference within a country, it would be in keeping with the spirit and purpose of SSAP 25 to treat the various geographically differentiable areas of that country as if they were different geographical segments.

Transfer pricing

Turnover must be disclosed for each segment, split between sales to external customers and sales to other segments. There is no requirement to disclose the basis of such inter-segment sales. Consequently, by manipulating the basis of transfer pricing adopted, segments may be made to appear more or less profitable than would otherwise be the case.

Cost apportionment

There is more than one way in which common costs may be apportioned, and it may be that the adoption of one basis over another results in segments appearing better or worse than if another basis were adopted. While the standard states (paragraph 23) that common costs should not be apportioned if to do so would be misleading, there will be many occasions when an apportionment produces a set of segmental results which, while not misleading, are less than clearly indicative of the 'true' performance they purport to portray.

The treatment of interest

Interest earned or incurred is described as being a result of the entity's overall financial policy, rather than a proper reflection of the results of the various segments (paragraph 22). As a result, segment results should normally be reported before interest *except* where all or part of the entity's business is to earn/incur interest, or interest is central to the business. Thus, the disclosure requirement relating to results, given in paragraph 34(b), needs to be read in conjunction with paragraph 22. This produces an amended requirement along the lines: disclose the *result, before accounting for* interest (except where earning/incurring interest is part of the entity's business or interest is central to the business) and *taxation, minority interests and extraordinary items* (the italicised words are taken from paragraph 34(b)).

Net assets disclosed should exclude those assets and liabilities which are interest-bearing *except* where the results have been disclosed after interest. The purpose of this requirement is to enable the appropriate calculation of return on capital employed to be made.

Associated undertakings

Apart from the self-inflicted problems of segmental identification and limited disclosure, one of the biggest problems in the application of SSAP 25 relates to associated undertakings. Firstly, it is unclear whether disclosure of their results should also exclude interest: on the grounds of consistency, it should. There is also the problem of the definition of associated undertakings - there is no definition in SSAP 25! However, the Interim Statement on Consolidated Accounts, which was issued six months after SSAP 25, explains that 'associated undertakings' is the term used in the Companies Act when it refers to what the accounting standards had hitherto described as 'associated companies'. (Also, while it could be argued that trade investments could also be said to form a part of the results and assets, the wording of paragraph 26 makes it clear that only associated undertakings are to be considered.)

Secondly, all the net assets of associated undertakings must be combined. Some will be at fair values, some at historic values, and some a mixture of the two - hardly a sound basis for comparison, but already an acceptable compromise under SSAP 1 (*Accounting for associated companies* - chapter 14). Therefore, SSAP 25 is simply trying to make the best of what is available: a not unworthy aim, though the users of such information need to be aware of its deficiencies.

Finally, the standard appears to rule out the inclusion of associated undertakings in the segmental report of an entity which does not prepare consolidated financial statements. [SSAP 1 requires that the group's share of the associated undertaking results and net assets (at acquisition date fair value if possible) be incorporated in the consolidated financial statements, with their inclusion in individual company accounts only as a supplement and only where no consolidated financial statements are prepared. In the investing company balance sheet, the investment will be carried at cost (less amounts written-off), or at valuation; and only associated undertaking dividends received and receivable are included in the investing company profit and loss account. Consequently, associated undertakings are not likely to form a significant part of the net assets or the results of a reporting entity which does not prepare consolidated financial statements.] It seems totally contrary to the spirit and purpose of SSAP 25 that associated undertakings should be excluded from the segmental reports of companies which do not prepare consolidated financial statements. At the very least, it would be reasonable to include a supplement to the segmental report relating to associated undertakings, just as is required under SSAP 1 for associated undertakings. There is nothing to stop companies doing so, even if SSAP 25 does not advocate it, so long as it is clearly labelled as being a supplement.

Major customer dependence

In the USA, if sales to one customer (or group of entities under common control) are ≥ 10% of total revenue, this fact must be disclosed along with the amount of revenue from each such customer and the industry segment making the sales. Given that dependence on major customers may be viewed as an indicator of potential weakness, it is unfortunate that SSAP 25 does not include a similar disclosure requirement.

Conclusions

It is clear that SSAP 25 could have been more realistic concerning the capabilities of smaller companies and, given its objective, it would be sensible to amend it to apply to all entities. It is illogical to argue that just because an entity is small, the users of its financial statements would not benefit from the inclusion of a segmental report.

Nevertheless, for all its faults, SSAP 25 represented a breath of fresh air in what had become a very unhealthy collection of both out-of-date and open to abuse standards. The last of the accounting standards issued by the ASC, it gave a good indication of the style and openness that the ASB was to adopt in its Financial Reporting Standards.

UITF 7:   True and Fair View Override Disclosures

Summary of the accounting treatment requirements

The purpose of UITF 7 is to clarify what should be disclosed when the true and fair view override is being invoked. It defines the three terms contained in the requirement of CA 95 (sch. 4, para 36A) that *particulars of any such departure*, the *reasons for it* and *its effect* shall be given in a note to the accounts. *Particulars of any such departure* are defined as *a statement of the treatment which the Act would normally require in the circumstances and a description of the treatment actually adopted*. The *reasons for it* are defined as *a statement as to why the treatment prescribed would not give a true and fair view*, and *its effect* is defined as *a description of how the position shown in the accounts is different as a result of the departure* (with quantification unless it is obvious from the accounts, or if it is impracticable). Corresponding amounts for the previous year should also be disclosed.

UITF 10:   Disclosure of Directors' Share Options

Summary of the accounting treatment requirements

The purpose of UITF 10 is to prescribe disclosure of some of the details relating to directors' share options. While such options were held by the UITF to be appropriately treated as giving rise to a benefit that should be included in the aggregate of directors' remuneration, it was held to be impracticable to require evaluation of such benefits. Rather, UITF 10 requires that information concerning the option prices applicable to individual directors, together with market price information at the year-end and at the date of exercise, should be disclosed.

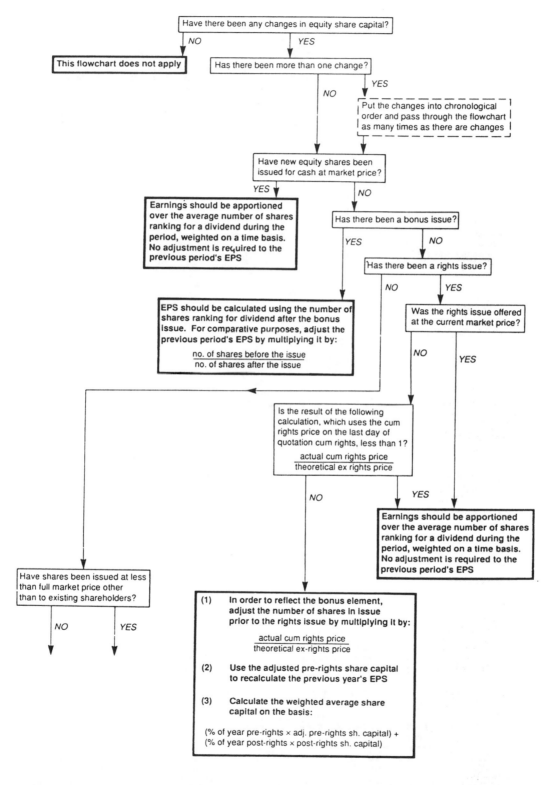

SSAP 3(a)   Approach to adopt when there are changes in equity share capital

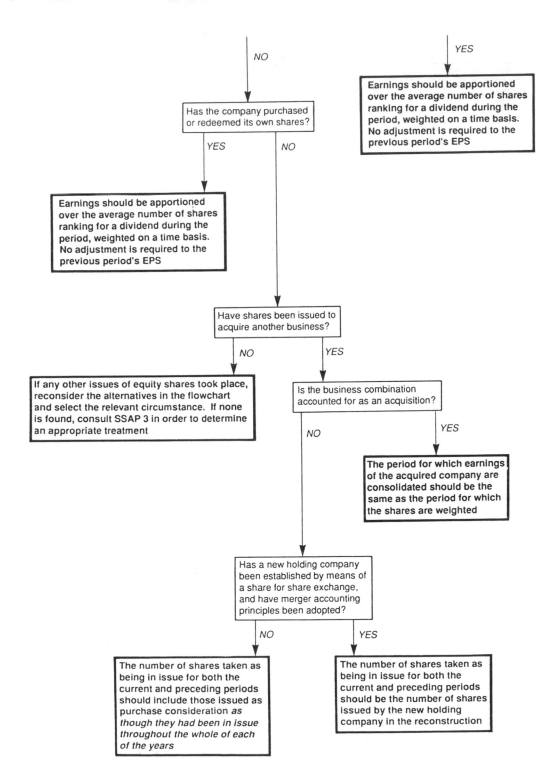

SSAP 3(b)   Approach to adopt when there are changes in equity share capital

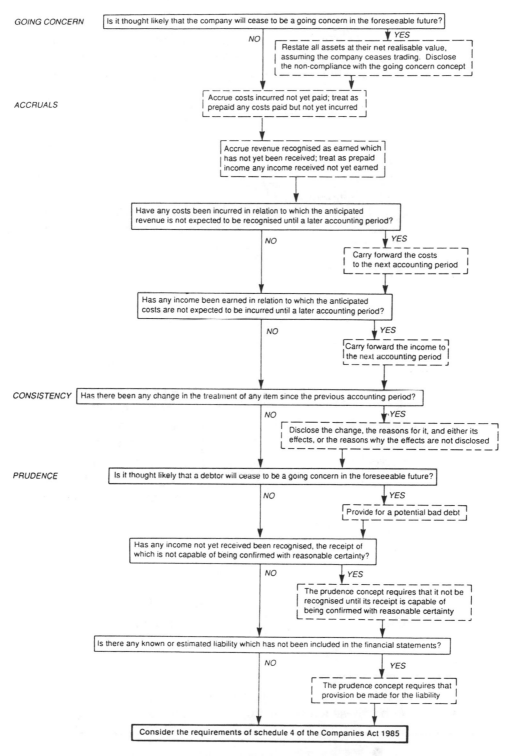

GOING CONCERN — Is it thought likely that the company will cease to be a going concern in the foreseeable future?

NO ↓ | ↓ YES

Restate all assets at their net realisable value, assuming the company ceases trading. Disclose the non-compliance with the going concern concept

ACCRUALS — Accrue costs incurred not yet paid; treat as prepaid any costs paid but not yet incurred

Accrue revenue recognised as earned which has not yet been received; treat as prepaid income any income received not yet earned

Have any costs been incurred in relation to which the anticipated revenue is not expected to be recognised until a later accounting period?

NO | YES

Carry forward the costs to the next accounting period

Has any income been earned in relation to which the anticipated costs are not expected to be incurred until a later accounting period?

NO | YES

Carry forward the income to the next accounting period

CONSISTENCY — Has there been any change in the treatment of any item since the previous accounting period?

NO | YES

Disclose the change, the reasons for it, and either its effects, or the reasons why the effects are not disclosed

PRUDENCE — Is it thought likely that a debtor will cease to be a going concern in the foreseeable future?

NO | YES

Provide for a potential bad debt

Has any income not yet received been recognised, the receipt of which is not capable of being confirmed with reasonable certainty?

NO | YES

The prudence concept requires that it not be recognised until its receipt is capable of being confirmed with reasonable certainty

Is there any known or estimated liability which has not been included in the financial statements?

NO | YES

The prudence concept requires that provision be made for the liability

Consider the requirements of schedule 4 of the Companies Act 1985

SSAP 2   Compliance with the four fundamental accounting concepts (adapted so as to comply with the explanatory forward to the accounting standards)

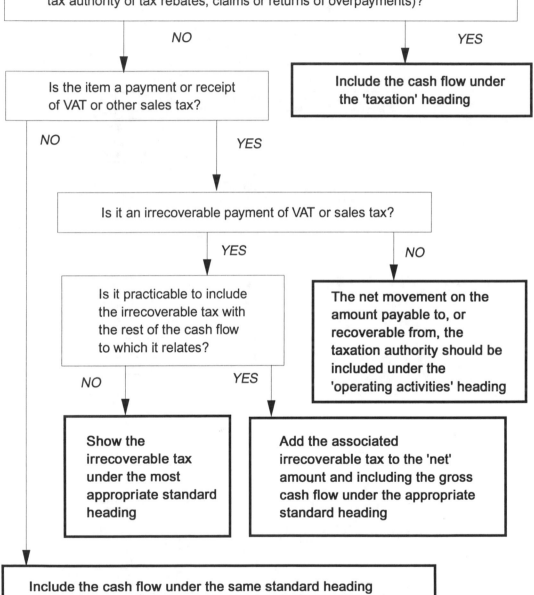

FRS 1   The treatment of taxation-related items in the cash flow forecast

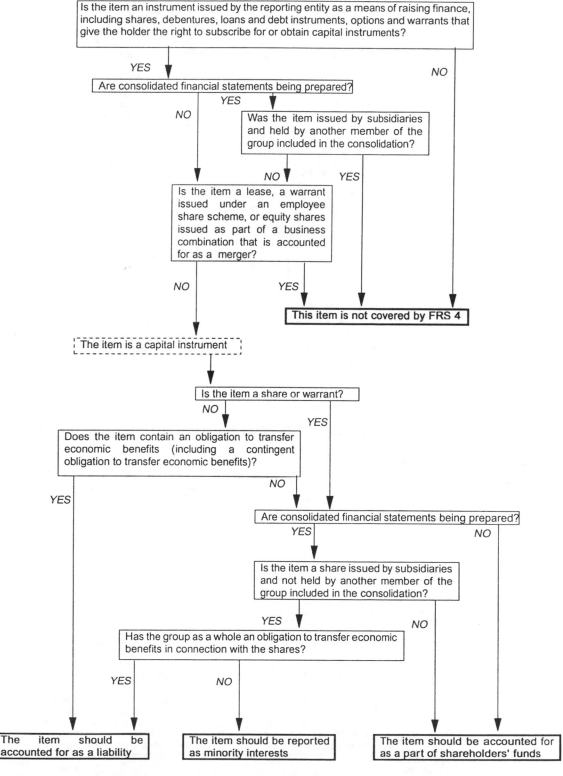

FRS 4   Initial classification of capital instruments

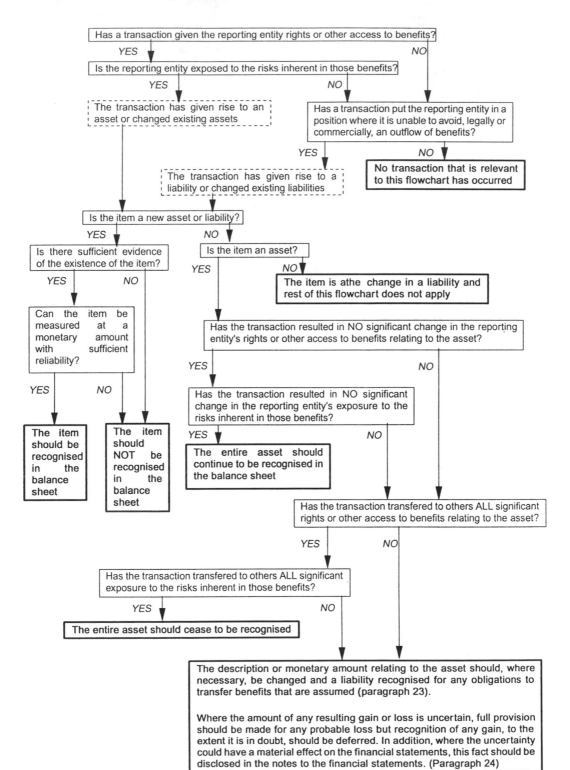

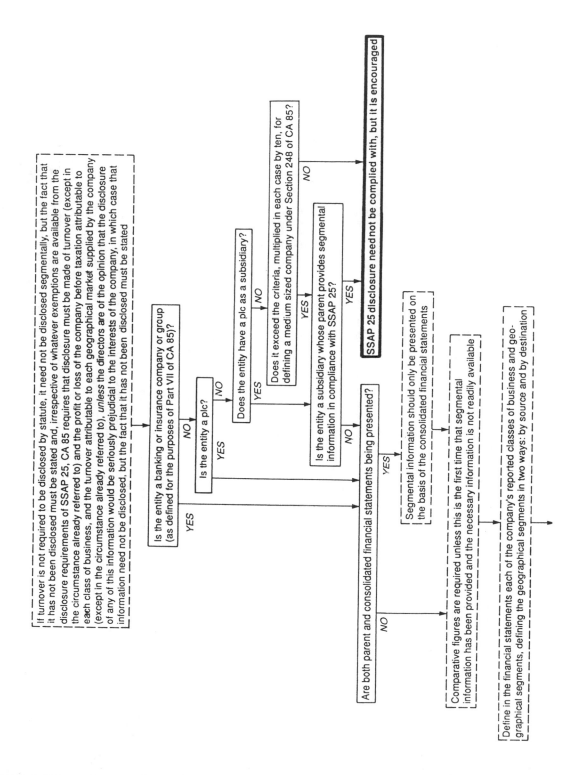

If turnover is not required to be disclosed by statute, it need not be disclosed segmentally, but the fact that it has not been disclosed must be stated and, irrespective of whatever exemptions are available from the disclosure requirements of SSAP 25, CA 85 requires that disclosure must be made of turnover (except in the circumstance already referred to) and the profit or loss of the company before taxation attributable to each class of business, and the turnover attributable to each geographical market supplied by the company (except in the circumstance already referred to), *unless* the directors are of the opinion that the disclosure of any of this information would be seriously prejudicial to the interests of the company, in which case that information need not be disclosed, but the fact that it has not been disclosed must be stated

Is the entity a banking or insurance company or group (as defined for the purposes of Part VII of CA 85)?

Is the entity a plc?

Does the entity have a plc as a subsidiary?

Does it exceed the criteria, multiplied in each case by ten, for defining a medium sized company under Section 248 of CA 85?

Is the entity a subsidiary whose parent provides segmental information in compliance with SSAP 25?

SSAP 25 disclosure need not be complied with, but it is encouraged

Are both parent and consolidated financial statements being presented?

Segmental information should only be presented on the basis of the consolidated financial statements

Comparative figures are required unless this is the first time that segmental information has been provided and the necessary information is not readily available

Define in the financial statements each of the company's reported classes of business and geographical segments, defining the geographical segments in two ways: by source and by destination

NO   YES   NO   YES   NO   YES   YES   NO   YES   NO

SSAP 25(a)   Segmental reporting

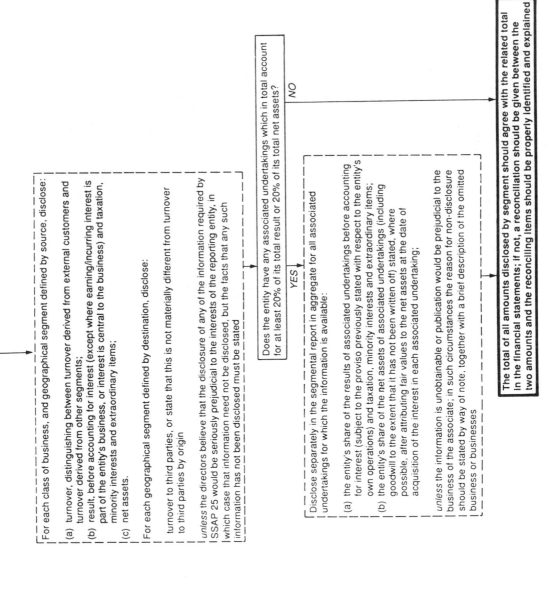

For each class of business, and geographical segment defined by source, disclose:

(a) turnover, distinguishing between turnover derived from external customers and turnover derived from other segments;

(b) result, before accounting for interest (except where earning/incurring interest is part of the entity's business, or interest is central to the business) and taxation, minority interests and extraordinary items;

(c) net assets.

For each geographical segment defined by destination, disclose:

turnover to third parties, or state that this is not materially different from turnover to third parties by origin

unless the directors believe that the disclosure of any of the information required by SSAP 25 would be seriously prejudicial to the interests of the reporting entity, in which case that information need not be disclosed, but the facts that any such information has not been disclosed must be stated

Does the entity have any associated undertakings which in total account for at least 20% of its total result or 20% of its total net assets?

YES

NO

Disclose separately in the segmental report in aggregate for all associated undertakings for which the information is available:

(a) the entity's share of the results of associated undertakings before accounting for interest (subject to the proviso previously stated with respect to the entity's own operations) and taxation, minority interests and extraordinary items;

(b) the entity's share of the net assets of associated undertakings (including goodwill to the extent that it has not been written off) stated, where possible, after attributing fair values to the net assets at the date of acquisition of the interest in each associated undertaking;

unless the information is unobtainable or publication would be prejudicial to the business of the associate; in such circumstances the reason for non-disclosure should be stated by way of note, together with a brief description of the omitted business or businesses

The total of all amounts disclosed by segment should agree with the related total in the financial statements; if not, a reconciliation should be given between the two amounts and the reconciling items should be properly identified and explained

Short Questions

*ASSUME THAT MATERIALITY EXISTS IN **EVERY** CASE*

SSAP 2:   **Disclosure of Accounting Policies**

Questions 1-2 relate to different companies, each of which has a balance sheet date of 31st December.

1   A clothing manufacturing company paid six months rent on a warehouse in August. The payment covered the six month period from August to January of the next accounting period inclusive.

2   The previous year's accounts of an engineering company had included warehouse salaries in administrative expenses. This year they are included in the distribution costs.

SSAP 3:   **Earnings per Share**

Questions 3-6 relate to a variety of companies, all of which have a balance sheet date of 31st December. In each case, at the start of the accounting period, there were 4 million ordinary £1 shares in issue. Earnings for EPS purposes are £2.5m (£2m in the previous year) and the companies have never had any irrecoverable ACT. Each question should be treated in isolation, i.e. no information contained in any question is applicable to any other question.

3   On 1st June, a supermarket company made a 1 for 10 rights issue at market price.

4   On 1st July, a publishing company placed 1 million ordinary shares at 82p with institutional investors who previously had no holdings in the company's shares. The market price on that date was 85p.

5   On 1st November, a chemical waste disposal company split its £1 ordinary shares into ordinary shares of 20p.

6   On 1st July, a cleansing company made a 1 for 8 rights issue at 70p. The market value of the shares on the last day of quotation cum rights was 65p.

Question 7 involves a company with a 31st December financial year end.

7   A house building company made a loss for EPS purposes of £1.2m during the accounting period. In the previous period it had made a profit of £3.6m. The company has never suffered irrecoverable ACT. There are 10 million ordinary £1 shares in issue.

FRS 1: Cash Flow Statements

Questions 8-11 relate to an aeronautic engineering company with a balance sheet date of 31st December. On turnover of £23.8m, the company has pre-tax earnings of £4.5m (last year £5.2m on turnover of £25.1m). Corporation tax is at 35% in all periods, and applies to all companies mentioned. Where the calculation of tax is required, assume that it is on the whole amount given, i.e. that there are no allowances available which could be used to reduce the liability. Treat each question in isolation, i.e. as if none of the others apply to the company.

8   On 15th February, the company paid a final dividend for the previous year of £600,000; on 15th August, an interim dividend was paid of £350,000; and, a final dividend of £650,000 is being proposed for the current year.

9   During the year, a cheque for £690,000 was received when plant with a net book value of £630,000 was sold.

10   Since the end of the previous period, debtors have risen by £200,000; trade creditors have fallen by £130,000; the provision for corporation tax has risen by £200,000; stocks have fallen by £190,000; dividends proposed have risen by £50,000; and, dividends receivable from associated companies have risen by £30,000.

11   On 1st July, the company issued £5m 5% convertible debenture stock. The conversion option will first be available in 5 years time, when each £1 of debenture stock will be convertible into one 10p ordinary share in the company. The £5m proceeds of the issue were applied to reduce the company's overdraft.

FRS 4:   Capital Instruments

Questions 12-16 are concerned with the disclosure requirements, treatment options, and definitions contained in FRS 4. There is no continuation from one question to the next, and each question should be considered in isolation from the rest.

12   If there is uncertainty as to whether an option to redeem or cancel a capital instrument will be exercised, when should the term of a capital instrument be deemed to end?

13   What is a 'warrant'?

14   How should the maturity of debt be disclosed?

15   Into which two categories should capital instruments be classified in the financial statements of an individual company?

16   In which circumstances should capital instruments (other than shares) be classified as liabilities?

FRS 5:   Reporting the Substance of Transactions

Questions 17-20 are concerned with the disclosure requirements, treatment options, and definitions contained in FRS 5. There is no continuation from one question to the next, and each question should be considered in isolation from the rest.

17   What is the definition of an asset according to FRS 5?

18   What is the definition of a liability according to FRS 5?

19   In the context of an asset, what is the definition of control according to FRS 5?

20   In the context of another entity, what is the definition of control according to FRS 5?

21   A businessman lent £1m to a football company on an interest free basis. The loan is to be repaid in five years time. At the same time, the company gave the businessman an executive suite at the football ground and free exclusive use of a car park during the week (the businessman runs a fruit market in the car park from Monday to Friday). Both these items have been given for a five year period.

SSAP 25:   Segmental Reporting

Questions 22-25 relate to Livro Plc, a publishing company with two subsidiaries. The group balance sheet date is 31st December. On turnover of £92.8m, the group has pre-tax earnings of £15.2m (last year £12.7m on turnover of £86.3m).

22   *Livro plc* has investments in three associated companies. Should they be included in its segmental report?

23   If the associated companies mentioned in question 22 are to be included in the segmental report, what should be disclosed?

24   Under what circumstances would disclosure of the associated undertakings not be required in the segmental report of the *Livro* group?

25   Under what circumstances would disclosure of group segments not be required in the segmental report of the *Livro* group?

Additional Questions

*ASSUME THAT MATERIALITY EXISTS IN **EVERY** CASE*

SSAP 2:   Disclosure of Accounting Policies

Questions 26-27 relate to a variety of companies, all of which have a balance sheet date of 31st December.

26   A mail order company has, over the previous five years, had a consistent level of bad debts of 6% of sales. The annual provision for bad debts has always been 5% but this year the policy is being changed and a 6% provision is to be made.

27   A shipbuilding company has been building a yacht for sale to a wealthy customer. The customer has died and the company has no claim on his estate for the expenditure incurred. The yacht is to a very unusual design and it is thought that there is probably only a 10% chance that another customer will be found. Costs to date are £35,000.

SSAP 3:   Earnings per Share

Questions 28-33 relate to a variety of companies, all of which have a balance sheet date of 31st December. In each case, at the start of the accounting period, there were 4 million ordinary £1 shares in issue. Earnings for EPS purposes are £2.5m (£2m in the previous year) and the companies have never had any irrecoverable ACT. Each question should be treated in isolation, i.e. no information contained in any question is applicable to any other question.

28   On 1st February, a leisure company redeemed 200,000 of its ordinary share capital. The market price was 35p.

29   On 1st May, an engineering company made a 1 for 2 bonus issue. On 1st December, it made a 5 for 8 rights issue at 60p. On the last day of quotation cum rights the share price was 80p.

30   On 1st August, a sports equipment company made a 3 for 20 rights issue at 95p. On the day the rights were declared, the market price of the company's shares was 110p. On the last day of quotation cum rights the share price was 95p.

31   On 1st October, a newspaper company issued 1 million ordinary shares in exchange for the entire share capital of a wholesale distribution company. The market price of the newspaper company's shares on that date was £3, and the wholesale distribution company's shares were worth £1.50p each. The business combination was accounted for as an acquisition and the date from which the earnings of the wholesale distribution company were consolidated was 1st October. The relevant earnings for EPS purposes of the acquired company, which are attributable to the period from 1st October are £400,000.

32   On 1st December, a brewery company issued ½ million ordinary shares in exchange for the entire share capital of a food processing company. The business combination was accounted for as a merger. The relevant earnings for EPS purposes of the acquired

company, are £200,000 for the current year, and £140,000 for the preceding period. The EPS of the food processing company was 42p in the previous year.

33   On 1st April, a timber preservation company made a 7 for 40 rights issue at 90p. The market value of the shares on the last day of quotation cum rights was 140p. On 1st October, a 3 for 47 bonus issue was made.

Questions 34-39 involve different companies. They each have a 31st December financial year end. Each question contains all the information required to answer it.

34   An electrical equipment company had earnings for EPS calculation purposes of £4.6m in the financial period. (Previous period £4.9m.) Company policy is to transfer £200,000 per annum out of the reserves to a sinking fund. The company has never had irrecoverable ACT. For the past ten years the company has had 3 million ordinary £1 shares in issue.

35   A transport company has 4 million ordinary £1 shares in issue. No shares have been issued in the last ten years. Last year, profits after tax and extraordinary items were £2.3m. This year, they were £0.6m. There was no irrecoverable ACT in the previous period, but this year there is irrecoverable ACT of £350,000.

36   A design company has 2.5 million ordinary 50p shares in issue. No shares have been issued in the last ten years. Last year, profits after tax and extraordinary items were £3.2m. This year, they were £1.4m. There was no irrecoverable ACT in the previous period, but this year there is irrecoverable ACT of £50,000.

37   An entertainment company has 1.6 million ordinary 'A' shares of 25p in issue. These shares have been in issue for the last ten years. Last year, profits after tax and extraordinary items were £0.8m. This year, they were £2.7m. There was no irrecoverable ACT in either period. On 1st July, the company made an issue of 400,000 ordinary 'B' shares of 25p at 35p per share. The newly issued shares do not rank for dividend on the profits of the period, but will do so on the profits of all future periods.

38   A television company has 10 million ordinary shares of 10p in issue. These shares have been in issue for the last ten years. Last year, losses after tax and extraordinary items were £0.65m. This year, they were £1.3m. There was no irrecoverable ACT in either period. The corporation tax rate has been 35% for the last 5 years. On 1st January, the company issued £500,000 of 6% convertible debentures. The terms of the conversion are that it may occur on:
       31st July next year at the rate of 80 ordinary shares for every £100 debenture stock, or,
       31st July in the year after next at the rate of 90 ordinary shares for every £100 of debenture stock.

39   An advertising company has 2 million ordinary shares of 50p in issue. These shares have been in issue for the last ten years. Last year, profits after tax were £3.3m. The current year profits after tax but before extraordinary items were £5.1m, but there was an extraordinary loss of £1.1m (£0.9m after tax). There were no extraordinary items in any of the previous five years. There was no irrecoverable ACT in either period. The

corporation tax rate has been 35% for the last 5 years. At the beginning of the current year, the company issued £500,000 of 5% convertible debentures. The terms of the conversion are that it may occur on:

> 30th April next year at the rate of 150 ordinary shares for every £100 debenture stock, or,
>
> 30th April in the year after next at the rate of 170 ordinary shares for every £100 of debenture stock.

What EPS disclosure must be made?

FRS 1: Cash Flow Statements

Question 40 relates to an engineering group with a balance sheet date of 31st December. On turnover of £28.4m, the group has pre-tax earnings of £5.8m (last year £4.1m on turnover of £25.2m). Corporation tax is at 35% in all periods, and applies to all companies mentioned. Any calculation of tax should assume that it is on the whole amount given, i.e. that there are no allowances available which could be used to reduce the liability.

40   During the period, an associated company paid the group holding company a final dividend of £80,000 in February, and an interim dividend of £70,000 in August. The pre-tax profits of the associated company were £950,000 and it declared a final dividend to be paid next February, of which the holding company will receive £110,000. The holding company has a 40% holding in the associated company.

41   At the end of a manufacturing company's accounting period, deferred tax had a balance of £430,000, and the corporation tax creditor was £1.1m. The corporation tax charge for the period was £990,000. The corporation tax creditor at the previous period end was £1.3m, and the deferred tax balance was £260,000. No associated undertaking investments are held.

FRS 4:   Capital Instruments

42   What are non-equity shares?

FRS 5:   Reporting the Substance of Transactions

43   How should a 'linked presentation' be shown in the balance sheet?

44   Under what circumstances may a vehicle recognised as a quasi-subsidiary be excluded from consolidation?

SSAP 25:   Segmental Reporting

45   Which items of financial information should be disclosed with respect to each class of business and geographical segment?

13   Taxation and Grants

Overview

This chapter deals with four accounting standards - SSAP 4 (Government grants); SSAP 5 (Value Added Tax); SSAP 8 (The imputation system); and SSAP 15 (Deferred tax).

SSAP 4:   Accounting for Government Grants

Summary of the accounting treatment requirements

Grants relating to fixed assets should be credited to revenue over the expected useful life of the asset concerned, either by setting the grant against the cost of the asset so that depreciation is only charged on the net figure (this approach may be contrary to Schedule 4 of the Companies Act 1985), or by carrying the grant as a deferred credit in the balance sheet and releasing it to income over the expected useful life of the asset on a basis consistent with the asset's depreciation provision.

Revenue grants should be recognised in the profit and loss account so as to match them with the expenditure towards which they are intended to contribute. If the expenditure has already been incurred when the grant is received, the grant should be recognised in the profit and loss account immediately. Where all the relevant expenditure has not yet been incurred, a proportionate part of the grant should be deferred and matched with the as yet unincurred expenditure at such time as it is incurred.

Grants should not be recognised in the profit and loss account until their receipt is reasonably assured.

Provision for repayment of grants should be made only to the extent that such repayment is probable. Any such repayment should be accounted for by setting it off against any unamortised deferred income relating to the grant, with any excess of the repayment being charged immediately to profit and loss.

Problems of interpretation and grey areas

The following items are discussed: the nature of government grants; the importance of the accruals and prudence concepts to this standard; 'fair value'; disclosure; grants receivable; timing differences on deferred income; grants received relating to earlier periods; the treatment of fixed asset grants and the true and fair view; treatment of the credit to profit and loss; and grant repayment.

The nature of government grants

Government grants are all forms of assistance from governments and government agencies, be they local, national, or international. The grants can take the form of cash or asset transfers, and can be given in return for past, present, or future compliance with the conditions of receiving them. The standard is not, therefore, restricted to the treatment of grants from UK sources. This could lead to problems of treatment in respect of foreign grants which have not been received at balance sheet date and for which there may not be the same level of certainty that they will be received as there would be for those from UK sources. If such a situation arose, the prudence concept should be applied in order to decide whether to account for the grant outstanding.

The importance of the accruals and prudence concepts to this standard

The standard puts great emphasis on the concepts of accruals and prudence (paragraphs 4 and 5), and the application of the former is particularly central to its application.

For the most part, the standard is fairly straightforward. It makes it clear that all grants, including those received in instalments, should be matched with the expenditure towards which they are intended to contribute. Where the expenditure is incurred over more than one accounting period, the grant should be apportioned appropriately, based on the proportion of the expenditure incurred in each period.

Prudence is applicable to two cases in particular. One, the treatment of grants receivable, was mentioned in the previous section. The other concerns a situation where it is probable (but not where only possible) that some of a grant will need to be repaid. When this occurs, provision must be made immediately by setting off the repayment against any unamortised deferred income relating to the grant. Any balance that remains unprovided for must be charged immediately to profit and loss. SSAP 18 (*Accounting for contingencies* - chapter 7) is the source of this treatment and, where the repayment is possible, disclosure should be made, unless the possibility is remote. (For a discussion of what would be considered 'probable', 'possible', and 'remotely possible', see page 68.)

'Fair value'

If the grant is in the form of non-monetary assets, a valuation must be put upon the assets received. The standard uses the term 'fair value' (paragraph 16), but does not attempt to define it. While this could be considered an unfortunate oversight, it is clearly intended that a realistic value be placed upon such assets. Such a valuation should be based on the condition and market value of the assets. For fixed assets, this should not present any great problems, nor for most of the other examples of assistance quoted in the standard (i.e. consultancy and advisory services, and subsidised loans). However, in the case of the other example given, credit guarantees, it may be difficult to evaluate the benefit, and care would be required in ensuring that an objective approach was taken in doing so.

Disclosure

The disclosure requirements are straightforward: disclosure should be made of the accounting policy adopted, the number and variety of the grants, and the periods over which they are credited to profit and loss. Where current or future results are/will be affected materially by grants received, the effects should be disclosed. In addition, the nature of any non-monetary, service-based assistance (e.g. consultancy) which has had a material effect upon the results for the period, should be disclosed along with its financial effect - a somewhat ambitious requirement which is qualified by limiting quantification to cases where it is possible to measure the financial effects of the assistance.

Grants receivable

Where a grant relates to expenditure incurred in the current period, but is not due to be received until a future period, it should be recognised (if, as already mentioned, it is prudent to do so) and (probably) treated as a deferred asset in the balance sheet. This suggested treatment is similar to that applied to recoverable advanced corporation tax (ACT) under SSAP 8 (*The treatment of taxation under the imputation system in the accounts of companies* - discussed later in this chapter): the circumstances would appear to be sufficiently similar to justify application of the same treatment, although it is not mentioned in SSAP 4. However, its nature is not similar to that of recoverable ACT and it is unlikely that it could be used in the same way to reduce the balance within the deferred tax account.

Timing differences on deferred income

When part of a grant received relates to a future period, that part should be treated as deferred income in the balance sheet. If the grant was taxable, there will be a timing difference on the part carried forward which should be treated as a deferred tax asset, and included in the computation of the balance on the deferred tax account at the balance sheet date.

Grants received relating to earlier periods

Where a grant, for which no provision had been made, is received relating to expenditure incurred in earlier periods, this does not constitute a prior period adjustment under FRS 3 (*Reporting financial performance* - chapter 2). The grant received should be recognised in the period during which it became reasonably certain that it would be received. This would normally be the same period as that in which it was received, but it is possible that receipt could occur in a later period.

The treatment of fixed asset grants and the true and fair view

In the case of a grant in respect of a fixed asset, two treatments are acceptable under the standard. *Either*, the amount of the grant is treated as deferred income and credited to profit and loss over the useful economic life of the asset to which it relates (on a basis consistent with the depreciation policy); *or*, the grant is deducted from the purchase price/production cost of the asset, and depreciation is based on the net amount. The standard considers that both treatments are capable of giving a true and fair view, but states that the second option is believed to be contrary to the requirements of paragraphs 17 and 26 of Schedule 4 of the Companies Act 1985 and, therefore, not available to companies which are subject to the requirements of these two paragraphs (i.e. most companies).

Thus it would appear that, in most cases, there is only one option rather than two. Nevertheless, the ultimate overriding principle is the provision of a true and fair view. Where it is necessary to do so, company law may be ignored, *if by observing it a true and fair view would be impossible*. The standard itself states that the second option is capable of giving a true and fair view (paragraph 15). Consequently, if the only way to present a true and fair view would be to net the grant against the cost of the asset, it would be appropriate to do so. Obviously, such non-observance of company law would require disclosure, and a statement that it was done so as to present a true and fair view. However, were a true and fair view also possible by using the first option, it could no longer be stated that the netted asset approach was applied on the grounds that it was the only way in which a true and fair view could be presented. Accordingly, the first option would have to be adopted, and the grant treated as deferred income.

Treatment of the credit to profit and loss

So far as grants other than those for fixed assets are concerned, the standard requires that they are matched with the expenditure which was incurred in qualifying for the grant. It does not make it clear whether the grant should be netted against the expenditure, or whether it should be credited directly to profit and loss. In view of the emphasis on matching, particularly in paragraphs 8 to 11, it could be argued that the grants should be netted against the relevant expenditure when possible; otherwise, the grant should be credited to profit and loss. However, the standard is too imprecise to make that interpretation mandatory. Accordingly, it would be reasonable to adopt either approach (i.e. credit profit and loss with all non-fixed asset grants received, or, offset all grants which can be specifically related to expenditure against that expenditure, and credit directly to profit and loss only those which cannot be matched with specific expenditure). Whichever approach is adopted should be disclosed.

Grant repayment

If a grant is required to be repaid, the amount to be repaid is first deducted from any unamortised deferred income relating to the grant. If this is not sufficient to cover the value of the repayment, the balance is charged to profit and loss. This can lead to some strange anomalies. For example, suppose an equipment grant of £100,000 is received in year 1 and amortised over four years at £25,000 per annum. In year 3, repayment of 50% (i.e. £50,000) is required. As £50,000 remains unamortised, no charge needs to be made to profit and loss for the repayment of the grant. Depreciation is £40,000 per annum (the equipment cost £160,000). Year 1 and year 2's depreciation was offset by £25,000 per annum in respect of the grant. The net profit and loss charge for each of those two years was, therefore, £15,000. In each of years 3 and 4, the charge to profit and loss will be £40,000. FRS 3 (*Reporting financial performance* - chapter 2) amended paragraph 14 of SSAP 4, making it clear that where the repayment is to be disclosed by virtue of either its size or incidence, if the financial statements are to give a true and fair view, the repayment should be treated as an exceptional item. The wording of the amendment appears to rule out the possibility of treating the item as a prior period adjustment.

SSAP 5:   Accounting for Value Added Tax

Summary of the accounting treatment requirements

Turnover should be shown in the profit and loss account net of value added tax (VAT). If the gross turnover is shown, the relevant VAT should be shown as a deduction in arriving at the figure for turnover net of VAT.

Irrecoverable VAT allocated to fixed assets and other separately disclosed items should be included in their cost.

Problems of interpretation and grey areas

The following items are discussed: the requirements of the standard; the problem of partial exemption; and the treatment of partially exempt fixed asset purchases.

The requirements of SSAP 5

This standard requires that turnover shown in the profit and loss should exclude VAT on taxable outputs (i.e. sales which included VAT). In addition, irrecoverable VAT should be allocated where practical and material, to those items to which it relates. VAT due to, or receivable from, Customs and Excise should be included in creditors (as part of 'other creditors including taxation and social security'), or in debtors, as appropriate, and need not be disclosed unless material. Finally, any capital commitments on which there is irrecoverable VAT, should include that VAT in the commitment disclosed.

The problem of partial exemption

Present-day bookkeeping systems make it a simple matter to comply with this standard *except in one case* - companies which trade in a mixture of exempt and non-exempt items. It is important that any irrecoverable VAT is included in the cost of the item to which it relates. If it is not, misleading performance indicators will result, and fixed assets will be misstated. In many cases, this will be a simple exercise. However, some companies which have a mixture of exempt outputs (no VAT on sales, VAT on purchases is irrecoverable) and non-exempt outputs, account for some of their VAT in proportion to the VAT mix within their turnover. The proportion found is applied to determine how much of their VAT on expenditure (input VAT), which cannot be traced directly to non-exempt outputs, can be reclaimed.

If, for instance, the proportion of turnover between exempt and non-exempt outputs is 1:4, 20% of VAT on expenditure which cannot be traced to either exempt or non-exempt outputs will be irrecoverable. The following example should help to clarify this approach:

		Sales	VAT
Outputs:	non-exempt	£4,000,000	£600,000
	exempt	1,000,000	-
		5,000,000	600,000
Inputs:	traceable as non-exempt	£2,400,000	£360,000
	traceable as exempt	200,000	30,000
	non-traceable	600,000	90,000
		3,200,000	480,000

The VAT of £30,000 traced to exempt outputs must be added to the cost of the items on which they were incurred. The non-traceable input VAT of £90,000 should be treated as 20% irrecoverable and that amount (£18,000) apportioned among the items which make up the non-traceable balance. The remaining input VAT of £432,000 (£360,000 + £72,000) can be reclaimed. (There are exemptions to these general irrecoverability rules for mixed supplies when the proportions or amounts fall below certain thresholds. For example, if exempt input VAT is less than £250 per month and less than 50% of total input VAT, it will be treated as recoverable.)

The treatment of partially exempt fixed asset purchases

The main problem which arises is how to treat fixed assets which will be used in the production of both exempt and non-exempt items. If the proportional usage is known, the costs can be split between the two categories. However, it is unlikely that an accurate figure would result - production levels change and, consequently, planned usage may not equate to actual usage. Where any such allocation has been agreed by the Customs and Excise, it should be applied in apportioning the irrecoverable VAT to the cost of the asset. However, this information will often not be readily available, in which case, previous similar examples must be considered in arriving at a suitable treatment. Should any apportionment made prove to have been materially incorrect, the following year's accounts should adjust the cost of the asset accordingly. This would not constitute a prior period adjustment under FRS 3 (*Reporting financial performance* - chapter 2).

SSAP 8: The Treatment of Taxation under the Imputation System in the Accounts of Companies

Summary of the accounting treatment requirements

The profit and loss account taxation charge should include the amount of UK corporation tax and the total overseas taxation. Where material, disclosure should be made of the amount of the UK corporation tax charge on the income for the year (any transfers between deferred tax and the profit and loss account included in that charge should be separately disclosed where material), tax attributable to franked investment income, irrecoverable advanced corporation tax (ACT), and relief for overseas taxation.

Where material, disclosure should be made of the total overseas taxation relieved and unrelieved, specifying that part of the unrelieved overseas taxation which arises from the payment or proposed payment of dividends.

Dividends proposed or payable should be included in current liabilities net of the related ACT (which should be included as a current tax liability). If the ACT on proposed dividends is regarded as recoverable, it should be deducted from the deferred tax account or, if this option is not available, shown as a deferred asset.

Irrecoverable ACT should treated as part of the tax on ordinary activities (paragraph 10, as amended by FRS 3).

Problems of interpretation and grey areas

This section begins by considering the outdated status of many items in the standard. The following items are then discussed under the heading of ACT and its treatment in the financial statements: the recoverability of ACT; the set off of ACT against chargeable gains; the treatment of irrecoverable ACT; the treatment of franked investment income (FII); the effect of overseas income; irrecoverable ACT on dividends relating to the previous period which were paid in the current period; tax rate apportionment; a summary of ACT set off; and tax law rules relating to ACT within groups.

The outdated status of many items in SSAP 8

This is one of the more straightforward accounting standards. It was issued in 1974, some 18 months after the adoption of the imputation scheme of company taxation in the UK. The intention was to establish a standard treatment of taxation in company accounts, particularly with reference to ACT and 'mainstream' corporation tax. As a result, there is a tendency for the standard to explain the imputation system in a manner which would probably not be considered appropriate today. Reference is also made (paragraph 18) to changes in the way in which preference shares should be described in the balance sheet -a not particularly relevant paragraph as it refers to changes brought about in the 1972 Finance Act! Paragraph 14 will soon be out of date: it concerns the possibility of companies paying corporation tax up to 21 months after the balance sheet date.

Thus, the standard contains three paragraphs which, due to the time lapse since it was issued, are of limited relevance. There is another example of potential obsolescence in paragraph 23, which refers to what should be done when the relevant rate of corporation tax is unknown. As tax rates have, in the recent past, been set one year in advance, rather than retrospectively as had been the case previously, this paragraph might appear to be redundant. However, it is conceivable that current practice may be changed, and it is also possible that the rate previously set could subsequently be amended. Accordingly, the use of the latest known rate, as advocated in paragraph 23, is still relevant and not in fact redundant.

Overall, SSAP 8 is embarrassingly out-of-date and, at its worst, confusing. Fortunately, it contains very little and, once the outdated elements are put aside or updated by the user, its application is reasonably straightforward. Clearly, however, updating of SSAP 8 would be useful.

ACT and its Treatment in the Financial Statements

The recoverability of ACT

The factor which most clearly suggests that the standard would benefit from updating concerns the effect of changes in tax law. Unlike standards dealing with rules of disclosure, SSAP 8 is primarily concerned with rules of computation. These rules were derived from the tax law of the day and there are now occasions when they are out-of-date - specifically, the two-year carry back of surplus ACT (paragraphs 2 and 5). All surplus ACT attributable to an accounting period ending after 31st March 1984 can be carried back to the previous six years. Thus, an ACT surplus attributable to the accounting period ending 31st December 1990, can be carried back to be offset against the corporation tax liability of the accounting period ending 31st December 1984.

The set off of ACT against chargeable gains

A further example of obsolescence arising from tax law occurs in paragraph 1, which states that 'ACT will normally be set off against the company's total liability for corporation tax on its income (but not on its chargeable gains)'. This restriction no longer applies. The same tax law changes make part of paragraph 7 obsolete: referring to ACT set off against the deferred tax account balance, the standard states that 'to the extent to which the deferred taxation account represents deferred chargeable gains, it is not available for this purpose'. In fact, it is available.

Application of the tax rules, rather than the obsolete SSAP 8 rules, would not require disclosure as a departure from the standard.

The treatment of irrecoverable ACT

Problems regarding the treatment of ACT are few. One concerns paragraph 2, which states that any ACT unrelieved against a company's corporation tax liability, can be carried back, or carried forward without time limit. There is no indication of which should be done first. Paragraph 5 repeats the option to carry back, and then states that ACT can also be carried forward *if necessary* - the implication being that it should first be carried back, and then any residue may be carried forward. Consideration of the remainder of the standard leaves the impression that unrelieved ACT should only be carried forward if there is a firm belief that future results will enable such a set off to be made - and it is recommended that only the following accounting period should be considered. In the absence of suitable conviction, the unrecovered ACT should be written-off in the current year. It would seem reasonable to suggest that the phrase 'if necessary' (paragraph 5) refers to the undesirability of carrying forward the balance of ACT unrecovered, rather than to the sequence of set off available. To conclude, either carry back, or carry forward may be used. However, carry back should logically be the preferred option as it will lead to short term receipts of refunded tax.

Paragraphs 2 and 5 are vague about which year should be used first when surplus ACT is carried back. This is clarified by tax law: later years must be used first.

The maximum offset of ACT against the corporation tax liability relating to an accounting period is limited to the proportion of the taxable profits equivalent to the tax rate used in computing the ACT. Thus, if the tax rate used to compute ACT is 25% (of the sum of the ACT + the dividend paid), then the ceiling is 25% of the taxable profits.

Where there is a deferred tax account, any unrelieved ACT should be debited to that account (paragraph 27), subject to a ceiling of the proportion of the value of the items giving rise to the deferred tax account balance, equivalent to the tax rate used in computing the ACT. Thus, if the tax rate used to compute ACT is 25% (of the sum of the ACT + the dividend paid), and there are £100,000 worth of timing differences giving rise to a deferred tax account balance of £35,000, then the ceiling is 25% of £100,000 (i.e. £25,000) (paragraph 7). It is, in effect, being carried forward in that account, rather than as a deferred asset. Consequently, it may be retrieved from that account in future years, and offset against future tax liabilities.

Irrecoverable ACT written-off should be included as part of the tax charge for the year, and the amount of irrecoverable ACT should be disclosed if material (paragraph 9). No alternative treatment is permitted. ACT written-off is not 'lost': it may still be recovered at a later date. If this occurs, the write-off may be reversed in that future accounting period. FRS 3 (*Reporting financial performance* - chapter 2) should be consulted to determine the appropriate treatment of the write-back.

Dividends received from UK companies can be paid out as dividends to members without any requirement to pay ACT (paragraph 12). This arises because the company can carry forward the tax credit on the dividend received, and then offset it against the ACT due when it pays its shareholders their dividend. Alternatively, if ACT has already been paid to the Inland Revenue during the same financial year as that when the dividend from the other company was received, a refund of the ACT paid, up to the value of the tax credit on the dividend received, can be reclaimed.

The treatment of franked investment income

Franked investment income (FII) should be brought into the financial statements at its gross value (i.e. dividend received + the associated tax credit). The tax credit should also be included in the taxation charge for the period (paragraph 13).

Tax credits on FII can be treated as reducing the ACT available for offset relating to an accounting period, up to the value of ACT payable during the same accounting period as that in which the tax credits are received. Any tax credit on FII not used to reduce, or obtain a refund of, an ACT payment made during the year, is normally carried forward to be offset against future ACT payments. If a tax credit on FII is carried forward, there can be no unrecovered ACT relating to the current accounting period.

If a tax credit preceded an ACT payment, it will either have been refunded, or will have been used to reduce the ACT actually paid. If any tax credit remains which preceded ACT payments made, it does so because the value of the tax credit was higher than the value of the ACT payable. In these circumstances, there will be no unrecovered ACT relating to the current accounting period.

There are two other possible ways in which a year end surplus of tax credits on FII may arise: when a company has made no dividend payments during the year, in which case there will be no unrecovered ACT relating to the accounting period; and when a tax credit is received after the last ACT payment was made, in which case it can be reclaimed up to the total value of all ACT paid during the accounting period - again there will be no unrecovered ACT relating to the current accounting period.

The effect of overseas income

If a company has overseas income, and the overseas tax is greater than the UK tax on the same income, part of the overseas tax will be unrelieved. Any dividends the company pays out of this overseas income will not qualify for ACT set off against the overseas tax suffered. For example, if the overseas tax rate is 60% and the company has taxable overseas profits of £100,000, it will pay £60,000 overseas tax. This will be relieved by tax at the UK rate, say £35,000, leaving £25,000 overseas tax which is not recoverable. The ACT on the dividends paid out of this income will be available for relief against the £35,000, but not the other £25,000. The unrelieved tax (i.e. the ACT paid) will not be available for carry forward (or carry back) and must be written-off in the same way as irrecoverable ACT (i.e. as part of the tax charge), and disclosed if material. It would be advisable not to offset the £35,000 against the UK tax liability which arose on the foreign income, as this would only serve to increase the amount of overseas tax unrelieved. It should, instead, be offset against taxation on UK income, or treated as surplus ACT and accounted for in the usual way (i.e. carried back, carried forward, or written-off) (paragraph 11 and appendix 2, sections 1 and 2).

Irrecoverable ACT on dividends relating to the previous period which were paid in the current period

Where a dividend relating to the previous accounting period is paid during the current accounting period, ACT will arise. According to SSAP 8, if at the end of the accounting period, any part of this ACT on prior period dividends is thought to be irrecoverable, it should be added to the taxation charge for the *previous* year (paragraph 8 states that it should be written-off in the profit and loss account in which the related dividend is shown). However, this does not constitute a fundamental error as defined in FRS 3 and thus, despite the suggestion in paragraph 8 that the previous period's profit and loss account figures should be restated, this should not be done. Rather, this would be treated in the same way as any under or over provision for tax in the previous period's accounts, and included in the profit and loss account for the current period.

Tax rate apportionment

When a company's balance sheet date is not 31st March, and does not therefore coincide with the date of a change of tax rate, it will be necessary to apportion the tax rates used in the ACT calculations in order to determine the effective tax rate for the period. Thus, if the balance sheet date is 31st December, and from January to March the corporation tax rate was 40%, but for the rest of the year it was 30%, the effective tax rate is 32.5% $[(40/4) + ((3 \times 30)/4)]$.

A summary of ACT set off

To conclude, the ACT available for set off against corporation tax arising on the profits of an accounting period, is that ACT payable which results from dividends paid *in* that accounting period at the current tax rate [currently ⅓(dividend)], less any tax credits received in the same accounting period up to the value of the ACT payable. (That is, the total ACT paid during the accounting period and available for set off, may be less than the ACT actually paid because tax credits on FII received during the accounting period were reclaimed; also, the amount actually paid may be less than the ACT payable because a tax credit received was offset against the ACT payable, and only the net amount paid.) The ACT available for set off should first be offset against the corporation tax liability of the company. Where there are insufficient profits to offset all the ACT available, it is advisable to carry it back, if possible, through each of the last six years, starting with the most recent, setting it off against the corporation tax liability of those earlier years. Where there are not sufficient prior year tax liabilities to offset all the surplus ACT, the balance should be debited to the deferred tax account. Where there is no deferred tax account, or where the balance in it is insufficient to permit debiting all the surplus ACT, the balance of ACT may be carried forward as a deferred asset under prepayments and accrued income, *provided that there is reasonable certainty that it will be recoverable in the next accounting period*. If this is not the case, the balance of irrecoverable ACT should be included in the tax charge for the year, and disclosed if material.

Tax laws relating to ACT within groups

Two further points, not contained in SSAP 8, are relevant. They both derive from tax legislation and concern ACT within groups. Firstly, a parent company may surrender any, or all ACT paid, to a 51% subsidiary. The subsidiary should then set off the transferred ACT before any arising from its own dividend payments. If the subsidiary is unable to utilise all the surrendered ACT, it may carry it forward. It cannot carry it back, though it can carry back any of its own ACT. Secondly, changes in the ownership of companies which have unrecovered ACT result in such ACT being unavailable for set off against future accounting periods if, within any period of three years, there is a change in ownership *and* a major change in the nature or conduct of the company's trade or business. This loss of set off also applies if there is a change in ownership at any time after a company's business has become negligible and before any revival.

SSAP 15:   Accounting for Deferred Tax

Summary of the accounting treatment requirements

Deferred tax should be calculated under the liability method *to the extent that it is probable that it will crystallise.*

The provision for deferred tax liabilities should be reduced by any deferred tax debit balances and any ACT available for set off. Deferred tax net debit balances should not be carried forward as assets, except to the extent that they are expected to be recoverable without replacement by equivalent debit balances.

Deferred tax relating to the ordinary activities of the enterprise should be shown separately as part of the tax on profit or loss on ordinary activities. Deferred tax relating to extraordinary items should be shown separately as part of the tax on extraordinary items. In both cases, disclosure should either be on the face of the profit and loss account or in a note.

Any unprovided deferred tax should be disclosed, analysed into its major components.

The deferred tax balance, and its major components, should be disclosed in the balance sheet or notes. Transfers to and from deferred tax should be disclosed in a note.

Where deferred tax has not been provided on a revalued asset because the revaluation does not constitute a timing difference, it should be stated that it does not constitute a timing difference and that tax has therefore not been quantified. Where the value of an asset has been shown in a note because it differs materially from its book amount, the note should also show the tax effects which would arise if the asset were realised at the balance sheet date at the noted value.

Problems of interpretation and grey areas

The following items are discussed: the aims of deferred tax, and the basis and method prescribed; permanent -v- timing differences; the global view requirement; deferred tax not included in profit and loss on ordinary activities; deferred tax assets; revaluation; disposal; future losses; deferred tax within groups; and disclosure requirements. This discussion is followed by concluding comments on the standard as a whole. (In order to facilitate understanding of the application of SSAP 15, 'pooling' of assets for capital allowance purposes has not been considered. The aspects of deferred tax relating to ACT and government grants are covered in the discussion of SSAP 8 (pages 182-186) and SSAP 4 (pages 177-180), respectively.)

The aims of deferred tax, and the basis and method prescribed

The standard is concerned with the situation where accounting profits/losses are different from taxable profits/losses for the same accounting period. In some circumstances, such differences, known as *timing differences*, may result in additional tax being due in later periods because the basis upon which the original tax assessment was made, ceased to apply. For example, a piece of machinery purchased for £1,000 may receive capital allowances at 25% written-down value, while it is being depreciated at 10% straight line. If sold after one year for £950, the tax written-down value of £750 is used to compute the taxable gain of £200, which is £150 greater than the accounting profit of £50. Tax will be assessed on the £200 gain, not on the £50 book profit. The standard also applies where the opposite arises (i.e. where the tax written-down value is higher than the book value), though prudence would be applied in deciding whether to provide for the deferred asset and, more often than not, no provision would result.

When timing differences occur, deferred tax should be provided to the extent that a liability or asset will crystallise (paragraph 2). It is this question of crystallisation that is the principal source of subjectivity in the application of SSAP 15.

In order to provide for deferred tax, with one exception, the standard makes mandatory the use of the *partial deferral* basis, as applied under the *liability method* (paragraph 24). Under earlier standards dealing with this topic, other methods were permitted. Such approaches are not acceptable under SSAP 15, and their use cannot be justified on the basis of a more true and fair view. The only exception is that the *full provision basis* (paragraph 8) may be used in accounting for the deferred tax implications of pensions and other post-retirement benefits (paragraph 32a).

Permanent -v- timing differences

Deferred tax is defined as tax attributable to *timing differences* (paragraph 17). The key point is that they originate in one period and are then capable of being reversed in later periods. Where an item has the appearance of a timing difference, but is incapable of subsequent reversal, it is classified as being a *permanent difference* and no deferred tax should be provided in respect of it. Examples of permanent differences are expenditure unallowable for tax purposes (for example, fines and most entertaining expenditure); and, tax-free income (for example, interest on tax repayments).

Although it has the appearance of being a permanent difference, depreciation (which is not allowable for tax purposes) does contribute towards a timing difference. This is because, while depreciation is not a tax-deductible expense, capital allowances are. The effect of the depreciation charge is to enable the tax written-down value to be related to a current book value which should, if SSAP 12 (*Accounting for depreciation* - chapter 4) is observed, be a good approximation of its true value. As a result, the potential tax liability on the disposal of the asset can be estimated. For example, if a piece of equipment which cost £5,000 has been depreciated to £2,000 and its tax written-down value is £1,500, there is a potential tax liability on the £500 difference (assuming it could be disposed of at its book value). Consequently, any provision made should be based on this potential liability, not on the difference between the original cost and the current tax written-down value.

The standard lists five principal areas of differences which may arise (appendix, section 2): permanent differences; timing differences; items not included in profit and loss on ordinary activities; losses; and ACT. Permanent differences have already been mentioned in the previous paragraph. Examples of timing differences are given in section 5 of the appendix, and include such items as development expenditure deferred (for tax purposes the expenditure is recognised when incurred), and interest receivable accrued (only assessable to tax when received).

The global view requirement

Timing differences should be treated as a whole, rather than individually, when attempting to assess whether a tax liability will crystallise. Potential assets are treated in the same way as potential liabilities: thus, there will be an element of set off amongst them. When considering the overall position, care must be taken to exclude those items which, although short-term in nature, are, in effect, permanent. For example, interest accrued on a long-term investment will create a permanent short-term timing difference which will not truly reverse until the investment is sold: the liability will not crystallise until the decision is taken to sell, and so it should not be provided for until that decision is taken.

In addition, the future must be considered - not just the next accounting period, but the years beyond. Financial plans and projections must be consulted over whatever future period is appropriate given the expected pattern of timing differences: the more irregular the expected pattern, the longer the time period that should be considered. The appendix suggests that the minimum period should be three years (section 4), but does not consider the difficulties of achieving accuracy in forecasts of any length. In practice, the accuracy of a one-year forecast is generally suspect; a three-year forecast is likely to be more than marginally imprecise, *except, possibly, where the pattern of the timing differences is regular*. As a result, considerable subjective judgment will be brought to bear in evaluating the probability of future tax liabilities and assets, especially when irregular timing difference patterns exist. Thus, two identical companies may make very different deferred tax provisions because one company's directors took a very different view, compared to the other's, concerning the accuracy of their future projections. The fact that prudence is advocated (paragraph 28) does little to reduce the possibility of widely different provisions being made.

For obvious reasons, the projections and plans must be not only physically feasible, but also financially possible. Attention must, therefore, be given to the financial basis of such projections.

Deferred tax not included in profit and loss on ordinary activities

Deferred tax on extraordinary items must be shown separately as part of the tax on extraordinary items in the profit and loss account, or as a note. Transfers to and from deferred tax relating to movements on reserves should be shown separately as part of such reserve movements (paragraphs 34 and 39).

Deferred tax assets

Tax losses can be offset against deferred tax credit balances. However, care must be taken when these are capital losses as they can only be offset against current and future capital gains. In addition, for capital losses to be utilised in this way, there must be an unrealised capital gain anticipated, which is not going to be covered by rollover relief, *and the asset(s) involved must not have been revalued in the financial statements to reflect the gain*, nor must the asset be essential to the future operations of the enterprise (i.e. it must be realistically disposable).

In general, deferred tax assets (of which tax losses are but one example) should be recognised only when they are expected to be recoverable without replacement by equivalent debit balances. For example, debenture interest payable accrued, which would give rise to a short-term debit timing difference, should not be recognised as it will be replaced in the following year by a similar amount relating to the next payment due. More specifically on trading losses, the appendix is very clear on when a loss should be treated as recoverable (and thus available for offset against credit balances in determining the deferred tax liability or asset): it must derive from an identifiable, non-recurring cause; there must be a history of profitability with any previous losses having been fully recovered; and there must be assurance, beyond a reasonable doubt, that future taxable profits will be sufficient to offset the loss *during the period of time permitted for such carry forward*.

Revaluation

One major area of confusion in the standard relates to asset revaluation. Paragraph 20 states: 'the revaluation of an asset ... will create a timing difference when it is incorporated in the balance sheet ... unless disposal of the revalued asset ... would not result in a tax liability, after taking account of any expected rollover relief'. Section 9 of the appendix states: 'when a fixed asset is revalued above cost a timing difference potentially arises in that, in the absence of rollover relief, tax on a chargeable gain may be payable if and when the asset is disposed of at its revalued amount. Where it is probable that a liability will crystallise, provision for the tax payable on disposal is required .... Whether or not a liability will crystallise can usually be determined ... at the time the enterprise decides to dispose of the asset'.

Taking both paragraphs together, it would appear that the required treatment is that no provision be made until it is planned that the asset will ultimately be disposed of. If there is no intention to dispose of the asset, there can be no potential tax liability, and so no provision should be made.

Accordingly, when a fixed asset is revalued above cost, a timing difference should only be recognised when there is an expectation that a tax liability will arise, and that expectation can only exist once there is a planned intention to dispose of the asset. At that time, any deferred tax provision must be made out of the revaluation surplus, based on the asset's carrying value in the balance sheet.

When there is a downward revaluation, it should be treated in the same way as depreciation, and used in the computation of timing differences on capital allowances, providing that a liability to future tax is foreseen in respect of that asset.

One problem concerning upwards revaluation arises over what value should be used when calculating timing differences arising from accelerated capital allowances. Consider the example of an asset which cost £5,000, has been depreciated to a net book value of £2,000, has a tax written-down value of £4,000, and is then revalued to £3,000. Should a timing difference computation use the revalued amount of £3,000, or the net book value of £2,000? It could be argued that the revaluation is a restatement of the true value and that any timing difference should only be calculated using the original cost, as that is what the capital allowances are based upon.

While this is logical, it is hard to see why it should be preferred to the argument that the revalued amount should be used as it more truly reflects the potential tax liability if it should crystallise. That, after all, is the reason why deferred tax is provided in the first place, or is it?

In the case of accelerated capital allowances, which arise when capital allowances and depreciation are unequal, and result in more or less tax being paid than would have been expected based on the accounting profit, the standard appears to attempt to achieve some degree of equality between the accounting profit and losses and the taxable profits and losses. This occurs because it requires that tax deferred or accelerated be accounted for to the extent that it is probable that a liability or asset will crystallise. The timing difference process apportions this tax saving/expense over the other periods in which there will have to be paid an amount of tax other than that which would have been expected on the basis of the accounting profit (i.e. those years when depreciation exceeds capital allowances, or *vice versa*). Under the prohibited full provision basis, equality could be achieved as each year's profit and loss would be charged with deferred tax based on the excess of capital allowances for the year over the depreciation for the year; or, when the depreciation charge exceeds the capital allowances received, by crediting profit and loss with the difference. Under the mandatory, partial provision basis, this provision is restricted to the extent that the originating difference (which arose because the capital allowances were greater than the depreciation charge, or *vice versa*) is foreseen as being reversed. The result is that equalisation of the two profit figures is not achieved, but there is a narrowing of the original imbalance. As the concept of accelerated capital allowances arises from the difference between capital allowances and depreciation based on the same cost figure, it would probably be more in keeping with the spirit of the standard to ignore any revaluation for the computation of timing differences based on accelerated capital allowances.

This view is given further weight by consideration of section 9 of the appendix (quoted on page 189) which states that if revaluation value is above cost, the potential tax liability for the chargeable gain should be provided for out of the revaluation surplus, based on the asset's carrying amount. To be consistent, the carrying amount of an asset prior to revaluation should also be the limit on which depreciation, applied to reverse timing differences on the capital allowances applicable to that asset, should be calculated. Thus, the standard does seem to suggest that timing differences arising from accelerated capital allowances should be based on the write-down of original cost, and that any upward revaluation should be ignored.

Accordingly, where the revaluation value exceeds the original cost, *and a tax liability is expected to arise*, the deferred tax provision on the chargeable gain should be calculated on the basis of the amount transferred to the revaluation surplus, and then transferred to deferred tax from that surplus. In the years that remain until disposal, the balance on the deferred tax account would be reduced because of the reversing timing differences generated by that part of the depreciation charge deriving from the revaluation surplus.

In all cases, including those where there is no revaluation, where no tax liability or asset is expected (probably because there is no intention to dispose of the asset, or, if disposal is intended, because of the availability of rollover relief), no provision should be made, not even for the timing differences arising from accelerated capital allowances (see section 8 of the appendix).

While paragraph 20 of the standard and section 9 of the appendix can be interpreted in this way, it should be realised that they are very imprecise and other interpretations are possible. There really is no 'correct' interpretation of the treatment of the revaluation of fixed assets, and it is very much up to each individual to decide how these parts of the standard should be applied. Students should be aware that there is an element of doubt in the appropriate treatment to adopt, a fact that is borne out by the conflicting approaches adopted in various textbooks dealing with the topic. As a result, it is important for students to be prepared to apply whichever approach is required by the question being tackled, not just the one which they, as individuals, believe to be 'best'.

Future losses

As previously mentioned (page 189), tax losses can, in certain circumstances, be offset against credit balances on the deferred tax account. If projections indicate that future tax losses will probably be incurred, all of which will probably be capable of offset, should these future losses be taken into account when determining the appropriate provision required for deferred tax? The standard states (paragraph 25) that 'tax deferred or accelerated by the effect of timing differences should be accounted for to the extent that it is probable that a liability or asset will crystallise'. The future tax losses would be a deferred asset. However, they are not yet a timing difference and it would not be appropriate to treat them as such until they are. [For a fuller explanation of this point, see *'UK GAAP'* (MacMillan, 1992, pp. 1044-5).]

Deferred tax within groups

Within groups, the elimination of intra-group profits upon consolidation might result in the need for a deferred tax provision. For example, if one company sells stock to another company in the group at a price which includes £50,000 profit then, if the second company still has the stock at the year end, the profit must be removed from the stock value upon consolidation. Tax will still be payable by the first company on the sale, but the extra cost will not be offset against the income of the second company until the stock is sold. The tax is being met by the group one year early. The consolidated accounts should, therefore, include a debit to deferred tax equal to the tax suffered.

A company within a group may be able to apply group relief to reduce its deferred tax provision. Where this occurs, the assumptions made, including details of compensatory payments to other group members, should be disclosed.

Individual companies within a group have to provide for deferred tax, if appropriate. Where a company has projected increases in its net timing differences, it will have no deferred tax provision. However, the net increase it forecast will be used within the group to offset net timing difference reversals in other companies in the group. Thus, the group deferred tax provision may be less than the sum of those of all the companies in the group. Also, where companies are subject to different rates of tax, the calculation of group deferred tax should be performed with reference to the tax expected to be paid (i.e. the tax on the timing difference), rather than the timing difference.

Disclosure requirements

Paragraphs 33-44 of the standard go into great detail regarding what requires to be disclosed in respect of deferred tax. In the profit and loss account, or as a note, deferred tax should be included and shown separately in the tax on profit or loss on ordinary activities. Any unprovided deferred tax in respect of the period should be disclosed in a note, analysed into its major components. Any adjustments to deferred tax resulting from changes in tax rates and allowances should normally be shown separately as part of the tax charge for the period.

In the balance sheet, or as a note, the deferred tax balance should be disclosed. Details should be given of any transfers to and from the account. Any deferred tax unprovided should be disclosed in a note, analysed into its major components. (This differs from the profit and loss requirement which only relates to the current period.) Where the potential deferred tax on a revalued asset is not shown because the revaluation does not constitute a timing difference, it should be stated and the reason declared. When an asset is shown in a note at a value materially different from its book value, the note should also reveal any tax effects which would arise should the asset be realised at that noted value.

Paragraph 47 states that the Companies Act requires that deferred tax provisions should be shown under the heading 'provisions for liabilities and charges'. Paragraph 50, following the same authority, states that any deferred tax carried forward as an asset should be included under the heading 'prepayments and accrued income'.

Conclusion

This is a somewhat vague standard which suffers in its interpretation from the fundamental changes which have taken place in both its aims and its approaches compared to those in its earlier versions. Three key areas in the standard are less than satisfactory. Firstly, there is the difficulty that any provision is dependent upon an assessment of the accuracy of future forecasts: if they are held to be unreliable, provision should not be made for future gains suggested by the forecasts (prudence); and, if provision cannot be made for future gains, it can hardly be made for future liabilities which will only result if the gains materialise. It could be argued that even the worst forecast will have some usefulness, and that it should always be possible to draw some conclusion from which an assessment of potential liability may be drawn. There is no doubt that this is true, but this is where the problem really arises: what is treated as a reasonably good forecast by one person will be dismissed as useless by another. Thus, consistency of treatment between companies is unlikely, and true comparability is impaired as a result.

Secondly, the area concerning asset revaluations is unsatisfactory. Apart from the lack of clarity in the standard over the appropriate treatment, which in effect leaves it very much up to the individual company as to whether or not any provision for a future tax liability should be provided for, there is a certain illogicality about the requirement. If one assumes that a lot of the equipment used by a company will eventually be scrapped, rather than sold, there will very often be no material tax liability. In addition, the majority of fixed asset revaluations are on land and buildings (i.e. fixed assets in respect of which there is often no intention of disposal). There is nothing to stop any company which revalues its fixed assets incorporating in its future plans no intention to resell those revalued assets, and thus no provision would be required. Besides which, rollover relief will often make any provision unnecessary. Again, consistency between companies is unlikely, and true comparability is impaired as a result.

Thirdly, despite the emphasis which most textbooks place on the subject, there is no mandatory requirement to provide for the reversal of timing differences arising from accelerated capital allowances. As stated in section 8 of the appendix, 'when ... originating timing differences ... reverse ... deferred tax should be provided unless it is probable ... that no tax liability will crystallise'. In other words, if the asset is not going to be disposed of in a way that will give rise to a charge for tax, no deferred tax should be provided.

The area of accelerated capital allowances is one over which students need to take care. Examiners tend to assume that, despite what their questions suggest, provision should be made if reversal of originating differences is foreseen. For example, a question which states: 'an asset will be bought for £10,000, has a useful life of four years, *after which it will be scrapped*' would probably expect provision to be made even though no taxable gain will arise on disposal. As a general guide, the relevant reversal is the largest net cumulative reversal from the current position over the projected period; and it should not exceed the current balance of originating differences. In addition, the opposite position, where depreciation initially exceeds capital allowances, is often overlooked. According to the standard, it should not be. A timing difference does arise and, assuming there is an expectation that future capital allowances will be received and utilised, an entry could be made in the deferred tax account. However, the prudence concept must be applied and for this reason it is unlikely that any such provision would be made. If it is, nevertheless, considered appropriate, and the overall effect is to create a debit balance on the account, then it should be carried forward as such, under prepayments and accrued income. Students need to take care: examiners will probably expect no provision to be made, on the grounds of prudence. The reason why examiners tend to make these assumptions is that they are testing students' knowledge of the mechanics. They usually want to know if an appropriate provision, assuming that it is required, can be computed. In an exam, a student who decides not to provide for a future tax liability, or who decides to provide for a future tax asset, would be wise to explain fully the reasons for doing so. Thankfully, recent professional exam questions in this area have tended to be either essay-based, or to contain information relating to one year only. As a result, the potential problems mentioned above are less likely to arise. The most important thing is that the main requirements of the standard are known, particularly, in view of the tendency to set narrative questions, those relating to disclosure.

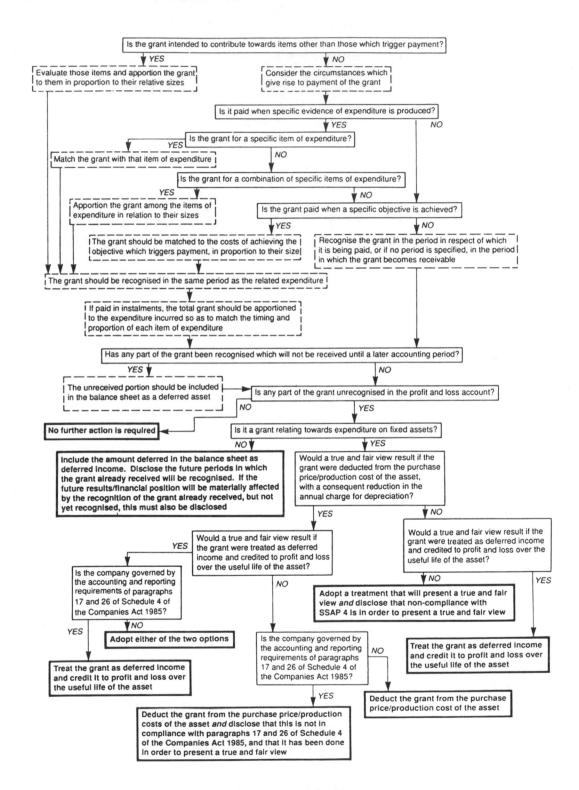

SSAP 4   Initial treatment of grants received and receivable

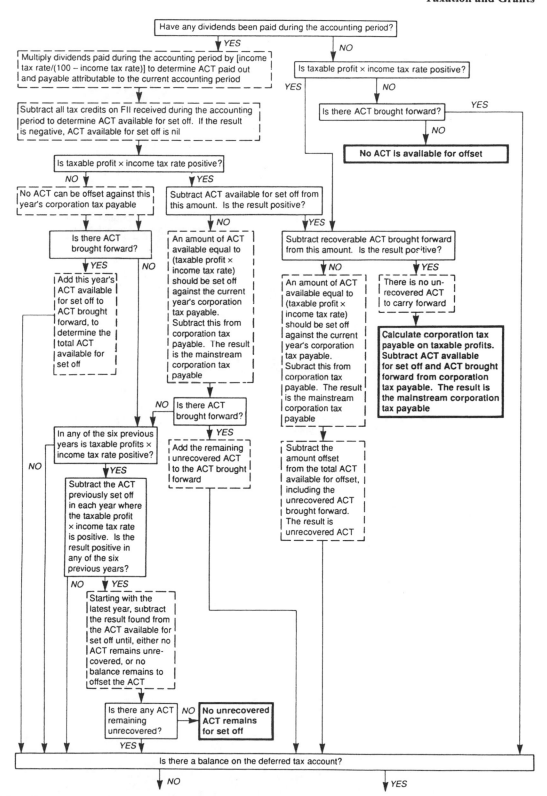

SSAP 8(a) Determination of ACT set off, carry forward, and write-off

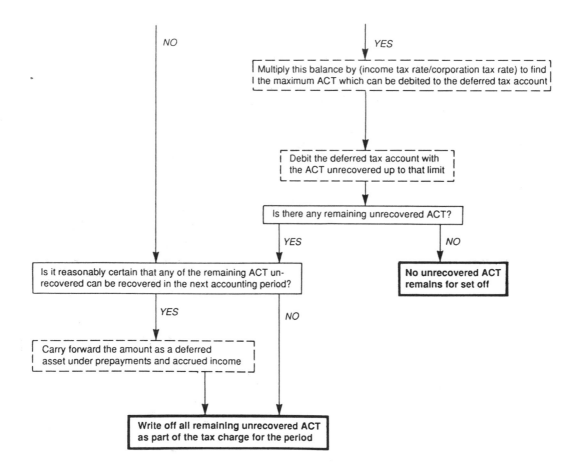

SSAP 8(b) Determination of ACT set off, carry forward, and write-off

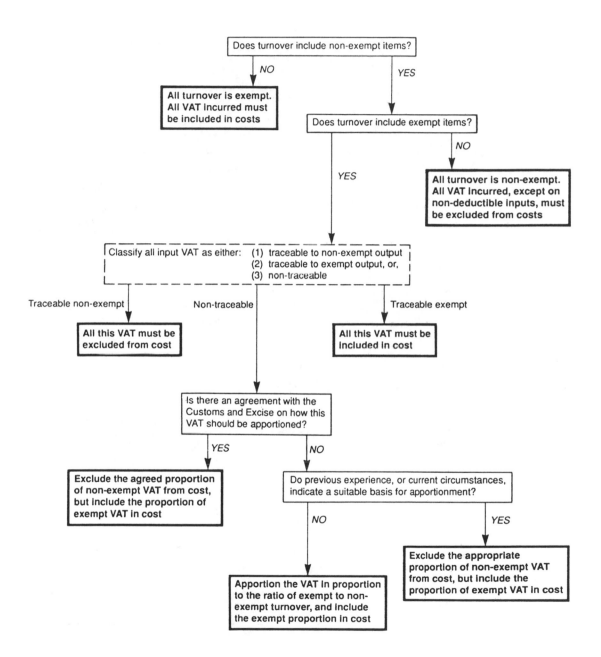

SSAP 5   Allocation of VAT to expenditure

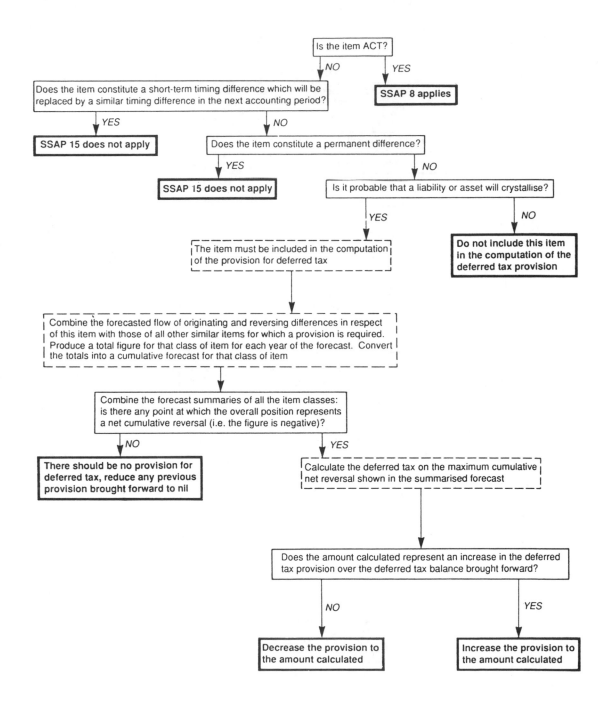

SSAP 15   Determination of the deferred tax provision required, assuming
the same tax rate throughout

Short Questions

*ASSUME THAT MATERIALITY EXISTS IN **EVERY** CASE*

SSAP 4: Accounting for Government Grants

Questions 1-6 relate to a steel manufacturing company with current turnover of £35m and net pre-tax profit of £7.5m. (Last year £33.6m and £6.2m respectively.) The company's financial year ends on 31st December. Company policy is to treat grants received in respect of fixed assets as deferred income, and to deduct all grants identified as relating to specific revenue expenditure against that expenditure. All other grants recognised are credited to profit and loss. The questions should be done in sequence, using the information contained in earlier questions where appropriate.

1   During the year the company received a grant from the European Community for £100,000 towards the cost of some new equipment. The equipment has an estimated useful economic life of ten years and cost £500,000.

2   Company policy is to depreciate all depreciable fixed assets by the straight line method.

3   In September, the company spent £60,000 on training, in respect of which it is due receive a government grant of 50%. The grant formalities have been completed but payment is not expected until mid-March.

4   In May, the company received 10 days free consultancy from a financial advisor under a local enterprise scheme. The market rate for this service was £500 per day.

5   In July, a grant of £30,000 was received from the Swedish government in recognition of the high quality that the company's production had maintained over the five years which had ended on 31st December the previous year.

6   The company had been advised to expect the award of the Swedish grant while the previous year's accounts were being prepared. As a result £20,000 had been included in the previous year's accounts as a deferred asset in respect of this grant.

SSAP 5: Accounting for Valued Added Tax

Questions 7-8 relate to a high street retailing company. The company's financial year ends on 31st December. The standard rate of VAT is 17½%. The two questions should be done in sequence, using the information contained in earlier questions where appropriate.

7   A trading company has gross turnover of £52.875m. One third of this is exempt output.

8   At the balance sheet date, the company was due to pay the Customs and Excise £50,000 in respect of VAT for the last quarter.

SSAP 8:   The Treatment of Taxation under the Imputation System in the Accounts of Companies

Questions 9-14 relate to a furniture manufacturing and redecoration company with current turnover of £15m and net pre-tax profit of £2.5m. (Last year £13.6m and £1.8m respectively.) The company's financial year ends on 31st December. The corporation tax rate applicable is 35%, and ACT is one third of the amount of qualifying distributions. The six questions should be done in sequence, using the information contained in earlier questions where appropriate.

9   During the year the company received two dividends from a UK company in which it has a minor shareholding. The first was £7,500 on 15th June, and the second, £11,250 on 15th December.

10   The company paid the final dividend (£150,000) for the previous accounting period on 28th March. On 28th September, it paid an interim dividend for the current accounting period (£60,000).

11   When the company received the dividend from the other company on 15th June, it reclaimed the tax credit.

12   The company included a proposed final dividend of £300,000 in the financial statements.

13   The taxable profit was £2.8m.

14   Included in the deferred tax account at the start of the accounting period, was unrecovered ACT of £118,000.

SSAP 15:   Accounting for Deferred Tax

Questions 15-25 all relate to an engineering company with current turnover of £12m and net pre-tax profit of £2.6m. (Last year £11.6m and £1.9m respectively.) The company's financial year ends on 31st December. The corporation tax rate applicable is 35%, the income tax rate is 25%, and the writing down allowance for all capital allowances available is 25%; these rates apply to all accounting periods involved. At 31st December, the company had claimed capital allowances that exceeded accumulated depreciation by £620,000, and there was no balance on the deferred tax account. The questions should be done in sequence, using the information contained in earlier questions where appropriate, except for the information in question 15, which should be treated in isolation from the rest.

[Note for tutors: the £620,000 excess of capital allowances claimed over depreciation charged results in all the reversals identified being provided for. It would be a worthwhile exercise to set some of the questions on the premise that a different initial excess existed.]

15   The company received a one-off government training grant of £100,000 in June. It covers the year to the end of next June. £50,000 has been treated as deferred income and carried forward to next year. Tax, at 35%, was payable on receipt of the grant.

Ignore the information contained in question 15 in all future questions

16   At the financial year end, the company had capital allowances of £70,000 and a depreciation charge of £50,000. In the absence of other information, assuming that a provision is required for deferred tax, what should it be?

17   The company has capital losses of £15,000 available which it believes will be recoverable. What should the provision now be?

18   The company has the following projection for accelerated capital allowance based timing differences occurring in each of the next five years (figures in brackets represent reversing differences):

1	2	3	4	5
£100,000	200,000	(350,000)	150,000	(80,000)

What provision should now be made? The capital losses mentioned in question 17 are no longer considered to be recoverable.

19   The forecast includes a timing difference in respect of a piece of equipment on which rollover relief will be available. The amounts included in respect of the equipment were:

1	2	3	4	5
£6,000	3,500	1,625	nil	nil

What provision should now be made?

20   Additional information has come to light which alters the forecasted year 5 timing difference. It is now believed that it will be a reversal of £180,000, rather than the £80,000 reversal previously forecast. What provision should now be made?

21   Other timing differences identified are:

1	2	3	4	5
£(54,000)	(115,000)	63,625	(58,000)	29,000

What provision should now be made?

22   After further analysis, the other timing differences given in question 21 were found to be incorrect. The revised forecast is as follows:

1	2	3	4	5
£(54,000)	115,000	63,625	(58,000)	29,000

What provision should now be made?

23   There is recoverable ACT of £20,000 at this balance sheet date (i.e. at the end of year 0).

24   One year has now passed and it is the end of year 1. Forecasts have been produced for the next five years. The forecasted accelerated capital allowance based timing differences are:

2	3	4	5	6
£184,000	(276,000)	97,000	(42,000)	221,000

Assume that there are no other timing differences, what amount should be credited/debited to the deferred tax account?

25   There is unrecovered ACT of £47,000 at the balance sheet date (i.e. at the end of year 1).

Additional Questions

*ASSUME THAT MATERIALITY EXISTS IN **EVERY** CASE*

SSAP 4:   Accounting for Government Grants

Questions 26-29 relate to the same steel manufacturing company as questions 1-6. It has current turnover of £35m and net pre-tax profit of £7.5m. (Last year £33.6m and £6.2m respectively.) The company's financial year ends on 31st December. Company policy is to treat grants received in respect of fixed assets as deferred income, and to deduct all grants identified as relating to specific revenue expenditure against that expenditure. All other grants recognised are credited to profit and loss. The questions should be done in sequence, using the information contained in earlier questions, including questions 1-6, where appropriate.

26   The company has learnt that it will be required to repay a grant of £75,000 which it received in March. When it was received, the company suspected that there had been an error. As a result, no entries have been made through the accounts other than to deposit it in the company bank account.

27   Whilst the grant received in error was being held in the company's bank account, it earned interest of £6,000. The government agency which had issued the money has indicated its gratitude that the company informed it of its error, and has indicated that the company will not be required to hand over the interest. (The company pays corporation tax at 35%.)

28   A grant previously awarded towards the planning and construction costs of a distribution warehouse has been recalled due to the company failing to meet the conditions relating to costs and design. It was received in the previous year, when £10,000 was applied to offset the planning costs incurred. The remainder of the grant was carried forward as deferred income to be amortised over the useful economic life of the warehouse. The warehouse was completed this year.

29   Under a central government scheme developed to enhance the international competitiveness of UK steel companies, the company was awarded £500,000 worth of computer controlled production monitoring equipment. The equipment was received in

April and has been in full use since its installation in July. It is expected to have a useful economic life of five years.

30   In May, an engineering company received a grant of £150,000 in compensation for loss of income resulting from a change in effluent control regulations.

31   In October, Fortunada Plc was awarded with £800,000 worth of engineering equipment under a government scheme to assist engineering output and performance. The equipment was received on 10th January and went into full use two months after the balance sheet date. It is expected to have a useful economic life of ten years. The company uses straight line depreciation. How should this item be treated in Fortunada Plc's financial statements?

SSAP 5:   Accounting for Valued Added Tax

Questions 32-33 relate to the same high street retailing company as featured in questions 7 and 8. The company's financial year ends on 31st December. The standard rate of VAT is 17½%. The two questions should be done in sequence, using the information contained in the earlier questions where appropriate.

32   During the year the company replaced its fleet of company cars. The cost included VAT of £15,000.

33   The company installed a new computer system costing £874,000, including VAT, in December. It is to be used throughout the company and will be used in connection with items related to both exempt and nonexempt supplies. The company has started negotiations with the Customs and Excise over the apportionment of the VAT on this equipment, but has yet to receive any response. No similar situation has previously arisen.

34   A household products company has signed an agreement to purchase a new fleet of cars for its salesmen over the next two accounting periods. The agreed cost, including VAT at 17½%, is £205,625.

SSAP 8:   The Treatment of Taxation under the Imputation System in the Accounts of Companies

Questions 35-38 relate to an electric goods manufacturing and distribution company with current turnover of £2m and net pre-tax profit of £400,000. (Last year £3.4m and £800,000 respectively.) The company's financial year ends on 31st December. The corporation tax rate applicable for all accounting periods is 35%, and ACT is one third of the amount of qualifying distributions. The four questions should be done in sequence, using the information contained in earlier questions where appropriate.

35   Previous accounting periods' corporation tax liabilities were as follows:

year	maximum ACT offset	ACT offset used	corpn. tax paid
last	£112,500	£80,000	£77,500
last-1	50,000	50,000	20,000
last-2	25,000	20,000	15,000
last-3	80,000	80,000	32,000
last-4	115,000	105,000	56,000
last-5	40,000	39,000	17,000
last-6	70,000	40,000	58,000

During the year, the company paid a final dividend relating to the previous year, of £300,000 and, at the year end, taxable profits amounted to £160,000.

36   The company has a deferred taxation account balance of £20,000 which stems from a timing difference arising from a chargeable gain of £70,000 expected on the anticipated sale of a small factory.

37   An error was made in the tax computation for the current year. Taxable profits were only £20,000.

38   The company paid an interim dividend of £60,000 on 18th December.

39   The board of an oil supply company wish to treat £65,000 irrecoverable ACT as an appropriation of profit, rather than as part of the tax charge upon the company to be deducted in arriving at profits after tax.

SSAP 15:   Accounting for Deferred Tax

Questions 40-44 continue from the scenario described in questions 15-25, and those questions should be referred to when answering these questions. As with questions 15-25, they all relate to an engineering company with current turnover of £12m and net pre-tax profit of £2.6m. (Last year £11.6m and £1.9m respectively.) The company's financial year ends on 31st December. The corporation tax rate applicable is 35%, the income tax rate is 25%, and the writing down allowance for all capital allowances available is 25%; these rates apply to all accounting periods involved. At 31st December, the company had claimed capital allowances that exceeded accumulated depreciation by £620,000, and there was no balance on the deferred tax account. The questions should be done in sequence, using the information contained in earlier questions where appropriate, except for the information in question 15, which should be treated in isolation from the rest.

[Note for tutors: the £620,000 excess of capital allowances claimed over depreciation charged results in all the reversals identified being provided for. It would be a worthwhile exercise to set some of the questions on the premise that a different initial excess existed.]

40   Another year has now passed (since the situation portrayed in question 25) and it is the end of year 2. Forecasts have been produced for the next five years. The forecasted accelerated capital allowance based timing differences for each year are:

3	4	5	6	7
£(142,000)	161,000	(48,000)	221,000	66,000

Assume that there are no other timing differences, what amount should be credited/debited to the deferred tax account?

41   There is unrecovered ACT of £35,000 at this balance sheet date (i.e. at the end of year 2).

42   At the end of year 2, the company consulted with an expert in capital taxes. As a result, the directors are now confident that rollover relief will be available in respect of some plant that has been included in the timing difference forecast for year 3. The same applies to other plant included in years 4-7. A revised forecast has been produced:

3	4	5	6	7
£(22,000)	43,000	(47,000)	98,000	32,000

Assume that there are no other timing differences, what amount should be credited/debited to the deferred tax account? Ignore the ACT mentioned in question 41.

43   What treatment is required in respect of the unrecovered ACT of £35,000 at this balance sheet date (i.e. at the end of year 2).

44   In year 8, the company was taken over. As a result it became a wholly owned subsidiary of another company. The forecasted timing differences, at the end of year 8, for each of the two companies were as follows:

	9	10	11	12	13
Company A	£ 56,000	42,000	53,000	(95,000)	(70,000)
Company B	£(40,000)	(66,000)	135,000	65,000	50,000

What is the overall group deferred tax provision required at the end of year 8?

45   An electronics company received a government training grant of £180,000 in December covering the first six months after the end of the financial period. Tax at 25% was payable on receipt of the grant.

Long Question

SSAP 15:   Accounting for Deferred Tax

Demora Plc

For some years, *Demora Plc* has been successful at developing new products and capturing new markets. It has built up a strong asset base, a point reflected in the draft accounts at 31st December which show that the company had fixed assets with a book value of £6.3m, and a tax written-down value of £5.14m. Unfortunately, the accounts also show that, for the first time, the company, as had been forecasted a year earlier, made a taxable loss. The company plan for the next four years reveals the following:

Year	Taxable Profits	Asset Net Book Value	Asset Tax Written-down Value
current	£(1.2m)	£6.3m	£5.14m
1	0.7m	5.8m	4.28m
2	1.3m	4.9m	3.72m
3	1.8m	4.0m	3.26m
4	2.1m	3.2m	2.60m

The taxable loss of £1.2m was due to a large reorganisation that the company had gone through during the last eighteen months. Included in the asset values is a new office block which the company purchased at the end of the previous year. The office block is situated in the centre of Edinburgh, two miles from the company's main factory site. It cost £1m and is being depreciated at 10% straight line, the first depreciation having been charged this year. For tax purposes, the office block does not qualify for any capital or building allowances.

The company does not plan to purchase any fixed assets which will give rise to future tax liabilities during the next four years. Thereafter, it is intended that the company will undergo a major expansion which will result in capital allowances exceeding depreciation for the foreseeable future thereafter. The balance brought forward from the previous year on the deferred tax account was £160,000 (credit).

Required:

In compliance with SSAP 15, calculate the amount that should be debited/credited to the deferred tax account at the current year end. (Assume that corporation tax is at 35% throughout and that there is a probable tax liability in respect of all the fixed assets other than the two factories.)

14   Groups

Overview

This chapter deals with five accounting standards - SSAP 1 (Associated companies); FRS 2 (Accounting for subsidiary undertakings); FRS 6 (Acquisitions and mergers); FRS 7 (Fair values in acquisition accounting); and SSAP 22 (Goodwill).

SSAP   1:   Accounting for Associated Companies

Summary of the accounting treatment requirements

The SSAP 1 definition of associated companies was amended by the ASB's *Interim Statement - Consolidated Accounts*, issued in December 1990. Associated companies (more accurately, associated *undertakings*) are those which are not subsidiaries of the investing group or company but in which the investing group or company has a long term interest and over which it is in a position to exercise significant influence. The investing company's own financial statements should show the dividends received and receivable, and the valuation or cost less any amounts written-off the investment in each associated undertaking.

  The investing group's financial statements should show its share of profits less losses of its associated undertakings; its share of the net assets other than goodwill of its associated undertakings (after attributing fair values at the time of acquisition, if possible); its share of any goodwill in the associated undertakings' own financial statements; and the premium or discount which arose on acquisition, in so far as it has not already been written-off or amortised.

  Extraordinary items dealt with in associated undertakings' financial statements which qualify as extraordinary items in the context of the group according to the criteria of FRS 3 (*Reporting financial performance* - chapter 2) should be included with the group's extraordinary items. However, they should be disclosed separately from those arising from companies belonging to the group if they are material in the context of the group's results.

  Tax attributed to the share of profits of associated undertakings should be disclosed separately within the group tax charge in the consolidated financial statements.

  If no consolidated financial statements are produced by the investing company and it is not exempt from preparing consolidated statements, or would not be if it had subsidiaries, a separate profit and loss account (or a supplement to the investing company's own profit and loss account) should be prepared showing the information that would have been included in respect of the associated undertaking had consolidated financial statements been prepared. Similar requirements apply to the balance sheet.

Problems of interpretation and grey areas

The following items are discussed: equity accounting; non-coterminous periods; goodwill, fair valuation, and associated undertaking asset depreciation, sales and revaluations; extraordinary items; negative investments; piecemeal investments; dividends; and the date of recognition of associated undertaking status.

Equity accounting

The concept applied in this SSAP is that of *equity accounting*. It is a modified form of consolidation that requires similar adjustments to be made as apply under FRS 2 (*Accounting for subsidiary undertakings*) for full, acquisition accounting-based, consolidations. In some cases, the requirements imposed could be considered excessive - for example, the preparation of the accounting information included in the investing company's accounts in respect of the associated undertaking, on the basis of accounting policies reasonably consistent with those adopted by the investing company (paragraph 39). However, where it is possible to do what is required by the standard, the quality of information contained in the investing company's financial statements should be enhanced, and the true and fair view improved. The fact that it may not always be possible to adopt the treatment required by SSAP 1 does not mean that it was inappropriate to include the requirement in the standard.

Non-coterminous periods

There are a number of areas where problems may arise: the standard requires that the financial statements used for the purpose of including the results of associated undertakings should be either coterminous with, or made up to a date which is either not more than six months before, or shortly after, the date of the financial statements of the investing company/group (paragraph 36). Why no more than six months earlier, and is there no difference between six months earlier and, for example, one day earlier? The six month rule does seem somewhat arbitrarily based upon the premise that interim accounts are produced every half year. In addition, what is meant by 'shortly after', and why not 'up to six months after'? It is all rather academic: the time difference, if large, will often be immovable: the investing company has, by definition, only the ability to influence, it cannot force a change. Investing companies will be faced with having to use non-coterminous financial statements in order to comply with SSAP 1, and provision is made in the standard concerning what to do in such a situation: the investing company should consider all information available relating to the intervening period in order to determine if any material event has arisen which affects the view shown by the 'old' financial statements. If such an event has occurred, the facts should be disclosed (paragraph 37). Unfortunately, when it is identified from information which, in respect of a company listed on a recognised stock exchange, has not been published, disclosure is not permitted (paragraph 36).

Goodwill, fair valuation, and associated undertaking asset depreciation, sales and revaluations

Paragraph 26 of the standard refers to 'the premium paid (or discount)', in other words, goodwill. The rules regarding goodwill are contained in SSAP 22 (*Accounting for goodwill*), not in SSAP 1. These are the same rules as those applicable to subsidiaries. The goodwill can either be written-off immediately to reserves, or capitalised and amortised. In order to identify the purchased goodwill on the investment, it is necessary to use 'fair' (i.e. arm's length transaction) asset values, and from this requirement a number of difficulties arise: it may be hard to determine the fair value of some assets (the investing company has no right to demand information from the associated undertaking); the associated undertaking's depreciation will be based on historical cost values and the depreciation charge in the associated undertaking's accounts would need to be adjusted to reflect the fair value attributed by the investing company to the assets depreciated, before the share of profit to be recognised is determined (or, for example, the associated undertaking may fully depreciate assets that the investing company still places a value upon); and associated undertaking asset sales and revaluations could be partially/completely absorbed by the fair value adjustment already being applied by the investing company. It follows that the inclusion of the investment in the investing company's consolidated financial statements could become a very complex exercise indeed.

Extraordinary items

Extraordinary items in the associated undertaking's financial statements may not be extraordinary to the investing company or group (see paragraph 21). In this case, the item must be restated as ordinary and the accounts and taxation adjusted accordingly, prior to the inclusion of the appropriate figures. Otherwise, the appropriate share of the extraordinary item should be included in the investing group's profit and loss account and, if material, disclosed separately from that arising from companies belonging to the group.

Negative investments

It is sometimes assumed that the equity method is always to be applied, even when the investment has a negative value. Thus, even when the liability of the investing company is limited to the investment made, the financial statements could indicate a liability well in excess of that legal limit. Paragraph 33 reveals that this interpretation of the inclusion requirement is not quite correct: only when the investment is still considered 'long-term' *and supported by its shareholders (by way of loans or guarantees)* should it continue to be accounted for under the equity method. Even in those circumstances, it does seem somewhat inappropriate to reveal a liability that does not, and never will, materialise; yet, it is required by the standard.

Piecemeal investments

There will be occasions when investments will be made piecemeal (i.e. built up over time). Should the total of all the investments made up to the date of the recognition of an investee company as an associated undertaking be used to calculate the goodwill arising? Or should a goodwill element be calculated and recognised at each investment point? The latter approach could be more appropriate, particularly if the intention was that the investment would be built up until it qualified as an associated undertaking. However, such treatment would be contrary to the *separate entity* principle (referred to in paragraph 2 of the standard) whereby it is not appropriate for an investing company to recognise earnings other than dividends unless it is able to significantly influence the investee company (i.e. unless the investee is at least an associated undertaking).

As the second option is inappropriate, is the first to be adopted? Yes, but at the date of the last investment, *not* at the status recognition date. Paragraph 26 of the standard states that fair values should be attributed to the net assets at the time of acquisition (i.e. investment). The fact that an investment is built up piecemeal does not affect the figure for goodwill which is calculated, and there is no need to calculate the fair value of the net assets when each investment is made, only at the date of the last investment. However, it is possible that some time will pass between the last investment being made and associated undertaking status being recognised. If this period is long, it may no longer be possible to ascertain fair values at the date of the last investment. Consequently, particularly when associated undertaking status is being sought, it would be prudent to keep a record of the fair value of the net assets of the investee company at the time each investment is made.

Dividends

Dividends paid out of pre-acquisition reserves normally reduce the cost of investment once the investee company is classified as an associated undertaking. If investments are classified as trade investments, they should (*theoretically*) be treated in the same way. However, it is common practice to recognise them as income and make no adjustment to cost. When investments are built up piecemeal, a dividend received may be partially pre-acquisition (i.e. paid on a later investment which was not held when the earnings distributed were made) and partially post-acquisition (i.e. paid on an earlier investment), but common practice would suggest that there is no need to make any distinction until associated undertaking status is recognised. If this approach is adopted and status recognition occurs on the date on which the last of a series of investments is made, the reserves at that date are treated as pre-acquisition and any future dividend paid out of those reserves would normally be applied to reduce the cost of the investments made. If instead, a theoretical approach is adopted, the distinction would need to be made between pre- and post-acquisition earnings in respect of each investment in order that only the relevant investment costs are adjusted.

This distinction between theory and practice is particularly relevant in this case as a significant difference may result if an investment is made cum dividend, and, even more significantly, if the investments were made some time before associated undertaking status was recognised. It would be appropriate to adhere to the theoretical approach whenever the effect would be material. In addition, paragraph 43 (which indicates the treatment to adopt when associated undertaking status is lost and the investment reverts to being a trade investment) implies that the theoretical approach is the one required under SSAP 1. Except where materiality is absent, the theoretically more appropriate approach, which is implicitly prescribed by SSAP 1, should be adopted (i.e. dividends paid out of pre-acquisition earnings should be adjusted against the cost of all investments).

The date of recognition of associated undertaking status

A further complication concerns the date on which associated undertaking status is recognised. An associated undertaking is recognised as such if the investing company/group is *in a position* to exercise *significant influence* over the company in which the investment is made. The date on which an investee company is recognised as an associated undertaking may bear little relationship to the date(s) upon which investment occurred. In the same way, an investment may lose associated undertaking status without there having been any reduction in the investment. In this case, according to paragraph 43, it should be frozen at the carrying amount under the equity method at that date, and any dividends subsequently paid out of profits earned prior to that date should be adjusted against that carrying value. It would be consistent to apply a similar approach to the recognition of status. Accordingly, the carrying amount under the equity method, including goodwill, should be established at the date on which the status was recognised using the values relating to the date of the last investment (in accordance with paragraph 26). Pre-associated undertaking status recognition date earnings attributable to investments made up to that date and received or receivable as dividends should be recognised in the consolidated financial statements *only to the extent of those dividends* (i.e. on the same basis as that which applies to trade investments, which is what the investment was up to that date). All attributable post-associated undertaking status recognition date earnings should be recognised in the consolidated financial statements and, any dividends paid out of pre-acquisition earnings with respect to any part of the total investment should be deducted from the cost of that part of the investment and not treated as income in any of the financial statements.

One interesting point related to this topic concerns the way in which the question of recognition of associated undertaking status has been simplified and underdeveloped in most textbooks and exam questions. The tendency is to look purely at the date on which investments were made and to concentrate on the 20% rule. (20% holding in the voting equity implies significant influence - paragraph 14.) In reality, this is not quite so cut and dried, and as previously mentioned there will be many occasions when associated undertaking status as defined in SSAP 1 will arise at a date distant from that on which an investment was made, though whether companies would be willing or able to pinpoint the recognition date is another matter. The ability to exercise influence depends on a great many things, not just voting equity shareholding. It is often a matter of personalities and/or circumstances. For example, if the composition of the investee company's board changed, it may be more disposed to listen to larger shareholders than before; if an equity investor makes a loan to a company, that investor may enter into a position whereby influence may be exerted where previously none was possible; and two or more investors may form an alliance which provides each of them with the opportunity to influence a company where individually there was none.

In the case of an exam question which considers the recognition of associated undertaking status, care should be taken to adopt the treatment which the examiner appears to expect. It should be assumed that the appropriate date is the investment date, unless another date is clearly implied.

FRS 2: Accounting for Subsidiary Undertakings

Summary of the accounting treatment requirements

A group consists of a holding company and its subsidiaries. (For a detailed analysis of what constitutes a subsidiary, see the flowchart on FRS 2, on page 225.) A holding company should prepare a single set of consolidated financial statements for the group.

Uniform group accounting policies should be adopted. Where different policies are used, and adjustment to bring them into line for consolidation purposes is felt by the directors to be inappropriate, the particulars of the departure, the reason for it and the effects of it must be disclosed (paragraph 41).

The financial statements of all subsidiaries in the group should have the same financial year end and be for the same accounting period as those of the parent undertaking of the group (paragraph 42). Where this is not the case, interim financial statements should be prepared to the same date as used by the parent undertaking and, if this is not practicable, the financial statements for the last financial year of the subsidiary may be used providing they are to a date not more than three months earlier than that used by the group. Where such earlier financial statements are used, the consolidated financial statements should be adjusted to account for any changes that occurred in the intervening period and disclosure must be made of the name of the subsidiary undertaking, the accounting date or period of the subsidiary (depending on which is different), and the reason for the use of a different accounting date or period for the subsidiary undertaking. (Paragraphs 43 and 44.)

Undertakings become subsidiaries on the date when control passes to the parent undertaking (paragraph 45).

Subsidiaries may only be excluded from consolidation under circumstances which are detailed in the flowchart on FRS 2.

Problems of interpretation and grey areas

The following items are discussed: the requirement to prepare group accounts and exemption from their preparation; exemption from the inclusion of a subsidiary in consolidated statements; partial disposal of subsidiaries; piecemeal acquisition of subsidiaries; goodwill and minority interest; the rationalisation of accounting bases for consolidation; and the control concept.

The requirement to prepare group accounts and exemption from their preparation

Holding undertakings are required to prepare group accounts in the form of a single set of consolidated financial statements covering the holding undertaking and *all* its subsidiary undertakings except where exempted by paragraph 21 of FRS 2.

Paragraph 21 exempts holding undertakings *not* listed on a stock exchange in the EC which are either wholly or majority-owned subsidiaries whose immediate parent undertaking is established under the law of a member state of the EC, subject to the conditions given in CA 85 s.228(2) and, for majority-owned subsidiaries, s.228(1)(b).

In addition, parent undertakings of small or medium-sized groups (as defined by CA 85 s.249) are exempted when none of their members is a public company, a banking institution, an insurance company or an authorised person under the Financial Services Act 1986. (A medium sized group cannot exceed more than one of the following conditions: aggregate turnover of £11.2m net (£13.44m gross; gross implies before consolidation adjustments for intra group sales, unrealised profit on stock, etc.); an aggregate balance sheet total of £5.6m net (£6.72m gross); an aggregate number of employees of 250.)

Finally, if all a holding undertaking's subsidiaries are permitted or required to be excluded from consolidation, the holding company is exempted from preparing consolidated financial statements.

Exemption from the inclusion of a subsidiary in consolidated statements

There are three grounds for exclusion of a subsidiary given in FRS 2 and, while they are based on those given in CA 85, paragraph 24 of the standard disallows one of the exclusions given by the Act (where information cannot be obtained without disproportionate expense or undue delay) and paragraph 25 requires rather than allows exemptions granted by two others - where severe long-term restrictions substantially hinder the rights of the parent undertaking over the assets or management of the subsidiary undertaking (for example, a foreign subsidiary may have restrictions placed upon the movement of its assets by its government); and where the interest in the subsidiary undertaking is held exclusively for subsequent resale.

A subsidiary that is excluded on the grounds of long-term restriction should be treated as a fixed asset investment. However, if the parent still exercises significant influence it should be treated as an associated undertaking. Subsidiaries excluded on the grounds that they are being held exclusively for resale should be included as current assets at the lower of cost and net realisable value. The final circumstance which gives rise to exclusion concerns subsidiaries whose activities are so different from those of other undertakings to be included in the consolidation that their inclusion would be incompatible with the obligation to give a true and fair view. In this case, they should be accounted for using the equity method.

Disclosures to be made concerning excluded subsidiaries are given in paragraphs 31 and 32 of FRS 2 and are in addition to those contained in CA 85 Schedule 5. While the Act is concerned with disclosure of the excluded undertakings' capital, reserves and profits for the period, the disclosures in the standard relate to intra group balances, transactions, dividends, write-downs of investments in or amounts due from excluded undertakings and, for any excluded on the grounds of different activities, their financial statements.

Partial disposal of subsidiaries

Where the interest in a subsidiary undertaking is reduced, the profit or loss arising is calculated by subtracting the carrying amount of the group's interest in the net assets of the subsidiary undertaking before the reduction from the total of the carrying amount attributable to the group's interest after the reduction and the proceeds of the disposal. The net assets compared should include any related goodwill not previously written-off through the profit and loss account. Where the undertaking remains a subsidiary undertaking after the disposal, the minority interest in that subsidiary undertaking should be increased by the carrying amount of the net identifiable assets that are now attributable to the minority interest because of the decrease in the group's interest. However, no amount for goodwill that arose on acquisition of the group's interest in that subsidiary undertaking should be attributed to the minority interest. UITF 3 requires that any goodwill written-off to consolidated reserves is to be included in the calculation of profit or loss on disposal, unless it has already been charged to profit and loss (paragraph 3). However, it is unclear from the wording of paragraph 52 of the standard whether the same goodwill amount is to be included in the pre and post-reduction net assets, or whether the post-reduction goodwill should be proportionally reduced - i.e. if the holding has been reduced from 100% to 90% and the pre-reduction goodwill was £5m, should the post-reduction goodwill be £5m or 90% of £5m? Clearly, the calculation of the profit or loss arising from the reduction could be significantly different depending on which interpretation was applied. Apportionment would seem the more appropriate interpretation and the profit or loss calculated by either of the following approaches:

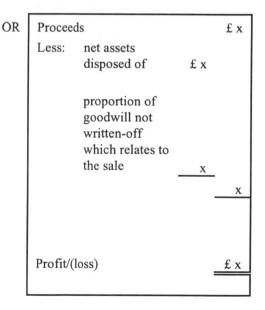

Piecemeal acquisition of subsidiaries

Piecemeal acquisitions of subsidiaries give rise to similar considerations as those resulting in associated undertaking status. At the point where an investment is to be treated as a subsidiary, fair values must be attributed, goodwill calculated, and the pre-acquisition reserves identified. If further investment follows, the fair values will have changed and there is again a need to calculate goodwill and identify the pre-acquisition reserves. Paragraph 51 states that this revaluation is not required if the difference between net fair values and carrying amounts of the assets and liabilities attributable to the increase in stake is not material; however, it is difficult to see how materiality could be determined without first calculating the current fair values and the resultant goodwill.

Goodwill and minority interest

Assets and liabilities attributable to minority interest should be included on the same basis as those attributable to the parent and its other subsidiary undertakings. However, the only goodwill recognised should be that which arises on acquisition which is attributable to the interest held by the parent and its other subsidiary undertakings. No goodwill should be attributed to the minority interest. (Paragraphs 38 and 82.) While this may appear contrary to the application of the 'entity' concept, paragraph 82 explains that the goodwill attributable to the minority interest that could be extrapolated from the goodwill arising on acquisition is hypothetical *because the minority is not a party to the transaction by which the subsidiary undertaking is acquired*; clearly a valid point, but hardly sufficient reason for the prescribed treatment. (A detailed discussion of the background to this approach is to be contained in a proposed chapter in the *Statement of principles* dealing with the reporting entity.)

The rationalisation of accounting bases for consolidation

Where the merger method of accounting is used, CA 85, Schedule 4A paragraph 11 requires the assets and liabilities of the subsidiary undertaking to be consolidated at the amounts at which they stand in that undertaking's financial statements, subject to any adjustments authorised or required by the Act. On the other hand, when the acquisition method of accounting is to be used in consolidating a subsidiary undertaking, CA 85, Schedule 4A paragraph 9 requires the identifiable assets and liabilities of the undertaking acquired to be included in the consolidation at their fair values as at the date of acquisition. Fair values must be adjusted whenever the stake in a subsidiary undertaking is altered such that the difference between the old and new fair values is material. Yet, the books of the subsidiary acquired do not require to be adjusted to reflect these fair values. Subsequent additions to the net assets of the subsidiary will be recorded at cost and some assets may be revalued. Clearly, rationalisation of the various cost bases for consolidation could become a very complex exercise if fair values are not adjusted in the books of the subsidiary undertaking.

The control concept

First introduced in ED 50 (*Consolidated accounts*), the control concept is central to FRS 2 - it is the 'accounting concept that underlies the presentation of consolidated financial statements for a group as a single economic entity.' (Paragraph 62) Paragraph 59 states that 'consolidated financial statements are required in order to reflect the extended business unit that conducts activities under the control of the parent undertaking'; and, paragraph 45 states that 'the date ... an undertaking becoming a subsidiary undertaking is the date on which control of that undertaking passes to its new parent undertaking.' While CA 85 section 258 contains a checklist which can be used to identify a parent:subsidiary relationship, it can result in more than one undertaking being classified as the parent. FRS 2 refines the result of applying the checklist and states that control ('the ability of an undertaking to direct the financial and operating policies of another undertaking with a view to gaining economic benefits from its activities' - paragraph 6) can only be held by one parent - 'the control that identifies undertakings as parent and subsidiary undertakings should be distinguished from shared control, for example, as in a joint venture. It is the parent undertaking's sole control of its subsidiary undertakings that gives it access to its subsidiary undertakings' resources. The parent undertaking extends economic activities through its subsidiary undertakings using their assets and liabilities in a similar way to its own.' (Paragraph 66)

FRS 6:   Acquisitions and Mergers

Summary of the accounting treatment requirements

FRS 6 defines a 'business combination' as *the bringing together of separate entities into one economic entity as a result of one entity uniting with, or obtaining control over the net assets and operations of, another* (paragraph 2). As a result, FRS 6 not only applies to situations where an entity has become a subsidiary of a parent entity that prepares consolidated financial statements, it also applies where an individual company or other reporting entity combines with a business other than a subsidiary undertaking (paragraph 4).

Merger accounting *should* be used only if a number of conditions are met. (These are shown in the flowchart on FRS 6, on page 227.) Otherwise, apart from two special cases, acquisition accounting *must* be used. In the case of group reconstruction, merger accounting *may* be used if (paragraph 13):

- permitted under CA 85, 4A, Sch 10 (see the first two boxes in the flowchart on FRS 6, on page 227);
- the ultimate shareholders remain the same, and the rights of each such shareholder, relative to the others, are unchanged; and,
- no minority interest in the net assets of the group is affected by the transfer.

When a combination is effected by using a newly formed parent company to hold the shares of each of the other parties to a combination, the treatment depends on whether the combination of the entities would have been an acquisition or a merger had the new parent company not been involved. However, in either case merger accounting is used for at least part of the accounting (paragraph 14):

- if the combination would have been an acquisition, the entity identified as having the role of acquirer and the new parent company should first be combined using merger accounting; then the other parties should be treated as acquired by this combined company using the acquisition method of accounting.
- if the substance of the combination is a merger, the new parent company and the other parties should all be combined using merger accounting.

Under merger accounting, carrying values need not be adjusted to fair value upon consolidation, but appropriate adjustments should be made to achieve uniformity of accounting policies in the combining entities (paragraph 16).

The results and cash flows of all the combining entities should be brought into the financial statements of the combined entity from the beginning of the financial year in which the combination occurred. They should be adjusted so as to achieve uniformity of accounting policies. The corresponding figures should be restated as if the new group structure had existed in the previous period, by including the results for all the combining entities for the previous period and their balance sheets for the previous balance sheet date, adjusted as necessary to achieve uniformity of accounting policies. (Paragraph 17)

The difference that arises on consolidation under merger accounting does not represent goodwill but is deducted from, or added to, reserves (paragraph Summary[c]). The difference, if any, between the nominal value of the shares issued plus the fair value of any other consideration given, and the nominal value of the shares received in exchange should be shown in a movement on other reserves in the consolidated financial statements. Any existing balance on the share premium account or capital redemption reserve of the new subsidiary undertaking should be brought in by being shown as a movement on other reserves. These movements should be shown in the reconciliation of movements in shareholders' funds. (Paragraph 18) This adjustment should not include merger expenses (paragraph 19).

In accordance with FRS3 (*Reporting financial performance*, chapter 2), merger expenses should be charged to the profit and loss account of the combined entity at the effective date of the merger, as *reorganisation or restructuring expenses* (paragraph 19).

Under acquisition accounting, fair values at the date of acquisition should be allocated to the identifiable assets and liabilities and they should be included in the acquirer's consolidated balance sheet at those values. Any difference between the fair value of the purchase consideration and the aggregate of the fair value of the net identifiable assets acquired is goodwill, positive or negative. (Paragraph 20)

Only the post-acquisition cash flows and results of the acquired company should be brought into the group accounts; and the figures for the previous period for the reporting entity should not be adjusted (paragraph 20).

If clarification is required, FRS 2 (*Accounting for subsidiary undertakings*, paragraphs 45, 50, 84, 85, 88, and 89) should be consulted concerning the identification of the date of acquisition and the acquisition of a subsidiary in stages.

In respect of all business combinations occurring in the financial year, the following should be disclosed in the financial statements of the acquiring entity if an acquisition, or of the entity issuing shares in the case of a merger (paragraph 21):

- the names of the combining entities (other than the reporting entity);
- whether the combination has been accounted for as an acquisition or as a merger; and,
- the date of the combination.

There are many detailed disclosure requirements contained in the standard and it should be referred to in order to identify the precise disclosure required.

Problems of interpretation and grey areas

The following items are discussed: the differences between acquisition accounting and merger accounting; the advantages of merger accounting to a group; the scope for avoiding the rules on eligibility for merger accounting; the accounting treatment under acquisition accounting; the distributability of pre-acquisition reserves; coterminous intra-group accounting periods; and Companies Act restrictions on the availability of merger accounting.

The differences between acquisition accounting and merger accounting

When a company becomes a subsidiary of another, there are two approaches which can be adopted when the investing group is accounting for the transaction: acquisition accounting, which would normally be applied; and merger accounting, which is restricted to specific circumstances. The first approach (acquisition accounting), is dealt with in FRSs 2 and 7. FRS 6 adds to it and presents the second approach (merger accounting).

One of the main differences between the two approaches arises because merger accounting can use book values throughout, whereas acquisition accounting requires that fair values be applied to the acquired company's assets and liabilities for consolidation purposes. Thus, depreciation will generally be higher under acquisition accounting. Also, by virtue of the rules on goodwill, while acquisition accounting will often give rise to goodwill, merger accounting never does - not because a difference cannot arise between the consideration given and the value received, but because such differences arising under the merger accounting approach do not conform to the definition of goodwill given in SSAP 22 (*Accounting for Goodwill*).

The advantages of merger accounting to a group

Merger accounting has a number of advantages from the perspective of the investing group: (a) the subsidiary's results are included in the group for the whole accounting period, not just for the post-acquisition period, and consequently, the group can appear to the casual reviewer as more profitable than it was - however, the amounts relating to pre-and post merger must be disclosed (paragraph 22) so this is not as great an advantage as it may appear; (b) the holding company can appear misleadingly successful if it is in receipt of pre-acquisition dividends which it treats as revenue income (the investment is normally recorded at the nominal value of the holding company shares issued, plus any other consideration given, and is unlikely to need to be reduced to account for the pre-acquisition distribution: this revenue recognition approach is far less likely to be appropriate under acquisition accounting); (c) assets may be understated (compared to equivalent situations where acquisition accounting has been applied), providing both an opportunity for instant earnings by selling assets, and resulting in higher returns on capital; (d) lower depreciation and an absence of goodwill will result in a correspondingly higher return on capital employed than would be the case were the acquisition accounting approach adopted; and, most importantly, (e) all the pre-acquisition distributable reserves of the companies involved are available for distribution to the group's shareholders (though this may be subject to a reduction resulting from the nominal value of the new shares exceeding the nominal value of the shares received).

The scope for avoiding the rules on eligibility for merger accounting

Given the advantages of merger accounting, it would not be surprising if companies were to prefer to adopt it yet, perversely, prior to the issue of FRS 6 they generally did not do so. Following the release of FRS 6, the combination of the quantitative Companies Act rules with the qualitative FRS 6 rules make it very unlikely that it would be possible to adopt merger accounting through choice, other than if the entire process of combination was undertaken with that in mind. Combined with reporting entities' previous reluctance to adopt the method, it is most unlikely that merger accounting will be other than a rare occurrence for the foreseeable future. In contrast, should a combination wish to avoid adopting merger accounting, it should be very easy to do so. Even if the Companies Act rules for merger accounting are satisfied, the inherent vagueness of the FRS 6 rules (despite the lengthy amplification of these rules in the explanation that follows the text of the standard) leaves plenty of scope for a combination to ensure it did not satisfy all of them.

The accounting treatment under acquisition accounting

The ASB viewed the fact that virtually all business combinations were applying acquisition accounting with some reservations. Previous rules were not very precise, particularly in the determination of *fair values* of assets and liabilities acquired, and of costs incurred. As a result, the ASB issued both FRS 6 and FRS 7 (*Fair values in acquisition accounting*, later this chapter) in September 1994. According to FRS 6, under acquisition accounting, the investment is shown at cost (= the fair value given) in the holding company's own financial statements. Any difference between the fair value of the net assets (excluding goodwill) acquired and the nominal value of any shares issued should be transferred to a share premium account, unless merger relief may be applied (in which case the share premium account is not required). It is beneficial if merger relief can be applied as it would allow any goodwill to be written-off against the merger reserve created in place of the share premium account, thereby leaving distributable reserves unaffected. In practice, an application can be made to the courts to use the share premium account to write-off goodwill, but it is far simpler if merger relief can be used to avoid the creation of the share premium balance in the first place. On consolidation, if the fair value of the net assets (excluding goodwill) acquired is less than the fair value of the purchase consideration, the difference should be treated as goodwill and written-off to reserves or capitalised and amortised; if the fair value of the net assets (excluding goodwill) acquired exceeds the fair value of the purchase consideration, the difference should be treated as a negative consolidation difference.

The distributability of pre-acquisition reserves

The treatment of distributions out of pre-acquisition reserves is, unfortunately, less regulated than it once was. The distinction between pre- and post-acquisition reserves is irrelevant under merger accounting: the new subsidiary is treated as if it was always part of the group and, therefore, the group can do what it wants with the distributable reserves that the subsidiary has accumulated since incorporation.

Under acquisition accounting, companies can either treat such distributions as repayments of their investment or as revenue income. The general rule in this case is: does the dividend received represent a *permanent* diminution in value of the investment? If it does, then it should be deducted from the book value of the investment. Where the holding company has treated such dividends as revenue income, it will be showing a level of revenue profitability which can only be misleading. If this treatment is adopted, the goodwill arising on consolidation will have been calculated to allow for the pre-acquisition distribution. For consolidation purposes, the distributable reserves of the acquired company are frozen at the date of the acquisition and, in the situation just described, there would need to be a reversing adjustment debiting the consolidated reserves and crediting goodwill with the amount treated as revenue income.

In paragraph 16 of Appendix 1 to FRS 6, it states that *where a dividend is paid out of pre-combination profits, it would appear that it need not necessarily be applied as a reduction in the carrying value of the investment in the subsidiary undertaking.* The standard does not explain why it may not be 'necessary' to do this, but states that *to the extent that this is not necessary, the amount received will be a realised profit in the hands of the parent company* - one of the most unhelpful explanatory paragraphs yet to appear in a document issued by the ASB.

While it is not mandatory to treat pre-acquisition distributions as repayments of capital invested, it still remains good accounting practice to do so and, if adopted, this approach will make consolidation more straightforward. However, there will be times when the book value is already so low that it would be wrong to reduce it further. This may be the case, for example, where merger relief has been adopted and the investment is recorded at the nominal value of the shares issued.

Coterminous intra-group accounting periods

Company law requires that the group financial statements be drawn up to the end of the holding company's accounting period. New subsidiaries may not initially have year ends which match those of the rest of the group. This can be particularly awkward when merger accounting is used, as comparative consolidated figures must be produced. The comparatives will often have to be based on internal records and management accounts, and the same degree of accuracy will not be possible as with current year figures: how, for example, can an annual stock-taking take place on 31st August when it is already 16th November? It is possible, for example, to apportion available figures of two financial periods in order to obtain an average figure for the required date, or to extrapolate the previous accounting period figures to cover the missing period. However, no ideal solution exists, and it will often be the case that the comparative figures produced relating to the period before the transaction occurred will not present as true and fair a view as would normally be the case.

Companies Act restrictions on the availability of merger accounting

As with FRS 2, the Companies Act has a direct impact upon the way in which FRS 6 is applied. FRS 2 refers frequently to the Companies Act and indicates where it extends or restricts the various clauses within the Act (for example, those relating to the exclusion of subsidiaries from consolidation). CA 85 returns the compliment by stating that the adoption of the merger method of accounting must accord with generally accepted accounting principles or practice (schedule 4A, 10(d)). Thus, the FRS 6 conditions which have to be satisfied before merger accounting must be used are reinforced and have the backing of law.

FRS 7:   Fair Values in Acquisition Accounting

Summary of the accounting treatment requirements

FRS 7 seeks to ensure that upon acquisition, all assets and liabilities that existed in the acquired entity at that date are recorded at *fair values* reflecting their condition at that date. In addition it seeks to ensure that all changes to the acquired assets and liabilities, and the resulting gains and losses that arise after control of the acquired entity has passed to the acquirer, are reported as part of the post-acquisition financial performance of the reporting group. (Paragraph 1)

Similarly to FRS 6, while FRS 7 clearly applies to situations where a parent company that prepares consolidated financial statements has acquired a subsidiary undertaking, it also applies where an individual company or other reporting entity acquires a business other than a subsidiary undertaking (paragraph 4).

There are a number of rules governing the determination of the appropriate *fair value*:

- the *fair value* of **tangible fixed assets** should be based upon either *market value* (if assets similar in type and condition are bought and sold on an open market) or *depreciated replacement cost* (reflecting the acquired business's normal buying process and the sources of supply and prices available to it). However, the *fair value* should not exceed the recoverable amount -i.e. the greater of the net realisable value and the value in use - of the asset. (Paragraph 9);
- the *fair value* of **intangible assets** should be based on their *replacement* cost, which is normally their estimated market value (paragraph 10);
- **stocks**, including commodity stocks, that **the acquired entity trades on a market in which it participates as both a buyer and a seller** should be valued at *current market prices* (paragraph 11);
- **other stocks and work-in-progress** should be valued at the lower of *replacement cost* and *net realisable value*. As with the use of *depreciated replacement cost* for *tangible fixed assets*, *replacement cost* for stock should be the cost at which it would have been replaced by the acquired entity, reflecting the acquired business's normal buying process and the sources of supply and prices available to it. The standard suggests that this is synonymous with 'the current cost of bringing the stocks to their present location and condition'. (Paragraph 12);
- **quoted investments** should be valued at *market price* (paragraph 13);
- **monetary assets and liabilities**, including accruals and provisions, should take into account their timing and the amounts expected to be received and paid. The *fair value* should be determined by reference to *market prices*, or by discounting to present value. (Paragraph 14);

- **contingencies** should be measured at *fair values* where these can be determined, using reasonable estimates of the expected outcome if necessary (paragraph 15).

The cost of acquisition is the amount of cash paid and the fair value of other purchase consideration given by the acquirer, together with the expenses of the acquisition (paragraph 26).

Problems of interpretation and grey areas

The following items are discussed: *fair values* of businesses sold or held exclusively with a view to subsequent resale; provisions or accruals for future operating losses or for reorganisation and integration costs expected to be incurred as a result of the acquisition; determination of the cost of the acquisition; and contingencies and other standards.

Fair values of businesses sold or held exclusively with a view to subsequent resale

If a separate business of the acquired entity is sold within *approximately* one year of the date of acquisition, the investment in that business should be treated as a single asset for the determination of *fair values*. Its *fair value* should be based on the net proceeds of the sale, adjusted for the *fair value* of any asset or liability transferred into or out of the business *except* when the adjusted net proceeds are *demonstrably* different from their *fair value* at the date of acquisition *as a result of a post-acquisition event*. (Paragraph 16)

This has an impact upon goodwill. The goodwill on the acquisition is effectively apportioned between the part retained and the part sold and there is, therefore, no need to make further adjustment to write-off the goodwill relating to the business disposed of. (Paragraph 65)

The wording of paragraph 16 throws-up some interesting terminology - 'approximately one year' and 'demonstrably different'. Is 'demonstrably different' any different from the difference being 'material'? No. And what is meant by 'approximately one year'? - eleven months, thirteen months; and does it really matter? Not really. The section that starts with paragraph 16 is entitled ' Business sold or held exclusively with a view to subsequent resale'. Paragraph 16 is written very much in the context of a prior intent to dispose of the part of the business. Viewed from that perspective, 'approximately one year' is merely a device by which to set a reasonable time limit on that intent being realised. However, what should be done when there is no intent at the date of acquisition to dispose of it, and disposal occurs after, say eight months. It is well within one year of the acquisition? If the financial statements of the reporting entity have not yet been approved, the paragraph 16 treatment *should* be followed (paragraph 16). However, if the financial statements had already been approved, the part disposed of would have been consolidated 'normally' with fair values attributed to the individual assets and liabilities as at the date of acquisition, and corresponding adjustment to goodwill. This is the same treatment as is adopted when a part of the business intended for resale has not been sold within approximately one year of the date of acquisition. The difference being that the part *intended for disposal* would not have been accounted for in this way in any financial statements approved prior to that one year period. Thus *intent to dispose* can delay 'normal' treatment of part of an acquisition, and intent is to be ascertained by evidence that a purchaser has been identified or is being sought and that disposal is 'reasonably expected to occur within one year of acquisition' - certainly vague enough to enable an entity that wished to defer 'normal' treatment of the relevant part of the acquired entity to do so. As a result, a reporting entity can show the assets of the part it 'intends' to dispose of within current assets. It can also, depending on the date on which the acquisition occurred and the date on which the financial statements are prepared, delay treating part of an acquisition 'normally' for up to two years after the date of acquisition. It must be arguable whether this is will provide as true and fair a view as 'normal' treatment accompanied by an explanatory note (subsequently revised if disposal occurs), would provide.

Provisions or accruals for future operating losses or for reorganisation and integration costs expected to be incurred as a result of the acquisition

Provisions or accruals for future operating losses or for reorganisation and integration costs expected to be incurred as a result of the acquisition, whether they relate to the acquired entity or to the acquirer are to be treated as post-acquisition items (paragraph 7). Paragraph 7 also states that this requirement is a consequence of two principles contained in paragraphs 5 and 6:

- the identification of assets and liabilities to be recognised should be those of the acquired entity that existed at the date of the acquisition; and
- the recognised assets and liabilities should be measured at *fair values* that reflect the conditions at the date of the acquisition.

This makes it very clear what treatment is to be adopted. The scope for abuse is minimal. Yet, this implies a very narrow meaning for the term 'exist'. If a major customer has indicated that it will cease trading with the acquirer if it proceeds with the acquisition, any costs resulting from the loss of that custom (e.g. staff redundancies resulting from reduced demand for a specific product) could not be off-set against the acquisition. As a result, goodwill may be significantly over- or under-stated, compared to how it could have been calculated before FRS 7. Effectively, items that would previously have been treated as adjusting capital are to be treated as adjusting revenue - i.e. they now must be passed through the profit and loss account.

Determination of the cost of the acquisition

Paragraphs 26-28 describe how the cost should be determined. It is the total of the amount of cash paid plus the *fair value* of other purchase consideration paid by the acquirer, together with the expenses of the acquisition. The cost of staged (or piecemeal) acquisitions is the total of the costs of the interests acquired, determined as at the date of each transaction. When the cost is contingent on one or more future events, the cost of acquisition should include a reasonable estimate of the *fair value* of amounts expected to be payable in future. The cost of acquisition should be adjusted when revised estimates are made, with consequential corresponding adjustments continuing to be made to goodwill until the ultimate amount is known. Apart from the issue costs of shares or other securities (that are accounted for as a reduction in the proceeds of a capital instrument - FRS 4, *Capital instruments*, chapter 12), fees and similar incremental costs incurred directly in making an acquisition should be included in the cost of acquisition. Internal costs, and other expenses that cannot be attributed to the acquisition should be charged to the profit and loss account.

In the case of staged acquisitions over a long period of time, there is no allowance in the standard for inflationary impacts on costs. However, that is entirely in keeping with the historical cost convention. There may also appear to be no inflationary provision in relation to the materialisation of contingencies, but this is not the case. If there were no such provision, a football club that today purchased a player for £2 million, with a contingency that a further £3 million should be paid if he gained 50 international caps during the next 10 years would, even at low, single figure, inflation rates, be providing significantly more in this period's financial statements than, in real terms, the payment of £3 million in 10 years would actually represent. It could be argued that inflation is being accounted for in these cases because the standard requires that the contingent costs be estimated on the basis of the *fair value* of the amounts expected to be paid in the future (paragraph 27); combined with what is stated in paragraph 6 - that 'the recognised assets and liabilities should be measured at fair values that reflect the conditions at the date of the acquisition' - it could be argued that this means the £3 million should be recognised at an amount more in line with the 'real cost' of the contingency at the acquisition date. Further support for this view is given and the correct treatment is identified in paragraphs 14 and 61, both of which are concerned with monetary assets and liabilities. Paragraph 61 provides greater detail of the requirements of paragraph 14 and it states that the *fair value* of monetary items other than quoted securities 'may be determined by ..... discounting to their present values the total amounts expected to be received or paid'.

Contingencies and other standards

Paragraph 15 requires that contingent assets and liabilities should be measured at fair values where they can be determined and that for this purpose reasonable estimates of the expected outcome may be used. In contrast to the conditions for recognition of contingent gains and losses under SSAP 18 (*Accounting for contingencies*, chapter 7), this is a very imprecise criterion. As a result, contingent gains in particular, but some losses also, will be recognised for *fair value* accounting purposes (and hence impact upon the financial statements) which would never be recognised under 'normal' circumstances of financial statement preparation. While this is an apparently significant change in direction away from the prudence concept (in relation to gains), it is consistent to treat as capital an item that should logically be treated as a capital item. (Compare this with the treatment required of provisions for future operating losses expected to be incurred as a result of the acquisition - paragraph 7c.)

SSAP 22: Accounting for Goodwill

Summary of the accounting treatment requirements

Purchased goodwill should not be carried in the balance sheet of a company or group as a permanent item. If positive, it should normally be eliminated from the accounts immediately on acquisition against reserves, but it may, alternatively, be eliminated by amortisation through the profit and loss account on a systematic basis over its useful economic life. It should not be revalued but, if there is a permanent diminution in its value, it should be written-down immediately through the profit and loss account to its estimated recoverable amount.

If the purchased goodwill is negative, it should be credited directly to reserves.

Non-purchased goodwill should not be included in the balance sheet of companies or groups.

Problems of interpretation and grey areas

The following items are discussed: the options available whenever positive purchased goodwill arises; the differing impact on financial statements of the two options; the treatment of negative purchased goodwill; the different treatment recommended in individual company financial statements; the selection of reserves for write-off of goodwill; the amortisation period; the avoidance of goodwill by assigning value to other intangible assets; the treatment of non-purchased goodwill; and the proposed revision of the standard.

The options available whenever positive purchased goodwill arises

A number of problems arise in the application of this accounting standard, the most frequently quoted of which concerns the options available whenever positive purchased goodwill arises. There are two options: either it must be written-off immediately to reserves, or it must be capitalised and amortised over its useful economic life.

The differing impact on financial statements of the two options

The two options can have quite different impacts upon the financial statements: immediate write-off reduces shareholders' funds and net assets (possibly to abnormally low levels), thereby resulting in a lower capital employed figure, a higher return (no amortisation cost is charged to the consolidated profit and loss account), and a higher resultant return on capital employed. However, it also causes the gearing ratio to rise.

The distinction between the two options becomes blurred in the case of an individual company which acquires an unincorporated entity. If it writes-off the goodwill arising to reserves other than because of a diminution in value, it is recommended in the appendix to the standard that it should do so through an unrealised reserve, for example a merger reserve, and then amortise the reserve entry over the useful economic life of the goodwill by systematic transfer to realised reserves. In effect this has the same final impact upon the realised reserves as capitalisation and amortisation, though it still results in the immediate reduction of shareholders' funds and net assets. The effect of the choice made may not, therefore, be quite as great as at first it appears to be.

The treatment of negative purchased goodwill

The choice in treatment does not apply to *negative* purchased goodwill: it must be credited directly to reserves. However, when this arises in the accounts of an individual company, the appendix recommends that the credit should be to an unrealised reserve, from where it should be transferred to realised reserves in line with the depreciation or realisation of the assets acquired (appendix 2(3)).

The different treatment recommended in individual company financial statements

Why is the recommended treatment in individual company financial statements different from that required in consolidated financial statements? It has much to do with distributable profits. Individual companies declare dividends from their distributable reserves; the consolidated reserves are an adjusted summary of the reserves of the companies in the group, and any distributions made by the group are sourced from the individual companies' distributable reserves, not the consolidated reserves. Therefore, it is irrelevant which reserve a group uses for the consolidation entry (though CA 85 prohibits the use of a revaluation reserve for this purpose - schedule 4, paragraph 34(3) and schedule 4A, paragraph 1). By using an unrealised reserve, the individual company will not experience a disproportionate initial impact upon its distributable reserves. Instead, as the amount put to the unrealised reserve is transferred systematically to realised reserves, so the distributable reserves will be reduced systematically to reflect the period to which the goodwill relates.

The selection of reserves for write-off of goodwill

The standard gives no guidance as to which reserve is to be used for immediate write-off of goodwill. Like revaluation reserves, share premium and capital redemption reserves cannot normally be chosen. However, in the case of these last two, application can be made to the courts to have them redesignated in order that they may be used for this purpose.

The amortisation period

The amortisation period selected is the estimated useful economic life of the goodwill, which is the best estimate possible *at the date of purchase*. Subsequently this can be reduced but it cannot be increased (paragraph 41(c)), even if the period selected is clearly seen to have been inappropriate. In contrast, while the goodwill should also not be revalued (paragraph 41(a)), if any of the fair values needed for the calculation can only be estimated, it may be adjusted subsequently if the estimates were materially inaccurate (paragraph 50). The difference in treatment presumably derives from the requirement to show assets and liabilities at fair values, and the desire not to permit an infinite economic life for goodwill. While the different treatment is justifiable on these grounds, it is not very consistent. Both involve estimates and both are liable to be inaccurate. Why should the same flexibility not apply when adjustments would be appropriate?

The avoidance of goodwill by assigning value to other intangible assets

It is possible to reduce the goodwill arising on an acquisition by allocating some of the difference arising between the net assets and the fair value of the consideration to other intangible assets, for example, trademarks and patents. This has the advantage that the amount so allocated is not subject to SSAP 22 and may, therefore, be carried indefinitely if the intangible asset is held to have an infinite life.

The treatment of non-purchased goodwill

Capitalisation and amortisation results in *purchased* goodwill being recognised as an asset. In contrast, *non-purchased* goodwill is not recognised. There are those who would argue that either both should be recognised, or neither, and that to do otherwise is inconsistent.

The proposed revision of the standard

As was the case with the original SSAPs 1, 14, and 23, this standard is in need of review. It is too much of a compromise having been issued as a stop-gap while a new standard was being developed. Seven months after it was issued, an exposure draft (ED 47 - *Accounting for goodwill*) was published. Among its proposals, it suggested that the choice in the treatment of goodwill be eliminated. Purchased goodwill would have to be capitalised and amortised. While this did not meet with great enthusiasm - in fact it was widely condemned - it would result in a more consistent treatment of goodwill, not just between groups, but also within groups which, under the current standard, may adopt either approach irrespective of which one they had used previously. However, ED47 never progressed beyond being an exposure draft and, in December 1993, the ASB issued a discussion paper - *Goodwill and intangible assets* - suggesting six possible ways in which goodwill could be accounted for. These ranged from 'capitalisation and predetermined life amortisation' to use of a 'separate write-off reserve'. It appears that we are still some considerable way from reaching a consensus on how to account for goodwill.

This area is going to remain a talking point for some time. Consequently, it would be advisable to know and understand the implications of the alternatives available in SSAP 22, as well as the suggestions that are being put forward for its revision, and the reasons for them.

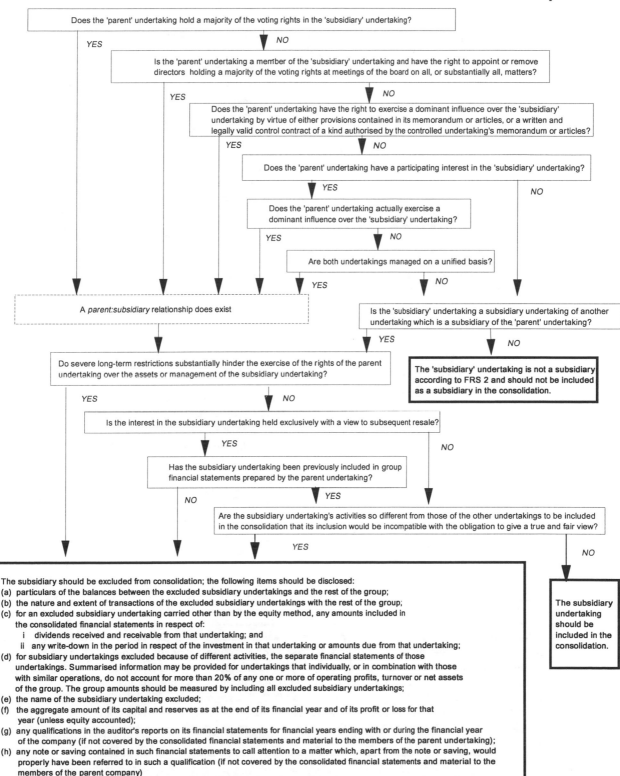

FRS 2 Exclusion of an undertaking from consolidation as a subsidiary

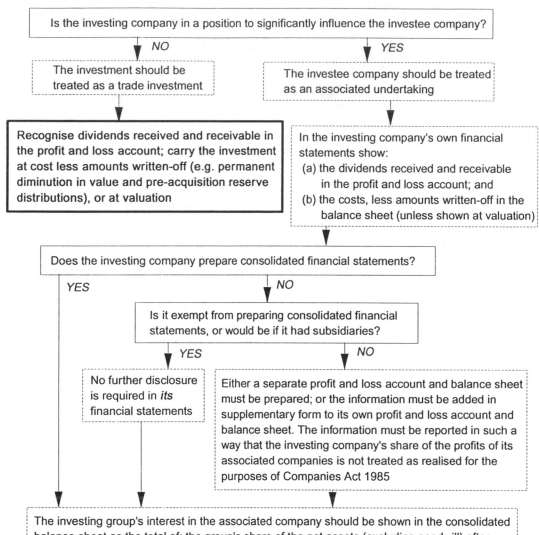

Is the investing company in a position to significantly influence the investee company?

NO → The investment should be treated as a trade investment

YES → The investee company should be treated as an associated undertaking

Recognise dividends received and receivable in the profit and loss account; carry the investment at cost less amounts written-off (e.g. permanent diminution in value and pre-acquisition reserve distributions), or at valuation

In the investing company's own financial statements show:
(a) the dividends received and receivable in the profit and loss account; and
(b) the costs, less amounts written-off in the balance sheet (unless shown at valuation)

Does the investing company prepare consolidated financial statements?

YES

NO → Is it exempt from preparing consolidated financial statements, or would be if it had subsidiaries?

YES → No further disclosure is required in *its* financial statements

NO → Either a separate profit and loss account and balance sheet must be prepared; or the information must be added in supplementary form to its own profit and loss account and balance sheet. The information must be reported in such a way that the investing company's share of the profits of its associated companies is not treated as realised for the purposes of Companies Act 1985

The investing group's interest in the associated company should be shown in the consolidated balance sheet as the total of: the group's share of the net assets (excluding goodwill) after attributing fair values at the time of the acquisition; the group's share of any goodwill in the associated company's own financial statements; and the premium paid/discount on acquisition of the interest in the associated company, so far as it has not been written-off or amortised

In the consolidated profit and loss account, the investing group's share of profits/losses before tax should be shown, and the attributable tax on the profits/losses should be disclosed separately within the group tax charge. The investing group's share of extraordinary items dealt with in the associated company's financial statements should be included with the group's extraordinary items (if this is appropriate under the criteria of FRS 3) and, where that share is material in the context of the group's results, it should be disclosed separately from the extraordinary items arising from companies belonging to the group.

SSAP 1   Recognition of associated company status and the general accounting treatment

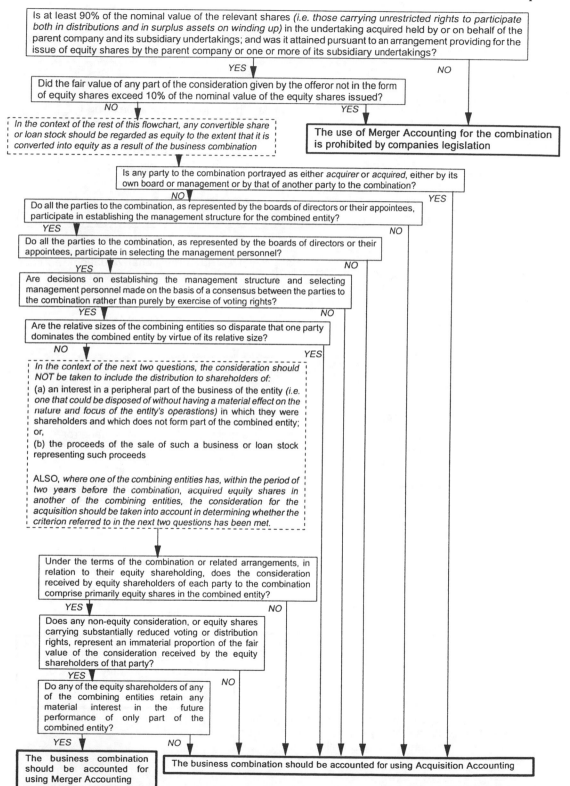

Is at least 90% of the nominal value of the relevant shares *(i.e. those carrying unrestricted rights to participate both in distributions and in surplus assets on winding up)* in the undertaking acquired held by or on behalf of the parent company and its subsidiary undertakings; and was it attained pursuant to an arrangement providing for the issue of equity shares by the parent company or one or more of its subsidiary undertakings?

YES ▼   NO

Did the fair value of any part of the consideration given by the offeror not in the form of equity shares exceed 10% of the nominal value of the equity shares issued?

NO   YES

In the context of the rest of this flowchart, any convertible share or loan stock should be regarded as equity to the extent that it is converted into equity as a result of the business combination

The use of Merger Accounting for the combination is prohibited by companies legislation

Is any party to the combination portrayed as either *acquirer* or *acquired*, either by its own board or management or by that of another party to the combination?

NO   YES

Do all the parties to the combination, as represented by the boards of directors or their appointees, participate in establishing the management structure for the combined entity?

YES   NO

Do all the parties to the combination, as represented by the boards of directors or their appointees, participate in selecting the management personnel?

YES   NO

Are decisions on establishing the management structure and selecting management personnel made on the basis of a consensus between the parties to the combination rather than purely by exercise of voting rights?

YES   NO

Are the relative sizes of the combining entities so disparate that one party dominates the combined entity by virtue of its relative size?

NO   YES

In the context of the next two questions, the consideration should NOT be taken to include the distribution to shareholders of:

(a) an interest in a peripheral part of the business of the entity (i.e. one that could be disposed of without having a material effect on the nature and focus of the entity's operastions) in which they were shareholders and which does not form part of the combined entity; or,

(b) the proceeds of the sale of such a business or loan stock representing such proceeds

ALSO, where one of the combining entities has, within the period of two years before the combination, acquired equity shares in another of the combining entities, the consideration for the acquisition should be taken into account in determining whether the criterion referred to in the next two questions has been met.

Under the terms of the combination or related arrangements, in relation to their equity shareholding, does the consideration received by equity shareholders of each party to the combination comprise primarily equity shares in the combined entity?

YES   NO

Does any non-equity consideration, or equity shares carrying substantially reduced voting or distribution rights, represent an immaterial proportion of the fair value of the consideration received by the equity shareholders of that party?

YES   NO

Do any of the equity shareholders of any of the combining entities retain any material interest in the future performance of only part of the combined entity?

YES   NO

The business combination should be accounted for using Merger Accounting

The business combination should be accounted for using Acquisition Accounting

FRS 6 Requirements to be met if merger accounting is to be used

By the date on which the first post-acquisition financial statements of the acquirer are approved by the directors, have *fair values* been identified for all the assets and liabilities acquired?

YES

NO

Apply SSAP 22 *(Accounting for goodwill)* in order to identify the correct accounting treatment of any goodwill arising on the acquisition.

Make provisional valuations and apply SSAP 22 *(Accounting for goodwill)* in order to identify the correct accounting treatment of any goodwill arising on the acquisition.

By the date the following year's financial statements of the acquirer are approved, have the *fair values* been identified for all the assets and liabilities acquired?

YES

NO

Incorporate appropriate adjustments to the provisional values and adjust goodwill accordingly. Apply SSAP 22 *(Accounting for goodwill)* in order to identify the correct accounting treatment of any remaining goodwill.

Treat the provisional valuations as final and continue to apply SSAP 22 *(Accounting for goodwill)* in order to identify the correct accounting treatment of any remaining goodwill.

Has the 'correct' *fair value* been identifed later than that date?

NO

YES

Continue to apply SSAP 22 *(Accounting for goodwill)* in order to identify the correct accounting treatment of any remaining goodwill.

Has a difference between the provisional *fair value* and the 'correct' *fair value* been found that is due to a fundamental error?

NO

YES

Account for that difference as a prior period adjustment

Has a difference between the provisional *fair value* and the 'correct' *fair value* been found that is NOT due to a fundamental error?

YES

NO

Recognise that difference identified as profits or losses in the period when they are identified

and

Continue to apply SSAP 22 *(Accounting for goodwill)* in order to identify the correct accounting treatment of any remaining goodwill.

Continue to apply SSAP 22 *(Accounting for goodwill)* in order to identify the correct accounting treatment of any remaining goodwill.

FRS   7 Treatment when *fair value* of acquired assets and liabilities has not been identified

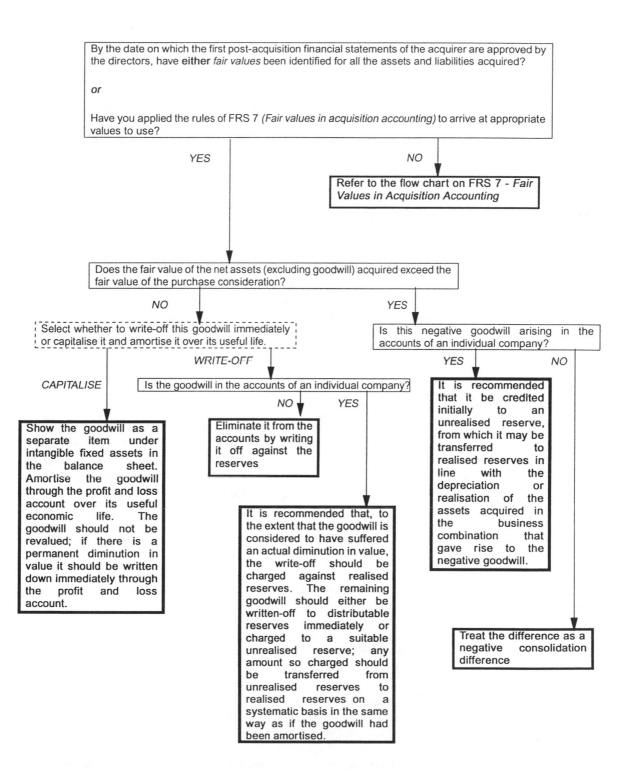

By the date on which the first post-acquisition financial statements of the acquirer are approved by the directors, have **either** *fair values* been identified for all the assets and liabilities acquired?

or

Have you applied the rules of FRS 7 *(Fair values in acquisition accounting)* to arrive at appropriate values to use?

YES   NO

Refer to the flow chart on FRS 7 - *Fair Values in Acquisition Accounting*

Does the fair value of the net assets (excluding goodwill) acquired exceed the fair value of the purchase consideration?

NO   YES

Select whether to write-off this goodwill immediately or capitalise it and amortise it over its useful life.

Is this negative goodwill arising in the accounts of an individual company?

CAPITALISE   WRITE-OFF   YES   NO

Is the goodwill in the accounts of an individual company?

NO   YES

Show the goodwill as a separate item under intangible fixed assets in the balance sheet. Amortise the goodwill through the profit and loss account over its useful economic life. The goodwill should not be revalued; if there is a permanent diminution in value it should be written down immediately through the profit and loss account.

Eliminate it from the accounts by writing it off against the reserves

It is recommended that it be credited initially to an unrealised reserve, from which it may be transferred to realised reserves in line with the depreciation or realisation of the assets acquired in the business combination that gave rise to the negative goodwill.

It is recommended that, to the extent that the goodwill is considered to have suffered an actual diminution in value, the write-off should be charged against realised reserves. The remaining goodwill should either be written-off to distributable reserves immediately or charged to a suitable unrealised reserve; any amount so charged should be transferred from unrealised reserves to realised reserves on a systematic basis in the same way as if the goodwill had been amortised.

Treat the difference as a negative consolidation difference

SSAP 22   Accounting for goodwill

Short Questions

*ASSUME THAT MATERIALITY EXISTS IN **EVERY** CASE*

SSAP 1:   Accounting for Associated Companies

Questions 1-8 relate to a manufacturing company with one 80% subsidiary and with current group turnover of £235m and net pre-tax profit of £46.3m. (Last year £223.4m and £41.8m respectively.) The financial year ends of all the companies in the questions are coterminous, ending on 31st December. Unless otherwise indicated, there is no continuation from one question to another and each question should be considered in isolation from the rest. (Assume that all equity has equal voting rights and that book value = fair value.)

1   During the year the company purchased a 25% holding of the equity of a paper processing company.

2   At the end of the previous year the company had a holding representing 10% of the equity of a clothing company. It had cost £80,000 when purchased at the start of the previous year. At that time the investee company had net assets of £560,000 which increased to £840,000 by the end of that year. At the start of the current year, the investment was increased by a further 11% of the equity at a cost of £110,000. The clothing company is not to be treated as an associated undertaking.

3   Repeat question 2, but this time the clothing company is to be treated as an associated undertaking.

4   An investment was made in a publishing company at the start of the year. It represented 15% of the equity of the publishing company, and cost £150,000. The pre-tax profits of the publishing company for the current year were £120,000. A final dividend of £6,000 was received in respect of the previous year; an interim dividend of £4,000 was received in respect of the current year; and a final dividend of £48,000 has been declared for the current year. The company can exercise significant control over the publishing company and it is to be treated as an associated undertaking in the current year's financial statements. Associated undertaking status is to date from when the investment was made. (Ignore taxation in any calculations.)

5   On 1st January, the company acquired 2,000 ordinary shares in a small engineering company. The cost was £95,000 and the holding represented 20% of the equity of the engineering company. It is to be treated as an associated undertaking. At that date, the reserves of the engineering company were £300,000. Its profits for the current year are £140,000 (on which tax of £35,000 is payable) and a dividend totalling £20,000 was declared by it at the end of the period. (Assume that no premium or discount arose on the investment.)

6   The company has a 30% investment in an associated undertaking. During the year, the associated undertaking suffered an extraordinary loss of £600,000 before tax at 35%.

7   The company's subsidiary has a 25% holding of the equity of a construction company. It is considered that the subsidiary has a significant influence upon the construction

company.

8   The fair value used in respect of the assets of an associated undertaking acquired at the start of the year was £200,000. The assets were shown at a carrying value of £100,000 in the financial statements of the associated undertaking at that time. During the year no additions or disposals were made. Depreciation of £10,000 was included in this year's profit and loss of the associated undertaking, whose accounts included the assets at a year end carrying value of £90,000. The associated undertaking's pre-tax profit was £310,000 (£240,000 after tax).

FRS 2: Accounting for Subsidiary Undertakings

Questions 9-14 relate to a variety of companies and groups. Unless otherwise indicated, the companies' financial year ends are all at 31st December and the groups are 'large' as defined by the Companies Act. In the absence of other information, assume that there is no continuation from one question to another and each question should be considered in isolation from the rest.

9   *Crescendo Plc* has had one 100% subsidiary, *Fugindo Ltd*, for the last two years. In November, the board decided to sell the subsidiary as soon as possible. An interested buyer was immediately contacted but so far (it is now two months after the financial year end) it has not been sold. However, this is believed to be only a temporary delay and it is expected that a sale should go through in April or May.

10   *Falisando Plc* has three subsidiaries: *Pequeno Ltd, Menor Ltd*, and *Maior Ltd*, all three were acquired on 1st January at the start of the financial year which has just ended. It has a 55%, 70%, and 95% holding respectively and holds a majority of the voting equity in *Pequeno and Menor*. It has changed the composition of both these companies' boards since they were acquired. However, despite its 95% holding in *Maior Ltd*, it only has a 45% holding of the voting equity and has so far failed in all its attempts to have a director appointed to the board.

11   *Dentro Plc* has two 60% subsidiaries, one of which, *Embaixo Ltd* has a 90% subsidiary. *Dentro Plc* is itself a subsidiary of *Jamais SA*, a French holding company.

12   *Outra Ltd* is a holding company with two subsidiaries and one associated undertaking. The group is 'large' as defined by CA 85. The directors have decided that the group financial statements will consist of a consolidated balance sheet, a consolidated cash flow statement, and the unconsolidated profit and loss accounts of each of the subsidiaries and the holding company. The associated undertaking will be included in the financial statements of *Outra Plc* as the investing company.

13   *Comprido Plc* is the holding company of a group. All of the companies in the group operate within the retail and distribution sectors, except for one subsidiary, *Seguranca Ltd*, which is a life assurance company whose accounts are subject to the rules and regulations relating to the insurance sector. As a result, the accounting policies adopted by *Seguranca Ltd* are very different from those adopted by the rest of the group.

14   The *Explicar* group consists of a holding company and two subsidiaries all of whom operate in the retail foods sector. None of the group undertakings is quoted on a recognised stock exchange. The group has always previously qualified as medium-sized under the Companies Act definition. However, this year, increases in its turnover and assets have resulted in it gaining 'large' company status. In the previous year it did not produce consolidated accounts, instead choosing to produce individual company accounts only.

FRS 6:   Acquisitions and Mergers

Questions 15-18 relate to a variety of companies and groups. Unless otherwise indicated, the companies' financial year ends are all at 31st December. In the absence of other information, assume that there is no continuation from one question to another and each question should be considered in isolation from the rest.

15   On 1st September, *Comendo Plc* issued 500,000 £1 equity shares in a one for two share exchange for all the (£1) equity shares in *Comida Ltd*. All the equity share capital of *Comida Ltd* was obtained. The merger method of accounting is to be used.

16   If the share exchange in question 15 had been a two for one exchange, what would be the accounting treatment on consolidation?

17   What disclosure should be made in respect of *all* business combinations occurring in the financial year, whether accounted for as acquisitions or mergers, in the financial statements of the acquiring entity or, in the case of a merger, the entity issuing shares?

18   *Criar Ltd* is a company which was formed five years ago to act as an ultimate group holding company in the event of an expansion of the *Criar* group. It has a 31st December year end. On 1st November, the shareholders of *Moreno Ltd* and *Azul Ltd* exchanged all their share capital in a one for one share exchange for shares of the same nominal value in *Criar Ltd*. *Moreno Ltd* has a financial year end at 30th April. *Azul's* financial year end is 31st December. Merger accounting is to be used for the group consolidation.

FRS 7:   Fair Values in Acquisition Accounting

Questions 19-21 relate to companies and groups all of which have financial year ends at 31st December and whose financial statements are approved on 31st March.

19   *Arvore plc* acquired *Boba Ltd* for £4.5 million on 1st June. At 31st March it was still investigating the *fair values* relating to the acquisition.

20   Repeat question 19, but this time *Arvore plc* identified the *fair values* in May.

21   Repeat question 19, but this time *Arvore plc* took three years to identify the *fair values*.

SSAP 22:   Accounting for Goodwill

Questions 22-25 relate to a variety of companies and groups. Unless otherwise indicated, the companies' financial year ends are all at 31st December. In the absence of other information, assume that there is no continuation from one question to another and each question should be considered in isolation from the rest.

22   When *Pereira Ltd* took over *Morango Ltd* in November of the previous year, purchased goodwill of £350,000 arose and was capitalised to be amortised over a twenty year period. On acquisition, a small warehouse belonging to *Morango Ltd* had been revalued to a fair value of £250,000. The warehouse was leased to another company in September at which time a valuation was placed on it of £300,000.

23   Repeat question 22, but this time the fair value originally applied was a provisional estimate.

24   Repeat question 22, but this time the goodwill was immediately written-off to reserves.

25   When *Carteira Ltd* took over *Carro Ltd* in December of the previous year, purchased goodwill of £475,000 arose and was capitalised to be written-off over a ten year period. On acquisition, some unused equipment belonging to *Carro Ltd* had been revalued to a fair value of £60,000. (The fair value was believed to be correct.) The equipment was sold in March when it realised £30,000.

Additional Questions

*ASSUME THAT MATERIALITY EXISTS IN **EVERY** CASE*

SSAP 1:   Accounting for Associated Companies

26   *Simples Ltd* is an independent medium-sized company as defined by the Companies Act 1985. During the financial period just ended, it purchased a 25% holding in *Aberto Ltd*. It ultimately intends taking-over the company but, for the time being, is content to play a major role in the financial and operating policy decisions of *Aberto Ltd* while leaving ultimate control over these policies in the hands of *Aberto Ltd*'s other directors.

FRS 2: Accounting for Subsidiary Undertakings

Questions 27-35 relate to a variety of companies and groups. Unless otherwise indicated, the companies' financial year ends are all at 31st December and the groups are 'large' as defined by the Companies Act. In the absence of other information, assume that there is no continuation from one question to another and each question should be considered in isolation from the rest.

27   The *Cama* group consists of a holding company (*Uma Plc*), one 100% subsidiary (*Prima Ltd*), and one 60% subsidiary of the subsidiary (*Duas Ltd*). There was an extraordinary item of £240,000 in the financial statements of *Duas Ltd* and its profit and loss account

shows a pre-tax profit of £400,000 and tax of £100,000. (Ignore taxation on the extraordinary item.)

28   At end of the previous year, *Novo Plc* had a holding representing 21% of the equity of a clothing company. It had cost £260,000 when purchased on 1st January that year, including goodwill of £30,000. In the previous year's financial statements, the clothing company was treated as an associated undertaking. Pre-acquisition reserves were identified as being £840,000. At the end of last year the reserves of the clothing company were £1.1m. On 1st January this year, the company increased its holding to 51%, and paid £520,000 on a total net asset value of £1.4m. At the end of the current year, the reserves of the clothing company were £1.45m. (Assume fair value is the same as net carrying amount and that no dividends have been paid or declared by the clothing company since *Novo Plc* invested in it.)

29   *Novo Plc* has two subsidiaries: *Grande Ltd* and *Gorda Ltd*. Both were acquired over three years ago and both were consolidated in the last *Novo* group accounts. It has a 52% and 85% holding in the companies respectively and holds a majority of the voting equity in *Gorda Ltd*. However, it only holds 49% of the voting equity in *Grande Ltd*. In October, *Grande Ltd*'s managing director resigned and sold his 2% of the voting equity to *Grande Ltd*'s finance director. The managing director had been in favour of the acquisition by *Novo Plc* and had agreed to side with *Novo* on all matters requiring a vote. The finance director did not agree with the acquisition and has always voted against *Novo*. In December, the two directors appointed by *Novo* were removed from the board.

30   The fair value attributed to the buildings of *Barata Ltd* when it became a 60% subsidiary of *Comendo Plc* was £450,000. The net book value of £240,000, which dated from the end of the previous year, was not changed. (It is based on a historic cost of £300,000.) *Barata Ltd* depreciates all buildings at 5% straight line, the same rate as that used within the *Comendo* group. The subsidiary was acquired on 1st July, half way through the financial year. At the year end, it had pre-tax profits of £260,000.

31   All companies in the *Mixturado* group have a 31st December financial year end except one 60% subsidiary (*Naomesmo Ltd*) of the holding company, *Mixturado Plc*. *Naomesmo Ltd* has its financial year end on 31st October because of the seasonal nature of its business.

32   A group consists of a holding company (*Ama*) with one subsidiary (*Boa*), which in turn has one subsidiary (*Cor*), which in turn has one subsidiary (*Dei*). All the subsidiaries are 100% owned by their immediate parent. The companies are incorporated in the following countries:

Ama	United States
Boa	Italy
Cor	New Zealand
Dei	Great Britain

Ignoring questions of size, which of the companies would be exempt from the preparation of group accounts?

33   A group consists of a holding company (*Era*) with one subsidiary (*Fez*), which in turn has one subsidiary (*Goz*), which in turn has one subsidiary (*Hei*). All the subsidiaries are 100% owned by their immediate parent. The companies are incorporated in the following countries:

Era	United States
Fez	Great Britain
Goz	New Zealand
Hei	Italy

Ignoring questions of size, which of the companies would be exempt from the preparation of group accounts?

34   A group consists of a holding company (*Iam*) with one subsidiary (*Jot*), which in turn has one subsidiary (*Kay*), which in turn has one subsidiary (*Lei*). All the subsidiaries are 100% owned by their immediate parent. The companies are incorporated in the following countries:

Iam	Italy
Jot	Great Britain
Kay	United States
Lei	New Zealand

Ignoring questions of size, which of the companies would be exempt from the preparation of group accounts?

35   A group consists of a holding company (*Mae*) with one subsidiary (*Nao*), which in turn has one subsidiary (*Ovo*), which in turn has one subsidiary (*Pao*). All the subsidiaries are 100% owned by their immediate parent. The companies are incorporated in the following countries:

Mae	Eire
Nao	Great Britain
Ovo	Great Britain
Pao	Canada

Ignoring questions of size, which of the companies would be exempt from the preparation of group accounts?

FRS 6:   Acquisitions and Mergers

Questions 36-37 relate to a variety of companies and groups. Unless otherwise indicated, the companies' financial year ends are all at 31st December. In the absence of other information, assume that there is no continuation from one question to another and each question should be considered in isolation from the rest.

36   As the result of an offer to the shareholders of *Morto Ltd*, 95% of its equity shares were obtained by *Subindo Plc*. The 950,000 equity shares obtained had a nominal value of £1

each. *Morto Ltd* has only one class of share in issue and all equity shares have voting rights. On the date the exchange took place, the net assets of *Morto Ltd* had a fair value of £2m and the market value of a share in *Subindo Plc* was £2. *Subindo Plc* has only one class of share in issue: £1 voting equity shares, and prior to the offer it had no loan stock. In consideration for every ten shares in *Morto Ltd*, *Subindo Plc* issued nine of its own shares and £5 loan stock. Assuming all conditions dependent upon other factors are satisfied, must merger accounting be applied?

37   90% of the 500,000 £1 equity shares of *Acabado Ltd* were acquired by *Emcima Plc*. *Acabado Ltd* has only one class of share in issue and all equity shares have voting rights. On the date that control passed to *Emcima Plc*, the net assets of *Acabado Ltd* had a fair value of £3m and the market value of a share in *Emcima Plc* was £1. *Emcima Plc* has only one class of share in issue: £0.25 voting equity shares, and prior to the offer it had no loan stock. In consideration for every five shares in *Acabado Ltd*, *Emcima Plc* issued 24 of its own shares and £0.50 loan stock. Assuming all conditions dependent upon other factors are satisfied, must merger accounting be applied?

FRS 7:   Fair Values in Acquisition Accounting

Questions 38-39 relate to companies and groups whose financial year ends are all at 31st December and whose financial statements are approved on 31st March.

38   In September, three months after acquiring *Casinha Ltd* at a cost, as calculated under FRS 7, of £2 million, giving rise to goodwill on consolidation of £0.5 million, *Cidade plc* decided that it would not, after all, be appropriate to retain the maintenance division of *Casinha*. In October, it sold the maintenance division of *Casinha Ltd* to *Tio plc* for £0.75 million.

39   Repeat question 38, but this time assume *Cidade plc* sold *Casinha Ltd* to *Tio plc* in April the following year.

SSAP 22:   Accounting for Goodwill

Questions 40-45 relate to a variety of companies and groups. Unless otherwise indicated, the companies' financial year ends are all at 31st December. In the absence of other information, assume that there is no continuation from one question to another and each question should be considered in isolation from the rest.

40   *Tinto Plc* acquired all the share capital of *Branco Ltd* on 1st January. The consolidated shareholders' funds after the acquisition were £6m (after capitalising goodwill of £1m which arose on the acquisition). The earnings for the group for the year were £1.5m. Based on the average shareholders' funds for the year, what is the return on shareholders funds if the goodwill remains capitalised and is amortised over its five year useful economic life?

41   Repeat question 40, but this time, what is the return on average shareholders' funds if the

goodwill is immediately written-off to reserves?

42   *Voo Plc* has an 80% shareholding in its supplier subsidiary *Anda Ltd*. During the year *Anda Ltd* sold stock to *Voo Plc* at a mark up over cost of 20%. The total charge to *Voo Plc* was £600,000. At the year end, £150,000 of this stock was included in the stock valuation of *Voo Plc*.

43   When a 100% shareholding in *Menos Ltd* was acquired by *Tinta Ltd*, a large-sized holding company (as defined by the Companies Act) for £7.2m, the aggregate of the fair values of the separable net assets acquired was £8.42m.

44   When *Chega Ltd* acquired a 100% shareholding in *Indo Ltd* in February of the previous year for £1.7m, purchased goodwill of £240,000 arose which was capitalised to be amortised over a twenty year period. In the last few months a major competitor of *Indo Ltd* has introduced a new product to the market which has resulted in a 50% fall in sales during that period. It is believed that the situation is permanent and that *Indo Ltd* will need to pursue new products and markets if it is to remain profitable in the foreseeable future. An independent consultant has suggested that the current market value of *Indo Ltd* is approximately £1.5m.

45   Repeat question 44, but this time the goodwill was written-off immediately to reserves.

15   Which Standard?

This chapter contains 60 short questions. Unless otherwise indicated, each of the questions is self-contained and should be considered in isolation from the others. There are one or more questions relating to each of the accounting standards currently in effect. While the solution to each question gives the appropriate treatment for one or two standards, there are many times when other standards will also need to be considered and it should not be assumed that those standards mentioned in the solutions are the only ones to which reference should be made.

The opportunity has been taken to include some questions purely on SSAP and FRS disclosure requirements.

Short Questions

*ASSUME THAT MATERIALITY EXISTS IN **EVERY** CASE*

The companies in the questions all have a financial year end of 31st December. In each case, the board of directors is scheduled to approve the financial statements on 31st March.

1   Costa Ltd depreciates all its plant over 5 years using the straight line method. Two years ago, the company had five new cutting machines built to its own specifications. The machines cost £35,000 each and had a resale value of £10,000 each at the end of the financial period. In February, the UK's leading manufacturer of cutting machines announced a new range of machines that effectively made the company's machines obsolete, reducing their resale value to nil. The company has been experiencing severe financing problems and it seems unlikely that it can continue to survive for much longer without a major injection of new funds. It is now mid-March and all attempts at raising this money have failed.

2   *Tempo plc*, is a building company with one subsidiary. The group balance sheet date is 31st December. On turnover of £94.7m, the group has pre-tax earnings of £16.1m (last year £11.4m on turnover of £79.3m). *Tempo plc* has investments in four associated undertakings, should they be included in the group's segmental report?

3   Last year, a company whose accounting policy is to defer and amortise development expenditure, wrote off £100,000 expenditure incurred in developing a new product which was held to have been unlikely to be commercially viable. In June, the company was approached by a retail hardware chain who were interested in selling the product. It is now in production and it is expected that all the costs will be recouped within the next twelve months and that, thereafter, it will generate a good profit for the next three to four years.

4   A building company is being sued for damages of £450,000 for breach of contract. Legal

opinion suggests that there is about a 40% chance that the company may lose the case. It also suggests that the £450,000 damages claim is excessive and 99% unlikely to be confirmed by the court. £350,000 is the most that the company should expect to be required to pay if it loses the case. £225,000 was given as an estimate of the likely level of damages that would be assessed. The action was started before the company's financial year end and is scheduled to be heard in court two months after the date on which the financial statements are to be approved by the board of directors.

5   On 23rd February, the company rolled-over the £800,000 investment for a further 90 days. How would these items be treated under FRS 1 (*Cash flow statements*)?

6   During the year, as a result of a steady stream of break-ins and subsequently mounting losses, a furniture discount store leased an infra-red security systems and employed four permanent security staff. The cost of this during the year was £45,000. The annual charge in future is expected to be around £55,000.

7   What information concerning government grants should be disclosed in the financial statements?

8   At the balance sheet date, a motor trader company was owed £37,000 by the Customs and Excise in respect of a refund of over-payments of VAT made by the company during the previous two years.

9   When *Janella Ltd* acquired a 60% shareholding in *Curtina Ltd* in September two years ago, it paid £1.4m and the £240,000 of purchased goodwill arising was immediately written-off to the reserves. In June of the current year, *Janella Ltd* acquired another 20% of the equity of *Curtina Ltd*. The fair value of the identifiable assets and liabilities of *Curtina Ltd* at that time was £2.3m.

10   A building company decided to apply SSAP 19 (*Accounting for investment properties -* chapter 8) and stop depreciating a building it has sub-leased on a 10 year lease to a firm in Dunfermline. The lease has 4 years to run. The thirty year leasehold to the property was bought by the company 6 years ago solely for letting purposes. It has been depreciated in each of the first five years at 15% reducing balance.

11   What is the *accounting objective* of SSAP 24 (*Accounting for pension costs* - chapter 11)?

12   On 1st August, a new holding company was created and it acquired the entire share capital of a chemical company in a 2 for 1 share exchange. The chemical company had earnings for EPS purposes of £4.5m in the current year (£3.8m in the previous period). Merger accounting has been applied. The chemical company had 3 million shares in issue prior to the share exchange. In the absence of any further information, what EPS should be disclosed?

13   What is deferred tax and what is the liability method of computing deferred tax?

14   A manufacturing company has one 60% subsidiary. and current group turnover of

£165m and net pre-tax profit of £22.3m. During the financial period just ended, the subsidiary acquired a 21% holding in the ordinary share capital of a raw material supplier company as security against a one year loan of £5m which the subsidiary made to the raw material supplier company's parent (of which that company was a 100% subsidiary).

15   What are the disclosure requirements of SSAP 12 (*Accounting for depreciation* - chapter 4) ?

16   If a holding company has a 30% investment in an associated undertaking, should the group's share of the associated undertaking's results be included in the group segmental report under 'results of associated undertakings' ?

17   After its chemical store was contaminated, a chemical company spent £11,000 on research into why the contamination had occurred.

18   A compact disc manufacturing company has a factory and a warehouse, both of which are included in the financial statements at cost less depreciation to date. A recent newspaper article by a local surveyor stated that while there was a shortage of factory space on the market, there was a glut of warehouse accommodation. From the value per square foot that he quoted, it appears that the factory is undervalued by approximately the same amount as the warehouse is overvalued. As the two value differences offset each other, no change has been made to the value at which these properties have been included in the balance sheet.

19   *Prediu plc*, whose main business is property leasing, recently completed construction of a multi-storey office block. It is to be treated as an investment property, as under SSAP 19. The first tenants are due to take possession of their offices in April. As the building was only completed in October, it has been decided that no valuation will take place at the end of the financial period.

20   *Cachoro Ltd* has two subsidiaries, *Pedra Ltd* and *Maca Ltd*. *Cachoro Ltd* is a 100% subsidiary of *Trem Plc*. What consolidated financial statements should *Cachoro Ltd* prepare?

21   A steel company purchased raw materials from an American supplier for $270,000. The goods were delivered on November 18th, when the exchange rate was £1=$1.85. Payment was not made by the year end but will be made on the 14th February. In order to avoid exchange rate losses, the company contracted to buy forward $270,000 on 14th February at £1=$1.87. The exchange rate at the year end was £1=$1.76.

22   According to SSAP 9 (*Stocks and long term contracts* - chapter 3), what disclosure must be made and what application requirements are there regarding accounting policies adopted in respect of stocks and long term contracts?

23   *Novinho Ltd* was formed on 1st January in order that two existing companies, *Velho Ltd* and *Juvem Ltd*, could merge. The shareholders of the two companies exchanged their equity shares in a one for one share exchange for shares in *Novinho Ltd*. Merger accounting is to be adopted. No difference exists between the investment's carrying value

and the nominal value of the shares transferred.

24   On 1st September, a fish processing company made a 1 for 6 rights issue at 20p. The market value of the shares on the last day of quotation cum rights was 21p. At the start of the accounting period, there were 3 million ordinary £1 shares in issue. Earnings for EPS purposes are £1.2m (£0.9m in the previous year) and the company has never had any irrecoverable ACT.

25   As a result of a production error, a clothing company lost stock worth £50,000. The company's insurers made good the loss and also paid the company £90,000 for consequential loss of profits.

26   A company has been developing a new product in a rented factory which is being used solely for the product. Production has been scheduled to start in three months time and sufficient orders have already been received to guarantee a sizeable profit.

27   According to SSAP 8 (*The treatment of taxation under the imputation system in the accounts of companies* - chapter 13), what disclosure must be made in the financial statements relating to overseas taxation?

28   Under what circumstances would a property owned by a company which was let to another group company be an 'investment property'?

29   A marketing company has a holding in an associated undertaking. The company's financial year end is the same as that of the associated undertaking. The company had assumed that a dividend of 5p per share would be declared by the associate and had provided for this in the financial statements. The associate company declared a dividend of 7p per share one week before the marketing company's board of directors were due to approve the financial statements.

30   Refer to question 29: if the associated undertaking's dividend had not been known until the week after the financial statements of the marketing company were approved, what treatment would be appropriate?

31   At the period end, deferred tax was credited with £120,000 relating to accelerated capital allowances. The corporation tax creditor at the previous period end was £1.4m, £1.7m tax was paid during the period, and a taxation liability for £1.6m is included in the draft balance sheet for the current period. How should this be treated under FRS 1 (*Cash flow statements* - chapter 12)?

32   Five years earlier, a small footwear company wrote off equipment with a book value of £40,000 when it reorganised its production facilities. At that time it was not believed likely that it could be sold. During the current year, the company sold the equipment for £70,000.

33   According to SSAP 22 (*Accounting for goodwill* - chapter 14), what disclosure should be made where goodwill is amortised?

34   In November, a company finished erecting a small laboratory in the grounds of its

Brechin factory. The lab is to be used on all general scientific research. It cost £52,000.

35   What segmental analysis is required under SSAP 25 (*Segmental reporting* - chapter 12) in respect of joint ventures which have been accounted for by proportional consolidation?

36   A company had a computer system in its old office which it was writing-down at 20% straight line. When it moved it agreed to lease the equipment to the estate agency which leased the building. The equipment had a net book value at the start of the year of £9,000 and was 2 years old. The lease is for 5 years and includes an option for the estate agency to buy the equipment at the end of the lease for £1. The estate agency is responsible for maintaining the equipment during the term of the lease.

37   A company has been developing a new product in a custom-built factory. Production has been scheduled to start in three months time and sufficient orders have already been received to guarantee a sizeable profit.

38   A plumbing company has been paid an advance of £65,000 on a contract for maintenance work on offshore oil rigs. The contract incorporated an advance payment bond (a guarantee that all advance payments made to the company would be reimbursed should the customer fail to fulfil the contract). Since signing the contract six months ago, the company has been unable to discover any qualified plumbers who were willing to work at the under-water depths required on the oil rigs. It is thought unlikely that anyone suitable will be found. It is now 31st March, and the board of directors are scheduled to approve the financial statements later today.

39   A mining company made a profit after tax and extraordinary items of £4.6m during the accounting period (previous period £3.8m). It has 5 million ordinary £1 shares, and 500,000 10% cumulative preference shares of £1 each in issue (no change since the previous period).

40   *Ficando Plc* has a number of subsidiaries. It bought a 60% holding in *Saindo Ltd* on 1st September. It was acquired with the intention of holding it for six months. A buyer has not yet been found and it seems unlikely that one will be found by the end of the six month period.

41   A shipping company made a profit after tax and extraordinary items of £6.4m during the accounting period (previous period a loss of £3.1m). It has 25 million ordinary £1 shares, and £3 million 10% non-cumulative preference shares in issue (no change since the previous period). During the previous period, no dividend was declared in respect of the preference shareholders. This period, a dividend of £250,000 has been declared on the preference shares.

42   A carpet company has stock of 1000 metres of high quality carpeting which was purchased direct from the supplier for £12,000 over two years ago on the basis of an expected contract which never transpired. All attempts to sell the carpet have failed and an offer has been received from a discount warehouse to buy the carpet from the company for £1,000.

43 A group consists of a holding company (*Tempo*) with one subsidiary (*Chapeau*), which in turn has one subsidiary (*Tocar*), which in turn has one subsidiary (*Repicar*). All the subsidiaries are 100% owned by their immediate parent. The companies are incorporated in the following countries:

Tempo	Isle of Man
Chapeau	Great Britain
Tocar	New Zealand
Repicar	Italy

Ignoring questions of size, which of the companies would be exempt from the preparation of group accounts?

44 What treatment should be adopted when the amount of purchase consideration is contingent on one or more future events?

45 Included in the year end trade debtors of a furniture manufacturing company is a balance of £70,000. The balance has been outstanding for the previous eleven months. The debtor is a national retailer which is known to be in serious financial difficulty.

46 What disclosure should be made of a quasi-subsidiary?

47 A double glazing company has been experiencing financial problems due to increased competition. It is thought unlikely that it will remain in business beyond the middle of the next financial year.

48 When *Fin Ltd* acquired a 100% shareholding in *Comeca Ltd* in April of the previous year for £1.2m, purchased goodwill of £130,000 arose which was immediately written-off to reserves. In November of the current year, *Comeca Ltd* was sold for £1.1m. Its net assets at that time were £1.3m. No changes had been made to the company during the time it was owned by *Fin Ltd*.

49 A toy making company has two major products *meninas* and *meninos*. At the year end stock valuation, the cost of the *menina* stock was greater than its net realisable value by £35,000. However, as the cost of the *menino* stock was £48,000 less than its net realisable value, both product stocks were included in the financial statements at cost.

50 On 1st April, a clothing company made a 1 for 4 bonus issue. At the start of the period it had 4 million ordinary £1 shares in issue; and earnings for EPS purposes were £2.5m (£2m in the previous period).

51 What are 'issue costs'?

52 On 1st May, a confectionery company made a 1 for 5 rights issue at 80p. The market value of the shares on the last day of quotation cum rights was 120p. At the start of the period it had 4 million ordinary £1 shares in issue; and earnings for EPS purposes were £2.5m (£2m in the previous period).

53 What is 'control in the context of an asset'? (FRS 5)

54   In May, a carpet manufacturing company received an order for custom-designed carpets from a Middle Eastern customer. The company expects to start work on the carpet in March. Due to the particularly exclusive nature of the order, it is worth £300,000 to the company, although the costs of meeting it are the same as those normally incurred on orders of £50,000. Included in the directors' report is a projection of turnover and profit for the coming year which includes the value and cost of this carpet order. The customer's country was invaded in November and he has not been heard of since.

55   The *Pensando* group consisted of *Pensando Ltd* and its 90% subsidiary, *Fazendo Ltd*, which it acquired fourteen years ago. In November, the board decided to sell the subsidiary as soon as possible and in mid-December, *Fazendo* was sold.

56   In its previous year's financial statements, a pharmaceutical company wrote off a bad debt of £25,000 in respect of a customer who was in serious financial difficulty. In March, the customer finally arranged the funding needed in order to continue in business and, in April, the £25,000 was received. The pharmaceutical company only made a profit of £20,000 in the previous year and the directors want to restate the previous year's accounts, eliminating the bad debt, in order to present a more realistic picture of the company's performance during that year. In previous years, any bad debt recovered has been credited to the profit and loss account of the period that recovery occurred.

57   £470,000 development expenditure incurred during the period by an engineering company has been deferred.

58   As the result of an offer to the shareholders of *Acordo Ltd*, 95% of its equity shares were obtained by *Descendo Plc*. The 950,000 equity shares obtained had a nominal value of £1 each. *Acordo Ltd* has only one class of share in issue and all equity shares have voting rights. On the date the exchange took place, the net assets of *Acordo Ltd* had a fair value of £2m and the market value of a share in *Descendo Plc* was £2. *Descendo Plc* has only one class of share in issue: £1 voting equity shares, and prior to the offer it had no loan stock. In consideration for every ten shares in *Acordo Ltd*, *Descendo Plc* issued nine of its own shares and £2 loan stock. Assuming all conditions dependent upon other factors are satisfied, must merger accounting be applied?

59   *Rapido Plc* acquired a controlling interest in each of three companies when it took over a small group in August. At the time of their acquisition, *Rapido Plc* intended selling one of the companies (*Segundo Ltd*) as soon as possible. By the year end, no buyer had been found. However, the directors of *Rapido Plc* believe that *Segundo Ltd* will be sold within the next few months.

60   What is 'value in use' of an asset? (FRS 7)

Solutions

FRS 3: Reporting Financial Performance

Short Question Solutions

*ASSUME THAT MATERIALITY EXISTS IN **EVERY** CASE*

Questions 1-18 relate to a household furniture manufacturing and retailing plc with current turnover of £8m and draft pre-tax profit of £1.4m. (Last year £6.6m and £1.1m respectively.) The company's financial year ends on 31st December. (Ignore the taxation effects.)

1   Normally the company breaks even on its currency exchange dealings but this year a currency exchange surplus amounting to £180,000 arose on a remittance from an overseas depot.

This is an exceptional item which should be incorporated into the computation of the figure of profit or loss on ordinary activities by inclusion under the statutory format headings to which it relates, and its nature and amount disclosed.

2   In September, the company entered into a contract with the Brazilian government for the supply of wood from the Queimar tree (which grows only in Brazil) to be used in the construction of an exclusive range of outdoor furniture. The company started work on the project in January and had spent £110,000 developing the product until, in November, the Brazilian government was replaced and all foreign contracts were cancelled. There is no possibility of reinstatement of the contract and no other source for the wood. Work on the project ceased immediately the supply contract was cancelled.

The £110,000 development expenditure must be written-off (see SSAP 13 - *Accounting for research and development* - chapter 5). The event which has resulted in the write-off is the action of the Brazilian government. According to paragraph 2 of FRS 3, ordinary activities include the effects on the reporting entity of any event in the environments in which it operates, irrespective of the frequency or unusual nature of the events. The paragraph gives four examples of 'environments' - political, regulatory, economic, and geographical. Clearly this event is, therefore, 'ordinary'. However, it is such that it needs to be disclosed if the financial statements are to give a true and fair view. It should, therefore, be treated as an exceptional item and incorporated into the computation of the figure of profit or loss on ordinary activities by inclusion under the statutory format headings to which it relates, and its nature and amount disclosed.

3   Eighteen months ago the company was informed that a shop that it had constructed the year before, at a cost of £12,000, had been built without proper planning permission and

that it was going to be issued with a directive to destroy it. As a result, it was held prudent at the time to write-off, as an exceptional item, the £11,400 book value of the building. (The company policy is to depreciate buildings over twenty years using the straight-line method.) The directive has never been issued and the shop has been used continuously since it was first built. During the last year a new local council was elected, and it now transpires that the destruction order will definitely not be issued.

This involves the write-back of a previous exceptional write-off for permanent diminution of the value of the building. The write-back should be made subject to an allowance for the first two year's depreciation and should take the form of an exceptional credit in the profit and loss account. Depreciation should be provided on the shop over its useful economic life. The amount written-back should be £11,400, less one year's depreciation of £600 which would have been charged in the previous year had the write-down not occurred. The building should be represented in the accounts at the year end at cost of £12,000, less accumulated depreciation of £1,800. The year end net book value should therefore be £10,200. Apart from the write-back of £10,800 for the reversal of the write-off to the extent that it is no longer required, the profit and loss account will also include an ordinary debit of £600 for this years' depreciation.

4   Previously, *development* expenditure was written-off over 5 years. The company has changed its policy this year and now writes it off as it is incurred. In last year's balance sheet, *development* was shown as £320,000. (This year's new [net] *research and development* costs were £145,000.)

This is a prior period adjustment arising from a change in accounting policy. It should be accounted for by restating the comparative figures for the preceding period in the primary statements and notes and adjusting the opening balance of reserves for the cumulative effect. The cumulative effect of the adjustment should be noted at the foot of the statement of total recognised gains and losses of the current period. The effect of the prior period adjustment on the results for the preceding period should be disclosed where practicable. The balance brought forward should be charged against the prior periods in which it arose. As a result there will be no unamortised balance brought forward at the start of the year. The current period's profit and loss charge for research and development will be £145,000.

5   In May, the company made an extra £200,000 contribution to the employees' pension fund.

This is an exceptional item. It should be incorporated into the computation of the figure of profit or loss on ordinary activities by inclusion under the statutory format headings to which it relates, and its nature and amount disclosed.

6   In April, the company entered into a contract to refurbish all hospitals in Strathclyde Region. It was expected to take two years to complete at a cost of £900,000. The contract price was £1.8m. Cost was expected to be spread evenly over the two years. Since the start, serious problems have been encountered due to the unforeseen complexity of the design of hospital interiors. As a result, costs are running at a rate of £100,000 per month and are not expected to fall. Completion is still on schedule.

This is an exceptional anticipated loss of £600,000 on a long term contract. SSAP 9 (*Stocks*

and long term contracts - chapter 3) requires that it be provided for in full in arriving at the figure of profit or loss. It should be treated as an exceptional item and incorporated into the computation of the figure of profit or loss on ordinary activities by inclusion under the statutory format headings to which it relates, and its nature and amount disclosed.

7   An overall cost of £800,000 was incurred in terminating production at the company's Edinburgh factory during the year.

FRS 3 requires that material profits or losses on the termination of an operation should be treated as exceptional and shown separately on the face of the profit and loss account after operating profit and before interest, and included under the appropriate heading of continuing or discontinued operations. In calculating the profit or loss in respect of the termination, consideration should only be given to revenue and costs directly related to it. Clearly, the costs have been identified and are known; but, until the income generated (if any) by the termination is known, it is not possible to state whether there is a profit or a loss on the termination. If the profit or loss is not material, it would clearly not be exceptional. However in that case, if the gross profit or loss is material, the relevant heading should still appear on the face of the profit and loss account with a reference to a related note analysing the profits and losses. Income information is needed before the appropriate treatment can be determined.

8   Over three years ago, the company bought four weaving machines, which are exclusively manufactured in the far east, for £10,000 each. The currency of their country of origin has consistently weakened against the pound since its government was overthrown by the army in the middle of the previous year (50% in the last 12 months). As a result, the current UK price of a machine is £4,000. The company had the machines professionally revalued at the end of the current year. The revalued amount is £3,000 per machine. They have an estimated useful economic life of 20 years (from when they were first used) and are being depreciated using the straight-line method. The estimated residual value at the time of purchase was £1,000 per machine. As a result of the change in the price of the machine, this is now felt to have been an overestimate and £600 is considered more appropriate. No revaluation has taken place previously.

There has been a permanent diminution in value of £5,650 per machine [(£10,000-(3×((£10,000-£1,000)/20=£450))=£8,650)-£3,000] per machine, i.e. £22,600 in total. The £22,600 should be written-off as an exceptional item and incorporated into the computation of the figure of profit or loss on ordinary activities by inclusion under the statutory format headings to which it relates, and its nature and amount disclosed.

9   Equipment which had a net carrying value of £128,000 had been written-off (as an exceptional item) in the previous period's financial statements (when the decision had been taken to terminate production of an old product). An overall profit of £320,000 arose when the termination was completed in May, including proceeds of £135,000 from the sale of the equipment. Apart from the asset write-down, no provisions in respect of the termination had been made in the previous period's financial statements.

This represents an exceptional item as it arises directly from the termination of an operation (production of a product). The previous period's exceptional write-down should be reversed. Consideration should be given as to whether the circumstances constitute a fundamental error (which would give rise to a prior period adjustment) and, if not, there should be an exceptional credit in the profit and loss account reversing the £128,000 charge made in the previous period. The overall profit calculation should be based on the equipment's previous carrying value of £128,000, not the zero value resulting from the exceptional write-off. The overall profit or loss on the termination should be shown separately on the face of the profit and loss account after operating profit and before interest, and included under the heading of discontinued operations.

10   In September, an art expert who was visiting the company secretary discovered that one of the paintings in the company boardroom was a valuable masterpiece. It was sold at auction in December for £300,000. No value had ever been placed on the painting in the company's financial statements. (Assume that company policy has never been to revalue its fixed assets.)

This is an extraordinary item. The extraordinary profit should be shown separately on the face of the profit and loss account, after the profit or loss on ordinary activities after taxation but before deducting any appropriations such as dividends paid or payable. Where not shown individually on the face of the profit and loss account, the amount of this extraordinary item should be shown individually in a note and an adequate description of the item should be given to enable its nature to be understood. The tax on the extraordinary profit should be shown separately as a part of the extraordinary item either on the face of the profit and loss account or in a note. Any subsequent adjustments to the tax on this extraordinary profit in future periods should be shown as an extraordinary item.

11   If the company decided not to sell the painting in question 10, what would be the appropriate treatment?

There is no requirement to adjust understated fixed asset values, even if they have been formally revalued. However, the company could seek a valuation of the painting and incorporate the revalued amount in the financial statements according to the procedures given in SSAP 12 (*Accounting for depreciation* - chapter 4).

12   What would be the treatment if the painting sold in question 10 had been received as a gift from the founding chairman 150 years ago, at which time he had entered in the board minutes that it was the work of a famous artist, but that no-one had ever believed his claim? (Assume that company policy has never been to revalue its fixed assets.)

The treatment would be the same as in question 10. While an error had occurred in the past (the value had been understated) this would not constitute a prior period adjustment as the error had made no difference to the content of the financial statements and no change would have been made to the financial statements had the true situation been known.

13   Assume all the information concerning the painting referred to in questions 10, 11 and 12. However, if it was not sold, but valued by the art expert valued it at £250,000 when he saw it and also, for this question only, assume that the company policy had always been to revalue its fixed assets every five years and incorporate the revalued amount in the financial statements. What would be the appropriate treatment?

This would be a prior period adjustment (the information that it was valuable was available at the time the previous financial statements were prepared) and an extraordinary item. (Keeping the painting is not an activity undertaken by the company as part of its business or part of related activities in which it engages in furtherance of, incidental to, or arising from, those activities - see paragraph 2 of FRS 3 - i.e. it is not part of the 'ordinary' activities of the company to keep the painting *and*, as the painting can only be identified once, discovering it was valuable cannot recur.) The extraordinary prior period adjustment would require that the value which would have appeared in the previous period's financial statements be identified.

14   As a result of a reorganization of its distribution network, the company incurred redundancy costs of £50,000.

If the reorganisation satisfies the requirements of paragraph 20 of FRS 3 (that it had a material effect on the nature and focus of the reporting entity's operations) the costs should be shown separately on the face of the profit and loss account after operating profit and before interest, and included under the heading of continuing operations. Relevant information regarding its effect on the taxation charge should be shown in a note to the profit and loss account. If there are other exceptional items in the financial period, and the tax effect differs between them, further information should be given, where practicable, to assist users in assessing the impact of the different items on the net profit or loss attributable to shareholders.
 If it does not meet the paragraph 20 requirements, it should be charged in arriving at the profit or loss on ordinary activities by inclusion under the statutory format headings to which it relates and attributed to continuing operations. The amount of the exceptional item, either individually or as an aggregate of items of a similar type, should be disclosed separately by way of note, or on the face of the profit and loss account if that degree of prominence is necessary in order to give a true and fair view; and an adequate description of the exceptional item should be given to enable its nature to be understood.

15   Due to an error in raw material ordering, the company used the wrong grade of material in its production of lounge suites for two weeks during the summer. As a result, the entire production for that period had to be recalled and re-upholstered. The cost of the error has been estimated at £70,000.

This derives from within the ordinary activities of the company and is, therefore, an exceptional item. It should be incorporated into the computation of the figure of profit or loss on ordinary activities by inclusion under the statutory format headings to which it relates, and its nature and amount disclosed.

16   All the company's cloth cutting machines were wrongly set for the last three months of the year. As a result, £30,000 more raw material was used in production than would normally have been the case.

This item is exceptional spoilage and must be eliminated from any overhead allocation to stock - see SSAP 9 (*Stocks and long term contracts*, chapter 3) - and treated as an exceptional item in arriving at the figure of profit or loss on ordinary activities by inclusion under the statutory format headings to which it relates, and its nature and amount disclosed.

17   Last year's accounts included in turnover an amount of £700,000 relating to sub-contracted manufacturing of a product for *Sonno Plc* who went into liquidation in the first month of the current year still owing the entire amount. No payment is expected and the whole debt has been written-off as bad. (Total bad debts for this year are £745,000.)

This is an exceptionally large charge for a bad debt and should be treated as an exceptional item. It should be treated as such in arriving at the figure of profit or loss on ordinary activities by inclusion under the statutory format headings to which it relates, and its nature and amount disclosed.

18   During the year, as a result of public pressure, the government banned the use of kangaroo skin in household furniture. As a result, the company had to scrap £40,000 stock of kangaroo skin suites. The company recovered this amount from their insurers, along with a further £55,000 for loss of profits resulting.

The relevant item is the £55,000 compensation received for loss of profits. It should be treated as an exceptional item (it arises from a change in the environment in which the company operates - the government ban) and treated as such in arriving at the figure of profit or loss on ordinary activities by inclusion under the statutory format headings to which it relates, and its nature and amount disclosed.

Questions 19-20 relate to an industrial holding company with current group turnover of £19.3m and draft pre-tax profit of £4.65m. (Last year £18.2m and £3.1m respectively.) The company's financial year ends on 31st December. (Ignore the taxation effects.)

19   In June, the company disposed of a small portion of its shareholding in a subsidiary company resulting in a loss of £70,000.

This is an exceptional item. Investing and disinvesting in subsidiary companies would fall within activities which are undertaken by a holding company (see paragraph 2 of FRS 3). It should be incorporated into the computation of the figure of profit or loss on ordinary activities by inclusion under the statutory format headings to which it relates, and its nature and amount disclosed.

20   In September, the company disposed of its 100% shareholding in a company which it had acquired in the previous financial period. As it was acquired solely with the intention to resell it, the company had not been consolidated as a subsidiary into the previous period's financial statements. A gain of £220,000 was made when the holding was sold.

[According to FRS 2 (*Accounting for subsidiary undertakings* - chapter 14) the investment would have been accounted for in the previous period's consolidated financial statements as a current asset at the lower of cost and net realisable value.] Such investing activity may be outwith the 'ordinary' activities of the company, in which case the gain would be extraordinary; or it may be within the 'ordinary activities, in which case it would be exceptional. It is possible that this is an extraordinary event. However, more information is required concerning the activities in which the company engages before a decision can be made.

Questions 21-25 relate to a chemicals company with current turnover of £11m and draft pre-tax profit of £4.8m. (Last year £11.6m and £4.6m respectively.) The company's financial year ends on 31st December. (Ignore the taxation effects.)

21   As a result of changes in the rules relating to the availability of capital allowances on scientific research, the company made an adjustment of £300,000 to its deferred taxation account.

This is an exceptional item arising from a change in one of the environments in which the company operates. However, it relates solely to the taxation computation and should, therefore, be included in the computation of the tax charge for the period and separately disclosed on the face of the profit and loss account.

22   Some highly specialised equipment that the company used in its research laboratory was found to emit a highly dangerous form of radiation. As a result, the equipment was scrapped. The makers went into liquidation just before the dangerous nature of the equipment was detected and no compensation is likely to be received. The net book value of the equipment at the start of the year was £120,000.

This is an exceptional item arising in an activity (use of the specialised equipment) incidental to the pursuit of the company's main activities. It should be incorporated into the computation of the figure of profit or loss on ordinary activities by inclusion under the statutory format headings to which it relates, and its nature and amount disclosed.

23   As a result of the equipment having to be scrapped (see question 22) the company spent £200,000 replacing it.

While this arises from the exceptional event, it is a normal capital transaction and should be treated as such.

24   In October, the company sold a sterilisation purifier for £125,000. The machine had cost £60,000 exactly four years earlier and had been revalued to £140,000 at the end of the previous financial period (net carrying amount £120,000 after depreciation of £20,000). Straight-line depreciation is applied to all the company's equipment.

Paragraph 21 of FRS 3 states that 'the profit or loss on the disposal of an asset should be accounted for in the profit and loss account of the period in which the disposal occurs as the difference between the net sale proceeds and the net carrying amount, whether carried at historical cost (less any provisions made) or at a valuation.' In this case, the profit on disposal is £5,000 (£125,000-£120,000) and that is the amount that should be entered in the profit and loss account. However, paragraph 26 requires that 'where there is a material difference between the result as disclosed in the profit and loss account and the result on an unmodified historical cost basis, a note of the historical cost profit or loss for the period should be presented. ... The note of the historical cost profit or loss should include a reconciliation of the reported profit on ordinary activities before taxation to the equivalent historical cost amount and should also show the retained profit for the financial year reported on the historical cost basis. The note should be presented immediately following the profit and loss account or the statement of recognised gains and losses. The gain on a historical cost basis would be £89,000 [£125,000-(£60,000-(4×(£60,000÷10))] and the amount that would be disclosed in the note of historical gains and losses would be £84,000 (£89,000-

£5,000) described as, for example, 'realisation of equipment revaluation gain of previous periods'.

25   The company moved its laboratory to new premises during the year and made a gain of £210,000 when it sold the old building.

Profits on the disposal of fixed assets is one of the items listed for special treatment in paragraph 20 of FRS 3. It should be shown separately on the face of the profit and loss account after operating profit and before interest, and included under the heading of continuing operations. Relevant information regarding its effect on the taxation charge should be shown in a note to the profit and loss account. If there are other exceptional items in the financial period, and the tax effect differs between them, further information should be given, where practicable, to assist users in assessing the impact of the different items on the net profit or loss attributable to shareholders.

SSAP 9:   Stocks and Long Term Contracts

Short Question Solutions

*ASSUME THAT MATERIALITY EXISTS IN **EVERY** CASE*

Questions 1-39 relate to a furniture manufacturing and redecoration company with current turnover of £15m and net pre-tax profit of £2.5m. (Last year £13.6m and £1.8m respectively.) The company's financial year ends on 31st December and the Board of Directors are scheduled to approve the accounts on 31st March.

1   During the year the company sub-contracted to develop a new range of garden furniture for an Australian hardware company incorporating the company's newly discovered sun-proof furniture varnish. Total costs in the year, £37,000.

SSAP 9 should be applied to the extent that this sub-contracted development expenditure has not been recovered. Further information regarding costs and income are required before the appropriate treatment can be determined.

2   In December the company paid £42,000 for all the remaining toilet suites from a bankrupt manufacturer. They are to be sold to the trade. In order to generate orders a circular was produced and distributed at a cost of £1,800.

The stock value, which should be entered in the accounts at cost, is £42,000; the other £1,800 is advertising and should be treated as such in the P&L a/c.

3   All the company's cloth cutting machines were wrongly set for the last three months of the year. As a result, £30,000 more raw material was used in production than would normally have been the case.

The exceptional spoilage cost must be eliminated from any overhead allocation to stock and, according to FRS 3 (*Reporting financial performance* - chapter 2), included as an exceptional item in arriving at the figure of profit or loss on ordinary activities. Its nature and size should be disclosed.

4   Early in the year, the company was sub-contracted to develop a new exclusive range of bedroom furniture for Marks & Spencer. It incorporates the company's newly discovered mirrored glass effect finish. Total costs in the year were £22,000. On 31st December, the company received a cheque for £22,000 from Marks & Spencer.

As all the sub-contracted development costs have been reimbursed this item does not come within the scope of SSAP 9.

5   At the balance sheet date, the company had 4,000 wooden ceiling panels in stock. Their total cost was £14,000. Due to foreign competition, the market for these panels had slumped in the last three months of the year and the balance sheet date sale price was £2.

Net realisable value of £8,000 should be used in respect of this stock.

6   In order to sell the wooden ceiling panels (see question 5), they require to be packaged and shipped. Costs per panel are £0.30 and £0.20, respectively.

Net realisable value should be reduced to £6,000 [£8,000 - (4,000 @ £0.50)]

7   At the balance sheet date, the company had stock of furniture fitments valued at cost of £30,000. The fitments are used in the production of kitchen units. Four fitments (total cost £5) are used in the manufacture of each completed unit. The kitchen units have a total cost of £23 and their balance sheet date sale price was £25. Net realisable value of the fitments at the balance sheet date (based on replacement cost) was £21,000.

The stock of fitments should be included at its cost of £30,000 as the kitchen units into which they are incorporated are expected to make a profit (£25 - £23).

8   Two weeks after the balance sheet date, the net realisable value (based on replacement cost) of the furniture fitments referred to in question 7 was still £21,000, but the sale price of the kitchen units was reduced to £22, as a result of increased competition. No other costs incurred in the manufacture of the kitchen units had changed since the balance sheet date. All of the balance sheet date stock of furniture fitments was still held by the company, though half of it was in kitchen units held in the company's warehouse.

The kitchen units are now selling at a loss when calculated using the original cost of the fitments [£22 - £23]. The fitments should be revalued at their net realisable value of £21,000. The value of any still unsold balance sheet date kitchen unit work in progress and finished goods stock will also require to be reduced to net realisable value. [This treatment also complies with SSAP 17 (*Accounting for post balance sheet events* - chapter 6).]

9   The company has stock of 1,200 glass-topped coffee tables which was purchased direct from a foreign supplier for £14,000 over three years ago on the basis of an expected contract which never transpired. All attempts to sell the coffee tables have failed and an offer has been received from a discount warehouse to buy them from the company for £2,000.

The value of this stock should be included in the balance sheet at its net realisable value of £2,000.

10   Early in the year, the company was sub-contracted to develop a new exclusive range of kitchen furniture for MFI. MFI agreed to reimburse all development costs incurred. Total costs in the year were £55,000, in respect of which £30,000 has been received to date from MFI.

£25,000 should be included in stocks as contract work in progress (see SSAP 13, *Accounting for research and development*, paragraph 17).

11   The company produces three different beds in its Dundee factory. In each of the previous two years, the total labour hours worked in the factory was 450,000. Fixed overheads are apportioned to production on the basis of standard hours per unit. In the current year, the total labour hours worked was, as before, 450,000. The same products are being

produced as in the previous two years. The standard hours per single bed is 8, per queen-sized bed 10, and per king-sized bed 12. These standards were set three years ago and have remained unchanged. Actual labour hours per bed during the current year were 9, 10 and 11, respectively. 15,000 of each type of bed were produced during the year. There was no work in progress at the balance sheet date. Stock of finished beds comprised: 3,000 single beds, 2,000 queen-sized beds, and 1,500 king-sized beds. The stocks are at a similar level to that in previous years.

The standard apportionment is resulting in an under-apportionment to the single beds, and an over-apportionment to the king-sized beds. An adjustment should be made to the closing stock values of these two items in order to bring costs apportioned into line with actual costs incurred. This will result in the stock value of single beds being increased, and that of the king size beds, reduced. The overall effect will be to increase the stock value of beds. (The standard hours being used should be revised if it is to be of any further practical use.)

12   Included in the company's stocks at the balance sheet date is a large holding of plywood boards. This stock is stored on wooden pallets and is withdrawn for use by taking the uppermost board first. Additions to stock are placed on top of existing stocks. The stock is approximately ten metres high. During the year, four consignments were received, each of 1000 boards. During the year, stocks never fell below 1,100 boards. The cost per board rose at each delivery and was £12, £13, £14, and £15 respectively. Closing stock is 1,300 boards. This is the first year the company has held stocks of these boards.

This is a situation where it may be appropriate to use LIFO. It seems probable that the closing stock consists of stock which had been purchased for £12 (1000 boards) and £13 (300 boards). Use of LIFO will probably result in the fairest practicable approximation to cost (see section 12 of appendix 1). Attention should be paid to the possibility of stock deterioration: some downward adjustment to the valuation may be required. It would be inappropriate to adopt FIFO as it would result in the stock of boards being stated at an amount that bears little relationship to its cost. (FIFO value = £19,200; LIFO value = £15,900)

13   The company manufactures card tables. The total cost per table, as calculated by the chief management accountant, is £26. This comprises material costs of £13.50 (after deducting a 10% cash discount received from the supplier); delivery charges on the materials of £0.20; direct labour and expenses of £10; other production overheads apportioned of £1.65; £0.55 central service department costs (derived from the original apportionment to the production function of £35,000); and general administration costs apportioned at a rate of £0.10 per table. At the year end, the company had 120 finished card tables in stock.

The £26 valuation is inappropriate. The cash discount of £1.50 should be added back and the general administration costs should be eliminated (unless the daily administration of the production function - see s6 of appendix 1). The unit cost for stock valuation purposes is, therefore, £27.40, giving a total stock value of £3,288.

14   There were 30 half-finished and 40 three-quarter finished card tables in stock at the balance sheet date (see question 13). All the materials are incorporated at an early stage in the production process.

The half-finished tables should be valued at £21.30 [£13.50 + £1.50 + £0.20 + ½£(10 + 1.65 + 0.55)] = £639, and the three-quarter finished ones at £24.35 [£13.50 + £1.50 + £0.20 + ¾£(10 + 1.65 + 0.55)] = £974.

15   The company sells all waste from its production of laminated worktops to a local foundry. The sale takes place every three months. The company had stock of this waste valued at a net realisable value of £1,200 at the balance sheet date. This represented the result of two months production. One months production of laminated worktops was also in stock at that date.

Half of the waste stock value should be deducted from the cost of the stock of laminated worktops as it derives from waste created in the production of that stock. The other £600 should be credited to profit and loss as it arose in the production of goods sold and should be set against the costs of producing those goods.

Questions 16 - 42 are concerned with long term contracts

16   In October the company entered into a contract to furnish and decorate every new house built in Scotland by Wimpey during the following 12 months. Costs to date are £50,000 and a further £70,000 is expected to be incurred before completion. The work done so far will be invoiced at £85,000 when the company raises an invoice at the end of the first six months.

This is a long term contract. Allowance should be made for profits to date and they should be passed through the P&L a/c - the balance sheet should show the amount of £50,000, plus the profit taken to P&L a/c, as amounts recoverable on contracts within debtors. *However, there is not enough information provided to enable a decision to be taken on whether a profit should be recognised: there is no information regarding overall profitability expectations.*

17   During the year, the company entered into a contract to refurbish an Edinburgh concert hall. Costs to date of £120,000 have been transferred to cost of sales. A further £70,000 is expected to be spent prior to completion. The contract price is £160,000. The contract is 65% complete.

This is contract work in progress on which there is an expected overall loss of £30,000. All the loss must be provided for now. As 65% of the contract is complete, turnover should be entered in profit and loss as £104,000 [65% of £160,000]; as costs to date are £120,000, a £16,000 loss has already been recognised in this year's accounts. The overall loss on the contract is £30,000, consequently, a further £14,000 must be provided this year. Cost of sales should be increased to £134,000 and a £14,000 provision/accrual for foreseeable losses should be included, under creditors, or under provision for liabilities and charges.

18   In March the company agreed to fully refurbish a chain of supermarkets. It is anticipated that a profit will result and the contract is expected to take eighteen more months to complete. No payment will be received until three months after the contract is completed.

This is a long term contract. Allowance should be made for profits to date and they should be passed through the P&L a/c. The balance sheet should include, within debtors, the total

of cost transferred to cost of sales and the profit taken to P&L a/c, as amounts recoverable on contracts.

Questions 19 - 21 concern a contract to redecorate all the chalets in three timeshare resorts. It was started in July and is scheduled to take two years.

19   Turnover recognised in this year's accounts is £50,000. No profit has been recognised this year. At the end of September the company raised an invoice for £10,000 and sent it to the customer, another invoice, this time for £20,000, was sent at the beginning of December. At the year end, payments on account from the customer totalled £35,000. Total costs to balance sheet date are £95,000, of which £76,000 are to be recorded as cost of sales. The remaining eighteen months of the contract are expected to break-even.

Debtors should include £15,000 under amounts recoverable on contracts [cumulative turnover - cumulative payments on account]. Stocks should include £19,000 under long term contract balances [£95,000 - £76,000]. There will be a gross loss of £26,000 in respect of this contract. However, it has all been incurred in the accounting period under review and no further loss is anticipated, therefore no entry is required for a provision/accrual for foreseeable losses.

20   An error has been discovered in the amounts posted to the timeshare customer's account: the year end payments on account from the customer totalled £53,000, not the £35,000 mentioned in question 19.

No amount should appear in debtors as the original balance of £15,000 has now been replaced by an excess payment on account of £3,000 [cumulative turnover - cumulative payments on account (£50,000 - £53,000)]. Stocks should include £16,000 under long term contract balances [total costs incurred to date - costs transferred to cost of sales (£121,000-£76,000=£19,000) - excess payments on account (£3,000)]. A note must be included giving the net cost (£19,000) of the stock and the £3,000 excess payments on account applied to reduce it to £16,000.

21   After reconsideration of the timeshare contract, an additional £30,000 is to be provided to cover losses on the contract as a whole.

Cost of sales in the profit and loss account is increased to £106,000 [£76,000 + £30,000]. The previous stock figure of £16,000 is replaced by an £11,000 provision/accrual for foreseeable losses under creditors, or under provision for liabilities and charges [total costs incurred to date - transferred to cost of sales - future foreseeable losses on the contract (95,000 - £76,000 = £19,000 - £30,000)]. Creditors should include £3,000 as payments received on account.

22   The company is replacing all sleeper furnishings on ScotRail trains. The contract is worth £2.6m, total costs were estimated at £1.4m and were expected to be spread evenly over twenty months. Work began at the start of April and costs so far are £0.9m due to a mistake in the price used in the contract quotation calculation. All the estimates have now been checked and it is anticipated that a further £1.1m will be incurred over the remainder of the contract. All costs to balance sheet date are to be included in cost of sales. (£200,000 payment on account has been invoiced, but has not yet been paid by British Rail.)

The original expected profit was £1.2m. The forecasted costs to the end of this year were £630,000. The actual costs to the end of this year were £900,000. However, an overall profit of £600,000 is still anticipated. Profit has been earned during the year (the fact that costs exceeded the estimate previously made is irrelevant) and should be recognised. As total costs are expected to be £2m, and £900,000 has already been incurred, the contract could be said to be 9/20 complete. Expected profit has been revised to £600,000, thus £270,000 (9/20×£600,000) may be recognised in this year's accounts. Turnover should be credited with £1,170,000. Debtors should include £970,000 in respect of this contract, as amounts recoverable on contracts, and a further £200,000 which derives from the payment on account receivable.

23   A contract to supply and fit all the restaurants in the *Dormebem* hotel chain with kitchen furniture was started during the year. The contract is expected to take a further six months to complete. Turnover recognised in this year's accounts is £80,000, including profit of £25,000. At the end of November, the company raised an invoice for £70,000 and sent it to the customer. At the year end, payments on account from the customer totalled £60,000. Total costs to date are £65,000.

Debtors should include £10,000 under amounts recoverable on contracts [cumulative turnover - cumulative payments on account] and £10,000 in respect of the payment on account receivable. Stocks should include £10,000 under long term contract balances. [total costs to date (£65,000) - amounts transferred to cost of sales (£80,000 turnover - £25,000 profit = £55,000)]

24   In January the company entered into a contract to fully refurbish a chain of hotels, one at a time. It is expected to take three years. The work on each hotel is individually priced within the contract and payment of the contracted amount is due on each hotel one month after the work on it has been certified complete. The refurbishment costs estimated for each hotel varied considerably across the chain. The fourth hotel was certified complete in mid December. Of the four completed to date, three have been profitable and one was not. Work has not yet started on the next hotel scheduled for refurbishment. Payment has been received in respect of the first three hotels completed.

While this has all the appearance of being, not one contract, but several, it is in fact a single long term contract comprising of a number of sub-contracts. Each hotel refurbishment can be individually costed and priced - a situation referred to in section 22 of appendix 1. Turnover should be credited with the sum of the revenue received and receivable in respect of the four hotels completed. Their costs should be charged to cost of sales in the normal way. Debtors will include an amount in respect of the outstanding payment on account due for the fourth hotel. In addition, the remaining sub-contracts should be reviewed in order to determine whether an overall future loss on them is anticipated. If one is, provision will be required to be made in this year's accounts.

25   At the beginning of April the company started on a contract to refurbish all the offices of Grant Thornton in Scotland. It was expected to take three years to complete, at a cost of £590,000. The contract price was £860,000. Cost and profitability was expected to be spread evenly over the three years. Costs are running at a rate of £30,000 per month and are not expected to fall. All costs have been transferred to cost of sales. £100,000 has been received as payments on account. Completion is still on schedule.

There is an anticipated loss of £220,000 on this contract which should be provided for in full. The transfer to turnover should be £215,000 [£860,000×(9/36)]; cost of sales should be charged with £435,000 (£270,000 costs + £165,000 future loss [total loss £220,000 - loss already recognised £55,000]); the balance sheet entry under debtors (amounts recoverable on contracts) would be £115,000 [£215,000-£100,000].

Long Question Solutions

(1) *Estrada Plc*

(A) Motorway	M20	M30	M40
Costs to date (£m)	6.8	11.0	1.0
Additional costs to complete	0.4	1.4	3.5
	7.2	12.4	4.5
Contracted Sum	8.0	10.0	5.0
Expected profit/(loss)	0.8	(2.4)	0.5

M20

Profit should be recognised. The certified value of work completed should be treated as cumulative turnover to date; profit will be found by deducting costs transferred to cost of sales from that figure.

£7.1m-£6.6m= £500,000

The overall profit anticipated on the contract is £800,000, thus a further £300,000 is expected to be earned over the rest of the contract.

[If the proportion of costs to date - v- total costs (i.e. 6.8/7.2) were used to calculate profit to date, it would be £755,556. This does not produce a profit to date which reflects the proportion of the work carried out to date.]

M30

The loss should be written-off. The certified value of work completed should be treated as cumulative turnover to date (£9m). When costs to date transferred to cost of sales (£10.5m) are subtracted from that figure, it can be seen that a loss of £1.5m has already been recognised. The additional foreseeable future loss of £0.9m (£2.4m - £1.5m) must be recognised now and added to cost of sales.

M40

This contract has made a substantial profit to date. If the costs to date transferred to cost of sales (£1m) are subtracted from the certified value of work completed (£2.5m) a profit to date of £1.5m results. If the outcome of the contract could be assessed with reasonable certainty, these figures would be entered through profit and loss and an adjustment for the foreseeable future losses of £1m (overall profit of £0.5m - profit recognised of £1.5m) would be made. However, the outcome of the contract cannot be assessed with reasonable certainty. In these circumstances, the costs to date transferred to cost of sales (£1m) should be matched by a similar figure for turnover.

(B) Profit and loss account values:	M20	M30	M40
Turnover	7.1	9.0	1.0
Cost of sales	6.6	11.4	1.0
Profit/(Loss)	0.5	(2.4)	-

(C) Balance sheet values:	M20	M30	M40
a) Stock - *long term contract balances*	0.2	-	-
b) Debtors - *amounts recoverable on contracts*	0.6	-	-
c) Debtors - *trade debtors*	-	1.0	-
d) Creditors - *payments received on account*	-	-	1.7
e) Creditors/Provisions for liabilities and charges			
(*provision/accrual for foreseeable losses*)	-	0.4	-

workings:

	M20	M30	M40
Costs to date	6.8	11.0	1
Less: transferred to P&L	6.6	10.5	1
	0.2	0.5	-
Less: foreseeable future losses	-	0.9	-
	0.2	(0.4)	-
Less: excess payments on account	-	n/a	n/a
a) Stock - *long term contract balances*	0.2	-	-
e) Creditors/Provision for liabilities & charges			
(*provision/accrual for foreseeable losses*)	-	(0.4)	-

	M20	M30	M40
Turnover	7.1	9.0	1.0
Less: payments on account	6.5	9.0	2.7
excess payments on account	-	-	1.7
b) Debtors - *amounts recoverable on contracts*	0.6	-	-
d) Creditors - *payments received on account*	-	-	1.7

	M20	M30	M40
Payments on account invoiced	6.0	9.0	2.0
Less: payments on accounts received	6.5	8.0	2.7
c) Debtors - *trade debtors*	-	1.0	-

(2) *Navio Ltd*

(A) *Calculation of attributable profits and foreseeable losses*

		Anda		Briga		Canta
Contract price		805		990		660
Estimated costs for the whole contract						
Direct materials	148		196		340	
Direct labour	180		252		150	
Production overheads	360	688	504	952	300	790
Expected profit/(loss)		117		38		(130)
Calculation of costs to date						
Direct material		120		182		30
Direct labour		150		228		6
Production overheads		300		456		12
		570		866		48

Anda

There is no certified value available, thus costs to date (£570,000) in relation to total costs anticipated (£688,000) should be used to arrive at a suitable figure for turnover.

$$\frac{570,000}{688,000} = 82.8\%$$

82.8% of £805,000 (the contract price) is £666,540. When used as turnover, this figure results in a profit to date of £96,540.

The overall profit anticipated on the contract is £117,000, thus a further £20,460 is expected to be earned over the rest of the contract.

[If 570/688 is not rounded to 82.8%, the turnover is £666,933, and the profit to date is £96,933.]

Briga

The contract is expected to make a profit of £38,000. The certified value of work completed should be treated as cumulative turnover to date (£920,000). When costs to date transferred to cost of sales (£866,000) are subtracted from that figure, it can be seen that a profit would be recognised of £54,000. There is, therefore, a foreseeable future loss of £16,000 which must be recognised now and added to cost of sales.

[If it was felt that it would be more prudent to delay the recognition of some of the overall contract profit, attributable profit could be based on the percentage that costs to date are of total estimated costs, i.e. £38,000 × 866/952 = £34,567.]

Canta

This contract has made a loss of £12,000 already (costs to date of £48,000 transferred to cost of sales subtracted from the certified value of work completed of £36,000). There is a further foreseeable loss of £118,000 which must be provided for now by adding that amount to cost of sales.

(B) Profit and loss account values:

	Anda	_Briga_	_Canta_
Turnover	666.54	920	36
Cost of sales	570.00	882	166
Profit/(Loss)	96:54	38	(130)

(C) Balance sheet values:

	Anda	_Briga_	_Canta_
a) Debtors - _amounts recoverable on contracts_	126.54	320	30
b) Debtors - _trade debtors_	30	60	-
c) Creditors/Provision for liabilities & charges			
(_provision/accrual for foreseeable losses_)	-	(16)	(118)

---

workings:

	Anda	_Briga_	_Canta_
Costs to date	570	866	48
Less: transferred to P&L	570	866	48
	-	-	-
Less: foreseeable future losses	-	16	118
c) Creditors/Provision for liabilities & charges			
(_provision/accrual for foreseeable losses_)	-	(16)	(118)

	Anda	_Briga_	_Canta_
Turnover	666.54	920	36
Less: payments on account	540.00	600	6
a) Debtors - _amounts recoverable on contracts_	126.54	320	30

	Anda	_Briga_	_Canta_
Payments on account invoiced	540	600	6
Less: payments on accounts received	510	540	6
b) Debtors - _trade debtors_	30	60	-

(3) *Fazer Ltd*

Production during the year

	tonnes
Raw materials (26 deliveries of 5,000 tonnes)	130,000
Less: closing stock	13,000
Used in production	117,000

Output of coisas (⅔ tonnes of raw materials used)	78,000
Weekly production (78,000 tonnes/52)	1,500

Overhead recovery rate

$$\frac{\text{fixed production costs}}{\text{normal activity level}} = \frac{£90,000}{1,500} = £60 \text{ per tonne produced}$$

Raw material stock cost

	£ per tonne
Purchase cost	420
Handling charges (£20,000/5,000)	4
	424

Cost of year end stock (13,000 tonnes at £424 per tonne)   £5.512m

---

Finished stock of 6,000 coisas cost

	£ per tonne
Raw material cost (1.5 × £424)	636
Direct costs	80
Fixed production overheads (as above)	60
	776

Cost of year end stock (6,000 tonnes at £776 per tonne)   £4.656m

---

Delivery costs per tonne

Annual fixed cost	£432,000
Tonnes delivered (78,000 - 6,000)	72,000
Cost per tonne delivered	£6

Net realisable value of raw material stock

		£ per tonne produced
Selling price		£899

Less:	Additional costs to completion		
	Direct costs	80	
	Fixed production overheads	60	
		140	
	Packaging costs	30	
	Delivery costs	6	
			176
			723

Net realisable value per tonne at ⅔ of £723 = £482

Net realisable value of year end stock (13,000 tonnes at £482 per tonne) = £6.266m

---

Net realisable value of finished stock

		£ per tonne produced
Selling price		£899

Less:	Packaging costs	30	
	Delivery costs	6	
			36
			863

Net realisable value of year end stock (6,000 tonnes at £863 per tonne) = £5.178m

---

Year end stock valuation

	£m
Raw materials	5.512
Finished goods	4.656
	10.168

SSAP 12:   Accounting for Depreciation

Short Question Solutions

*ASSUME THAT MATERIALITY EXISTS IN **EVERY** CASE*

Questions 1-25 relate to a household furniture manufacturing and retailing company with current turnover of £5m and net pre-tax profit of £0.5m. (Last year £4.6m and £0.6m respectively.) The company's financial year ends on 31st December. (Unless otherwise indicated, estimated residual value is zero.)

1   During the year, the company purchased 20 acres of freehold land for £100,000.

Do not provide any depreciation on this land, unless it is subject to depletion.

2   The company owns a binding machine which cost £72,000 over two years ago. At the end of each of the previous two years it was depreciated using 25% straight-line. This year the company is adopting a 20% straight-line basis for all its machinery depreciation.

Write-off the remaining £36,000 over the 3 years left = £12,000 instead of £18,000 per annum. There can be no claw-back of the difference in accumulated depreciation brought forward (£36,000-£28,800 = £7,200) had the new system been in operation when the machine was acquired - SSAP 12 prohibits such treatment of depreciation already provided. SSAP 12 also does not require disclosure of the effects of the change in estimated life on the depreciation charge for the year. If there are sufficient assets affected by the change to make the overall effect material, the effects of the change on the depreciation charge for the year should be disclosed by way of a note to the financial statements. Also, if future results will be materially affected by the change in estimated life, FRS 3 (*Reporting financial performance* - chapter 2) should be applied and the adjustment treated as an exceptional item.

3   At the start of the year, the company revalued its head office at £220,000. It had cost £115,000 four years earlier and this was the first revaluation of this property the company have undertaken.

The effect of the revaluation on the depreciation charge, if material, must be disclosed along with the names, or qualifications, of the valuers and the bases of valuation used. Transfer the difference between the net book value brought forward at the start of the year and the new valuation to a revaluation reserve. Depreciate for a full year on the basis of a carrying value of £220,000.

4   The depreciation method applied to the head office (see question 3) was changed during the year from 5% straight-line to 25% reducing balance.

As was stated in the solution to question 3, the effect of the revaluation on the depreciation charge, if material, must be disclosed along with the names, or qualifications, of the valuers and the bases of valuation used. There is the apparent complication of a change in depreciation method (presumably on the basis that it will give a fairer presentation of the results and of the financial position -this must be checked to ensure compliance with SSAP

12). However, due to the revaluation, the change in the method of depreciation involves no adjustment as there is no accumulated depreciation. The depreciation charge for the year will be £55,000 and the net book value at the year end, £165,000.

5   During the year, the Icelandic government passed a law forbidding foreign-based companies from having sales outlets on Icelandic territory. All such outlets must be closed and vacated by the end of the year after next at which time they are to be confiscated with no compensation. As a result, the company have revised the expected useful economic life of their custom built (and now legally unsellable) shop in Iceland from 43 years to 3. The shop cost £300,000, had an original expected useful economic life of 50 years, and was being depreciated at 2% straight-line.

To depreciate this over the remaining three years of useful economic life would involve an annual depreciation charge of £86,000. Had the useful economic life always been 10 years, the annual depreciation charge would have been £30,000 [£300,000/10]. The difference of £56,000 per year would probably materially distort future results. If so, it should be treated as an exceptional item and £168,000 written-off now. If a ten year life is the basis for the depreciation entry in each of the final three years of its existence, the total depreciation charge for the shop for the period would be   £   90,000
        add the accumulated depreciation to date = 7 years@£6,000   =   42,000
        giving a total depreciation charge over the ten year life   =   132,000
        the balance is the exceptional item   =   168,000
                                                £   300,000

6   The company has previously used a 5 year life when calculating depreciation on its computers. It has now decided to change this to 10 years. The method of depreciation has not been changed.

Write-off the unamortised cost/revalued amount over the remaining useful life. If the change causes future results to be materially distorted then FRS 3 should be referred to and the distorting amount treated as an exceptional item.

7   One of the company's computers is now 6 years old. It originally cost £6,000 and was written-down to zero last year.

Normally the unamortised cost should be written-off over the remaining useful life but, as it has no remaining value, no charge will be put through the profit and loss. The effect is unlikely to be sufficiently material to impair the true and fair view.

8   At the end of the year, the company, as a result of a purchasing error, had sufficient stocks of computer stationery for the next 2 years. It was valued at £19,000.

This is a current asset: SSAP 12 does not apply.

9   The depreciation method on company motor vehicles has been changed to straight-line from reducing balance.

Write-off the unamortised cost/revalued amount over the vehicles' remaining useful economic lives.

10   The company's shop in Paisley was revalued two years ago at £22,000.

The year of valuation and the value given must be disclosed in this year's accounts.

11   During the year, the company bought a furniture shop building in Greenock for £170,000. The value of the freehold was £140,000.

The £30,000 difference between the value and the purchase price is goodwill. SSAP 22 (*Accounting for goodwill* - chapter 14) should be consulted for the appropriate treatment of the £30,000. The £140,000 shop value should be depreciated using the most appropriate method over its estimated useful economic life.

12   The asset values of the freehold of the Greenock shop (see question 11) were £60,000 for the land and £80,000 for the building.

Depreciate the building using the most appropriate method. Do not depreciate the land.

13   A small shop which the company bought for £15,000 over 10 years ago was closed at the same time as the company closed its Edinburgh factory. It was being depreciated by 1% per year, straight-line. The company has no plans to re-open the shop. Instead, it plans to retain it for a few years and then sell it when its value has appreciated appreciably, probably in about five years' time. In the meantime it is allowing a local hospice to use the premises rent free.

SSAP 12 does not apply as the shop is no longer being used in the business. It is now being held as an investment and is not therefore subject to the requirements of SSAP 12. The net book value at the start of the year should be transferred to an investment account and shown as an investment in the accounts at the year end. The fact that the shop was in use for part of the year does imply that some depreciation charge should be made. However, the effect would not be material and consequently need not be charged.

14   The company has the leasehold of a warehouse in Greenock. The lease was originally for 30 years and still has 22 years to run. It was revalued at the start of the year from a net book value of £88,000 to a value of £132,000. No change has been made to the depreciation method (which is straight-line).

The effect of the revaluation on the depreciation charge, if material, must be disclosed along with the names, or qualifications, of the valuers and the bases of valuation used. The depreciation calculation should be based on £132,000. This will give an annual charge of £6,000 (£132,000/22) compared to £4,000 (£88,000/22). Unless the difference of £2,000 is going to have a material effect on the total depreciation charge for the year, it need not be disclosed.

15   At the start of the year, the company renegotiated the lease on its shop in Troon. Under the renegotiation, which cost £25,000, the unexpired term was increased by 5 years. At the start of the year there was 5 years left on the old lease. After the re-negotiation, the company adopted the valuation which the lessor had undertaken at the end of the previous year and the shop is now shown at a value of £50,000 compared to the £20,000 net book value it had at the start of the year. It is to continue to be written-off using the

straight-line method.

There has been a revaluation and, as a result, the circumstances have changed: the useful economic life has been revised. If the purchased element of the revaluation (£25,000) is put aside, the change in useful economic life and consequent revaluation has resulted in an annual depreciation charge of £2,500 (£25,000/10) as compared to £4,000 (£20,000/5): this is unlikely to be material and, if so, would not need to be disclosed. Future results will not be distorted by following normal depreciation practice therefore the depreciation provision should be based on £50,000 over 10 years = £5,000. The other revaluation rules must be followed, namely, the names, or qualifications, of the valuers and the bases of valuation used must be disclosed. Transfer the total of the net book value brought forward at the start of the year (£20,000), plus the cost of the extension to the lease (£25,000), subtracted from the new valuation (£50,000) to a revaluation reserve (£5,000).

16   During the year the company purchased three new wood-steel-binding machines at a total cost of £210,000. It only has need of two and has leased the third on a 25 year lease to *Joga Fora Plc*, a company specializing in office furniture. The company has adopted a general policy of depreciating all machines over a period of 5 years, straight-line.

In view of the length of the lease it appears that the useful economic life of these machines is in excess of 5 years. If this is the case, under SSAP 12 they must be written-off over their useful economic life, rather than the five year period normally used by the company. SSAP 21 (*Accounting for leases and hire purchase contracts* - chapter 10) should be referred to concerning the leased machine as it may require to be treated as being leased under a finance lease, in which case it will not be depreciated.

17   During the year the company increased its holding in *Boots Plc* to 50,000 ordinary shares. The total cost of its holding is £90,000.

This is an investment: SSAP 12 does not apply

18   The company's small tools are revalued every year due to the frequency with which they are lost. Prior to this year's revaluation, the small tools account was showing a value of £16,000. After the revaluation this figure was reduced to £11,500.

The depreciation charge for the year is £5,500.

19   During the year, the company invested £70,000 on a new water cooling system for the administration block at head office.

Depreciate over its estimated useful economic life using the most appropriate method.

20   During the year, the company spent £120,000 repairing the roof of the Motherwell factory.

This is not a fixed asset but a revenue expense (no mention is made of improvement). As a result, SSAP 12 does not apply, and no depreciation should be charged.

21   At the end of the year, the company had almost completed the building of a new

bungalow for retired single ex-employees. Total costs to date are £16,000.

The almost completed bungalow should be included in the balance sheet at cost. The standard states that depreciation is the measure of the wearing out, consumption, or other reduction in the useful economic life and should be allocated so as to charge a fair proportion of cost ... to each accounting period expected to benefit from its use. It also states that it is necessary for there to be a charge against income in respect of the use of ... assets. This asset has not been completed. It has not therefore been used. It would not be appropriate to depreciate it.

22   A company car used by one of the directors, with a book value of £14,000 was stolen in December. It had only been bought the day before and, due to an error by a clerk in the office, it was not yet insured. It has not yet been recovered.

On the grounds of prudence, the car should be written-off, *unless* there is evidence to suggest that it may be found.

23   At the start of the year, the company revalued its Glasgow shop. Its net book value at the start of the year was £15,000 and it was revalued at £112,000. Two years earlier, the company had reduced the useful economic life of the shop from 20 years to 5 as the local council had indicated they would condemn it as unsafe when a new inner-city motorway was built. This had caused the company to charge an exceptional depreciation write-off to that year's accounts. (The plan to built the inner-city motorway was scrapped during the year.)

There have been two years' depreciation since the exceptional depreciation write-off. The £15,000 remaining at the start of the year represents three years further depreciation (though there may be a residual value involved). The exceptional write-off must be added back to the extent it is no longer required. The write-back value (which will presumably be equal to the original write-off) must then be added to the £15,000 balance at the start of the year. The result must then be subtracted from the revaluation amount in order to find the amount to be transferred to an asset revaluation reserve. Depreciation for the year will be based on the revalued amount of £112,000 and an expected useful economic life of 18 years (20-2).

24   The company has a rainwear subsidiary, *Abaixo Ltd*, which is leasing the company's old Edinburgh factory at full market rental. At the start of the year the factory had a net book value of £180,000 (cost £200,000). Previously it was being depreciated at 2% straight-line. Now it is to be depreciated at 4% straight-line.

Remaining useful economic life has been reduced from 45 years to 25. The effect is to have a total life from acquisition of 30 years instead of 50. Had this been in effect since acquisition, total depreciation to date would have been (£200,000/30) × 5 ≈ £33,333 instead of the £20,000 charged to the start of the year. The difference of £13,333 represents an increase of only £533 (£13,333/25) per year in the depreciation charge over this and future years (compared to what it would have been had a 30 year life been used from the outset): it is not going to distort future results if the annual charge is £7,200 (£180,000/25) instead of £6,667 (£200,000/30). From another viewpoint, if depreciation to date (£20,000) is added to the depreciation which would have been charged over the remaining 25 years had the 30

year life been in operation throughout (£166,667), the total depreciation charged over the 30 years would be £186,667. This represents a shortfall of £13,333 which, when spread over the 25 years remaining, represents an annual charge of only £533. Under no circumstance could that amount be said to be capable of materially distorting future results. The £180,000 should therefore be depreciated at 4% straight-line over the 25 years revised useful economic life. (The fact that it is being leased is irrelevant as it is an intra-group rental.)

25   The company purchased a new machine in February for £45,000. It paid for it by cheque in April but the cheque has not been cashed and has now lapsed. It transpires that the supplier (a sole trader) disappeared on a scuba-diving holiday in the Bahamas in March. The sole trader has no lawyer and no dependents and paid all his bills prior to leaving for his holiday.

Depreciate it normally. No special rules apply. The fact that it is still unpaid, and seems unlikely to ever be, is irrelevant.

Long Question Solution

Casa Linda Plc

(i)

Casa Linda Plc
(extract from balance sheet notes)

	Land & Buildings	Vehicles	Equipment	Under Construction
Cost at 1st January	25,000	20,000	40,000	12,000
Additions	-	16,000	-	8,000
Transferred complete	20,000	-	-	-
Revaluation Adjustments	70,500	-	-	-
	115,500	36,000	40,000	20,000
Disposals	(500)	(8,000)	-	-
Transferred complete	-	-	-	(20,000)
	115,000	28,000	40,000	-
Acc. Depn. at 1st January	800	15,000	16,000	-
Depreciation on Disposals	-	(6,000)	-	-
Depreciation for year	800	7,000	8,000	-
Acc. Depn. at 31st December	1,600	16,000	24,000	-
Net Book Value at 31st December	113,400	12,000	16,000	-
Net Book Value at 1st January	24,200	5,000	24,000	12,000

* * * * * * * *

Other matters which must be disclosed:
The names or qualifications of the valuers of the land and the valuation bases used;
The depreciation methods and rates (or useful economic lives).

* * * * * * * *

(ii)   The profit and loss figure for depreciation is £14,800. This represents the depreciation for the year (£15,800) less the gain on the trade-in of the car (£1,000). The gain on the sale of the land (£9,500) should be separately disclosed; FRS 3 (*Reporting financial performance* - chapter 2) should be applied in order to determine the appropriate treatment to adopt.

* * * * * * * *

Workings: 1) land cost £5,000. 90% is left. £5,000 × 90%=£4,500; the revaluation adjustment=£75,000-£4,500=£70,500.

2) Building cost = original cost-land cost = £20,000; the addition cost is £20,000 (£12,000+£8,000); total cost is therefore £40,000. Depreciation at 2% straight-line is £800.

SSAP 13:   Accounting for Research and Development

Short Question Solutions

*ASSUME THAT MATERIALITY EXISTS IN **EVERY** CASE*

Questions 1-3 concern Diga Ltd, a private independent engineering company with 100 employees, current turnover of £8m and net pre-tax profit of £700,000. (Last year £7.6m and £780,000 respectively.) The company's financial year ends on 31st December.

1   The company's accounting policy on research and development expenditure is that, where permissable, development expenditure should be deferred and amortised over the period during which the item it relates to is expected to be sold or used, starting in the first such period.

The accounting policy on research and development expenditure should be disclosed.

2   Until the current accounting period, research and development expenditure was written-off as it occurred.

The new accounting policy should be disclosed. FRS 3 (*Reporting financial performance -* chapter 2) should be referred to as this will constitute a prior period adjustment.

3   The company charged £80,000 to profit and loss for the current year's expenditure on research and development, this was in addition to an amortization charge in the accounts for £10,000 relating to deferred development expenditure.

As paragraph 22 of SSAP 13 exempts the company from disclosing the total amount of research and development expenditure charged in the profit and loss account, it need only disclose and explain its accounting policy on research and development expenditure, the movements on deferred development expenditure, and the amount carried forward at the beginning and the end of the period. The deferred development expenditure should be disclosed under intangible fixed assets in the balance sheet.

Questions 4-17 relate to Casabonita Plc, a household furniture manufacturing and retailing company with current turnover of £28m and net pre-tax losses of £3.4m. (Last year £26.6m and £3.1m [profit] respectively.) The company's financial year ends on 31st December.

4   During the year, the company bought a mobile laboratory for £42,000 which it is using to develop a new range of kitchen worktops incorporating the company's newly discovered cigarette burn resistant furniture laminate.

This fixed asset acquired to provide facilities for development activities should be capitalised and written-off over its useful life through the profit and loss account. The depreciation should be included in the depreciation disclosed in the accounts and should also be included as part of the expenditure on research and development. If the kitchen worktops project qualifies as development expenditure and is deferred, the depreciation charge should be added to the amount deferred.

5   During the year, work commenced on an attempt to identify a new scratch-proof wood coating using a newly discovered process. By the end of the year, £62,000 had been spent on this work.

This is applied research and must be written-off.

6   After some prototypes had been made to verify feasibility, the company entered into a contract with the Sri Lankan government for the company to be supplied with a natural furniture dye whose only source is a large forest on the Sri Lankan eastern seaboard. It was to have been used in the finishing of an exclusive range of dining furniture. The company spent £110,000 on the feasibility study and use of the dye is believed to be potentially highly profitable. In November the Sri Lankan government cancelled all foreign contracts pending a review of the methods whereby such contracts were negotiated. In view of the generous compensation payments made by the company to the Sri Lankan negotiators, it is thought unlikely that the contract will be reinstated. However, it is thought possible that another dye could be substituted: tests will be required before a decision can be taken on the use of the substitute dye.

In theory, the original project is no longer technically feasible and the development expenditure relating directly to the Sri Lankan dye should be written-off. The fact that a substitute *may* be available is not sufficiently positive and any balance of the expenditure which could possibly have been deferred as being part of the development costs of the substitute dye project, should also be written-off.

7   During the year, £37,000 was spent developing a bright yellow pigmentation which could be added to the colours available for customers when selecting a bathroom suite from the company's range. A large demand had been identified for the colour. Unfortunately, although the pigmentation was easily developed, all attempts to manufacture bright yellow bathroom suites have failed and the company's experts have stated that the colour cannot be incorporated using any known methods.

This is development expenditure on a project which is not technically feasible. It must be written-off.

8   During the year, the company spent £50,000 identifying consumer preference relating to a new type of collapsible table it is developing. A large and profitable market has been found to exist.

This is market research and would not normally be included in research and development expenditure. There are no grounds for it to qualify as an exception to that general rule and it should be charged to profit and loss accordingly.

9   During the year, the company sub-contracted to develop and then produce a new range of bedroom furniture for an American hotel chain, incorporating the company's newly-discovered cigarette burn resistant furniture laminate. Total development costs in the year were £120,000. Under the terms of the contract, the company will receive 80% of the costs incurred prior to completion and the remaining 20% after the furniture has been satisfactorily installed. The company had been reimbursed £78,000 by the balance sheet date. Production is expected to start in April or May.

This is development work carried out for a third party on a full reimbursement basis. The fact that full reimbursement is delayed is not relevant to its treatment under SSAP 13. The £42,000 unreimbursed at the balance sheet date should be treated as contract work in progress, in respect of which reference should be made to SSAP 9 (*Stocks and long term contracts* - chapter 3).

10   During the year, the company took out a two-year lease on a small workshop, in order that it could develop the new range of bedroom furniture for the American hotel chain, incorporating the company's newly-discovered cigarette-burn-resistant furniture laminate.

The leasing charges should be included in the contract work in progress.

11   The American hotel chain referred to in questions 9 and 10 went into liquidation at the end of the year. There is no prospect of any further payments being received. Under the terms of the contract, the company has full rights of disposal over any furniture produced.

The development expenditure unreimbursed should be written-off, *unless* the furniture can be sold elsewhere at a profit. If that is judged to be realistically certain then the amount unreimbursed may be deferred and amortised over the period when the furniture is being sold.

12   During the year, the company spent £100,000 exploring the possibility that it had a rich seam of coal on some land it owned within the grounds of its Motherwell factory.

Expenditure incurred in locating mineral deposits is not research and development and SSAP 13 does not therefore apply.

13   In July, the company started developing a new furniture fabric using a newly-discovered chemical, *Ficar*. The company is confident that this will enable them to lead the luxury furniture market for a number of years and are convinced they will make enormous profits on the production of furniture incorporating the fabric. The development work has been undertaken in his quiet moments by the site chemist at the Motherwell factory. No records of his time on this have been kept and unfortunately he died just after the year end before telling anyone how much time he had spent. The company believe he may have spent something between 1,000 and 2,000 hours on the project during the year.

As this development expenditure is not separately identifiable, it should be written-off.

14   The company is considering using the new flush-pan wood-waterproofing technique on a new range of garden furniture. During the year it spent £44,000 undertaking research on prototypes into the functionality of the product.

This is development expenditure and may be deferred and amortised over the period during which the item it relates to is expected to be sold.

15   During the year, the company spent £45,000 on research into attitudes to waterbeds and peoples' comfort needs. This is directly related to a new type of waterbed, consisting of

an air mattress within a bed of water, which the company is developing and intends to sell exclusively through its London showroom. As a result of the research, the design was changed substantially and it is believed that the research has given the company the knowledge to dominate the market for up-market beds over the next two to three years. Consequently, the bed is expected to realise a considerable profit.

This is market research but it may be argued that it was aimed at the discovery of new knowledge in order to substantially improve an existing product. If this argument is accepted, the expenditure should be classified as applied research and included in the total research and development expenditure charged in the profit and loss account.

16   During the year, the company started trying to identify a new water-resistant coating solution. Unfortunately, the records relating to this project were stolen and the company are unable to precisely state the amount incurred. It is thought to have been between £30,000 and £45,000.

This is applied research and the costs incurred must be written-off, in so far as it is possible, given the absence of conclusive evidence as to what the actual expenditure was.

17   During the year, the company started to develop the production process necessary in order to add its newly-discovered *Neve* fabric strengthener to its curtain and furnishing-cover range. The process is certain to be successfully implemented, but there is some doubt as to whether the costs will ever be recovered. Nevertheless, the company is carrying on with the development as it sees it as a means of field-testing the fabric strengthener as a possible future do-it-yourself product, if the recent law relating to the sale of poisonous substances were ever to be repealed.

The curtain and furnishing fabric strengthening project is not financially feasible, and on that basis should be written-off. It could be argued that it is evaluation of a product - *Neve* - and should therefore be treated as development expenditure relating to its launch as a do-it-yourself product. However, even if this viewpoint were adopted, the expenditure would still require to be written-off as the do-it-yourself product is not likely to be commercially viable, because of legislation.

Questions 18-34 relate to, Inventar plc, a chemicals and pharmaceuticals company with current turnover of £120m and net pre-tax profit of £19m. (Last year £81m and £13.6m respectively.) The company's financial year ends on 31st December.

18   The company spent £37,000 during the year attempting to discover whether a newly-discovered virus could be used in the treatment of toothache.

This is applied research and must be written-off.

19   £60,000 was spent during the year developing a new brand of toothpaste. Most of the expense has been incurred in trying to eliminate the repulsive flavour of the newly-

discovered fluoride substitute which was the reason for the new product's development. Despite all the company's efforts, the flavour is as obnoxious as ever, and the chief research chemist is of the opinion that it cannot be eradicated.

This is development expenditure, but the project is technically infeasible. The £60,000 must be written-off.

20   The company brought forward deferred development expenditure of £103,000 at the start of the year relating to the development of a new coating for emery boards. A further £54,000 was spent on development of the project during the year. The potential profits are large, and the market is certainly there for the taking. It had been felt that development work would be completed by the middle of next year, and that production could follow soon after. However, in December the Romanian government announced an export ban on *Duro*, the mineral employed in the emery board construction, as it was needed as a cheap source of raw material in the construction of the country's new motorway network. No other known source exists.

The project is now technically infeasible and all the £157,000 development costs must be written-off.

21   The company introduced a new range of breath freshener in September. It has been a huge commercial success due to the fact that it is effective for three times as long as any other product on the market. Development took place in the Spring and cost £71,000.

The development expenditure of £71,000 may be deferred and amortised over the period during which the breath freshener is expected to be sold.

22   In the previous period, the company wrote off £130,000 deferred development expenditure incurred on a project which led to the marketing of a new product, *Gosto*. Sales of the product had slumped to zero in the middle of that year after a competitor brought out a similar product at one third of the selling price of *Gosto*. The company was unable to match the competitor's price and production of *Gosto* ceased. In May of the current year, the competitor's product was found to contain some very dangerous banned chemicals. As a result the product was withdrawn and, one month later, the competitor went into liquidation. The company recommenced production of *Gosto* in August and has subsequently regained its original share of the market at the same selling price as before.

The £130,000 written-off can be reinstated, as the expenditure had previously been capitalised.

23   £39,000 was spent during the year on developing techniques for putting more toothpaste into the tube.

This is applied research and must be written-off.

24   The company spent £89,500 during the year researching the durability characteristics of the five leading types of toothbrush. This was with a view to entering into a joint promotional campaign for the company's new fluoride toothpaste (see question 19) and

the brush which came out best in the test.

It could be argued that this expenditure constitutes applied research which has been undertaken in the pursuit of technical knowledge, the aim being to identify the best toothbrush to promote along with the company's toothpaste. If so, it would require to be written-off. The product (the toothpaste) already exists (though it is unmarketable) and the expenditure is not going to improve it. It cannot therefore be classified as development expenditure; even if it could be classified as development expenditure relating to the toothpaste, as the toothpaste is not technically feasible, this expenditure would require to be written-off. It is probably market research rather than applied research but expert opinion would be required before a firm judgement could be given. If it was determined that it was research expenditure then it would require to be included in the total for research and development expenditure charged to profit and loss.

25   The company's chief research chemist has spent £36,000 on the development of a new toothpaste preservative, or it might be a dental floss preservative, or it might be a toothpick steriliser - he's not too sure which, but he is sure that one of them will result.

This project is not clearly defined and the development expenditure must therefore be written-off.

SSAP 17:   Accounting for Post Balance Sheet Events

Short Question Solutions

*ASSUME THAT MATERIALITY EXISTS IN **EVERY** CASE*

Questions 1-40 relate to a household furniture manufacturing and retailing company with 100 employees, current turnover of £8m and net pre-tax profit of £700,000. (Last year £7.6m and £780,000 respectively.) The company's financial year ended on 31st December. It is now 31st March and the Board of Directors are meeting to approve the accounts. (All references to January, February, March and April relate to the year following the accounting period under review.)

1   In February, the company bought a new warehouse for £500,000. The purchase was funded by a 10 year loan and the loan is secured by a fixed charge over the company's offices and central warehouse assets.

This event has arisen in the 'post balance sheet period'. It is not an adjusting event. (The standard cites the acquisition of fixed assets as an example of a non-adjusting event.) The nature and financial effects of the purchase should be disclosed as non-disclosure will affect the ability of those using the accounts to have a proper understanding of the company's position.

2   In late January, the company's entire stock of recliner chairs (which had been water damaged in a small fire in the warehouse in the first week in January) were sold for £20,000 to an overseas customer. The value in the accounts was £45,000.

This event has arisen in the 'post balance sheet period'. It is a non-adjusting event as it relates to conditions which did not exist at the balance sheet date. The nature and financial effects of the fire should be disclosed if non-disclosure will affect the ability of those using the accounts to have a proper understanding of the company's position.

3   In February, a defect was found in the material used in some batches of furniture awaiting shipment to an overseas customer. It was discovered that these were the only batches affected and that they were all manufactured in the last week of December. As a result, the customer was offered a 40% discount on the agreed price. This was accepted and the sale proceeded at a value of £60,000. (The value placed on the stock in question in the year-end accounts was £80,000.)

This event has arisen in the 'post balance sheet period'. It is an adjusting event as it relates to a condition which existed at the balance sheet date (the faulty stock). The figure for stock in the year-end accounts should be adjusted accordingly. There is no requirement for separate disclosure.

4   After negotiating for six months, the company finally sold its Dundee factory 2 days after the year end. It was sold for £160,000. This was £28,000 less than the value it was shown at in the accounts which was based on an independent valuation carried out in mid-December.

This event has arisen in the 'post balance sheet period'. It is an adjusting event. Clearly, two days is unlikely to have been a sufficient time for any new circumstances to have developed which could have caused the loss. While the sale did not precede the year end (one of the examples quoted in the standard of an adjusting event), and despite the standard citing post-year end sales of fixed assets as an example of a non-adjusting event, the conditions surrounding the sale certainly did exist at the year end and thus it is an adjusting event. The fixed asset figure in the balance sheet should be adjusted accordingly. There is no need for separate disclosure.

5   The warehouse fire in January gave rise to a claim for loss of profits with the company's insurers. In March the company received a cheque for £12,000.

This event has arisen in the 'post balance sheet period'. It is a non-adjusting event. The nature and financial effects of the fire should be disclosed if non-disclosure will affect the ability of those using the accounts to have a proper understanding of the company's position.

6   Some land that the company owned was sold in November at a price to be set by independent valuers. It was included in the year end accounts at a figure of £23,000, pending a decision on the sale value. In January it was agreed that the land should be sold for £41,000.

This event has arisen in the 'post balance sheet period'. It is an adjusting event. (The standard specifically refers to this as being an adjusting event.) The accounts should be adjusted to reflect the value of the sale.

7   For some years the company has been running a wallpaper division. This has never been very profitable - approximately 2% on turnover of £1.2m in the last year. In order to improve profitability of what the company then believed to be a potentially profitable venture an industrial consultant was appointed in January to undertake a feasibility study of the operation. Unfortunately he concluded that, due to the company's failure to keep up-to-date in both design and manufacture, huge losses would be incurred if it were not closed immediately. As a result, at an emergency board meeting in 18th February, the wallpaper division was disbanded and steps were taken to sell off all the equipment and plant as quickly as possible. By mid-March this had been achieved and the sale raised £129,000 as against a book value in the year end accounts of £335,000.

This event has arisen in the 'post balance sheet period'. It is a non-adjusting event. (The standard specifically refers to the closure of a significant part of the trading activities if not anticipated at the year end as being a non-adjusting event.) However, the consultant's report has shown that it would be inappropriate to consider the wallpaper division as a 'going concern' at the year end. Consequently, it would be prudent to treat this item as an adjusting event and adjust the figures in the financial statements accordingly. While disclosure would not be required under SSAP 17, it would be required under SSAP 2 (*Disclosure of accounting policies* - chapter 12).

8   Due to the company being under-insured since it changed insurers last year, a claim for

equipment worth £20,000 which was destroyed in the January fire realised only £5,000 from the insurance company.

This event has arisen in the 'post balance sheet period'. It is a non-adjusting event. The fact that the company was underinsured prior to the year end is irrelevant: it is the fire that is the event, not the underinsurance. The nature and financial effects of the fire should be disclosed if non-disclosure will affect the ability of those using the accounts to have a proper understanding of the company's position.

9   In February, the company's subsidiary *Menor Ltd* declared a dividend for the year to 31st December.

This event has arisen in the 'post balance sheet period'. It is an adjusting event. (The standard specifically refers to this as being an example of an event which, because of statutory requirements or customary practice is reflected in financial statements and so falls to be treated as an adjusting event.) The accounts should be adjusted to reflect the dividend.

10   In late December, the company sold stock worth £300,000 to a furnishing company for £350,000. In February, the company bought back all this stock for £355,000 and resold it to a foreign customer for £390,000. It has subsequently been discovered that the stock never left the company's warehouse until it was shipped overseas in mid-March - i.e. the temporary owner never had possession of the stock.

This event has arisen in the 'post balance sheet period'. It may be an example of 'window dressing', which is a non-adjusting event. Further investigation regarding the intention behind the initial transaction will be required. Why, for example, was the stock never delivered to the furnishing company? Should it transpire that the intention was to alter the appearance of the company's balance sheet, then the nature and financial effects should be disclosed as non-disclosure will affect the ability of those using the accounts to have a proper understanding of the company's position.

11   In January, a ship carrying a consignment of custom-built furniture which had been sold in December sank. All the furniture was lost. The company had forgotten to arrange insurance cover. The buyer demanded an immediate refund of the deposit paid and refused to accept a replacement consignment.

This event has arisen in the 'post balance sheet period'. It is a non-adjusting event as it concerns something which did not exist at the balance sheet date, i.e. the sinking of the ship. The nature and financial effects of the loss should be disclosed if non-disclosure will affect the ability of those using the accounts to have a proper understanding of the company's position.

12   The board decided at a special board meeting on 23rd December that its investment in an associate company should be sold as soon as possible. The investment was valued in the balance sheet at £80,000. On 9th January the entire holding was sold and raised £110,000.

This event has arisen in the 'post balance sheet period'. It is given in the standard as an example of a non-adjusting event. The nature and financial effects of the sale should be

disclosed if non-disclosure will affect the ability of those using the accounts to have a proper understanding of the company's position.

[It can be argued that the sale provides evidence that the conditions existing at balance sheet date, i.e. the value of the investment, were not as stated in the financial statements. If on investigation this was found to be the case, then this would clearly be an adjusting event.]

13   The board decided at the January 12th board meeting that, following the profitable sale of its investment in one associated undertaking it should sell its holding in another as soon as possible. The investment was valued in the balance sheet at £90,000. On 23rd February the entire holding was sold and raised £140,000.

This event has arisen in the 'post balance sheet period'. It is given in the standard as an example of a non-adjusting event. The nature and financial effects of the sale should be disclosed if non-disclosure will affect the ability of those using the accounts to have a proper understanding of the company's position.

[The longer time that has elapsed compared to the January sale makes it less likely that this sale provides evidence that the value as stated in the balance sheet was inappropriate. Nevertheless, it will require investigation and, should it be found that the value was understated then this will also be an adjusting event.]

14   The board decided at the 14th March board meeting that, following the profitable sale of its investments in two associated undertakings, it should sell another similar holding as soon as possible. The investment was valued in the balance sheet at £70,000. No sale has yet been negotiated.

This event has arisen in the 'post balance sheet period'. This SSAP does not, however, apply as the event has not resulted in any transaction arising. Should information regarding the sale become available after the post balance sheet period, and before the accounts are published, then consideration may be given to disclosure of the nature and financial effects of the sale if non-disclosure would affect the ability of those using the accounts to have a proper understanding of the company's position.

15   The board also decided at the March board meeting that it should consider selling a wholly-owned subsidiary which is valued in the financial statements at £240,000. The finance director was instructed to investigate the financial implications and determine whether there may be any interested buyers. The proposal is to be discussed again at the June board meeting.

This event has arisen in the 'post balance sheet period'. The standard specifically excludes from its scope preliminary consideration of a matter which may lead to a decision by the board of directors in the future. The standard does not, therefore, apply.

16   On 19th December, the union safety officer drew the management's attention to a potentially dangerous area in the Aberdeen factory. This was noted and it was agreed that

it would be looked at. On December 29th a painter slipped and fell 30 feet, breaking an arm and a leg. He is unlikely to work for the next year and, in a letter dated February 7th, is suing the company for £60,000. The company's lawyers advise that the company was negligent and that, even allowing for contributory negligence on the part of the employee (who did know the floor was unsafe) they would be unlikely to avoid a damages payment of £30,000. The company's insurance will not meet the claim as the company had taken no steps to improve a dangerous situation. No allowance has been entered in the financial statements as it was assumed that the company's insurance would meet any claim arising.

This event has arisen in the 'post balance sheet period'. It is an adjusting event. The accounts should be adjusted to reflect the 'realistic' estimate of loss of £30,000 and SSAP 18 (*Accounting for contingencies* - chapter 7) should be applied in respect of the contingency of further loss.

17   After a painter was badly injured at the end of December, some repair work was undertaken to improve the safety level in part of the Aberdeen factory. However, before it could be completed, on January 4th a security guard slipped and fell 30 feet, breaking his back. He is unlikely to ever work again and is suing the company for £350,000. The company's lawyers advise that the company was negligent and that, even allowing for contributory negligence on the part of the security guard (who did know the floor was unsafe) they would be unlikely to avoid a damages payment of £150,000. The company's insurance will meet the claim as they had approved the company's plan and timetable for the safety improvement work being undertaken.

This event has arisen in the 'post balance sheet period'. It is not an adjusting event - the injury to the security guard is the event *not* the potential danger. It is a non-adjusting event but, as the liability will be met in full by the company's insurers, there will be no financial impact and the ability of those using the accounts to have a proper understanding of the company's position will not be affected by non-disclosure. Accordingly, it need not be disclosed.

18   On 29th December, the company repaid a £300,000 loan from an Iraq-based finance company which had been taken out in June in order to fund the establishment of an overseas distribution network. On 2nd January the loan was taken out again from the same source.

This event has arisen in the 'post balance sheet period'. It is an example of 'window dressing', which is a non-adjusting event. It would appear that it has been done in order to avoid the shareholders and other readers of the accounts being aware of the Iraq connection. As the intention was to alter the appearance of the company's balance sheet, then the nature and financial effects should be disclosed as non-disclosure will affect the ability of those using the accounts to have a proper understanding of the company's position. The fact that doing so will highlight the directors' actions is irrelevant. A misleading impression is being given which must be disclosed if a true and fair view is to be provided by the financial statements.

19   In order to finance the temporary repayment of the Iraq loan, trade creditors were unpaid for three months, instead of the normal one month. When the loan was reactivated in January the creditors were immediately paid.

This event has arisen in the 'post balance sheet period'. It is an example of 'window dressing', which is a non-adjusting event. Clearly it has been done in order to maintain a 'normal' cash balance and avoid high short-term borrowing from appearing in the balance sheet. It is up to the company how it chooses to fund its short-term operations but, due to the event stemming from the Iraq loan its nature and financial effects should also be revealed, though in this case the financial benefits will be positive as they represent interest saved by delaying the paying of creditors.

20   A contract to supply hospital fixtures (built-in wardrobes and private rooms facilities) throughout Highland region was due to have been completed by the end of February. The company had sub-contracted the work to a highly successful, private company, *Malsorte Ltd,* and work had been proceeding on schedule up to the end of the year when profit of £20,000 was recognised in the accounts. In January the entire board, management and workforce of *Malsorte Ltd* were killed when the charter flight taking them for a week's holiday in Egypt to celebrate the company's 50th anniversary crashed. As a result of having to identify and appoint another firm to take over the sub-contract work, the expected completion date is now mid-July and an overall loss is expected of £40,000 on the contract thanks to a combination of penalty costs for late completion and the higher cost of employing the new sub-contractors compared to *Malsorte Ltd*. (There is no possibility of any contribution towards the costs being recoverable from either *Malsorte Ltd* or their insurers.)

This event has arisen in the 'post balance sheet period'. It is a non-adjusting event and, according to the standard, the nature and financial effects of the sale should be disclosed if non-disclosure will affect the ability of those using the accounts to have a proper understanding of the company's position. However, two factors indicate that the accounts should be adjusted. Firstly, in the appendix to the standard it is stated that 'in exceptional circumstances, to accord with the prudence concept, an adverse event which would normally be classified as non-adjusting may need to be reclassified as adjusting'. What is meant by 'exceptional' is unclear and it could be argued that this event is not sufficiently 'exceptional' to warrant this treatment. The doubt surrounding whether or not it would be correct to apply the reclassification is overcome by the second factor - SSAP 9 (*Stocks and long term contracts* - chapter 3), which requires that the loss now identified should be reflected in the accounts. Consequently, the SSAP 17 disclosure requirement is superseded and the adjustment should be made.

21   A contract to supply restaurant furnishings to a fast-food chain was due to have been completed by the end of next July. The contract had been proceeding on schedule up to the end of the year when a profit of £30,000 was included in the accounts. It has just been discovered that the table tops, which were manufactured in December, are not of the correct grade of burn-resistant plastic. Consequently all the table tops will have to be scrapped and replaced with new production. It is anticipated that the contract completion date will still be met but the cost of the extra work will cause the contract to make an overall loss of £22,000.

This event has arisen in the 'post balance sheet period'. It is one of the examples of an adjusting event given in the standard (receipt of evidence that the previous estimate of accrued profit on a long-term contract was materially inaccurate). The accounts should be adjusted accordingly.

22   At the end of December the company tendered for a contract to refurnish Holyrood Palace in Edinburgh. The price quoted would result in a loss of around £30,000 but it was felt that the publicity benefits would more than compensate for this. On 6th February the tender was accepted at the price proposed.

This event has arisen in the 'post balance sheet period'. It is a non-adjusting event and, according to the standard, the nature and financial effects of the sale should be disclosed if non-disclosure will affect the ability of those using the accounts to have a proper understanding of the company's position. (The contract did not exist prior to the year end and so SSAP 9 does not apply.)

23   The company instructed a firm of surveyors to conduct a full structural survey of the Dundee offices following the appearance of cracks in the ceiling in mid-February. The surveyors have reported that there is considerable evidence of long-standing subsidence and have recommended extensive structural repairs be carried out. The value they place on the building is £30,000 less than the £90,000 at which it was included in the year end balance sheet.

This event has arisen in the 'post balance sheet period'. It relates to conditions existing at the balance sheet date and is one of the examples of an adjusting event given in the standard ('a valuation which provides evidence of a permanent diminution in value' [of property]). The accounts should be adjusted accordingly.

24   Stocks of invalid furniture, which had been valued at £26,000 in the year end balance sheet, had to be sold-off at vastly reduced prices (£12,000 was received) when the market for the company's product collapsed in mid-January as a result of a competitor introducing a new range of invalid furniture using a far superior type of material. The new material is readily available but the company had had an informal agreement with the competitor that neither would use it until existing stocks of the old material-based furniture had been exhausted. (On 5th January the company sold a batch of the furniture to Grampian Health Board at the company's usual selling price.)

This event has arisen in the 'post balance sheet period'. It does not relate to conditions existing at the balance sheet date. There is no suggestion that the company was aware at the balance sheet date that its competitor intended to break their agreement. Nor is it reasonable to suggest that the company should have been aware that the competitor was on the verge of introducing the new product range. There is evidence that the value at balance sheet date was accurate. Accordingly this should be treated as a non-adjusting event and the nature and financial effects of the event should be disclosed if non-disclosure will affect the ability of those using the accounts to have a proper understanding of the company's position.

25   The company has, for many years, sold deck chairs to the main high street chain stores. At the year end, the stock of deck chairs was valued at £40,000. In the first week of January, the company's salesmen started to report that they were hearing rumours of cheap Taiwanese deck chairs becoming available. No sales of deck chairs were made in January - usually the peak month for deck chair sales. After making some enquiries, it

was discovered that these were being offered to the stores for half the price the company charged. Not surprisingly, the stores' buyers were not keen to place any orders for the company's deck chairs. The production of deck chairs always occurs in November and December. The company never manufactures them outside these months unless a customer places an order of sufficient size to warrant production being undertaken. In response to the Taiwanese competition, the company decided to offer all the deck chairs in stock at a 40% discount to existing customers and to wait until the autumn before deciding whether or not to produce deck chairs in future. The stock has consequently now been revalued at £28,000 and sufficient orders are being received to suggest that it will all be sold by the end of April.

This event has arisen in the 'post balance sheet period'. It does seem likely that the arrival of the cheap imported deck chairs could have been foreseen at the balance sheet date. It is unlikely that the conditions at the balance sheet date were that either that no production of deck chairs for sale to the UK was planned, in progress, or had been undertaken in Taiwan, or that no excess stocks had been built up which could be sold in the UK. In other words, the conditions at the balance sheet date were that there was a competitor's product which made the year end valuation incorrect. There is no evidence that the value placed on the stock at balance sheet date was correct, there is evidence that it was incorrect. This should be treated as an adjusting event and the values in the financial statements amended accordingly.

SSAP 18:   Accounting for Contingencies

Short Question Solutions

*ASSUME THAT MATERIALITY EXISTS IN **EVERY** CASE*

Questions 1-40 relate to a household furniture manufacturing and retailing company with 100 employees, current turnover of £8m and net pre-tax profit of £700,000. (Last year £7.6m and £780,000 respectively.) The company's financial year ended on 31st December. It is now 31st March and the Board of Directors are meeting to approve the accounts. (All references to January, February, March and April relate to the year following the accounting period under review.) **[You should ignore the taxation implications referred to in paragraphs 7 and 20 of the standard.]**

1   In February a very successful and profitable subsidiary purchased a new warehouse for £400,000. The purchase was funded by a 10 year loan and the company, under group policy, guaranteed the subsidiary's loan.

This event has arisen in the 'post balance sheet period' and its manner of disclosure in the accounts is dependent upon SSAP 17 (*Accounting for post balance sheet events* - chapter 6) rather than SSAP 18. However, the details to be disclosed are determined by SSAP 18 under which there is a contingent loss of £400,000. The possibility that the liability will be realised appears remote and there is therefore no requirement to disclose this under SSAP 18. (The same conclusion will result if consideration is given to this under SSAP 17 - the financial statements will not be misleading if they do not contain this information.)

2   In December, a ship carrying a consignment of custom-built furniture, which had been sold in November, sank. All the furniture was lost. The company had not arranged insurance cover, believing it to be the responsibility of the buyer. The buyer insists that it was not his responsibility and is suing the company for a refund of the payment he made in respect of the goods. (Full payment for the goods - amounting to just over £38,000 - was required prior to shipment being sent.) The company's lawyers are of the opinion that it has a reasonable chance of success unless the buyer can produce evidence that the company agreed to insure the cargo. (The buyer has indicated that he has evidence that the company made a commitment to insure the cargo and the lawyers do find it strange that the case should be going to court unless the buyer has such evidence. The company maintains that no evidence can exist, as it is against company policy to make such a commitment.) No provision has been made in the accounts for the potential loss.

On the face of it there is a contingent liability for £38,000. Whether it is possible or probable is unclear and considerable subjective judgement will be required. If the buyer has evidence of a commitment to insure having being made by the company then it appears probable that the liability will be realised. Otherwise, it seems to be possible, not probable. For it to be treated as probable is to admit that the company policy may not have been upheld which may prejudice the pending court case and it is unlikely that the company will agree to this treatment. Given the uncertainty involved, it would be appropriate to treat it as a possible loss and disclose it by way of note.

3   In December, one of the company's delivery lorries was left double parked while the driver went into a shop to buy a newspaper. The street was on a steep hill and, within seconds, sixteen cars had been damaged and the delivery lorry was a write-off. Expert examination revealed that the hand-brake had failed and that neither the driver, nor anyone else, was to blame. The company carries its own motor insurance. Repair and replacement claims received to date amount to £32,000 and there are also two court cases pending, one for consequential loss (£4,000) and another in respect of personal injury (£45,000). The company's lawyers have recommended that the company settle all the repair and replacement claims, that the consequential loss claim should be settled out of court, and would be if £1,500 were offered, and that the personal injury case should be taken to court where an award of about £30,000 was probable, though it was possible that as much as £65,000 could be awarded.

There is a certain loss of £32,000 which should be provided for. The company should also provide £1,500 for the consequential loss claim (but if they decide to contest the case then a possible contingent liability for £2,500 should be disclosed). £30,000 should be provided for the personal injury claim and a contingent liability for a further £35,000 should be disclosed.

4   Some land that the company owned was sold in December at a price to be set by independent valuers. It was included in the year end accounts at a figure of £23,000 despite the expected sale value being £50,000 to £60,000.

This is not a contingency. It is specifically excluded from the scope of the standard (paragraph 1).

5   In December, the company invested £100,000 in shares in a well established chain of hardware stores which had just 'gone public'. The shares are partly paid and the hardware company is expected to make a call for the rest of the investment in the mid-April. At that time, the company will be required to pay a further £120,000.

There is a reasonably certain liability for £120,000. It should be provided for.

6   Due to the company being under-insured since it changed insurers last year, a claim for building repairs costing £50,000 (which arose because of storm damage in November) remains unsettled. £20,000 has been offered by the insurers and at best this may be raised to £30,000, though the company's lawyers are doubtful that it will be increased.

There is a reasonably certain contingent gain of £20,000. This should be accrued and set against the loss incurred. The possible contingent gain of £10,000 does not appear probable and so should not be disclosed.

7   The company is awaiting results for the year ending 31st December of a subsidiary company (*Tarde Ltd*) before deciding on the amount of dividend to declare for the year. The results, which are expected to show unusually high losses due to the excessively bad autumn weather's effect on demand for *Tarde's* products, should have arrived last week but have been delayed due to problems with a new management information system *Tarde* has recently had installed.

This is outwith the scope of this standard. The amount will be included in the financial

statements when available. (The approval of the financial statements will require to be postponed.)

8   In February, a defect was found in the material used in some batches of furniture which had been made in December. Some of these batches had already been shipped to customers. There has been an insignificant return of these items so far. The company is of the opinion that the defect (a slight fault in the colour match) is unlikely to result in significant returns.

There appears to be a remote contingent liability. Disclosure is not required.

9   On 19th December the union safety officer drew the management's attention to a potentially dangerous area in the Aberdeen factory. This was noted, and it was agreed that it would be looked at. On December 29th a painter slipped and fell 30 feet, breaking an arm and a leg. He is unlikely to work for the next year and, in a letter dated February 7th, is suing the company for £60,000. The company's lawyers advise that the company was negligent and that, even allowing for contributory negligence on the part of the employee (who did know the floor was unsafe) they would be unlikely to avoid a damages payment of £30,000. The company's insurance will not meet the claim as the company had taken no steps to improve a dangerous situation. No allowance has been entered in the financial statements as it was assumed that the company's insurance would meet any claim arising.

There is a highly probable contingent loss of £30,000 which should be provided for in the financial statements. (The event in question - legal action - occurred in the 'post balance sheet period' and SSAP 17 could also be applied. If it were, the same conclusion would result.) There is also a possibility of further loss depending on how the courts view the question of the employees alleged contributory negligence. It is more than a remote possibility and so should be disclosed by way of note.

10   In August, the Spanish government expropriated some land that the company had bought two years earlier with a view to building a factory and distribution warehouse. The land is valued in the financial statements at its cost of £50,000. Compensation amounting to between 50% and 80% of the original cost is to be paid once all the formalities have been completed. It is expected that payment will be received in June or July.

The balance sheet value of the land requires to be adjusted. There is a reasonably certain gain of £25,000 which should be treated as being the value of the land in the financial statements. A further £15,000 is possible, but not, on the basis of information supplied, probable. No disclosure should be made of this £15,000.

11   The company guarantees all furniture sold to the public through its own department store, and by mail order, for a period of ten years. This normally results in annual refund, repair and replacement costs of approximately 4% of these sales. Last year these sales totalled £750,000. Events in the period since the year end indicate that a similar level of claims can be expected this year.

**There is a contingent liability for £30,000. It is probable and should be provided for. If this represents a change in accounting policy, FRS 3 (*Reporting financial performance year* *adjustments* - chapter 2) may need to be applied in respect of prior period adjustments.

12   In September, a special order of a new design of bedroom furniture was completed and despatched to a customer in the United States. The total value of the order was £120,000. In October, the company were contacted by the customer and informed that one of the beds on display had collapsed when lain on by an overweight prospective purchaser, and that they were being sued for the equivalent of £80,000 for injuries sustained. The company has been advised by its lawyers to do nothing unless the American firm raises an action for compensation.

There is not enough information here to indicate whether the company has any contingent liability - there is not even word of there being any likelihood of a claim being made by the US company. As no other information is available the degree of probability of the loss is indeterminable, though common sense would suggest that it may arise. The directors would probably prefer not to disclose the possibility of legal action but they have no justification for treating the possibility of loss as remote. It should be disclosed along with a statement that it is impracticable to estimate the financial effect - the American firm's being sued for £80,000 does not limit the company's potential loss to that amount, it all depends on what the American company claims, if anything, that it has lost as a result of the case.

13   The company, along with three subsidiaries has a group registration for VAT purposes. (This means that the company is jointly and severally liable, along with the other three companies, for the whole of the VAT group's VAT liability.) At the balance sheet date the total VAT the company was due to remit to Customs and Excise was £70,000. The total for the whole VAT group was £160,000. All the amount due was paid. It is estimated that the equivalent figures for the quarter just ending will be £85,000 and £190,000.

The contingent liability at the year end has not been realised. It could be argued that it should not therefore be disclosed. However, the company always has a contingent liability for the VAT due by the other VAT group members, and it could be argued that it would be misleading not to disclose this. Nevertheless, there appears to be little chance of the contingent liability crystallising and therefore, on the grounds of remoteness, it should not be necessary to disclose it. [Whether this would be an acceptable approach under the Companies Act requirements is debatable and it may well be that disclosure will be necessary after all.]

14   In September, a special order of a new design of lounge furniture was completed and despatched to a firm in London. The total value of the order was £110,000. In October the company were contacted by the customer and informed that an electric bed settee on display had closed and trapped a customer inside. The customer had suffered severe trauma and a broken arm and was suing the London firm for undisclosed damages. The company examined the bed settee in question and found that the electric control on the bed settee was faulty. Further examination of the rest of the London firm's stock has revealed that all the bed settee controls were faulty, as were all those held in the company's own warehouse. No sales of the bed settee have been made to the public. The electric switch company that supplied the electric controls denies all responsibility insisting that the controls were designed for fold-down beds of the type that is concealed behind a built in panel in the wall. The company has contacted an electrical specialist

who is of the opinion that the controls should have been modified by the manufacturer, if the manufacturer had been told of the use to which they were to be put. The company has a copy of the letter sent with the order to the electric switch company in which it was stated what they were to be used for. The company's lawyers feel that there is a good case for the company to sue the electric switch company for failing to supply goods as specified. They are also of the opinion that the London firm's customer will receive a substantial award and that a claim for damages will be raised by the London firm in respect of the effect the case has had upon its image and trade, in addition to the damages the court awards to the injured customer.

The company has a reasonably certain liability for whatever damages the London firm has to meet. If the amount of damages that the London firm's customer is probably going to be awarded were known then that amount should be provided for in the financial statements. Unfortunately, the amount is not known and so the probable loss cannot be provided but should be disclosed. There may also be an action for damages from the London firm in respect of the impact that the case has had upon their image and trade. This should be disclosed along with a statement that it is impracticable to estimate the financial effects at this time.

The company appears to have a probable contingent gain available to offset these losses but it is only probable, rather than reasonably certain and so the details of the claim against the electric switch company should be disclosed separately from the contingent losses to which it relates.

15   A warehouse fire in January gave rise to a claim for loss of profits with the company's insurers. There is some dispute as to how much will be received. The insurers are claiming that the company was negligent and are offering £30,000. The company is claiming £90,000. The company's lawyers have recommended that it stick to its original claim and, if necessary, take the matter to arbitration where it will be guaranteed at least the £30,000 currently on offer.

This event has arisen in the 'post balance sheet period' and its manner of disclosure in the accounts is dependent upon SSAP 17, rather than SSAP 18. However, the details to be disclosed are determined by SSAP 18, under which there is a reasonably certain gain of £30,000 and a possible contingent gain of £60,000. The £60,000 should not be disclosed, the £30,000 should be set against the loss, and a non-adjusting post balance sheet event will be disclosed under SSAP 17 for a £60,000 loss as a result of the fire.

[It could be argued that there is a contingent loss of £60,000 and, as there is a possibility that this loss will be realised, it should be disclosed. (This analysis assumes that the cost of the fire was £90,000 and that £30,000 will be recovered, leaving £60,000 of a contingent loss.) However, as the contingency relates to the possible gain and not to the loss (which has already occurred) this alternative approach would not be appropriate.]

16   The company engaged a building firm to build a new multi-storey car park for employees to use at the Aberdeen factory. In November, just as the car park was due to be completed, the structure collapsed, destroying a raw material store and a works canteen. The company is suing for compensation and the case comes to court in June.

The builders' insurers have offered to settle out of court for £130,000. The company is claiming £290,000. The company's lawyers belief that their claim is uncontestable and the company is proceeding with the case.

There is reasonable certainty that the gain will be realised. £290,000 should be accrued.

17   The company ran an advertising campaign in respect of its children's bedroom furniture during December. The campaign involved the distribution of 200,000 £20 discount vouchers for purchases made up to the end of June. Since these were issued, 4,000 vouchers have been redeemed and it is estimated that a further 2,000 will be redeemed during the remaining three months of the offer.

The £80,000 already redeemed will be covered by SSAP 17. The remaining £40,000 probable contingent liability should be provided for.

18   Rumours have been circulating since November that a Japanese company is close to world-wide marketing of a new synthetic wood substitute which would make the use of wood in furniture building obsolete. The company has wood valued at £150,000 (3 months supply) in stock on a permanent basis. Were the rumours to prove true, the stock value would fall to about £25,000.

The value of inventories is covered by SSAP 9 (*Stocks and long term contracts* - chapter 4) and is outside the scope of this standard. (The year end stock has, in any case, all been used and so the situation will not affect the year end stock value.)

While the contingent loss that existed at the balance sheet date has not, and cannot now arise (none of the stock remains), there is an ongoing contingent loss which it could be argued would be misleading not to disclose. This contingent loss does fall within the scope of this standard but insufficient information is given in order to determine what the probability of the loss is. In addition, even though the stock value would fall by £125,000, that assumes the company would ignore any clear signs that the new material was about to be marketed. The actual stock of wood when (if ever) the new material is launched would be likely to be very much lower than the above estimate suggests. The maximum possible loss would appear to be £125,000 but there may be no loss at all if the company were to react promptly to any warning of the introduction of the new product. Overall, taking the fact that it is only a rumour together with the possibility that any loss will be minimal, the possibility of loss would appear to be remote and should not be disclosed.

19   At the year end, the company had discounted £200,000 bills of exchange without recourse. By the end of March, £50,000 were still outstanding and are due to mature in two months time.

As these are non-recourse bills, there is no contingent liability should they fail to be met when due.

20   On December 28th the company discounted, with recourse, a bill of exchange for £70,000 from a small private company. It is not normal practice for the company to discount bills with recourse. The bill was met when due earlier this week.

There was a contingent liability at the balance sheet date, but there is no contingent liability now. There should be no disclosure of the contingent liability that existed at the balance sheet date as there is no habitual discounting with recourse of bills by the company.

21   The company uses recourse factoring for credit sales to private individuals made through its department store, and by mail order. At the year end there was £70,000 outstanding in factored credit. Of this, £2,100 was not met when due (which was around the normal percentage level of recourse the company experiences) and the company had to purchase it back. The other £67,900 has been cleared. There is currently £110,000 of outstanding factored debt.

The contingent liability at the year end has now been realised. It could be argued that it should not, therefore, be disclosed. However, the company habitually discounts credit sales to private individuals, and it would be misleading not to reveal this in the accounts. In addition there is a current contingent liability for £110,000 which appears likely to be realised at around £3,300 (based on the example given showing a 'normal' percentage recourse of 3%). There is a virtual certainty of a loss of about £3,300 being incurred and a remote possibility that it may be £110,000. As SSAP 18 does not relate directly to conditions which did not exist at the balance sheet date, it would be inappropriate to make adjustments now for the probable loss of £3,300. Consideration of SSAP 17 indicates that the £2,100 loss is an adjusting event. SSAP 18 should be applied by disclosing that the company habitually uses recourse factoring, that the total contingent liability at the balance sheet date was £70,000, that £2,100 of this amount materialised and has been adjusted for in the financial statements, and that the current (31st March) level of the contingent liability is £110,000 of which £3,300 is thought probable to be realised.

22   A retail customer who heard about the problem the company was having over electric controls on its bed settees, asked that the company provide a performance bond guaranteeing that the goods it bought will meet the standards stipulated. The performance bond includes a legally enforceable penalty clause which would result in the company meeting all costs of supplying replacement goods from a competitor at retail prices if more than the normal fault rate of 2% is found. If the whole consignment were to be faulty it is estimated that this would cost the company about £150,000. The contract was for toilet suites and had a value of £90,000. The sale occurred in December since when no claims have been received.

On the assumption that the company usually supplies goods to a high standard and that not even the 'normal' 2% fault rate has materialised in over three months, there is a contingent liability but there is no evidence to suggest that it is other than remote. No disclosure is required. [The Companies Act requirements would suggest that it should be disclosed.]

23   A contract to supply hotel fixtures (built-in wardrobes and en-suite facilities) throughout the north of England was started in May and completed at the end of November. It was discovered in December that someone in the company forgot to apply for planning permission to put in the en-suite facilities and that, as a result, the company was liable to be sued for loss of profits and all the costs related to the removal of the en-suite facilities. At that time, the contingent liability was estimated at £140,000. It has transpired that the company is being sued, but only in respect of two Newcastle hotels

(where the local council has refused to retrospectively grant planning permission - all the other councils involved gave retrospective permission). The total claim is for £30,000 and the company's lawyers advise that they have no defence to it. The company has no insurance cover for this type of employee negligence.

The original contingent liability of £140,000 has now been reduced to £30,000 and is reasonably certain. Provision should be made for the £30,000 and no disclosure need be made regarding the other £110,000 which has failed to materialise.

24   A contract to refurbish a private school in Edinburgh was started in December. In the process of doing the work, one of the company's painters accidentally started a fire and the work had to be abandoned in mid-January. The school has indicated that it will be suing the company for the full costs of repair and other losses incurred. The total has been estimated at being somewhere between £50,000 and £200,000. The company's lawyers have indicated that the company is wholly liable and that there is no point in suing the painter.

The first point to be considered is: when did the fire occur? If it occurred before the year end then SSAP 18 would apply. If not, then SSAP 17 would apply (where it would be a non-adjusting event) and SSAP 18 would be used in order to determine what was to be disclosed. SSAP 9 would also apply in respect of value of contract work in progress.

So far as SSAP 18 is concerned, there is an apparent reasonably certain loss of £50,000 which, if the fire occurred prior to the year end, should be provided for. If the fire occurred after the year end then it should be disclosed in a note according to SSAP 17.

The maximum possible potential liability of £200,000 should be disclosed whether the fire occurred prior to the year end (SSAP 18) or after it (SSAP 17, after reference to SSAP 18).

25   The company bought £200,000 in German marks in December. This was done on the advice of the company's bankers who viewed the move as a good hedge against a rise in the mark versus the pound, especially as the company was due to pay that amount to a German sub-contractor in about six months time. Unfortunately the opposite has occurred and the investment is now worth about £180,000 and is expected to fall further before starting to rise again in the autumn. It is thought 20% likely that it will have risen back to its original value by the time the company is due to pay for the work done, 50% likely that it will be at about the current level and 30% likely that it will have fallen to about £160,000. The work has to be paid in marks but is priced in £sterling.

This is not a contingency. It is specifically excluded from the scope of the standard (paragraph 1).

SSAP 19:   Accounting for Investment Properties

Short Question Solutions

*ASSUME THAT MATERIALITY EXISTS IN **EVERY** CASE*

Except where otherwise indicated, all the questions relate to a household manufacturing and retailing company with 100 employees, current turnover of £18m and net pre-tax profit of £2.7m. (Last year £16.2m and £1.9m respectively.) The company's financial year ends on 31st December and the board of directors are scheduled to approve the financial statements on 31st March.

1   The company has the leasehold of a warehouse in Greenock. The lease still has 22 years to run.

The company is lessor not lessee, therefore, SSAP 19 does not apply. The lease should be depreciated according to SSAP 12 (*Accounting for depreciation* - chapter 4).

2   As a result of the closure earlier in the year of the company's Edinburgh factory, the company was left with a large empty and unused warehouse on the east side of the city. The warehouse, which was originally acquired on a 50 year lease 39 years ago, has a net book value of £120,000. The situation is causing the company some concern because no other company has expressed an interest in sub-leasing it. The main problem lies in its wording which prevents it from selling-on the lease - i.e. it has no option but to continue leasing the property itself and sub-leasing it to a third party, should it no longer have any use for it. The company's lease, which cost £5,000, also prohibits any change in use of the warehouse and requires that the company maintain it. The company is of the opinion that it will never be sub-leased.

As the warehouse is not being held for its investment potential, it is not an investment property and SSAP 19 does not apply. The expected useful economic life is unchanged and it should be subject to depreciation as before. If it were clear that no further use could be made of the warehouse, it could be argued that the net book value should be written-off between the revaluation reserve (in respect of the amount transferred to that reserve in respect of the warehouse) and the profit and loss. The net realisable value appears to be zero - it may, in the light of the maintenance requirement, even be negative - if that is the case, it should be written-down to zero against the revaluation reserve, to the extent that it has contributed to the balance held therein, and, (probably) as an ordinary item, the profit and loss account.

3   The company used an independent firm of professional surveyors to determine the open market value of most of its property.

The names of the persons making the valuation, or particulars of their qualifications, should be disclosed together with the bases of valuation used.

4   *A property unit trust* has revalued its investment properties this year. It had a balance of £460,000 on its investment revaluation reserve at the start of the year. Due to depressed market conditions, the revaluation showed a fall in value and a revaluation deficit for the

year of £190,000 has resulted.

The changes in market value should be taken to the statement of total gains and losses (being a movement on the investment revaluation reserve).

5   *A pension fund* found a deficit when revaluing its investment properties this year.

The deficit should be dealt with in the relevant fund account.

6   In October the company signed an agreement to lease one of its shops to the local housing association for £1 per month. It had closed the shop earlier in the year when it opened up a new one further down the same street.

The shop is not an investment property (as it is not an arm's length rental) and it should continue to be depreciated over its useful economic life.

7   The company has a shop in Dunblane which has a garage attached that had been converted into a small store. It was decided to rent it separately from the shop but, despite being advertised for lease, at a very competitive rental, as yet there have been no positive enquiries. The company is of the opinion that it will eventually be leased and wishes to retain the property for this purpose.

The garage is an investment property (the fact that it is not currently being leased is irrelevant). It should not be depreciated and should be included in the balance sheet at full market value.

8   The company erected a number of advertising hoardings in the south of Scotland. The total cost was £59,000. These are all leased for 3 months at a time. They have an expected useful life of 50 years.

SSAP 19 does not apply as these are not investment properties. Depreciate them over their 50 year expected useful life as required by SSAP 12.

9   The company holds a 30 year lease on a shop in Dumfries which it purchased 8 years ago. The shop was a disaster and was closed and leased to a chemist on a 12 year lease which still has 6 years to run.

This is an investment property and need not be depreciated. It should be included in the balance sheet at its open market value.

10   The company intends to use the year end open market value of the Dumfries shop (see question 9) which it has been supplied with by the shop's owners. The valuer was a fully qualified surveyor employed in their estates department.

The names of the persons making the valuation, or particulars of their qualifications, should be disclosed together with the bases of valuation used. In addition, the fact that the valuer was an employee of the company which owns the shop should be disclosed.

11   *An insurance company* found a deficit when it revalued its long-term business

investment properties this year.

The change in market value should be included in the profit and loss account.

12 At the start of the year, a *Companies Act investment company* had a balance of £230,000 on its investment revaluation reserve. The annual revaluation showed a fall in value and a revaluation deficit for the year of £310,000 resulted.

The change in market value should be taken to the statement of total recognised gains and losses (being a movement on the investment revaluation reserve).

13 After a decision earlier in the year to buy-in more items, the company closed its Edinburgh factory. It had been acquired on a 99 year lease 81 years ago and the terms of the lease permit sub-leasing but not re-sale. The company has successfully negotiated a lease to a local co-operative at a fair rental.

While the factory is an investment property, it is subject to the depreciation rules of SSAP 12 (as it is held on a lease with less than 20 years to run). It should continue to be depreciated over its useful economic life. As it is now redesignated as an investment property, it should be revalued and carried in the financial statements at its open market value.

14 The company acquired a 10 year leasehold on a shop in Carluke during the year.

Depreciate over the 10 years of the lease. While it is common practice to charge a full year's depreciation in the year of acquisition, it may be more appropriate to apportion the cost according to the actual period the lease was effective during the year. By doing so a fairer proportion of the cost would be allocated to both this period and the period during which the lease expires, particularly if the lease was acquired towards the end of the year.

15 On purchasing a new shop in Greenock, the company closed its existing Rothesay shop and transferred all stock and staff to the new premises. The old shop building, which has a net book value of £15,000, was then leased to the managing director's brother at a nominal rental of £52 per year, plus all rates and upkeep costs. (The company is going to re-assess the situation in five year's with a view to re-opening the shop at that time.)

The shop should continue to be depreciated normally. It is not an arm's length rental and is not, therefore, an investment property as defined by SSAP 19.

16 *A D-I-Y chain* has a number of investment properties. When they were revalued this year a revaluation deficit resulted which exceeded the balance on the investment revaluation reserve brought forward.

The excess deficit on revaluation should be taken to profit and loss.

17 The company owns a building in Brodick which it has let on a 10-year lease to a local garage proprietor.

This is an investment property and should not be depreciated. It should be carried in the financial statements at its open market value.

18   The company owns ten completed bungalows which it lets out to retired single ex-employees with more than 20 years service. The rental on these bungalows has been set by the local government rents tribunal. The bungalows, which are being depreciated at 1% straight line per annum, were built over ten years ago at a cost of £100,000 and were revalued at the start of the year at £126,000. The net book value at the end of the previous year was £90,000. No revaluation has been undertaken at the current year end as the directors do not believe it is necessary.

The directors are correct, revaluation is not necessary: the bungalows are not investment properties as they are not held for their investment potential, but as a welfare exercise for the benefit of ex-employees. The requirements of SSAP 12 should therefore be applied. The difference between the new valuation and the net book value (£36,000) should be transferred to a revaluation reserve. The depreciation charge for the year will be £1,400 [£126,000/(100-10)]. The effect of the revaluation is to increase the depreciation for the year on the bungalows from £1,000 to £1,400. If the extra £400 is material (which is unlikely) in relation to the total depreciation charge for the year, it should be disclosed. The names or qualifications of the valuers must be disclosed, as must the bases of valuation used.

19   *A pension fund's* annual property revaluation resulted in an increase in value on investment properties held of £76,000.

The changes in market values should be dealt with in the relevant fund account.

20   The company opened a new office in Cumbernauld. A 25 year lease, which cost £80,000, is held on the property. The lease restricts the use of the building to offices and the property cannot be sub-let. The company is responsible for all maintenance and upkeep of the property during the term of the lease. At the end of the lease, the company has no right to require renewal of the lease and full rights revert to the lessor. The property must be returned to the lessor in its present state.

The company is lessee not lessor and therefore this is not an investment property. SSAP 12 should be applied and the lease should be depreciated over its 25 year term in a manner appropriate to the nature of the property. There will be no residual value on the lease but there may be a residual cost incurred in returning the property to its present state. If material, the anticipated costs of returning it to its present state should be provided for over the period of the lease.

21   The company has 14 years to run on a 30 year lease of a warehouse which it took out for its investment potential. It sub-let it from the start to an associated undertaking at an 'arm's length' rental.

The warehouse is an investment property (an associated undertaking is not a group company) but, as the lease has less than 20 years to run, it should be depreciated. It should be included in the financial statements at its open market value.

22   In February, the company obtained, at no cost, a cottage in Wishaw on a 25 year cost-free lease from a grateful ex-employee who won £1.5m on the football pools. It rents the cottage to a local policeman at full market rental.

This is an investment property and should be carried in the financial statements at its open market value. It should not be depreciated.

23   When it moved to its new Cumbernauld office at the start of this year, the company leased its old Cumbernauld branch office to an estate agent. Its net book value at that time was £17,000. It has been revalued at £35,000. The lease is for 10 years.

The office is redesignated as an investment property. The difference between the net book value and the new valuation (£18,000) should be transferred to an investment property reserve, the accumulated depreciation set to zero, and the building should be shown in the financial statements at the valuation figure of £35,000. No depreciation should be charged on it.

24   The revaluation of the old Cumbernauld branch office (see question 23) was done by the company's marketing director. She has no formal qualifications but has often been involved in property valuations.

The name of the marketing director (particulars of her qualifications can not be given instead, as she has none), should be disclosed together with the bases of valuation used. As she is an officer of the company this must be disclosed.

25   A *Companies Act investment company* has purchased investment properties costing £2.1m this year. At the start of the year it had a surplus of £211,000 on its investment revaluation reserve. The annual property revaluation resulted in an increase in value on investment properties held at the start of the year of £87,000; none of the properties experienced a fall in valuation.

The increase of £87,000 should be disclosed in the statement of total recognised gains and losses (being movement on an investment revaluation reserve).

Long Question Solution

Devagar Plc

The solution to this question assumes the following:

(1) depreciation at the end of the first accounting period is for ¼ of a year

(2) depreciation for accounting period 13 is for the ¼ of the year prior to it becoming an investment property

(3) depreciation for accounting period 21 is for the last ¼ of the year, i.e. it starts from when the lease had 20 years or less to run

\	\	\	\	\	\	\	\
Devagar Plc - year end balances and depreciation charges							
End Acc	Inv	Lease	Cost/	P&L a/c	Accum	Net Book	Revaluation
Period	Prop	Life o/s	Valuation	Depn	Depn	Value	Reserve
1		39.75	1,500	9	9	1,491	
2		38.75	1,500	38	47	1,453	
3		37.75	1,500	38	84	1,416	
4		36.75	1,500	38	122	1,378	
5		35.75	3,450	38	159	3,450	2,109
6		34.75	3,450	97	97	3,353	2,109
7		33.75	6,400	97	193	6,400	5,252
8		32.75	6,400	190	190	6,210	5,252
9		31.75	6,400	190	379	6,021	5,252
10		30.75	6,400	190	569	5,831	5,252
11		29.75	6,400	190	759	5,641	5,252
12		28.75	16,000	190	948	16,000	15,801
13	✓	27.75	28,000	139	139	28,000	27,940
14	✓	26.75	38,000			38,000	37,940
15	✓	25.75	64,000			64,000	63,940
16	✓	24.75	88,000			88,000	87,940
17	✓	23.75	78,000			78,000	77,940
18	✓	22.75	92,000			92,000	91,940
19	✓	21.75	104,000			104,000	103,940
20	✓	20.75	108,000			108,000	107,940
21	✓	19.75	124,000	1,350	1,350	124,000	125,290

Proof of the final figures	
Total Depreciation	2,790
Plus: Net Book Value	124,000
	126,790
Less: Revaluation Reserve	(125,290)
Original Cost	1,500

SSAP 20:   Foreign Currency Translation

Short Question Solutions

*ASSUME THAT MATERIALITY EXISTS IN **EVERY** CASE*

The Individual Company Stage:

Questions 1-20 relate to a large (as defined in the Companies Act) manufacturing company which has many overseas customers and suppliers. It has invested in some overseas companies and is highly geared, having both sterling and foreign currency borrowings of a long and short-term nature. The company's balance sheet date is 31st December.

1   The company purchased raw materials from a German supplier for DM 21,000. At the request of the supplier, the purchase was paid in cash the day the raw materials were delivered.

Translate the DM 21,000 into £sterling at the rate of exchange ruling on the date of the transaction (the date of delivery).

2   The company has two lorries which were bought in Denmark in June for kr420,400 when the exchange rate was £1=kr10.51. At the balance sheet date the exchange rate was £1=kr10.38.

This is a non-monetary asset and it should be translated at the date ruling on the transaction date (£40,000). It should not subsequently be retranslated.

3   The company purchased raw materials from an Italian supplier for IL400m. The goods were delivered on May 5th, when the exchange rate was £1=IL2,000. Payment was made in lire on August 15th, when the exchange rate was £1=IL2,200.

Translate the purchase at the exchange rate ruling at the date of the transaction (£1=IL2,000) and the payment at the rate ruling on the day it was paid (£1=IL2,200). The exchange rate gain of £18,182 should be included in the profit and loss account under profit or loss from ordinary activities.

4   The company purchased raw materials from a French supplier for Ffr150,000. The goods were delivered, on September 19th when the exchange rate was £1=Ffr9.13. Payment was not made by the year end but will be paid by the due date of 19th March. The exchange rate at the balance sheet date was £1=Ffr9.16.

Translate the purchase at the exchange rate ruling at the date of the transaction (£1=Ffr9.13). The closing creditor should be retranslated at the balance sheet date (£1=Ffr9.16). The exchange rate gain of only just over £50 is certainly not material but the correct treatment is to include it in the profit and loss account under profit or loss from ordinary activities. A gain or loss will arise on the settlement of the debt on 19th March, which will be accounted for in the following year's financial statements.

5   The company purchased raw materials from an American supplier for $34,000. The goods were delivered on December 14th when the exchange rate was £1=$1.70. Payment was not made by the year end but will be made on the 14th January in £sterling. £20,000 will be paid. The exchange rate at the year end was £1=$1.66.

This is not a foreign currency transaction. SSAP 20 does not apply.

6   The company purchased raw materials from a Portuguese supplier for esc2.4m. The goods were delivered, on December 21st when the exchange rate was £1=esc240. Payment was not made by the year end but will be made on the 11th March. The company estimate that it will cost them £10,526. The exchange rate at the year end was £1=esc220.

The transaction should be translated at the transaction date rate (£10,000). The creditor should be retranslated using the balance sheet date rate (£10,909). The exchange rate loss should be included in the profit and loss account under profit or loss from ordinary activities. The company's estimate of the exchange rate on 11th March is irrelevant. A gain or loss will arise on the settlement of the debt on 11th January which will be accounted for in the following year's financial statements.

7   The company purchased raw materials from a Spanish supplier for pes3.1m. The goods were delivered on November 28th when the exchange rate was £1=pes240. Payment was not made by the year end and is to be made on 28th February. The company has arranged to buy pesetas on that date at an agreed rate of £1=pes245. The exchange rate at the balance sheet date was £1=pes242.

As the transaction is covered by a matching forward contract, the option exists to record the transaction at that rate. Otherwise, it should be recorded at the 28th November rate (£1=pes240), in which case the gain arising when settlement is made should be included in the profit and loss account under profit or loss from ordinary activities for the period. To add further complication, the creditor balance may be retranslated using the balance sheet date rate or the forward contract rate. If the balance sheet date rate of £1=pes242 were used, it would create a gain or loss (depending on what rate was used to translate the initial transaction).

However, as the forward contract was negotiated during the accounting period, the profit which it will generate should be accrued within that period: the closing creditor should, therefore, be translated using the forward contract rate, as should the original transaction. Any other treatment would not give a true and fair view of these two related transactions.

8   On 6th December, the company purchased raw materials for £110,000 from a Swedish supplier. The exchange rate on 6th December was £1=kr11.14. Payment in £sterling is to be made on 6th February. The balance sheet date exchange rate is £1=kr11.12.

SSAP 20 does not apply as there is no foreign currency involved in the transaction.

9   On 3rd August, the company supplied goods with a sterling sales price of £70,000 to the Brazilian government. The exchange rate ruling when the payment was made on 8th September was £1=Cz70 (on 3rd August it had been £1=Cz60). The contract was in Brazilian cruzados and under it the company agreed to accept payment of Cz4.2m on the settlement date.

The transaction should be translated at the rate which applied at the transaction date (£1=Cz60). This gives the transaction a sales value of £70,000. The payment should be translated at the rate ruling on the date it occurred (8th September). Payment was therefore worth £60,000. The £10,000 exchange rate loss should be included in the profit and loss account under profit or loss from ordinary activities.

10   Having learnt from experience, when the company sold a second shipment of goods to the Brazilian government for Cz1.5m on 19th November they contracted to sell forward Cz1.5m on the settlement date (17th December). The exchange rate on 19th November was £1=Cz90. The forward contract rate was £1=Cz120. The exchange rate on 17th December was £1=Cz130.

The transaction should be translated at the forward contract rate. It does appear to represent the value that the company placed on the sale. To do otherwise would be to clearly overstate the value of the transaction. The settlement should also be recorded at the contracted exchange rate.

11   The company purchased equipment from an American supplier for $34,000. The goods were delivered, on December 12th when the exchange rate was £1=$1.70. Payment was not made by the year end but will be made on the 12th March. In order to avoid exchange rate losses, the company contracted to buy $34,000 on 12th March at £1=$1.67. The exchange rate at the year end was £1=$1.66.

The transaction should be translated using the forward contract rate of £1=$1.67. There will be no exchange rate gain or loss. The balance sheet date creditor will also be based on the forward contract rate translation (£20,359), as will the depreciation charge on the equipment.

12   The company bought raw materials from a Belgian supplier on 21st June. The cost was BFr4m and the exchange rate on that date was £1=BFr50. Payment was made on 19th August when the exchange rate was £1=BFr46. The balance sheet date rate is £1=BFr49.

The purchase should be translated and recorded at the transaction date rate (£1=BFr50)=£80,000. The settlement should be translated and recorded at the rate ruling on 19th August (£1=BFr46)=£86,957. The £6,957 exchange rate loss should be included in the profit and loss account under profit or loss from ordinary activities.

13   The company bought raw materials from a Belgian supplier on 15th February. The cost was BFr4m and the exchange rate on that date was £1=BFr50. In keeping with company policy, all foreign currency based transactions undertaken in January and February and due for payment after UK Budget Day (mid-March) are always covered by forward

currency contracts. In this case, payment was due on 15th April. On 15th February the company contracted to buy BFr4m on 15th April at a rate of £1=BFr51. On 15th April the exchange rate was £1=BFr46.

The purchase should be translated and recorded at the forward contract rate (£1=BFr51). On 15th April the company paid £78,431 for the francs, the same price as that recorded for the initial transaction.

14   The company bought goods valued at HK$720,000 from a Hong Kong supplier on 16th October. The exchange rate on that date was £1=HK$12. The goods were to be paid for in three monthly instalments of HK$240,000. The first payment was made on 16th November (exchange rate=£1=HK$12.2), the second was made on 16th December (exchange rate=£1=HK$12.1), the third is due to be made on 16th January. The balance sheet date exchange rate is £1=HK$11.9.

The initial transaction should be translated at the rate ruling on 16th October (£60,000). The first payment should be translated at the rate ruling on that payment date (£19,672) and an exchange gain of £328 recorded. The second payment should be made at the rate ruling on the date it was paid (£19,835) and an exchange gain of £165 recorded. The year end creditor should be retranslated at the balance sheet date rate (£20,168) and an exchange loss of £168 recorded. The overall exchange rate gain of £325 will be included in the profit and loss account under profit or loss from ordinary activities.

15   At the start of the year the company owed a Japanese supplier Yen7.5m. This had been translated and recorded in the financial statements at the previous balance sheet date rate of £1=Yen250 (£30,000). The supplier was paid on February 19th when the exchange rate was £1=Yen258. The balance sheet date exchange rate is £1=Yen251.

The payment should be translated at the settlement day rate (£29,070) and the resulting exchange rate gain of £930 included in the profit and loss account under profit or loss from ordinary activities. The current balance sheet date rate is irrelevant.

16   On September 16th, the company sold goods to a German customer for £5,000. The German customer has the option to pay for the goods in German marks. The exchange rate on the transaction date was £1=DM2.7. On the balance sheet date the customer still had not paid. The exchange rate was then £1=DM2.55. A fax was sent to the customer requesting immediate payment on December 28th and the customer's cheque is now 'in the post'.

The transaction should be entered at £5,000. At the balance sheet date, if the debtor were translated using the closing rate it would translate at £5,294. That is greater than the original £sterling value. As the debtor has the option to pay in either £sterling or marks, payment will logically be in that currency which is cheaper for the debtor. Thus payment will be in £sterling. The exchange rate gain that retranslation identifies is not expected to materialise and prudence requires that it not be accounted for. The debtor should be entered at the original £sterling price of £5,000.

17   All American and Canadian customers have the option to pay for goods in their local

currency, but they must indicate which currency they are going to use at the date of purchase. On December 9th, the company sold a large consignment of goods to a Canadian customer for £42,000. The exchange rate on that date was £1=Cn$1.88. The customer has indicated that payment will be in Canadian dollars. Payment is due on 9th February. The company has taken out a forward contract to sell Cn$75,600 on 9th February at £1=Cn$1.87. The exchange rate on balance sheet date is £1=Cn$1.90.

The transaction, while initially denominated in £sterling, is actually denominated in Cn$ at a value of Cn$78,960. The company has the option to use the forward contract rate (in so far as it covers the transaction), and translate the rest of the transaction at the transaction date rate, or to use the transaction date rate for the initial translation. The former would provide a more true and fair view (it more truly reflects the actual value of the transaction) and should be adopted. The transaction is therefore recorded at £42,215.

[£42,000 × 1.88 = Cn$78,960: Cn$78,960 - Cn$75,600 = Cn$3,360: Cn$75,600 @£1=Cn$1.87 = £40,428: Cn$3,360 @£1=Cn$1.88 = £1,787: £40,428 + £1,787 = £42,215]

At the balance sheet date, the debtor owes Cn$78,960, of which Cn$3,360 is not covered by the forward contract and should therefore be retranslated using the balance sheet date rate (=£1,768). This produces a revised figure for the debtor of £42,196. The resulting exchange rate loss of £19 should be included in the profit and loss account under profit or loss from ordinary activities.

18   On May 3rd, the company borrowed $200,000 from an American bank. The rate of exchange at that time was £1=$1.75. The loan was outstanding at the balance sheet date when the rate of exchange was £1=$1.66.

The transaction should be recorded at the transaction date rate (£114,286). At the balance sheet date it should be retranslated and recorded in the financial statements at £120,482. The exchange rate loss of £6,196 should be included in the profit and loss account under profit or loss from ordinary activities.

19   The company took a 5% equity investment in a Swiss company costing Sfr200,000 on May 7th when the exchange rate was £1=Sfr2.3. The balance sheet date exchange rate is £1=Sfr2.1.

The transaction should be translated at the exchange rate ruling on the transaction date (£86,957). It should not be retranslated at the balance sheet date.

20   The company took a 5% equity investment in an Australian company costing A$200,000 on June 7th when the exchange rate was £1=A$2.1. At the same time, as a hedge against the exchange risk in the investment, the company borrowed A$200,000. The balance sheet date exchange rate is £1=A$2.2.

The transactions should be translated using the transaction date rate (£95,238). As the borrowing appears to comply with the requirements for offset, they should both be retranslated at the balance sheet date rate (£90,909) and entered into the financial statements at this figure. The exchange rate loss on the investment (£4,329) should be taken direct to reserves where it should be offset by the exchange rate gain on the borrowing to produce an overall associated loss/gain on the exchange rate change of nil.

[If the cover method were not used, the investment would be translated at £1=A$2.1 (£95,238). It would not be retranslated at balance sheet date. The loan would first be translated at the same rate (£95,238) and would be retranslated as a monetary item at the balance sheet date rate (£90,909). The resulting exchange rate gain (£4,329) would be taken to profit and loss.]

The Consolidated Financial Statements Stage:

Questions 21-25 relate to groups, each of which comprises a UK holding company and many foreign enterprises. The balance sheet date is 31st December. [You should ignore goodwill on consolidation.]

21   *Menino plc* is a UK holding company. It has a wholly owned American subsidiary, *Terivel*, which it acquired four years ago for $1.2m when the exchange rate was £1=$1.9. The exchange rate at the balance sheet date is £1=$1.7. It was £1=$1.65 at the previous balance sheet date and the average rate was £1=$1.67. The profit and loss account for *Terivel* for the current year is:

	$
Turnover	1,560,000
Cost of Sales	(900,000)
Depreciation	(100,000)
Interest	(60,000)
Profit before tax	500,000
Tax	(200,000)
Profit after tax	300,000

If *Menino* adopts the policy of using the closing rate to translate the profit and loss account of subsidiaries when producing consolidated accounts, what would be the effect on the consolidated balance sheet of the above profit and loss account under the net investment method?

The reserves would have been increased by £176,471, which is the profit of £300,000 translated at the closing rate. There could never be an exchange rate difference on the profit for the period under this approach though exchange rate differences arising in the balance sheet could be introduced subsequently.

22   Repeat question 21, but this time assume that *Menino* adopts the policy of translating the profit and loss account at the average rate.

The reserves would have been increased initially by £179,641, which is the profit of £300,000 translated at the average rate. The exchange rate difference of £3,170 between the two translations would have been treated as a movement on the reserves and would have had the effect of reducing the reserve increase back to the £176,471 obtained under the closing rate approach. The difference in impact upon the financial statements between the two approaches is that the £3,170 exchange rate loss, resulting from the difference between the exchange rates applied, goes through the consolidated profit and loss when the closing rate is used, but direct to the reserves when the average rate is used.

23   The balance sheet of *Terivel* (see question 21) at the balance sheet date is as follows (the previous balance sheet date figures are in the left-hand column):

	$(then)	$(now)
Fixed Assets	1,700,000	1,600,000
Current Assets		
Stock	300,000	520,000
Debtors & Cash	580,000	810,000
	880,000	1,330,000
Current Liabilities		
Creditors	220,000	250,000
Tax	180,000	200,000
	400,000	450,000
Net Current Assets	480,000	880,000
	2,180,000	2,480,000
Long Term Loans	680,000	680,000
	1,500,000	1,800,000
Share Capital	800,000	800,000
Reserves	700,000	1,000,000
	1,500,000	1,800,000

(The fixed assets were bought when the exchange rate was £1=$1.8)

If *Menino* applies the closing rate method when incorporating *Terivel* into the consolidated accounts, what would be the exchange rate differences arising from the incorporation of *Terivel's* balance sheet, and what treatment would apply to them?

The opening net assets of $1.5m when retranslated (from £1=$1.65 to £1=$1.7) at the balance sheet date result in an exchange rate loss of £26,738 (£909,091-£882,353). It should be taken direct to the reserves.

24   Repeat question 23, but this time assume that *Menino* applies the temporal method. (You will find relevant information for this in question 21.)

The exchange rate differences will arise only on the monetary items - i.e. debtors & cash, creditors, tax and long-term loans. Everything else will continue to be treated at the original translation rate. The average rate should be used when appropriate as it is provided, whereas the individual transaction rates are not. The opening monetary items had a value of $(500,000) and there was an improvement of $180,000 during the period. The exchange difference (gain) on the opening value is £8,912 [$(500,000)@£1=$1.7 - $(500,000)@£1=$1.65]. This should be adjusted, using the average and closing rates, to take account of the monetary cash flows during the period: the adjustment is £(1,902) [($180,000@£1=$1.7) - ($180,000@£1=$1.67)]. The overall exchange rate gain on monetary items of £7,010 should be taken to profit and loss.

The relevant translations of the *Terivel* values used for incorporation in the consolidated accounts are:

	Opening Balance		Cash Flows	
	£(then) @1.65	£(now) @1.70	£(avge) @1.67	£(now) @1.70
Drs & Cash	351,515	341,176	137,724	135,294
Creditors	(133,333)	(129,412)	(17,964)	(17,647)
Tax	(109,091)	(105,882)	(11,976)	(11,765)
L T Loans	(412,121)	(400,000)	-	-
	(654,545)	(635,294)	(29,940)	(29,412)
	(303,030)	(294,118)	107,784	105,882
	(294,118)		105,882	
Difference	8,912		1,902	
	1,902			
Overall Gain	7,010	*taken to profit and loss*		

25   *Poco plc* is a UK holding company. It bought a 5% equity investment in a French company which cost Ffr1.2m at the start of the accounting period, when the exchange rate was £1=Ffr10. At the same time, as a hedge against the exchange risk in the investment, the company borrowed Ffr1m. The balance sheet date exchange rate is £1=Ffr9.5 and the market value of the investment is Ffr1.3m. How should any exchange rate differences arising on this investment be treated in the consolidated financial statements if the cover method was applied when *Poco* prepared its accounts?

Under the cover method, the transactions would first have been translated using the transaction date rate. On that basis, the investment cost £120,000 and the loan was for £100,000. They would then have been retranslated at the closing rate. This produces values of £126,316 for the investment and £105,263 for the loan. The exchange rate gain on the investment of £6,316 would then have been taken direct to the reserves where it would have been offset by the exchange rate loss of £5,263 on the loan. Nothing would have been entered in the profit and loss account in respect of the exchange rate differences. On consolidation, the same procedure would be repeated - i.e. there would be full offset and no entry in respect of the exchange rate differences would appear in the profit and loss account.

Long Question Solutions

(1) *Terivel*

The stock needs to be removed from the cost of sales in order to apply the appropriate rates. Cost of sales was $900,000. Opening stock was $300,000 and closing stock $520,000 (question 30). The purchases figure on which the average rate is to apply is therefore $1,120,000.

Translated Profit and Loss Account for Consolidation (based on the temporal method)

	$	Rate	£
Turnover	1,560,000	1.67	934,132
Opening stock	(300,000)	1.66	(180,723)
Purchases	(1,120,000)	1.67	(670,659)
Closing stock	520,000	1.69	307,692
Depreciation	(100,000)	1.80	(55,556)
Interest	(60,000)	1.67	(35,928)
Exchange rate gain	-		7,010[a]
Profit before tax	500,000		305,968
Tax	(200,000)	1.67	(119,760)
Profit after tax	300,000		186,208

[a]*from analysis of balance sheet monetary items - see solution to short question 24.*

(2) *Cansada*

Translated Balance Sheets for Consolidation (based on the temporal method)

	A$(then)	Rate	A$(now)	Rate
Fixed Assets	434,783	2.30	391,304	2.30
Current Assets				
Stock	303,030	1.98	265,700	2.07
Debtors & Cash	358,974	1.95	380,952	2.10
	662,004		646,652	
Current Liabilities				
Creditors	307,692	1.95	152,381	2.10
Tax	107,692	1.95	133,333	2.10
	415,384		285,714	
Net Current Assets	246,620		360,938	
	681,403		752,242	
Long Term Loans	102,564	1.95	95,238	2.10
	578,839		657,004	
Share Capital	384,615	2.60	384,615	2.60
Reserves	194,224[b]		272,389[b]	
	578,839		657,004	

[b]*balancing figure*

SSAP 21:   Accounting for Leases and Hire Purchase Contracts

Short Question Solutions

*ASSUME THAT MATERIALITY EXISTS IN **EVERY** CASE*

Questions 1-40 relate to an electronic engineering company with current turnover of £18m and net pre-tax profit of £3.4m. (Last year £14.3m and £1.9m respectively.) The company's financial year ends on 31st December and the Board of Directors are scheduled to approve the accounts on 31st March. [Apart from observing the principle of substance over form, unless otherwise indicated, you should concentrate upon the treatment as prescribed by SSAP 21.]

1   During the year, the company entered into a 10 year lease on a workshop near to the main company site. The lease can be cancelled at any time by the company, providing that six months notice is given. However, the company would be required to meet any deficit arising between the residual value anticipated and that which actually arose upon cancellation.

The fact that the company is bearing the risk in the event of cancellation of the lease would suggest that this may be a finance lease. More information would be required before a firm conclusion could be drawn.

2   The fair value of an item of equipment which the company leased in February for a 3 year period, is £15,000. The company has guaranteed a residual value of £1,000 to the lessor. After discounting at an estimated implicit interest rate of 12%, the present value of the minimum lease payments, including an initial payment of £500, is £13,000.

The lease fails the 90% of fair value rule. (90% of fair value is £13,500.) The residual guarantee is included in the present value of the minimum lease payments of £13,000. Consequently, in the absence of any information to the contrary, the lease should be treated as an operating lease.

3   The fair value of an electronic digitiser the company leased in May for a 4 year period, is £250,000. The company has the option at the end of the period to purchase the digitiser for £50,000, which it intends to exercise.

This is a hire purchase contract and the company does intend to own the digitiser at the end of the lease. It should be treated as if it were a finance lease and depreciated over its useful economic life. (Although SSAP 21 refers to 'useful life', depreciation is governed by SSAP 12 (*Accounting for depreciation* - chapter 4) which uses the term 'useful economic life'. Throughout these solutions, these two terms shall be treated as being synonymous.)

4   The company has a five year lease on a laboratory at the local university. Under the terms of the lease, the company must pay £5,000 per year and is responsible for maintaining the decor of the laboratory during the period of the lease. The laboratory is covered for insurance purposes by the university's policy. At the end of the five year term, the company has the option to extend the lease annually for the following five years. Thereafter, use of the laboratory will revert to the university. The university has the right to terminate the lease upon giving 1 month's notice, at any time within the term

of the lease. In the event of such cancellation, no compensation will be payable to the company. The company has no option to cancel the lease until the end of the first five year period.

The company has no option to acquire title. At the end of the lease the company has the right to extend the lease - which is more accurately a right to request that the lease be extended - but only for a maximum of a further five years and the university can cancel the lease at any time. The company will have to bear any costs incurred arising from termination of the lease by the university. While the company is responsible for maintaining the laboratory, it is not responsible for the insurance of it. Although the laboratory is a specialised building, there is no suggestion that it would be unusable by another party. Overall, it is not clearly demonstrable whether this is a finance or operating lease. The 90% fair value rule will require to be applied before any decision can be made.

5   The fair value of a machine leased by the company in July is £12,000. The present value of the minimum lease payments is £11,000.

The present value of the minimum lease payments is within 10% of the fair value. It should, in the absence of other information be treated as a finance lease. Either of the two values may be used in recording the lease. However, the same value must be used for both the asset and liability entries. (Strictly speaking the present value of the minimum lease payments should be used, rather than the fair value, but the standard does permit either.)

6   The company entered into a five year hire purchase contract on some sensory monitoring equipment. The equipment could have been purchased for £120,000. The total of the minimum lease payments is £135,000, and the present value of the minimum lease payments is £115,000. Under the contract, maintenance of the equipment is the responsibility of the seller. The contract has an option for the company to acquire title to the equipment at the end of the lease term for £80,000. It is believed that the equipment will have a useful life of 8 years. The company intends claiming 100% capital allowances on the grounds that the equipment is being used solely for scientific research.

A hire purchase contract is usually treated in the same way as a finance lease, however, where its substance is that of an operating lease, substance should take precedence over form and it should be treated on the same basis as an operating lease. In this case, the option to purchase is exercisable at a relatively high price such that the buyer may not take it up. It does seem to be of an operating nature and should be accounted for accordingly. £80,000 for some five year old equipment which currently costs £135,000, and which will only have a remaining useful life expectancy of three years does seem less than likely to be considered a good investment by the company. In addition, the fact that the seller is responsible for maintenance indicates that some of the risks of ownership are not passing to the company. The substance of the contract appears to be that of an operating lease, the form adopted having been selected in order to benefit from the relatively early receipt of the capital allowances, as opposed to the tax deductible rental payments. In fact, the main difference arising from whether the capital allowances are received, or the payments are treated as an expense is one of timing; the total tax saving (probably) being the same in both cases.

7   A lease on an industrial lathe has a primary term of four years. It may then be extended for a further two years, if the company wishes. The lathe has an expected useful life

(based on the use that the company intend to make of it) of three years.

In the absence of further information, this appears to be a finance lease, as the useful life of the lathe is less than the lease term. The asset should be depreciated over the shorter of the useful life of the asset and the term of the lease. In this case, three years.

8   A three year lease on image processing equipment, which had a fair value of £20,000 when the lease was implemented in November, has a complex clause related to the residual value of the equipment. The expected residual value is £8,000, and the lessor will sell the equipment when the lease term ends; if the lessor receives more than £8,000 the company will receive 90% of the excess; if the lessor receives less than £8,000, the company must pay the lessor the deficit subject to a limit of 1p for every time the image processing equipment was used to generate a page of output above the annual level of 50,000 pages which the company expected to produce. The equipment is expected to output 250,000 pages during its useful life.

It is clear that the guarantee by the company is unlikely to be activated in any material sense. In addition, SSAP 18 (*Accounting for contingencies* - chapter 7) states that unless a liability is probable, it should not be provided for, though it should be disclosed if considered possible. It may, therefore, be inappropriate to include the guarantee in the determination of the 90% rule. It is not sufficient that there is a guarantee clause, there must be a probability that it will be activated *and* that the amount incurred will be material before it should be recognised, to do otherwise would be to put form over substance, i.e. it would be the complete opposite of what the standard is attempting to achieve. In addition, even if the company were to use up the entire 250,000 pages of output that the machine is expected to deliver, the charge would only be £1,000 (100,000 pages at 1p each). Consequently, £7,000 of the £8,000 residual value is not guaranteed. As a result, even if the £1,000 guarantee is recognised, the lease will fail the 90% rule and, subject to other information, be classified as an operating lease. To add further weight to the argument that this is an operating lease, the residual value is 40% of the fair value, and this, combined with the terms of the guarantees make it hard to argue that the company is in receipt of substantially all the risks and rewards of ownership.

9   Three years ago, the company leased a surplus acetator to a small manufacturing company. The lease was classified as a finance lease and at the end of the previous year the net investment debtor balance was £7,000. The manufacturing company terminated the lease during the year and paid the amount required (£3,000) under the early termination clause in the lease. The acetator is now technically obsolete and is believed to be both unreleasable and unsaleable.

The company is the lessor in this case. The net investment debtor balance should be reduced to £4,000. This represents a loss which would normally be deducted from any other finance lease income which the company has. If it is considered that this loss is exceptionally large, it should be separately disclosed.

10   The company leased a power modulator to another electronic engineering company six years ago. The modulator was new, and had an estimated useful life of ten years. The original lease was classified as a finance lease and, at the end of the primary term of six years, the lessee company terminated the lease. The company immediately leased the

modulator to a scientific laboratory on a five year lease.

This new lease has the appearance of an operating lease - the lease term is longer than the useful life of the modulator. In the absence of other information, the lease should be classified as an operating lease, the modulator recorded as a fixed asset and depreciated over its useful life (*not* over the term of the lease), and the rental income should be recognised on a straight line basis, unless a more representative basis is identified.

11   The fair value of a machine which the company leased from the manufacturer's agents in April, is £14,000. The present value of the minimum lease payments is £12,000.

The present value of the minimum lease payments is not within 10% of the fair value (i.e. £12,600). It should, in the absence of other information be treated as an operating lease. The rental being paid should be charged to profit and loss on a straight line basis, unless another systematic and rational basis is identified as being more appropriate.

12   Under a clause in a finance lease which the company has on some duplicating equipment it is using, should tax rates change so as to disadvantage the lessor, the company will be required to compensate the lessor by paying correspondingly higher rental charges.

Should this occur, the company should spread the additional finance charge over the remaining period of the lease in the same way as this was done when the lease was first recognised, i.e. it should be done so as to achieve a constant periodic rate of charge on the remaining balance of the obligation for each accounting period. No attempt should be made to adjust the original calculation so as to achieve a constant periodic rate of return over the entire lease term. This would result in an adjusting profit or loss in the current period which would not be a fair reflection of what has occurred.

13   During the year, the company sold its head office building to a property company, and then immediately leased it back. The lease is for 99 years and is a finance lease. The sale price was £240,000; the net book value at the end of the previous accounting period was £220,000.

The profit should be deferred and amortised over the shorter of the lease term and the useful life of the building (unless it includes an element arising from the building having been undervalued, in which case it should be revalued and only the balance treated as the gain on sale). This could be done by recording the lease asset and the obligation at the sale value, and writing off the book value (or the revalued book value) in order to recognise the profit which is to be deferred and subsequently amortised. Alternatively, the lease asset could be retained at the written-down value of £220,000 (or the revalued book value), and the sale value of £240,000 treated as if it were a loan; then, when payments are made, they would be apportioned between repayment of the liability, and partly transferred to profit and loss as finance charges. In the case of the second option, the gain is automatically spread over the appropriate period through the reduced depreciation charge that results from the lower value being used for the lease asset valuation.

14   The present value of the minimum lease payments on a four year lease on a sizing machine is £28,000. The company could have purchased the machine at the time the

lease was signed in March, for £32,000. The quarterly payments on the lease are £2,500.

The present value of the minimum lease payments is not within 10% of the fair value (i.e. £28,800). It should, in the absence of other information be treated as an operating lease. The rental being paid should be charged to profit and loss on a straight line basis (£10,000 per year).

15   Five years ago, the company entered into a finance lease on some robotics kit. The lease included a clause whereby the company guaranteed to meet the first £20,000 of any deficit arising from the actual residual value being below the anticipated residual value of £80,000. The guarantee of £20,000 was included in the computation of the asset and liability amount at the start of the lease and by the end of the lease the lease asset account had a zero balance. When the lease expired the lessor sold the robotics kit and a shortfall of £20,000 resulted, which the company duly paid.

The payment of the guarantee equals the expected guarantee payment. The charge will be met by the remaining balance on the liability account. No further entry is necessary as the cost has already been charged to profit and loss in the form of depreciation.

16   During the year, the company sold an equipment store to a property company, and then immediately leased it back. The lease is an operating lcase. The sale price was £70,000; the net book value at the end of the previous accounting period was £62,000; and the fair value was £65,000.

The profit of £3,000 (fair value - book value) should be recognised immediately. The remaining profit of £5,000 (sale price - fair value) should be deferred and amortised over the shorter of the lease term and the period to the next rent review (if any).

17   During the year, the company sold a filter machine to an equipment leasing company, and then immediatcly leased it back. The lease is an operating lease. The sale price was £20,000; the net book value at the end of the previous accounting period was £26,000; and the fair value was £24,000.

The loss of £2,000 (book value - fair value) should be recognised immediately. The remaining loss of £4,000 (fair value - sale value) should be recognised immediately, unless the lease rental payments are low in order to compensate for the loss on sale. If this is the case, the amount compensated should be deferred and amortised over the shorter of the lease term and the period during which the lease rentals are chargeable. The remaining loss should be recognised immediately.

18   During the year, the company sold a computer to a leasing company, and then immediately leased it back. The lease is an operating lease. The sale price was £15,000; the net book value at the end of the previous accounting period was £16,000; and the fair value was £13,000.

The loss of £3,000 (book value - fair value) should be recognised immediately. The profit of

£2,000 (sale price - fair value) should be deferred and amortised over the shorter of the lease term and the period to the next rent review (if any).

19   During the year, the company sold a thermo masking machine to a leasing company, and then immediately leased it back. The lease is an operating lease. The sale price was £13,000; the net book value at the end of the previous accounting period was £11,000; and the fair value was £14,000.

The profit of £2,000 (sales value - book value) should be recognised immediately. No treatment is required in respect of the fair value.

20   During the year, the company sold a generator to a leasing company, and then immediately leased it back. The lease is an operating lease. The sale price was £75,000; the net book value at the end of the previous accounting period was £72,000; and the fair value was £70,000.

The loss of £2,000 (book value - fair value) should be recognised immediately. The profit of £5,000 (sale price - fair value) should be deferred and amortised over the shorter of the lease term and the period to the next rent review (if any).

21   During the year, the company sold an electronic expansion chamber to a leasing company, and then immediately leased it back. The lease is an operating lease. The sale price was £55,000; the net book value at the end of the previous accounting period was £57,000; and the fair value was £61,000.

The loss of £2,000 (book value - sale price) should be recognised immediately, unless the lease rental payments are low in order to compensate for the loss on sale. If this is the case, the proportion of the loss compensated should be deferred and amortised over the shorter of the lease term and the period during which the lease rentals are chargeable. The remaining loss should be recognised immediately. No treatment is required in respect of the fair value.

22   The fair value of a machine leased in November for five years, for use at the company's Inverness site, is £44,000. The present value of the minimum lease payments is £37,500. The quarterly payments on the lease are £1,500 in the first year, £2,000 in the second, £2,500 in the third, £3,000 in the fourth, and £3,500 in the fifth.

The present value of the minimum lease payments is not within 90% of the fair value (i.e. £39,600). It should, in the absence of other information be treated as an operating lease. The total rental being paid (£50,000) should be charged to profit and loss on a straight line basis (£10,000 per year), unless another systematic and rational basis is more appropriate.

23   A few years ago, the company leased an unused acrylic binding machine to a chemical research company. The lease was classified as a finance lease and at the end of the previous year the net investment debtor balance was £11,000. The engineering company terminated the lease during the year and paid the amount required (£5,000) under the early termination clause in the lease. The equipment was then sold for £4,500.

The company is the lessor in this case. The net investment debtor balance should be reduced to £6,000. This represents a loss which would normally be deducted from any other finance

lease income which the company has. However, the company then sold the machine for a further £4,500. This must also be taken into account in arriving at the overall loss on the termination of the lease. This overall loss is £1,500, and it should be deducted from any other finance lease income which the company has.

24   Under a clause in a finance lease which the company has on some spacial measuring equipment, should tax rates change so as to disadvantage the lessor, the company will be required to compensate the lessor by paying a lump sum surcharge in any period where the lessor pays more tax than was anticipated at the time the lease was enacted.

Any surcharges should be treated as one-off additional rentals and accounted for in the period they arise. However, should the surcharges clearly be of a permanently recurring nature (for example, if the government announces that tax rates are changing and will remain at the new level for the foreseeable future), then the anticipated overall surcharge should be calculated and incorporated into a revised finance charge applicable to the remainder of the lease term - see question 12. No attempt should be made to adjust earlier amounts charged.

25   Ten years earlier, the company entered took out a lease on a small warehouse. The lease included a clause whereby the company guaranteed to meet any deficit arising from the actual residual value being below the anticipated residual value of £30,000. The guarantee of £30,000 was included in the computation of the asset and liability amount at the start of the lease. It was estimated that a realistic value to place on the guarantee was £10,000. The warehouse lease, which was classified as a finance lease, was written-down to the £20,000 of the guarantee which was not expected to be payable. When the lease expired the lessee sold the warehouse and a shortfall of £15,000 resulted, which the company duly paid.

The payment of the guarantee meant that the residual value on the lease asset was overstated by £5,000. This amount represents a loss on termination of the lease which must be charged to profit and loss.

Long Question Solution

Fazendo Plc

(a)

Qtr	NCI b/f	Cash Flow	Rental	Avge NCI	Interest	Profit	NCI c/f
1		(20000)	2500	(17500)	(700)	(562)	(18762)
2	(18762)		2500	(16262)	(650)	(523)	(17435)
3	(17435)		2500	(14935)	(597)	(480)	(16013)
4	(16013)		2500	(13513)	(541)	(434)	(14487)
			10000		(2488)	(1999)	
5	(14487)		2500	(11987)	(479)	(385)	(12852)
6	(12852)		2500	(10352)	(414)	(333)	(11099)
7	(11099)		2500	(8599)	(344)	(276)	(9219)
8	(9219)	(879)	2500	(7598)	(304)	(244)	(8146)
			10000		(1541)	(1238)	
9	(8146)		2500	(5646)	(226)	(181)	(6053)
10	(6053)		2500	(3553)	(142)	(114)	(3810)
11	(3810)		2500	(1310)	(52)	(42)	(1404)
12	(1404)	(1648)	2500	(552)	(22)	(18)	(592)
			10000		(442)	(355)	
16	(592)	592		0	0	0	0
totals		(20000)	30000		(4472)	(3593)	
net tax paid		(1935)					
Interest % per quarter		4	after tax profit				3593
Profit % per quarter		3.2132	tax wdv at end of lease				8438

The tax payable is calculated on the basis of capital allowances, interest paid and rentals. As the computer equipment will be scrapped, its tax written-down value of £8,438 represents a balancing allowance which has been added to the computation at the end of the lease, and is included in the tax receivable in quarter 16. *Fazendo Plc* has overall receipts of £30,000 arising from the loan it took out to purchase the equipment. Total interest paid on the loan was £4,472; tax paid was £1,935; and profit was £3,593.

(b)	Actuarial After Tax Method Basis Gross Earnings Allocation[a]				
Qtr	Profit	Tax@35/65	Pro+Tax	Interest	Gr. Earnings
1	562	303	865	700	1565
2	523	281	804	650	1454
3	480	258	738	597	1336
4	434	234	668	541	1208
5	385	207	593	479	1072
6	333	179	512	414	926
7	276	149	425	344	769
8	244	131	376	304	680
9	181	98	279	226	505
10	114	61	176	142	318
11	42	23	65	52	117
12	18	10	27	22	49
total	3593	1934	5527	4472	9999

([a]differences are due to rounding, as is the total, which should be £10,000)

(c)	Investment Period Method Gross Earnings Allocation				
Qtr	NCI c/f	×	Total Gross Earnings/Total NCI	=	Gr.Earn.
1	18762				1565
2	17435		(10,000/119,873)		1454
3	16013				1336
4	14487				1209
5	12852				1072
6	11099				926
7	9219				769
8	8146				680
9	6053				505
10	3810				318
11	1404				117
12	592				49
total	119873				10000

SSAP 24:   Accounting for Pension Costs

Short Question Solutions

*ASSUME THAT MATERIALITY EXISTS IN **EVERY** CASE*

In contrast to the questions in the rest of this workbook, those on SSAP 24 are a mixture of short questions concerning disclosure requirements, treatment options, definitions, and others involving computation. Unless otherwise indicated, assume that the company involved maintains a funded defined benefit pension scheme. Also, there is no continuation from one question to another unless indicated and, unless instructed to do otherwise, each question should be considered in isolation from the rest.

In questions 1-10 you should indicate what disclosure, if any, is required.

1   The company operates a defined benefit pension scheme.

The nature of the scheme (i.e. defined benefit) should be disclosed (paragraph 88a).

2   The latest actuarial valuation revealed a large funding deficiency.

The amount of the deficiency and the action (if any) being taken to deal with it in the current and future accounting periods should be disclosed (paragraph 88g).

3   At the end of the year a formal actuarial valuation was undertaken.

The following should all be disclosed: the actuarial method used; a brief description of the main actuarial assumptions, including those regarding new entrants; the market value of scheme assets at the valuation date; the percentage level of funding; comments on any material actuarial surplus or deficiency identified (paragraphs 48 and 88h).

4   A company has a wholly owned foreign subsidiary. The subsidiary contributes to a defined benefit pension scheme which is governed by the regulations of the country in which it is based. These regulations are very different from those which are used in the United Kingdom. It is felt to be financially and realistically impractical to convert the subsidiary's obligation so as to incorporate it into the consolidated financial statements.

The amount charged to profit and loss by the subsidiary and the basis of the charge should be disclosed in the consolidated financial statements (paragraph 91).

5   During the year, the company received a refund of surplus pension contributions subject to deduction of tax.

The accounting treatment adopted in respect of the refund should be disclosed (paragraphs 29, 83 and 88j).

6   This is the first period for which SSAP 24 has been implemented.

The way in which the transitional provisions have been applied should be disclosed in the financial statements for the current period (paragraph 92).

7   The company operates a defined contribution pension scheme.

The nature of the scheme (i.e. defined contribution) should be disclosed (paragraph 87a).

8   The company maintains two pension schemes, one for salaried staff and the other for manual staff. At the last actuarial revaluation a deficiency was found on the manual staff scheme, and a surplus was identified on the salaried staff scheme.

The deficiency should not be offset against the surplus, but should be disclosed separately along with the action, if any, being taken to deal with it in the current and future accounting periods (paragraphs 89 and 88g).

9   The company made contributions to the pension scheme during the year which were less than the profit and loss pension charge.

The pension provision for the year will have adjusted the balance sheet provision or prepayment brought forward. The resulting net provision or prepayment should be disclosed. (paragraph 88f)

10   The profit and loss pension charge was 50% higher than the charge made in the previous period.

The charge should be disclosed, together with an explanation for the significant change from that made in the previous period (paragraph 88e).

In questions 11-15 you should indicate what treatment(s) should be adopted.

11   For the first time since the company started its own pension scheme, an *ex gratia* pension was awarded during the year to a long serving employee who had never joined the company pension scheme. The company had not planned to make the award, and there are no current employees who are not members of the scheme.

If there is no surplus available to set off the capital cost of the award, it should be charged in the current year (paragraph 38).

12   The company made contributions of £500,000 to the pension scheme during the year. The profit and loss charge was £450,000.

The opening balance sheet balance should be adjusted for the £50,000 prepayment made during the year (paragraph 86).

13   During the year the company changed to an inflation proofed pension scheme. As a result, the level of the regular cost has doubled and special contributions amounting to 50% of the new regular cost will be required over the next ten years in order to take

account of the deficiency that has arisen from the increased benefits being provided. There was no commitment by the company to provide inflation proofed pensions and the actuarial assumptions previously applied did not allow for their introduction. There was no surplus on the fund at the start of the year.

This is a discretionary increase in the pension provision. As such, the capital amount of the increase must be provided for in the current year. (paragraph 85)

14   During the year, the company made 30% of the employees redundant. As a result, there has been a significant fall in the level of contributions to be made while the funding surplus which resulted is eliminated.

The reduction in contributions should be recognised when made. It should not be spread over the working lives of the current employees. Nor should it be recognised in advance of the reduction being received. In other words, the accounting treatment should follow the funding treatment. (paragraph 81)

15   During the year, the company received a refund of £2m surplus pension contributions subject to deduction of tax.

The refund may be spread across the remaining service lives of the current employees, or it may be recognised in the current period and the surplus or deficiency arising in the period may be accounted for in the period (paragraphs 22, 23, 29 and 83).

In questions 16-21 you should define the terms listed.

16   What is the *employer's obligation* in relation to a defined contribution pension scheme?

The amount of contributions payable to date (paragraph 17).

17   What is the *level of funding*?

The level of funding is the proportion at a given date of the actuarial value of liabilities for pensioners' and deferred pensioners' benefits and for members' accrued benefits that is covered by the actuarial value of assets (which, for this purpose, does not include the actuarial value of future contributions). (paragraph 66)

18   What is the difference in the assumptions used by *accrued benefit* methods and *prospective benefit* methods in order to project a stable contribution rate?

Accrued benefit methods measure the cost of providing the pension by putting a value directly on each incremental year's service so that it builds up towards the final liability which will arise on retirement; in order to project a stable contribution rate they rely on the assumption that the flow of new entrants will preserve the existing average age of the workforce. Prospective benefit methods look directly at the expected eventual liability for the current workforce and seek to provide for it evenly over the whole period of their service. (paragraphs 14, 56 and 71)

19   What is meant by the *regular cost* of defined benefit pension schemes?

The consistent ongoing cost recognised under the actuarial method used (paragraph 20).

20   What is the difference between an *ex gratia* pension and an *ex gratia* increase?

Both are pension amounts which the employer had no obligation to provide. An *ex gratia* pension is one awarded to someone who was not a member of the pension scheme and, in respect of whom, no contributions had been made. An *ex gratia* increase is (usually) a non-recurring, one-off increase made for the current period which will not affect pensions paid in future periods. (paragraphs 35, 37, 38, and 60)

21   What is the *average remaining service life*?

It is a weighted average of the expected future service of the current members of the scheme up to date when they are expected to retire or, if earlier, withdraw or die. The weightings can have regard to periods of service, salary levels of scheme members and future salary growth in a manner which the actuary considers appropriate having regard to the actuarial method and assumptions used. (paragraph 58)

Questions 22-25 are computational. They relate to an electronic engineering company with current turnover in excess of £100m and net pre-tax profits of approximately 30% of turnover. It has performed consistently over the last five years, experiencing profit growth of between 5 and 7% per annum.

22   In the actuarial valuation at 31st December Year 0, the company pension scheme showed a surplus of £22m. It was recommended by the actuary that this be eliminated by taking a contribution holiday in Years 1 and 2 and then paying contributions of £1m per annum for eight years. From that point onwards the standard contribution would be £3m per annum. The average remaining service life of employees in the scheme at 31st December Year 0 was ten years. What should the annual charge to profit and loss be for years 1 to 10; and what is the balance sheet amount in respect of the pension contributions and charges for years 1 to 10?

Year	Funded(£m)	Charge(£m)	(Provision)/Prepayment
1	-	0.8 [(30-22)/10]	(0.8)
2	-	0.8	(1.6)
3	1	0.8	(1.4)
4	1	0.8	(1.2)
5	1	0.8	(1.0)
6	1	0.8	(0.8)
7	1	0.8	(0.6)
8	1	0.8	(0.4)
9	1	0.8	(0.2)
10	1	0.8	(-)

23   In the actuarial valuation at 31st December Year 0, the company pension scheme showed a surplus of £22m. Of that surplus, £8m arose because of the decision to sell a business

segment and is treated as an exceptional item in Year 1. It was recommended by the actuary that the surplus be eliminated by taking a contribution holiday in Years 1 and 2 and then paying contributions of £1m per annum for eight years. From that point onwards the standard contribution would be £3m per annum. The average remaining service life of employees in the scheme at 31st December Year 0 was ten years. What should the annual charge to profit and loss be for years 1 to 10; and what is the balance sheet amount in respect of the pension contributions and charges for years 1 to 10?

Year	Funded(£m)	Charge(£m)	(Provision)/Prepayment
1	-	1.6 [(30-(22-8))/10]	
		(8.0) (exceptional credit)	
		(6.4)	6.4
2	-	1.6	4.8
3	1	1.6	4.2
4	1	1.6	3.6
5	1	1.6	3.0
6	1	1.6	2.4
7	1	1.6	1.8
8	1	1.6	1.2
9	1	1.6	0.6
10	1	1.6	-

24   Assume the situation and the treatment adopted in question 22. In year 3, an actuarial revaluation took place which identified a surplus of £13m. It was recommended by the actuary that the surplus be eliminated by taking a contribution holiday in Year 4, and then paying contributions of £1.5m per annum for two years, followed by seven years at £2m. From that point onwards the standard contribution would be £3m per annum. Assuming that the original accounting treatment of the elimination of the Year 0 surplus is to continue, and that the intra valuation deficit is to be treated separately, what should the annual charge to profit and loss be for years 4 to 13; and what is the balance sheet amount in respect of the pension contributions and charges for years 4 to 13?

Year	Funded(£m)	Charge(£m)	(Provision)/Prepayment
provision b/f			(1.4)
4	-	0.8 + 0.1 = 0.9 [(3-(22/10))+(1/10)]	(2.3)
5	1.5	0.8 + 0.1 = 0.9	(1.7)
6	1.5	0.8 + 0.1 = 0.9	(1.1)
7	2.0	0.8 + 0.1 = 0.9	-
8	2.0	0.8 + 0.1 = 0.9	1.1
9	2.0	0.8 + 0.1 = 0.9	2.2
10	2.0	0.8 + 0.1 = 0.9	3.3
11	2.0	3.1 [3+(1/10)]	2.2
12	2.0	3.1	1.1
13	2.0	3.1	-

25   Using the information from question 24, if the decision was taken to combine the old surplus with the intra valuation deficit and spread the combined figure evenly over years 4 to 13, what should the annual charge to profit and loss be for years 4 to 13; and what is the balance sheet amount in respect of the pension contributions and charges for years 4 to 13?

Year	Funded(£m)	Charge(£m)	(Provision)/Prepayment
provision b/f			(1.40)
4	-	1.56 [3-(14.4/10)]	(2.96)
5	1.5	1.56	(3.02)
6	1.5	1.56	(3.08)
7	2.0	1.56	(2.64)
8	2.0	1.56	(2.20)
9	2.0	1.56	(1.76)
10	2.0	1.56	(1.32)
11	2.0	1.56	(0.88)
12	2.0	1.56	(0.44)
13	2.0	1.56	-

Presentation Standards

Short Question Solutions

*ASSUME THAT MATERIALITY EXISTS IN **EVERY** CASE*

SSAP 2:   Disclosure of Accounting Policies

Questions 1-2 relate to different companies, each of which has a balance sheet date of 31st December.

1   A clothing manufacturing company paid six months rent on a warehouse in August. The payment covered the six month period from August to January of the next accounting period inclusive.

The accruals concept must be applied. The unexpired part of the expenditure should be carried forward as a prepayment and included in the rent expenditure of the following accounting period.

2   The previous year's accounts of an engineering company had included warehouse salaries in administrative expenses. This year they are included in the distribution costs.

The consistency concept is not being applied. Either, revised figures for administrative expenses and distribution costs in the previous year should be produced to enable comparison with the current year's figures, or the previous basis should be returned to. There should be no prior period adjustment as these circumstances would not merit such treatment under FRS 3 (*Reporting financial performance* - chapter 2).

SSAP 3:   Earnings per Share

Questions 3-6 relate to a variety of companies, all of which have a balance sheet date of 31st December. In each case, at the start of the accounting period, there were 4 million ordinary £1 shares in issue. Earnings for EPS purposes are £2.5m (£2m in the previous year) and the companies have never had any irrecoverable ACT. Each question should be treated in isolation, i.e. no information contained in any question is applicable to any other question.

3   On 1st June, a supermarket company made a 1 for 10 rights issue at market price.

EPS for the period is based upon the average shares in issue during the period. The current period's EPS is derived from:

(5/12) × 4 million	1,666,667
(7/12) × 4.4 million	<u>2,566,666</u>
	<u>4,233,333</u>

EPS = £2.5m/4,233,333 = 59.06p

The previous period's EPS remains at 50p.

4   On 1st July, a publishing company placed 1 million ordinary shares at 82p with

institutional investors who previously had no holdings in the company's shares. The market price on that date was 85p.

This should be treated as if it were at market value. The current period's EPS is derived from:

½ × 4 million	2,000,000
½ × 5 million	2,500,000
	4,500,000

EPS = £2.5m/4,500,000 = 55.56p

The previous period's EPS remains at 50p.

5   On 1st November, a chemical waste disposal company split its £1 ordinary shares into ordinary shares of 20p.

There are now 20 million shares in issue. EPS is £2.5/20 = 12½p. The comparative figure is 50p × (4/20) = 10p.

6   On 1st July, a cleansing company made a 1 for 8 rights issue at 70p. The market value of the shares on the last day of quotation cum rights was 65p.

The theoretical ex-rights price is [(70p × 500,000) + (65p × 4 million)]/4.5 million = £2.95/4.5 = 65.56p. The actual cum rights price was 65p. As the actual price is smaller, the issue should be treated as if it were at full market price. The current period's EPS is derived from:

½ × 4 million	2,000,000
½ × 4.5 million	2,250,000
	4,250,000

EPS = £2.5m/4,250,000 = 58.82p

The previous period's EPS remains at 50p.

Question 7 involves a company with a 31st December financial year end.

7   A house building company made a loss for EPS purposes of £1.2m during the accounting period. In the previous period it had made a profit of £3.6m. The company has never suffered irrecoverable ACT. There are 10 million ordinary £1 shares in issue.

EPS for the current period is derived from £(1.2)/10 = 12p (loss), and the EPS for the previous period = £3.6/10 = 36p

FRS 1: Cash Flow Statements

Questions 8-11 relate to an aeronautic engineering company with a balance sheet date of 31st December. On turnover of £23.8m, the company has pre-tax earnings of £4.5m (last year £5.2m on turnover of £25.1m). Corporation tax is at 35% in all periods, and applies to all companies mentioned. Where the calculation of tax is required, assume that it is on the whole amount given, i.e. that there are no allowances available which could be used to reduce the liability. Treat each question in isolation, i.e. as if none of the others apply to the company.

8   On 15th February, the company paid a final dividend for the previous year of £600,000; on 15th August, an interim dividend was paid of £350,000; and, a final dividend of £650,000 is being proposed for the current year.

The net dividends actually paid during the year (£950,000) should be included under the *returns on investment and servicing of finance* section. The ACT should be included in the corporation tax figure within the *taxation* section.

9   During the year, a cheque for £690,000 was received when plant with a net book value of £630,000 was sold.

The £690,000 received would be included in the *investing activities* section of the statement. The £60,000 gain would be included in the reconciliation of operating profit to net cash inflow from operating activities.

10   Since the end of the previous period, debtors have risen by £200,000; trade creditors have fallen by £130,000; the provision for corporation tax has risen by £200,000; stocks have fallen by £190,000; dividends proposed have risen by £50,000; and, dividends receivable from associated companies have risen by £30,000.

The changes in the taxation creditor and the dividends proposed and receivable should be ignored for the purposes of the statement. The fall in stocks, the increase in debtors (assuming 'debtors' is comprised only of debtors arising from operating activities and does not include, for example, debtors arising from the sale of fixed assets) and the fall in trade creditors should all be included in the reconciliation of operating profit to net cash inflow from operating activities.

11   On 1st July, the company issued £5m 5% convertible debenture stock. The conversion option will first be available in 5 years time, when each £1 of debenture stock will be convertible into one 10p ordinary share in the company. The £5m proceeds of the issue were applied to reduce the company's overdraft.

The £5m received would be included under *financing*; but the £5m applied to reduce the overdraft would not be included in the statement as it represents an investment of cash in cash.

FRS 4:   Capital Instruments

Questions 12-16 are concerned with the disclosure requirements, treatment options, and definitions contained in FRS 4. There is no continuation from one question to the next, and each question should be considered in isolation from the rest.

12   If there is uncertainty as to whether an option to redeem or cancel a capital instrument will be exercised, when should the term of a capital instrument be deemed to end?

The term should be taken to end on the earliest date at which the instrument would be redeemed or cancelled on exercise of such an option. (Paragraph 16)

13   What is a 'warrant'?

A warrant is an instrument that requires the issuer to issue shares (whether contingently or not) and contains no obligation for the issuer to transfer economic benefits. (Paragraph 17)

14   How should the maturity of debt be disclosed?

An analysis of the maturity of debt should be presented showing amounts falling due in one year or less, on demand; between one and two years; and in five or more years. (Paragraph 33)

15   Into which two categories should capital instruments be classified in the financial statements of an individual company?

The capital instruments should be accounted for in the balance sheet between liabilities and shareholders' funds. (Paragraph 23)

16   In which circumstances should capital instruments (other than shares) be classified as liabilities?

When they contain an obligation to transfer economic benefits (including a contingent obligation to transfer economic benefits). (Paragraph 24)

FRS 5:   Reporting the Substance of Transactions

Questions 17-20 are concerned with the disclosure requirements, treatment options, and definitions contained in FRS 5. There is no continuation from one question to the next, and each question should be considered in isolation from the rest.

17   What is the definition of an asset according to FRS 5?

An asset is the right or other access to future economic benefits controlled by an entity as a result of past transactions or events (paragraph 2).

18   What is the definition of a liability according to FRS 5?

A liability is an entity's obligation to transfer economic benefits as a result of past transactions or events (paragraph 4).

19   In the context of an asset, what is the definition of control according to FRS 5?

Control in the context of an asset is the ability to obtain future economic benefits relating to an asset and to restrict the access of others to those benefits (paragraph 3).

20   In the context of another entity, what is the definition of control according to FRS 5?

Control of another entity arises where the reporting entity has the ability to direct the financial and operating policies of that entity with a view to gaining economic benefit from its activities (paragraph 8).

21   A businessman lent £1m to a football company on an interest free basis. The loan is to be repaid in five years time. At the same time, the company gave the businessman an executive suite at the football ground and free exclusive use of a car park during the week (the businessman runs a fruit market in the car park from Monday to Friday). Both these items have been given for a five year period.

This transaction is hiding the real transactions which are the five year rental of an executive suite and the car park. The market rental of these two items should be determined and then compared to the interest payable on a £1m five year loan. The price paid can then be accounted for, along with the benefit received.

SSAP 25:   Segmental Reporting

Questions 22-25 relate to Livro Plc, a publishing company with two subsidiaries. The group balance sheet date is 31st December. On turnover of £92.8m, the group has pre-tax earnings of £15.2m (last year £12.7m on turnover of £86.3m).

22   *Livro plc* has investments in three associated companies. Should they be included in its segmental report?

As the company is a plc it must prepare consolidated accounts. It should, therefore, prepare a group segmental report, not a company one.

23   If the associated companies mentioned in question 22 are to be included in the segmental report, what should be disclosed?

The group's share of their profits or losses before interest, taxation, minority interests and extraordinary items; the groups share of their net assets (including goodwill to the extent that it has not been written-off) stated, where possible, after attributing fair values to their net assets at the dates they were acquired; the information should be shown separately from the group's own operations.

24   Under what circumstances would disclosure of the associated undertakings not be required in the segmental report of the *Livro* group?

If they do not amount to a significant part of the group results or assets, if the information is unobtainable or if publication might be prejudicial to the business of the associate; however, the reason for non disclosure should be given together with a brief description of the omitted business or businesses.

25   Under what circumstances would disclosure of group segments not be required in the segmental report of the *Livro* group?

If the directors are of the opinion that the disclosure of certain information would be seriously prejudicial to the interests of the group, that information need not be disclosed but the fact that it has not been disclosed must be stated.

Taxation and Grants

Short Question Solutions

*ASSUME THAT MATERIALITY EXISTS IN **EVERY** CASE*

SSAP 4:   Accounting for Government Grants

Questions 1-6 relate to a steel manufacturing company with current turnover of £35m and net pre-tax profit of £7.5m. (Last year £33.6m and £6.2m respectively.) The company's financial year ends on 31st December. Company policy is to treat grants received in respect of fixed assets as deferred income, and to deduct all grants identified as relating to specific revenue expenditure against that expenditure. All other grants recognised are credited to profit and loss. The questions should be done in sequence, using the information contained in earlier questions where appropriate.

1   During the year the company received a grant from the European Community for £100,000 towards the cost of some new equipment. The equipment has an estimated useful economic life of ten years and cost £500,000.

The grant should be amortised over the same period as the equipment is depreciated. The amount unamortised at the balance sheet date will be carried forward as deferred income under creditors or separately as accruals and deferred income.

2   Company policy is to depreciate all depreciable fixed assets by the straight line method.

This year, depreciation on the equipment will be one tenth of its cost (£100,000). The amortisation of the grant should also be at one tenth per annum. Thus, the credit to profit and loss in respect of the grant should be for £10,000. The balance at the year end of £90,000 should be carried forward as deferred income.

3   In September, the company spent £60,000 on training, in respect of which it is due receive a government grant of 50%. The grant formalities have been completed but payment is not expected until mid-March.

This grant should be treated as receivable, and included in the balance sheet as a deferred asset. It should also be offset against the £60,000 incurred, thereby resulting in a net expense in profit and loss of £30,000.

4   In May, the company received 10 days free consultancy from a financial advisor under a local enterprise scheme. The market rate for this service was £500 per day.

The consultancy should be treated as a grant received, and evaluated. (A fair value, based on the market rate, would probably be £5,000.) It should not be recognised in the profit and loss account, but, if it has had a material effect upon the results for the period, the nature and, if quantifiable, the effects of the assistance should be disclosed.

5   In July, a grant of £30,000 was received from the Swedish government in recognition of the high quality that the company's production had maintained over the five years which had ended on 31st December the previous year.

Assuming no provision had been made for this grant, it should be credited to profit and loss in the current year.

6   The company had been advised to expect the award of the Swedish grant while the previous year's accounts were being prepared. As a result £20,000 had been included in the previous year's accounts as a deferred asset in respect of this grant.

£20,000 should be used to write-off the deferred asset brought forward. The remaining £10,000 should be credited to profit and loss in the current period.

SSAP 5:   Accounting for Value Added Tax

Questions 7-8 relate to a high street retailing company. The company's financial year ends on 31st December. The standard rate of VAT is 17½%. The two questions should be done in sequence, using the information contained in earlier questions where appropriate.

7   A trading company has gross turnover of £52.875m. One third of this is exempt output.

The net of VAT turnover figure (£30m+£17.625m=£47.625m) should be shown in the profit and loss account, either after deduction of the £5.25m VAT from the gross figure, or as a single figure. There may also be apportionment of untraceable input VAT required.

8   At the balance sheet date, the company was due to pay the Customs and Excise £50,000 in respect of VAT for the last quarter.

Include this amount within creditors under 'other creditors including taxation and social security'. There is no need to disclose it separately.

SSAP 8:   The Treatment of Taxation under the Imputation System in the Accounts of Companies

Questions 9-14 relate to a furniture manufacturing and redecoration company with current turnover of £15m and net pre-tax profit of £2.5m. (Last year £13.6m and £1.8m respectively.) The company's financial year ends on 31st December. The corporation tax rate applicable is 35%, and ACT is one third of the amount of qualifying distributions. The six questions should be done in sequence, using the information contained in earlier questions where appropriate.

9   During the year the company received two dividends from a UK company in which it has a minor shareholding. The first was £7,500 on 15th June, and the second, £11,250 on 15th December.

This franked investment income should be brought into the financial statements at its gross value (i.e. dividend received + the associated tax credit) of £25,000. The total associated tax credits of £6,250 should also be included in the taxation charge for the period.

10   The company paid the final dividend (£150,000) for the previous accounting period on 28th March. On 28th September, it paid an interim dividend for the current accounting period (£60,000).

The company will have paid ACT of £67,500 [(£210,000/3) - (£7,500/3)]. It, therefore, has ACT of £67,500 available for offset on the corporation tax liability arising from the current accounting period. However, the tax credit of £3,750 on the second dividend received, can be refunded. Assuming this is done, the ACT available for offset is reduced to £63,750.

11   When the company received the dividend from the other company on 15th June, it reclaimed the tax credit.

The tax credit was £2,500. The company will have paid £70,000 ACT during the year, but the refund of the tax credit received reduces the amount of ACT available for offset to £67,500, which again is further reduced to £63,750. That is, the overall effect is the same, the only difference being that in this case a refund was obtained where previously a deduction was made to the amount of ACT due to be paid.

12   The company included a proposed final dividend of £300,000 in the financial statements.

Current liabilities should include £300,000 as proposed dividend, and £100,000 as ACT payable. If assumed recoverable, a deferred asset under prepayments and accrued income should be included for the £100,000 ACT recoverable, unless there is a balance on a deferred tax account, in which case an appropriate proportion of the £100,000 can be debited to that account. Any proportion of the £100,000 not considered recoverable should be written-off and included in the taxation charge for the current year.

13   The taxable profit was £2.8m.

Corporation Tax of £980,000 is payable. The maximum amount of ACT which could be offset against this is £700,000 [£2.8m×25%]. The tax payable will be reduced by the (net of FII tax credits) amount of ACT paid and payable attributable to the accounting period (£63,750). Thus the mainstream corporation tax liability is £916,250. There is no surplus ACT.

14   Included in the deferred tax account at the start of the accounting period, was unrecovered ACT of £118,000.

This unrecovered ACT brought forward should now be credited out of the deferred tax account and offset against the corporation tax liability of £916,250. As a result, the mainstream corporation tax liability is £798,250.

SSAP 15:   Accounting for Deferred Tax

Questions 15-25 all relate to an engineering company with current turnover of £12m and net pre-tax profit of £2.6m. (Last year £11.6m and £1.9m respectively.) The company's financial year ends on 31st December. The corporation tax rate applicable is 35%, the income tax rate is 25%, and the writing down allowance for all capital allowances available is 25%; these rates apply to all accounting periods involved. At 31st December, the company had claimed capital allowances that exceeded accumulated depreciation by £620,000, and there was no balance on the deferred tax account. The questions should be done in sequence, using the information contained in earlier questions where appropriate, except for the information in question 15, which should be treated in isolation from the rest.

[Note for tutors: the £620,000 excess of capital allowances claimed over depreciation charged results in all the reversals identified being provided for. It would be a worthwhile exercise to set some of the questions on the premise that a different initial excess existed.]

15   The company received a one-off government training grant of £100,000 in June. It covers the year to the end of next June. £50,000 has been treated as deferred income and carried forward to next year. Tax, at 35%, was payable on receipt of the grant.

There is a timing difference of £17,500 (£50,000 @ 35%) which should be treated as a deferred tax asset and applied to reduce any deferred tax liability and, if a debit balance results, it should be included in the balance sheet under prepayments and accrued income.

Ignore the information contained in question 15 in all future questions

16   At the financial year end, the company had capital allowances of £70,000 and a depreciation charge of £50,000. In the absence of other information, assuming that a provision is required for deferred tax, what should it be?

There is an originating timing difference of £20,000. Provision should be made for deferred tax of £7,000.

17   The company has capital losses of £15,000 available which it believes will be recoverable. What should the provision now be?

The losses represent a deferred asset which can be offset against the deferred liability arising from the accelerated capital allowances. The net provision becomes £1,750 [£5,000@35%].

18   The company has the following projection for accelerated capital allowance based timing differences occurring in each of the next five years (figures in brackets represent reversing differences):

1	2	3	4	5
£100,000	200,000	(350,000)	150,000	(80,000)

What provision should now be made? The capital losses mentioned in question 17 are no longer considered to be recoverable.

The annual amounts must be converted into cumulative totals. The resultant net position is:

1	2	3	4	5
£100,000	300,000	(50,000)	100,000	60,000

The provision made should be based on the maximum cumulative net reversal over the projected period, in this case, £50,000 in year three. The amount credited to deferred tax will be £17,500.

19   The forecast includes a timing difference in respect of a piece of equipment on which rollover relief will be available. The amounts included in respect of the equipment were:

1	2	3	4	5
£6,000	3,500	1,625	nil	nil

What provision should now be made?

The annual amounts become:

1	2	3	4	5
£94,000	196,500	(351,625)	150,000	(80,000)

and the cumulative totals become:

1	2	3	4	5
£94,000	290,500	(61,125)	88,875	8,875

The provision should be based on the maximum cumulative net reversal of £61,125. The amount credited to deferred tax will be £21,394.

20   Additional information has come to light which alters the forecasted year 5 timing difference. It is now believed that it will be a reversal of £180,000, rather than the £80,000 reversal previously forecast. What provision should now be made?

The revised forecast is now:

1	2	3	4	5
£94,000	196,500	(351,625)	150,000	(180,000)

and the cumulative totals:

1	2	3	4	5
£94,000	290,500	(61,125)	88,875	(91,125)

The provision should be based on the maximum cumulative net reversal of £91,125. The amount credited to deferred tax will be £31,894.

21   Other timing differences identified are:

1	2	3	4	5
£(54,000)	(115,000)	63,625	(58,000)	29,000

What provision should now be made?

The overall position must be considered. The two streams of timing differences must be combined to produce an overall net position:

	1	2	3	4	5
acc.c.l.	£ 94,000	196,500	(351,625)	150,000	(180,000)
others	£(54,000)	(115,000)	63,625	(58,000)	29,000
	£ 40,000	81,500	(288,000)	92,000	(151,000)

and the net cumulative totals are:

1	2	3	4	5
£40,000	121,500	(166,500)	(74,500)	(225,500)

The provision should be based on the maximum cumulative net reversal of £225,500. The amount credited to deferred tax will be £78,925.

22   After further analysis, the other timing differences given in question 21 were found to be incorrect. The revised forecast is as follows:

1	2	3	4	5
£(54,000)	115,000	63,625	(58,000)	29,000

What provision should now be made?

The overall position must be considered. The two streams of timing differences must be combined to produce an overall net position:

	1	2	3	4	5
acc.c.l.	£ 94,000	196,500	(351,625)	150,000	(180,000)
others	£(54,000)	115,000	63,625	(58,000)	29,000
	£ 40,000	311,500	(288,000)	92,000	(151,000)

and the net cumulative totals are:

1	2	3	4	5
£40,000	351,500	63,500	155,500	4,500

No provision should now be made as there is no overall net reversing difference in the period covered by the forecast.

23   There is recoverable ACT of £20,000 at this balance sheet date (i.e. at the end of year 0).

As there is no balance on the deferred tax account, the ACT cannot be offset against that account. The ACT should be included in the balance sheet as a deferred asset under prepayments and accrued income.

24   One year has now passed and it is the end of year 1. Forecasts have been produced for the next five years. The forecasted accelerated capital allowance based timing differences are:

2	3	4	5	6
£184,000	(276,000)	97,000	(42,000)	221,000

Assume that there are no other timing differences, what amount should be credited/debited to the deferred tax account?

There was a nil balance brought forward in the deferred tax account. The amount entered in the account will be the provision identified as being required. The annual amounts must be converted into cumulative totals. The resultant net position is:

2	3	4	5	6
£184,000	**(92,000)**	**5,000**	**(37,000)**	**184,000**

The provision made should be based on the maximum cumulative net reversal over the projected period, in this case, £92,000 in year three. The amount credited to deferred tax will be £32,200.

25   There is unrecovered ACT of £47,000 at the balance sheet date (i.e. at the end of year 1).

The ACT unrecovered can be set off against the deferred tax balance up to the limit permitted by SSAP 8. That limit is 25/35 of £32,200 (the balance on the deferred tax account), i.e. £23,000. Therefore, the deferred tax account may be debited with £23,000 in respect of recoverable ACT. If the remaining £24,000 is irrecoverable - i.e. if there is no apparent prospect of it being recovered in the next accounting period - it should be included in the tax charge for the year within the profit and loss account. If recovery is reasonably certain in the next accounting period, it should be carried forward as a deferred asset under prepayments and accrued income.

Long Question Solution

Demora Plc

The asset values need to be adjusted to eliminate the office block which is not involved in the deferred tax computation. The net book value should be reduced by its net book value in each year (£900,000 in the current year, £800,000 in year 1, etc.). The tax written-down value will be reduced by its cost of £1m (which is also its tax written-down value) in each year.

Year	Asset Net Book Value	Asset Tax Written Down Value
current	£6.3m - £0.9m = £5.4m	£5.14m - £1m = £4.14m
1	5.8m - 0.8m = 5.0m	4.28m - 1m = 3.28m
2	4.9m - 0.7m = 4.2m	3.72m - 1m = 2.72m
3	4.0m - 0.6m = 3.4m	3.26m - 1m = 2.26m
4	3.2m - 0.5m = 2.7m	2.60m - 1m = 1.60m

The depreciation and capital allowances for each of the years can then be calculated:

Year	Asset Net Book Value	Depreciation	Asset Tax Written Down Value	Capital Allowances
current	£5.4m		£4.14m	
1	5.0m	£0.4m	3.28m	£0.86m
2	4.2m	0.8m	2.72m	0.56m
3	3.4m	0.8m	2.26m	0.46m
4	2.7m	0.7m	1.60m	0.66m

The net timing difference for each of the forecasted years is:

Year	Depreciation	Capital Allowances	Timing Difference
1	£0.4m	£0.86m	£ 0.46m originating
2	0.8m	0.56m	(0.24m) reversing
3	0.8m	0.46m	(0.34m) reversing
4	0.7m	0.66m	(0.04m) reversing

The net cumulative timing differences for the forecast period can then be derived:

Year	Timing Difference	Net Cumulative Timing Difference
1	£ 0.46m originating	£ 0.46m
2	(0.24m) reversing	0.22m
3	(0.34m) reversing	(0.12m)
4	(0.04m) reversing	(0.16m)

The company should provide deferred tax of £56,000 in respect of the maximum potential liability of £160,000 arising in year 4. There is a credit balance brought forward of £160,000, therefore, the account must be debited with £104,000. In addition, the taxable losses of £1.2m give rise to a £420,000 deferred asset which may be debited to the deferred tax account, resulting in a balance carried forward to year 1 of £364,000 (debit) which should be included under the heading of prepayments and accrued income in the balance sheet.

Groups

Short Question Solutions

*ASSUME THAT MATERIALITY EXISTS IN **EVERY** CASE*

SSAP 1:   Accounting for Associated Companies

Questions 1-8 relate to a manufacturing company with one 80% subsidiary and with current group turnover of £235m and net pre-tax profit of £46.3m. (Last year £223.4m and £41.8m respectively.) The financial year ends of all the companies in the questions are coterminous, ending on 31st December. Unless otherwise indicated, there is no continuation from one question to another and each question should be considered in isolation from the rest. (Assume that all equity has equal voting rights and that book value = fair value.)

1   During the year the company purchased a 25% holding of the equity of a paper processing company.

Unless it can be clearly demonstrated that it cannot, it should be presumed that the company has the ability to exercise significant influence over the paper processing company. As a result, the investee company should be treated as an associated undertaking and appropriate disclosure made.

2   At the end of the previous year the company had a holding representing 10% of the equity of a clothing company. It had cost £80,000 when purchased at the start of the previous year. At that time the investee company had net assets of £560,000 which increased to £840,000 by the end of that year. At the start of the current year, the investment was increased by a further 11% of the equity at a cost of £110,000. The clothing company is not to be treated as an associated undertaking.

There are two acquisition points. Any dividends received from pre-acquisition (of the first investment) profits should be applied to reduce the initial investment of £80,000. Similar treatment should be applied to the £110,000 investment. The investment should be shown in the company's balance sheet at cost of £190,000 less any such dividends received (or it could be shown at valuation). Dividends received and receivable should be shown in the profit and loss account after adjustment for any pre-acquisition element.

3   Repeat question 2, but this time the clothing company is to be treated as an associated undertaking.

At the time the investment became 21%, the net assets of the clothing company were £840,000. The company's share of this is £176,400. The premium paid on acquisition, subject to adjustment for pre-acquisition reserves distributed, is £13,600 [£80,000 + £110,000 - £176,400] and, after any such adjustment required, it should either be written-off to the reserves, or capitalised and amortised. Disclosure in the company's own financial statements is as for trade investments. The group profit and loss should show the company's share of the publishing company's pre-tax profits/losses and its attributable share of the associated undertaking's tax charge on those profits/losses. The group balance sheet carrying value in

respect of this investment will comprise the cost of the investment plus the company's share of post-acquisition retained profits, less any amounts written-off either of these.

4   An investment was made in a publishing company at the start of the year. It represented 15% of the equity of the publishing company, and cost £150,000. The pre-tax profits of the publishing company for the current year were £120,000. A final dividend of £6,000 was received in respect of the previous year; an interim dividend of £4,000 was received in respect of the current year; and a final dividend of £48,000 has been declared for the current year. The company can exercise significant control over the publishing company and it is to be treated as an associated undertaking in the current year's financial statements. Associated undertaking status is to date from when the investment was made. (Ignore taxation in any calculations.)

The investment in the associated undertaking occurred at the start of the current year. The £6,000 dividends received relating to earlier periods should be offset against the £150,000 cost in order to identify the net investment of £144,000. This is the figure that should be used in order to identify the premium or discount arising on acquisition. The group's balance sheet should show the investment at a carrying value of £150,800 [£150,000 - £6,000 + (15% × £120,000) - £4,000 - (15% × £48,000)]. The group's profit and loss account should show its share of the publishing company's pre-tax profit, i.e. £18,000. It should also show the attributable share of the associated undertaking's tax charge on the pre-tax profits.

5   On 1st January, the company acquired 2,000 ordinary shares in a small engineering company. The cost was £95,000 and the holding represented 20% of the equity of the engineering company. It is to be treated as an associated undertaking. At that date, the reserves of the engineering company were £300,000. Its profits for the current year are £140,000 (on which tax of £35,000 is payable) and a dividend totalling £20,000 was declared by it at the end of the period. (Assume that no premium or discount arose on the investment.)

Assuming the price paid was a fair representation of the net worth of the engineering company, the net assets at 1st January were £475,000 [£95,000/.2]. Net assets at the end of the year are £560,000 [£475,000 + £105,000 - £20,000]. The investment should be shown at cost of £95,000 in the company's balance sheet, and the dividend receivable of £4,000 [£20,000 × 20%] included in its profit and loss account. In the group profit and loss account, the group's attributable share (£28,000) of the associated undertaking's profit before tax should be shown, and its attributable share (£7,000) of the tax charge on those profits should be disclosed separately within the group tax charge. The group balance sheet carrying value in respect of this investment will comprise the cost of the investment plus the company's share of post-acquisition retained profits, less any amounts written-off either of these, i.e. £112,000 [£95,000 + £21,000 - £4,000] This is the same as the group's attributable proportion of the net assets, i.e. £560,000 × 20%. Had there been any premium paid/discount at the time of acquisition, the second formula would incorporate that amount and again, the two approaches would agree. The SSAP requires that the second of the two approaches be adopted for disclosure purposes, i.e. it is necessary to disclose that the carrying value comprises the amount of the attributable proportion of net assets plus/minus goodwill. Goodwill appearing in the associated undertaking's own financial statements, should be excluded from the value of the attributable proportion of the net assets; the investing company's attributable proportion of such goodwill can either be disclosed separately or combined with the goodwill which arose on acquisition.

6   The company has a 30% investment in an associated undertaking. During the year, the associated undertaking suffered an extraordinary loss of £600,000 before tax at 35%.

If the item should be classified as extraordinary for the purposes of the group's financial statements (FRS 3: *Reporting financial performance* **- chapter 2 - would need to be consulted to determine this), the group's attributable share of the extraordinary item and the related taxation should be disclosed separately from any extraordinary items arising from companies belonging to the group. If it would not be considered as being extraordinary within the context of the financial statements of the group, the group's share of the pre-tax profits, and taxation thereon, of the associated undertaking should be restated to reflect the different treatment adopted. The entries in the company's own financial statements will be unaffected by the way this item is treated in the consolidated financial statements.**

7   The company's subsidiary has a 25% holding of the equity of a construction company. It is considered that the subsidiary has a significant influence upon the construction company.

If the subsidiary does not prepare consolidated accounts, it should show its share of the construction company's pre-tax profit/loss and its attributable share of the tax charge on that profit/loss either in a separate profit and loss account, or as a supplement to its own profit and loss account (which will already show any dividends received and receivable). If the latter course is taken, it should be made clear that its share of those profits retained/losses is not being treated as realised. It should also produce either an additional balance sheet, or a supplement to its own, showing the same information as that which would have been required had it prepared a group balance sheet. (However, this will differ from that which its own holding company would prepare as in that case the minority interest in the subsidiary becomes relevant where obviously it is not in the subsidiary's own accounts.) In the group's consolidated profit and loss account, its share of the construction company's profit/loss for the year should be shown, as should its share of the tax on this profit/loss. The group balance sheet should include the total of the group's share of the net assets (excluding goodwill) of the construction company (after revision to fair value at the time of acquisition); the group's share of any goodwill in the construction company's financial statements; and the premium paid/discount which arose on the acquisition of the construction company, in so far as it has not been written-off. In addition, the minority share of the subsidiary's interest in the results and net assets of the construction company should be included in the minority interests figure shown in the group financial statements.

8   The fair value used in respect of the assets of an associated undertaking acquired at the start of the year was £200,000. The assets were shown at a carrying value of £100,000 in the financial statements of the associated undertaking at that time. During the year no additions or disposals were made. Depreciation of £10,000 was included in this year's profit and loss of the associated undertaking, whose accounts included the assets at a year end carrying value of £90,000. The associated undertaking's pre-tax profit was £310,000 (£240,000 after tax).

The company must adjust the pre-tax profit by adding back the £10,000 depreciation charged, and then subtracting depreciation based on the fair value of £200,000 rather than the carrying value of £100,000. A charge of £20,000 would probably be appropriate. This results in the pre-tax profits being restated at £300,000. It does not affect the taxation charge. It is this revised figure which should be used when constructing the entries for the group's consolidated financial statements. The adjustment will not affect the entry in the investing company's own financial statements, nor will it result in the associated undertaking adjusting its financial statements.

FRS 2: Accounting for Subsidiary Undertakings

Questions 9-14 relate to a variety of companies and groups. Unless otherwise indicated, the companies' financial year ends are all at 31st December and the groups are 'large' as defined by the Companies Act. In the absence of other information, assume that there is no continuation from one question to another and each question should be considered in isolation from the rest.

9   *Crescendo Plc* has had one 100% subsidiary, *Fugindo Ltd*, for the last two years. In November, the board decided to sell the subsidiary as soon as possible. An interested buyer was immediately contacted but so far (it is now two months after the financial year end) it has not been sold. However, this is believed to be only a temporary delay and it is expected that a sale should go through in April or May.

While control is expected to cease in the near future, this is not an example of the type of temporary control which leads to exclusion from consolidation. While the interest in *Fugindo Ltd* is now held exclusively with a view to subsequent resale, it has previously been consolidated in group accounts by *Crescendo Plc* and cannot, therefore, be excluded from consolidation on the grounds of its impending sale. *Crescendo Ltd* should be included in the consolidation.

10   *Falisando Plc* has three subsidiaries: *Pequeno Ltd*, *Menor Ltd*, and *Maior Ltd*, all three were acquired on 1st January at the start of the financial year which has just ended. It has a 55%, 70%, and 95% holding respectively and holds a majority of the voting equity in *Pequeno and Menor*. It has changed the composition of both these companies' boards since they were acquired. However, despite its 95% holding in *Maior Ltd*, it only has a 45% holding of the voting equity and has so far failed in all its attempts to have a director appointed to the board.

If *Falisando Plc* is unable to exercise significant influence over *Maior Ltd*, the group comprises the holding company and two subsidiaries. *Maior Ltd* should be excluded from consolidation on the grounds of severe long-term restrictions and treated as a fixed asset investment at cost. If *Falisando Plc* is able to exercise significant influence over *Maior Ltd*, it should treat it as an associated undertaking using the equity method.

11   *Dentro Plc* has two 60% subsidiaries, one of which, *Embaixo Ltd* has a 90% subsidiary. *Dentro Plc* is itself a subsidiary of *Jamais SA*, a French holding company.

Despite the fact that *Dentro Plc* is a subsidiary, it must still prepare group accounts as it is a plc and is, therefore, quoted on the stock exchange.

12   *Outra Ltd* is a holding company with two subsidiaries and one associated undertaking. The group is 'large' as defined by CA 85. The directors have decided that the group financial statements will consist of a consolidated balance sheet, a consolidated cash flow statement, and the unconsolidated profit and loss accounts of each of the subsidiaries and the holding company. The associated undertaking will be included in the financial statements of *Outra Plc* as the investing company.

This approach is contrary to the CA 85 and FRS 2 requirement that consolidated financial statements be prepared.

13   *Comprido Plc* is the holding company of a group. All of the companies in the group operate within the retail and distribution sectors, except for one subsidiary, *Seguranca Ltd*, which is a life assurance company whose accounts are subject to the rules and regulations relating to the insurance sector. As a result, the accounting policies adopted by *Seguranca Ltd* are very different from those adopted by the rest of the group.

If it would be appropriate not to include *Seguranca Plc* in the consolidation on the grounds that its activities are so different from those of the other undertakings in the group that its inclusion would be incompatible with the obligation to give a true and fair view, it should be included in the consolidated financial statements under the equity method of accounting. However, it is most unlikely that its inclusion as a subsidiary in the consolidation would be misleading - the objective of FRS 2 is to require parent undertakings to provide financial information about the economic activities of their groups and the fact that groups often comprise a number of different undertakings operating in a range of different industries means that many consolidations will contain amalgamated data which is less than identical in terms of its background. Simply because one of the undertakings in a group is involved in activities which none of its fellow group members are engaged in is not sufficient grounds for exclusion from consolidation as a subsidiary. Segmental reporting (chapter 12) is far more revealing and should be used to highlight any such differences, rather than equity accounting. Although the amounts reported by *Seguranca Ltd* should normally be adjusted to the values that would be reflected if the group's accounting policies were applied, exceptionally it may be inappropriate to do so, in which case the different accounting policies should be disclosed

14   The *Explicar* group consists of a holding company and two subsidiaries all of whom operate in the retail foods sector. None of the group undertakings is quoted on a recognised stock exchange. The group has always previously qualified as medium-sized under the Companies Act definition. However, this year, increases in its turnover and assets have resulted in it gaining 'large' company status. In the previous year it did not produce consolidated accounts, instead choosing to produce individual company accounts only.

As the qualifying conditions were met in the previous year, the group can adopt the same approach this year and only produce individual company accounts, even though this year the qualifying conditions have not been met. To continue in future to produce only individual company accounts, the qualifying conditions will have to be met next year. Otherwise, it will only be available as an option when for two successive periods the qualifying conditions are met.

FRS 6:   Acquisitions and Mergers

Questions 15-18 relate to a variety of companies and groups. Unless otherwise indicated, the companies' financial year ends are all at 31st December. In the absence of other information, assume that there is no continuation from one question to another and each question should be considered in isolation from the rest.

15   On 1st September, *Comendo Plc* issued 500,000 £1 equity shares in a one for two share exchange for all the (£1) equity shares in *Comida Ltd*. All the equity share capital of *Comida Ltd* was obtained. The merger method of accounting is to be used.

The cost of the investment (£500,000) is less than the nominal value of the equity share capital of *Comida Ltd*. The difference should be treated as a movement on other reserves in the consolidated financial statements.

16   If the share exchange in question 15 had been a two for one exchange, what would be the accounting treatment on consolidation?

The cost of the investment (£500,000) is greater than the nominal value of the equity share capital of *Comida Ltd*. The difference should be treated as a movement on other reserves in the consolidated financial statements.

17   What disclosure should be made in respect of *all* business combinations occuring in the financial year, whether accounted for as acquisitions or mergers, in the financial statements of the acquiring entity or, in the case of a merger, the entity issuing shares?

The names of the combining entities (other than the reporting entity); whether the combination has been accounted for as an acquisition or as a merger; and the date of the combination.

18   *Criar Ltd* is a company which was formed five years ago to act as an ultimate group holding company in the event of an expansion of the *Criar* group. It has a 31st December year end. On 1st November, the shareholders of *Moreno Ltd* and *Azul Ltd* exchanged all their share capital in a one for one share exchange for shares of the same nominal value in *Criar Ltd*. *Moreno Ltd* has a financial year end at 30th April. *Azul's* financial year end is 31st December. Merger accounting is to be used for the group consolidation.

All companies in the group must have accounting periods coterminous with the ultimate holding company. *Moreno Ltd* should change its year end to 31st December. The comparative figures for the previous year may be difficult to determine and may, for example, be derived from internal records and management accounts of *Moreno Ltd*, or apportioned using the two previous financial years' accounts. Whatever approach is

adopted, it must produce as true and fair a view as possible of the comparative position and results for the group.

FRS 7:   Fair Values in Acquisition Accounting

Questions 19-21 relate to companies and groups all of which have financial year ends at 31st December and whose financial statements are approved on 31st March.

19   *Arvore plc* acquired *Boba Ltd* for £4.5 million on 1st June. At 31st March it was still investigating the *fair values* relating to the acquisition.

Provisional values should be used. In the next financial statements, if necessary, they should be amended to the correct values and goodwill adjusted accordingly. (Paragraphs 23 and 24)

20   Repeat question 19, but this time *Arvore plc* identified the *fair values* in May.

The provisional values used should be revised and goodwill adjusted accordingly. (Paragraph 24)

21   Repeat question 19, but this time *Arvore plc* took three years to identify the *fair values*.

Any necessary adjustments should be incorporated in the financial statements for the first full financial year following the acquisition. In this case, that period has expired. As a result, if there was a fundamental error in the provisional values, that should be accounted for as a prior period adjustment. Any other differences should be recognised as profits or losses in the financial statements for the period in which the *fair values* were identified. (Paragraph 25)

SSAP 22:   Accounting for Goodwill

Questions 22-25 relate to a variety of companies and groups. Unless otherwise indicated, the companies' financial year ends are all at 31st December. In the absence of other information, assume that there is no continuation from one question to another and each question should be considered in isolation from the rest.

22   When *Pereira Ltd* took over *Morango Ltd* in November of the previous year, purchased goodwill of £350,000 arose and was capitalised to be amortised over a twenty year period. On acquisition, a small warehouse belonging to *Morango Ltd* had been revalued to a fair value of £250,000. The warehouse was leased to another company in September at which time a valuation was placed on it of £300,000.

In order for the increase in value to be treated as a goodwill adjustment, it is necessary that the fair value at the acquisition date was incorrect. The fact that it was valued only ten months later at 20% more than the fair value adopted would suggest that the fair value may have been understated. However, the mere suggestion is not enough, there must be conclusive evidence that the higher amount would have been a true reflection of fair value at the acquisition date. If the original fair value were found to have been incorrect, FRS 3

would have to be consulted in order to determine whether it constituted a prior period adjustment and, if it does not constitute a prior period adjustment, the goodwill should be adjusted against the restatement of the fair value of the warehouse. If the original fair value was found to have been correct, no adjustment should be made.

23   Repeat question 22, but this time the fair value originally applied was a provisional estimate.

The answer remains the same. Unless there is conclusive evidence that the conditions existing at the acquisition date were such that the higher amount would have been a true reflection of fair value at that date, no adjustment to the goodwill figure should be made. The fact that a provisional fair value was used (which would have had to have been disclosed along with the reasons for its use in the previous year's consolidated financial statements) is irrelevant. Only if the new value were the fair value of the item at the acquisition date is adjustment possible.

24   Repeat question 22, but this time the goodwill was immediately written-off to reserves.

The same principles apply as with questions 22 and 23. If the fair value was incorrectly stated, the excess amount written-off could be recovered this year, unless it results from a fundamental error and should, therefore, be treated as a prior period adjustment under FRS 3.

25   When *Carteira Ltd* took over *Carro Ltd* in December of the previous year, purchased goodwill of £475,000 arose and was capitalised to be written-off over a ten year period. On acquisition, some unused equipment belonging to *Carro Ltd* had been revalued to a fair value of £60,000. (The fair value was believed to be correct.) The equipment was sold in March when it realised £30,000.

Goodwill should not be revalued. However it may be adjusted, if based on a fair value which subsequently was shown to have been incorrect. It is irrelevant whether the fair value used was provisional or not. The only way that the goodwill could be increased retrospectively would be if the difference arose from an error in the determination of the fair value used and it would qualify as a prior period adjustment arising from a fundamental error as defined by FRS 3. If it does not qualify as a prior period adjustment, the adjustment would be accounted for in the current year. If the original fair value was correct, no adjustment is possible. SSAP 22 does not consider the treatment of any goodwill relating to individual assets subsequently disposed of, only to businesses and business segments.

Which Standard?

Short Question Solutions

*ASSUME THAT MATERIALITY EXISTS IN **EVERY** CASE*

The companies in the questions all have a financial year end of 31st December. In each case, the board of directors is scheduled to approve the financial statements on 31st March.

1   Costa Ltd depreciates all its plant over 5 years using the straight line method. Two years ago, the company had five new cutting machines built to its own specifications. The machines cost £35,000 each and had a resale value of £10,000 each at the end of the financial period. In February, the UK's leading manufacturer of cutting machines announced a new range of machines that effectively made the company's machines obsolete, reducing their resale value to nil. The company has been experiencing severe financing problems and it seems unlikely that it can continue to survive for much longer without a major injection of new funds. It is now mid-March and all attempts at raising this money have failed.

SSAPs 2 and 17
The going concern concept should be applied (SSAP 2). This will require that the machines be written-down to their net realisable value. However, the resale value is now lower than it was at 31st December and SSAP 17 could be applied to support the view that the prudence concept should be applied to adjust the values of the machines to nil.

2   *Tempo plc*, is a building company with one subsidiary. The group balance sheet date is 31st December. On turnover of £94.7m, the group has pre-tax earnings of £16.1m (last year £11.4m on turnover of £79.3m). *Tempo plc* has investments in four associated undertakings, should they be included in the group's segmental report?

SSAP 25
Only if together they account for 20% of the group's total result or 20% of the group's total net assets.

3   Last year, a company whose accounting policy is to defer and amortise development expenditure, wrote off £100,000 expenditure incurred in developing a new product which was held to have been unlikely to be commercially viable. In June, the company was approached by a retail hardware chain who were interested in selling the product. It is now in production and it is expected that all the costs will be recouped within the next twelve months and that, thereafter, it will generate a good profit for the next three to four years.

SSAP 13 and FRS 3
This is an example of development expenditure written-off for a reason which has subsequently proved to have been incorrect. It is not the result of a fundamental error -it could not have been known at the time that the previous period's financial statements were prepared that the retail chain would make their approach - and so could not qualify as a prior period adjustment (FRS 3). Under SSAP 13, there is no facility for reversing the write-

off of development expenditure which was never capitalised. Accordingly, no adjustment can be made to the entries made.

4   A building company is being sued for damages of £450,000 for breach of contract. Legal opinion suggests that there is about a 40% chance that the company may lose the case. It also suggests that the £450,000 damages claim is excessive and 99% unlikely to be confirmed by the court. £350,000 is the most that the company should expect to be required to pay if it loses the case. £225,000 was given as an estimate of the likely level of damages that would be assessed. The action was started before the company's financial year end and is scheduled to be heard in court two months after the date on which the financial statements are to be approved by the board of directors.

SSAP 18

The potential financial effect of the case is £350,000. This amount should be disclosed. The other £100,000 appears to be remote and should not be disclosed. (The £225,000 likely level of damages may also be disclosed, but it should be clearly differentiated from the £350,000.)

5   On 23rd February, the company rolled-over the £800,000 investment for a further 90 days. How would these items be treated under FRS 1 (*Cash flow statements*)?

FRS 1

This investment will mature on 24th May. Strictly speaking it will not, therefore, mature within the three months time limit and should be included under investing activities rather than being excluded from the statement as the investment of cash in cash equivalents. (In a leap year this would qualify as a cash equivalent and would, therefore, be excluded from the cash flow statement.)

6   During the year, as a result of a steady stream of break-ins and subsequently mounting losses, a furniture discount store leased an infra-red security systems and employed four permanent security staff. The cost of this during the year was £45,000. The annual charge in future is expected to be around £55,000.

FRS 3

It is a normal activity for retail businesses to take security measures. However, as it is material, in order to give a true and fair view, its nature and amount should be disclosed.

7   What information concerning government grants should be disclosed in the financial statements?

SSAP 4

The accounting policy adopted for government grants; the effect of government grants on the results for the period and/or the financial position of the enterprise; where the results of the period are affected materially by the receipt of government assistance other than grants, the nature of that assistance and an estimate of its effects upon the financial statement (in so far as the effects can be measured); potential liabilities to repay grants may be subject to the disclosure requirements of SSAP 18 (*Accounting for contingencies* -chapter 7).

8   At the balance sheet date, a motor trader company was owed £37,000 by the Customs and Excise in respect of a refund of over-payments of VAT made by the company during the previous two years.

SSAP 5
Include this amount in the total for debtors. There is no need to disclose it separately. The refund will need to be entered through the appropriate ledger accounts. As a result, there will be some restatement of account balances. FRS 3 (*Reporting financial performance* - chapter 2) will require to be consulted in order to determine the appropriate treatment.

9   When *Janella Ltd* acquired a 60% shareholding in *Curtina Ltd* in September two years ago, it paid £1.4m and the £240,000 of purchased goodwill arising was immediately written-off to the reserves. In June of the current year, *Janella Ltd* acquired another 20% of the equity of *Curtina Ltd*. The fair value of the identifiable assets and liabilities of *Curtina Ltd* at that time was £2.3m.

FRS 2
When a group increases its interest in an undertaking that is already its subsidiary undertaking, the identifiable assets and liabilities of that subsidiary undertaking should be revalued to fair value and goodwill arising *on the increase in interest* should be calculated by reference to that fair value.

10   A building company decided to apply SSAP 19 (*Accounting for investment properties* - chapter 8) and stop depreciating a building it has sub-leased on a 10 year lease to a firm in Dunfermline. The lease has 4 years to run. The thirty year leasehold to the property was bought by the company 6 years ago solely for letting purposes. It has been depreciated in each of the first five years at 15% reducing balance.

SSAP 19 and FRS 3
This is a change in accounting policy. Under FRS 3, it should be accounted for by restating the comparative figures for the preceding period in the primary statements and notes and adjusting the opening balance of reserves for the cumulative effect. The cumulative effect of the adjustment should be noted at the foot of the statement of total recognised gains and losses of the current period. The effect of the prior period adjustment on the results for the preceding period should be disclosed where practicable. The effect will be that the depreciation provision should be set to zero (and the net book value amended accordingly) and the balance on the reserves increased by the amount previously provided.

11   What is the *accounting objective* of SSAP 24 (*Accounting for pension costs* - chapter 11)?

SSAP 24
The employer should recognise the expected cost of providing pensions on a systematic and

rational basis over the period during which he derives benefit from the employees' services (paragraph 77).

12   On 1st August, a new holding company was created and it acquired the entire share capital of a chemical company in a 2 for 1 share exchange. The chemical company had earnings for EPS purposes of £4.5m in the current year (£3.8m in the previous period). Merger accounting has been applied. The chemical company had 3 million shares in issue prior to the share exchange. In the absence of any further information, what EPS should be disclosed?

SSAP 3
Earnings must be divided by the number of shares issued by the holding company to find EPS:

$$\text{EPS for the current period} = \text{£4.5/6} = 75p$$
$$\text{EPS for the previous period} = \text{£3.8/6} = 63\frac{1}{3}p$$

13   What is deferred tax and what is the liability method of computing deferred tax?

SSAP 15
Deferred tax is the tax attributable to timing differences (differences between profits and losses as computed for tax purposes and results as stated in financial statements). The liability method calculates deferred tax at the tax rate that is estimated will be applicable when the timing differences reverse.

14   A manufacturing company has one 60% subsidiary. and current group turnover of £165m and net pre-tax profit of £22.3m. During the financial period just ended, the subsidiary acquired a 21% holding in the ordinary share capital of a raw material supplier company as security against a one year loan of £5m which the subsidiary made to the raw material supplier company's parent (of which that company was a 100% subsidiary).

SSAP 1
The holding is probably not for the long term, although this point could be argued. There must be considerable doubt over the extent of the influence that the group can have upon the raw material supplier company. Consequently, it should not be treated as an associated undertaking.

15   What are the disclosure requirements of SSAP 12 (*Accounting for depreciation* - chapter 4) ?

SSAP 12
In respect of each major class of depreciable asset: the depreciation methods used, the useful economic lives or the depreciation rates used, the total depreciation charged for the period, and the gross amount of depreciable assets and the related accumulated depreciation; where there has been a change in the depreciation method used, the effect, if material, should be disclosed in the year of change, along with the reason for the change; where assets have been revalued, the effect of the revaluation on the depreciation charge should, if material, be disclosed in the year of revaluation.

16   If a holding company has a 30% investment in an associated undertaking, should the group's share of the associated undertaking's results be included in the group segmental report under 'results of associated undertakings' ?

SSAP 25
Only if the aggregate of all group associated undertakings account for at least 20% of the total result or 20% of the total net assets of the group. The individual associated undertaking figures are irrelevant.

17   After its chemical store was contaminated, a chemical company spent £11,000 on research into why the contamination had occurred.

FRS 3
SSAP 13 does not apply. FRS 3 does. The event is the contamination of the chemical store. Contamination of its chemical store must be an unusual but, nevertheless, possible event for a chemical company. It cannot be considered to be an extraordinary event. If considered that disclosure is necessary in order that the financial statements give a true and fair view, the £11,000 incurred should be treated as exceptional and its nature and amount disclosed.

18   A compact disc manufacturing company has a factory and a warehouse, both of which are included in the financial statements at cost less depreciation to date. A recent newspaper article by a local surveyor stated that while there was a shortage of factory space on the market, there was a glut of warehouse accommodation. From the value per square foot that he quoted, it appears that the factory is undervalued by approximately the same amount as the warehouse is overvalued. As the two value differences offset each other, no change has been made to the value at which these properties have been included in the balance sheet.

SSAPs 2 and 12
This policy is not in accordance with the separate determination concept enforced by the Companies Act. Just because a liability is compensated by an asset it does not mean that they may be treated as capable of offset. The rules regarding profits and losses are very different: while profits should not be realised until it is prudent to do so, losses should be recognised as soon as they become apparent and not carried forward to future years. No formal revaluation has taken place and it could be argued that there is no requirement to take account of the valuation the article puts on the factory - it may, as it was an article dealing in generalities, be inappropriate. However, evidence does suggest that the value of the warehouse may have been overstated in the accounts. Accordingly, prudence would suggest that the warehouse should be revalued and the (probable) resulting reduction in valuation written-off. (SSAP 12 - *Accounting for depreciation* - should also be consulted, particularly paragraph 19 which is concerned with the treatment of permanent diminutions in value.)

19   *Prediu plc*, whose main business is property leasing, recently completed construction of a multi-storey office block. It is to be treated as an investment property, as under SSAP 19. The first tenants are due to take possession of their offices in April. As the building was only completed in October, it has been decided that no valuation will take place at the end of the financial period.

SSAP 19

This is in contravention of paragraph 6 of SSAP 19: investment properties are to be included in the balance sheet at open market value. The building will require to be valued at 31st December.

20   *Cachoro Ltd* has two subsidiaries, *Pedra Ltd* and *Maca Ltd*. *Cachoro Ltd* is a 100% subsidiary of *Trem Plc*. What consolidated financial statements should *Cachoro Ltd* prepare?

FRS 2

As *Cachoro Ltd* is a 100% subsidiary of a company incorporated in the EEC, it does not require to prepare group accounts, unless it has securities listed on a stock exchange in any member state of the EEC.

21   A steel company purchased raw materials from an American supplier for $270,000. The goods were delivered on November 18th, when the exchange rate was £1=$1.85. Payment was not made by the year end but will be made on the 14th February. In order to avoid exchange rate losses, the company contracted to buy forward $270,000 on 14th February at £1=$1.87. The exchange rate at the year end was £1=$1.76.

SSAP 20

The transaction should be translated using the forward contract rate of £1=$1.87. There will be no exchange rate gain or loss. The balance sheet date creditor will also be based on the forward contract rate translation (= £144,385).

22   According to SSAP 9 (*Stocks and long term contracts* - chapter 3), what disclosure must be made and what application requirements are there regarding accounting policies adopted in respect of stocks and long term contracts?

SSAP 9

The accounting policies that have been applied to stocks and long term contracts, in particular the method of ascertaining turnover and attributable profit, should be stated and applied consistently, within the business and from year to year.

23   *Novinho Ltd* was formed on 1st January in order that two existing companies, *Velho Ltd* and *Juvem Ltd*, could merge. The shareholders of the two companies exchanged their equity shares in a one for one share exchange for shares in *Novinho Ltd*. Merger accounting is to be adopted. No difference exists between the investment's carrying value and the nominal value of the shares transferred.

FRS 6

The problem in this case is that the holding company was not in existence in the period which would be covered by the comparative figures. There is no statutory facility for it to recognise a period when it did not exist. Nevertheless, it would be good accounting practice to produce comparative figures along with an explanatory note.

24   On 1st September, a fish processing company made a 1 for 6 rights issue at 20p. The market value of the shares on the last day of quotation cum rights was 21p. At the start of the accounting period, there were 3 million ordinary £1 shares in issue. Earnings for

EPS purposes are £1.2m (£0.9m in the previous year) and the company has never had any irrecoverable ACT.

SSAP 3

The theoretical ex-rights price is $[(20p \times 500,000) + (21p \times 3 \text{ million})]/3.5$ million = £0.73/3.5 = 20.86p. The actual cum rights price was 21p. As the actual price is less, the issue should not be treated as if it were at full market price. As a result, the previous period's EPS must be recalculated based on an adjusted number of shares of 3.02 million. $[(0.21/0.2086) \times 3$ million]. The previous period's EPS is restated at 29.8p (previously 30p). The current period's EPS is derived from:

$\frac{2}{3} \times 3.02$ million	2,013,333
$\frac{1}{3} \times 3.5$ million	1,166,667
	3,180,000

EPS = £1.2m/3,180,000 = 37.74p

25   As a result of a production error, a clothing company lost stock worth £50,000. The company's insurers made good the loss and also paid the company £90,000 for consequential loss of profits.

FRS 3

As it has arisen from the ordinary activities of the business, the loss of profits compensation should be treated as an exceptional item and its nature and amount disclosed.

26   A company has been developing a new product in a rented factory which is being used solely for the product. Production has been scheduled to start in three months time and sufficient orders have already been received to guarantee a sizeable profit.

SSAP 13

Include the rental charge in development expenditure. (SSAP 13 offers the choice of deferral or write-off of the development expenditure.)

27   According to SSAP 8 (*The treatment of taxation under the imputation system in the accounts of companies* - chapter 13), what disclosure must be made in the financial statements relating to overseas taxation?

SSAP 8

The taxation charge in the profit and loss account should include (and, where material, appropriate disclosure should be made of) the total overseas taxation, relieved and unrelieved, specifying that part of the unrelieved overseas taxation which arises from the payment or proposed payment of dividends; and disclosure should be made of relief for overseas taxation on the amount of UK corporation tax included in the profit and loss taxation charge.

28   Under what circumstances would a property owned by a company which was let to another group company be an 'investment property'?

SSAP 19

An investment property is an interest in land and/or buildings in respect of which construction work and development have been completed, and which is held for its investment potential with any rental income being negotiated at arm's length, *except* property owned and occupied by a company for its own purposes or let to and occupied by another group company. However, property owned by a company and let to another group company which then lets it to a non-group company, would be an investment property in the consolidated financial statements if the other conditions stated above were fulfilled.

29   A marketing company has a holding in an associated undertaking. The company's financial year end is the same as that of the associated undertaking. The company had assumed that a dividend of 5p per share would be declared by the associate and had provided for this in the financial statements. The associate company declared a dividend of 7p per share one week before the marketing company's board of directors were due to approve the financial statements.

SSAP 17
This event has arisen in the 'post balance sheet period'. It is an adjusting event. (The standard specifically refers to this as being an example of an event which, because of statutory requirements or customary practice is reflected in financial statements and so falls to be treated as an adjusting event.) The accounts should be adjusted to reflect the correct dividend.

30   Refer to question 29: if the associated undertaking's dividend had not been known until the week after the financial statements of the marketing company were approved, what treatment would be appropriate?

SSAP 17
This event has occurred in the post-post balance sheet period. If non-disclosure would cause the financial statements to be misleading, the actual dividend should be disclosed, otherwise it should not be disclosed.

31   At the period end, deferred tax was credited with £120,000 relating to accelerated capital allowances. The corporation tax creditor at the previous period end was £1.4m, £1.7m tax was paid during the period, and a taxation liability for £1.6m is included in the draft balance sheet for the current period. How should this be treated under FRS 1 (*Cash flow statements* - chapter 12)?

FRS 1
The actual tax paid of £1.7m should be shown under the *taxation* section of the cash flow statement.

32   Five years earlier, a small footwear company wrote off equipment with a book value of £40,000 when it reorganised its production facilities. At that time it was not believed likely that it could be sold. During the current year, the company sold the equipment for £70,000.

FRS 3
This represents an exceptional item arising from the ordinary activities of the business. its nature and amount (£70,000) should be disclosed. It does not qualify as a prior period adjustment as the sale could not have been foreseen five years ago.

33   According to SSAP 22 (*Accounting for goodwill* - chapter 14), what disclosure should be made where goodwill is amortised?

SSAP 22
Where amortised, purchased goodwill should be shown as a separate item under intangible fixed assets in the balance sheet until fully written-off; the movement on the goodwill account during the year should also be disclosed (showing the cost, accumulated amortisation and net book value of goodwill at the beginning and end of the year, and the amount of goodwill amortised through the profit and loss account during the year); disclosure should also be made of the period selected for amortising the goodwill relating to each major acquisition.

34   In November, a company finished erecting a small laboratory in the grounds of its Brechin factory. The lab is to be used on all general scientific research. It cost £52,000.

SSAPs 13 and 12
While this laboratory has been erected in order to provide facilities for general scientific research, no specific product or process is involved. Consequently, it would not be appropriate to treat it as development expenditure. It should be capitalised and written-off over its estimated useful life in accordance with SSAP 12. The annual depreciation should be disclosed in accordance with SSAP 12 and, as it does not qualify as development expenditure, it cannot be deferred and so should be included as part of the year's expenditure on research and development charged to profit and loss.

35   What segmental analysis is required under SSAP 25 (*Segmental reporting* - chapter 12) in respect of joint ventures which have been accounted for by proportional consolidation?

SSAP 25
None. Though it would be hard to argue that segmentalising the joint venture would not result in an improved true and fair view.

36   A company had a computer system in its old office which it was writing-down at 20% straight line. When it moved it agreed to lease the equipment to the estate agency which leased the building. The equipment had a net book value at the start of the year of £9,000 and was 2 years old. The lease is for 5 years and includes an option for the estate agency to buy the equipment at the end of the lease for £1. The estate agency is responsible for maintaining the equipment during the term of the lease.

SSAP 21
This should be treated as a finance lease under SSAP 21. It should be recorded in the balance sheet as a debtor at the amount of the net investment in the lease. The equipment and the accumulated depreciation should be written out of the fixed assets.

37   A company has been developing a new product in a custom-built factory. Production has been scheduled to start in three months time and sufficient orders have already been received to guarantee a sizeable profit.

SSAPs 12 and 13
The type of use is irrelevant so far as SSAP 12 is concerned. The exclusion of development expenditure from the scope of SSAP 12 does not affect the application of SSAP 12 in this case as the factory cost is not treated as a development cost, only the depreciation which is charged as a result. In order that there be any depreciation, SSAP 12 must be applied and the factory must be depreciated over its useful life. The depreciation charged for the period when development was taking place should be disclosed in the depreciation for the period, but should be included in research and development expenditure. If company policy is to defer development expenditure and the development meets the requirements of SSAP 13 regarding deferral, the depreciation charged would be included in the amount deferred.

38   A plumbing company has been paid an advance of £65,000 on a contract for maintenance work on offshore oil rigs. The contract incorporated an advance payment bond (a guarantee that all advance payments made to the company would be reimbursed should the customer fail to fulfil the contract). Since signing the contract six months ago, the company has been unable to discover any qualified plumbers who were willing to work at the under-water depths required on the oil rigs. It is thought unlikely that anyone suitable will be found. It is now 31st March, and the board of directors are scheduled to approve the financial statements later today.

SSAP 18
There is a contingent liability for the £65,000 which appears probable and it should be accrued in the financial statements.

39   A mining company made a profit after tax and extraordinary items of £4.6m during the accounting period (previous period £3.8m). It has 5 million ordinary £1 shares, and 500,000 10% cumulative preference shares of £1 each in issue (no change since the previous period).

SSAP 3
The preference dividend of £50,000 must be subtracted from the earnings figure prior to the EPS calculation. As a result, £4.55m is available this period (£3.75m last period). EPS for the current period = £4.55/5 = 91p. The previous period's EPS = £3.75/5 = 75p.

40   *Ficando Plc* has a number of subsidiaries. It bought a 60% holding in *Saindo Ltd* on 1st September. It was acquired with the intention of holding it for six months. A buyer has not yet been found and it seems unlikely that one will be found by the end of the six month period.

FRS 2
Control is intended to be temporary. The subsidiary should be excluded from consolidation. The investment should be stated in the consolidated balance sheet as a current asset at the lower of cost and net realisable value. (See paragraph 67 of FRS 7 - FRS 2 has precedence over this situation.)

41   A shipping company made a profit after tax and extraordinary items of £6.4m during the accounting period (previous period a loss of £3.1m). It has 25 million ordinary £1 shares, and £3 million 10% non-cumulative preference shares in issue (no change since the previous period). During the previous period, no dividend was declared in respect of the preference shareholders. This period, a dividend of £250,000 has been declared on the preference shares.

SSAP 3
The preference dividend of £250,000 must be subtracted from the earnings figure prior to the EPS calculation. As a result, £6.15m is available this period. A similar deduction is not required for the previous year as no dividend was paid. The earnings for the previous year, for use in the calculation of EPS was, therefore, a loss of £3.1m. EPS for the current period = £6.15/25 = 24.6p. The previous period's EPS = £(3.1)/25 = 12.4p (loss).

42   A carpet company has stock of 1000 metres of high quality carpeting which was purchased direct from the supplier for £12,000 over two years ago on the basis of an expected contract which never transpired. All attempts to sell the carpet have failed and an offer has been received from a discount warehouse to buy the carpet from the company for £1,000.

SSAP 9 and FRS 3
The stock should be included in the balance sheet at its net realisable value of £1,000. The remaining £11,000 should be written-off as an exceptional item and its nature and amount disclosed.

43   A group consists of a holding company (*Tempo*) with one subsidiary (*Chapeau*), which in turn has one subsidiary (*Tocar*), which in turn has one subsidiary (*Repicar*). All the subsidiaries are 100% owned by their immediate parent. The companies are incorporated in the following countries:

Tempo	Isle of Man
Chapeau	Great Britain
Tocar	New Zealand
Repicar	Italy

Ignoring questions of size, which of the companies would be exempt from the preparation of group accounts?

FRS 2
Chapeau **must prepare group accounts as its parent company is not incorporated in a member state of the EEC.**

44   What treatment should be adopted when the amount of purchase consideration is contingent on one or more future events?

FRS 7
The cost of acquisition should include a reasonable estimate of the *fair value* of amounts expected to be payable in future.

45   Included in the year end trade debtors of a furniture manufacturing company is a balance of £70,000. The balance has been outstanding for the previous eleven months. The debtor is a national retailer which is known to be in serious financial difficulty.

SSAP 2
The prudence concept requires that provision is made for the possible bad debt.

46   What disclosure should be made of a quasi-subsidiary?

FRS 5
The substance of the transactions entered into by the quasi-subsidiary should be reported in the consolidated statements (paragraph 15). The fact that a quasi-subsidiary has been included in the consolidated financial statements should be disclosed and a summary of the financial statements of the quasi-subsidiary should be provided in the notes (paragraph 38).

47   A double glazing company has been experiencing financial problems due to increased competition. It is thought unlikely that it will remain in business beyond the middle of the next financial year.

SSAP 2
The going concern concept should be applied and all assets should be valued on the basis of their net realisable value where that is less than net book value.

48   When *Fin Ltd* acquired a 100% shareholding in *Comeca Ltd* in April of the previous year for £1.2m, purchased goodwill of £130,000 arose which was immediately written-off to reserves. In November of the current year, *Comeca Ltd* was sold for £1.1m. Its net assets at that time were £1.3m. No changes had been made to the company during the time it was owned by *Fin Ltd*.

SSAP 22
The loss on sale is either £200,000 or £70,000. Which is reported depends on how the goodwill was previously written-off. Under FRS 2, the gain or loss on sale is the difference between the sale proceeds and the holding company's share of its net assets together with any goodwill (less any amounts written-off *through the profit and loss account*). Assuming that the write-off was directly to the reserves and did not pass through the profit and loss account, there was a loss on sale of £200,000. Under SSAP 22, the amount of purchased goodwill attributable to the business disposed of and how it has been treated in determining the profit or loss on disposal should be disclosed.

49   A toy making company has two major products *meninas* and *meninos*. At the year end stock valuation, the cost of the *menina* stock was greater than its net realisable value by £35,000. However, as the cost of the *menino* stock was £48,000 less than its net realisable value, both product stocks were included in the financial statements at cost.

SSAP 2
This policy is not in accordance with the separate determination concept enforced by the Companies Act. Just because a liability is compensated by an asset it does not mean that they may be treated as capable of offset. The rules regarding profits and losses are very different:

while profits should not be realised until it is prudent to do so, losses should be recognised as soon as they become apparent and not carried forward to future years. The treatment adopted is also contrary to SSAP 9 (*Stocks and long term contracts* - chapter 3). Accordingly, the *menina* stock must be restated at its net realisable value and the fall in value recognised in the current period's financial statements.

50   On 1st April, a clothing company made a 1 for 4 bonus issue. At the start of the period it had 4 million ordinary £1 shares in issue; and earnings for EPS purposes were £2.5m (£2m in the previous period).

SSAP 3
There are now 5 million ordinary shares in issue. EPS is £2.5/5 = 50p. The comparative figure is 50p × (4/5) = 40p.

51   What are 'issue costs'?

FRS 4
Issue costs are the costs incurred directly in connection with the issue of a capital instrument. They are those costs that would not have been incurred had the specific instrument in question not been issued.

52   On 1st May, a confectionery company made a 1 for 5 rights issue at 80p. The market value of the shares on the last day of quotation cum rights was 120p. At the start of the period it had 4 million ordinary £1 shares in issue; and earnings for EPS purposes were £2.5m (£2m in the previous period).

SSAP 3
The theoretical ex-rights price is [(80p × 800,000) + (120p × 4 million)]/4.8 million = £5.44/4.8 = 113⅓p. The actual cum rights price was 120p, therefore, the previous year's EPS of 50p must be multiplied by 113⅓/120 to produce a comparative EPS figure of 47.22p. The current period's EPS is derived from:

⅓ × 4 million × (120/113⅓)	1,411,765
⅔ × 4.8 million	3,200,000
	4,611,765

EPS = £2.5m/4,611,765 = 54.21p

53   What is 'control in the context of an asset'? (FRS 5)

FRS 5
The ability to obtain the future economic benefits relating to an asset and to restrict the access of others to those benefits (paragraph 3).

54   In May, a carpet manufacturing company received an order for custom-designed carpets from a Middle Eastern customer. The company expects to start work on the carpet in March. Due to the particularly exclusive nature of the order, it is worth £300,000 to the company, although the costs of meeting it are the same as those normally incurred on orders of £50,000. Included in the directors' report is a projection of turnover and profit for the coming year which includes the value and cost of this carpet order. The customer's country was invaded in November and he has not been heard of since.

SSAP 2
It seems likely that this order will not now be fulfilled. Consequently, the projections do not present a true and fair view. Prudence requires that no recognition be made of this order and that it should be excluded from the financial statements.

55   The *Pensando* group consisted of *Pensando Ltd* and its 90% subsidiary, *Fazendo Ltd*, which it acquired fourteen years ago. In November, the board decided to sell the subsidiary as soon as possible and in mid-December, *Fazendo* was sold.

FRS 2
There is no group in existence at the balance sheet date. Should consolidated financial statements be prepared up to the date of disposal of the interest in *Fazendo Ltd*? No. However the financial statements of *Pensando Ltd* should include sufficient detail of the performance of *Fazendo Ltd* to enable the users of those statements to isolate the performance of *Pensando Ltd*.

56   In its previous year's financial statements, a pharmaceutical company wrote off a bad debt of £25,000 in respect of a customer who was in serious financial difficulty. In March, the customer finally arranged the funding needed in order to continue in business and, in April, the £25,000 was received. The pharmaceutical company only made a profit of £20,000 in the previous year and the directors want to restate the previous year's accounts, eliminating the bad debt, in order to present a more realistic picture of the company's performance during that year. In previous years, any bad debt recovered has been credited to the profit and loss account of the period that recovery occurred.

SSAP 2
While the accruals concept may suggest that the treatment is appropriate, it is not a generally accepted approach to take; nor is it consistent with the previous accounting policy. On the grounds of consistency it would be inappropriate to restate the previous year's results, as it would be the opposite of what was previously done. (Under FRS 3, it does not qualify as a prior period adjustment as it arises from the modification of an accounting basis necessitated by events clearly different in substance from those previously occurring. It also would not qualify as a fundamental error as it arises from an adjustment of an accounting estimate made in the previous year. Restatement would not, therefore, be permitted under FRS 3.) However, if the directors are of the view that a true and fair view will only result if such a policy is adopted, they may do so, but must disclose that both the consistency concept, and FRS 3, have not been observed in order that the financial statements may present a true and fair view.

57   £470,000 development expenditure incurred during the period by an engineering company has been deferred.

FRS 1
The £470,000 cash flow should be included within the *investing activities* section of the Cash Flow Statement.

58   As the result of an offer to the shareholders of *Acordo Ltd*, 95% of its equity shares were obtained by *Descendo Plc*. The 950,000 equity shares obtained had a nominal value of

£1 each. *Acordo Ltd* has only one class of share in issue and all equity shares have voting rights. On the date the exchange took place, the net assets of *Acordo Ltd* had a fair value of £2m and the market value of a share in *Descendo Plc* was £2. *Descendo Plc* has only one class of share in issue: £1 voting equity shares, and prior to the offer it had no loan stock. In consideration for every ten shares in *Acordo Ltd*, *Descendo Plc* issued nine of its own shares and £2 loan stock. Assuming all conditions dependent upon other factors are satisfied, must merger accounting be applied?

FRS 6

The fair value of the consideration would be £1.9m [(£2 × 9 × 950,000/10) + (£2 × 950,000/10)]. The fair value of the consideration other than the issue of the equity shares (£190,000) is, at 22.2%, still in excess of 10% of the nominal value of the equity shares issued (£855,000). Under CA 85 Schedule 4A, paragraph 10(c) the merger accounting method can not be applied.

59   *Rapido Plc* acquired a controlling interest in each of three companies when it took over a small group in August. At the time of their acquisition, *Rapido Plc* intended selling one of the companies (*Segundo Ltd*) as soon as possible. By the year end, no buyer had been found. However, the directors of *Rapido Plc* believe that *Segundo Ltd* will be sold within the next few months.

FRS 2

This is an example of interest in a subsidiary undertaking which is held exclusively with a view to subsequent resale. The subsidiary has not been previously consolidated in group accounts prepared by *Rapido Plc* and it should, therefore, be excluded from the consolidation and recorded in the consolidated financial statements as a current asset at the lower of cost and its net realisable value.

60   What is 'value in use' of an asset? (FRS 7)

FRS 7

Present value of the future cash flows obtainable as a result of an asset's continued use, including those resulting frmo the ultimate disposal of the asset (paragraph 2).

Index